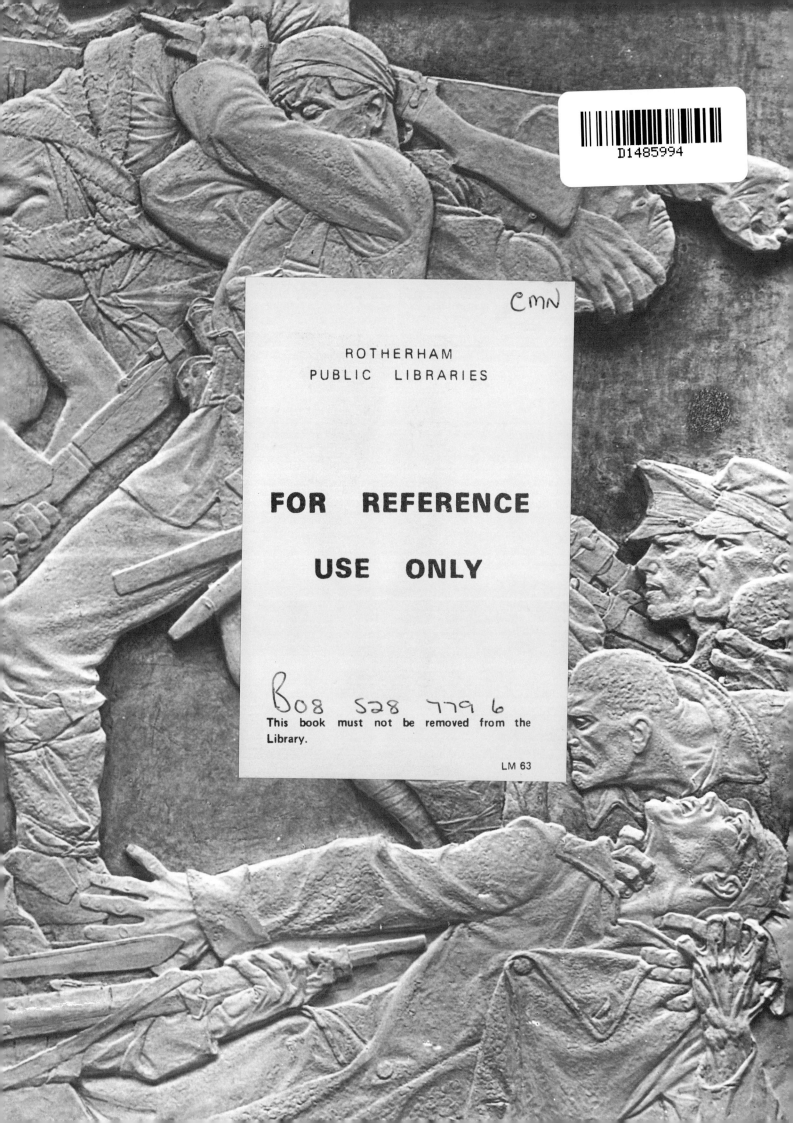

ILLUSTRATED HISTORY OF
20th CENTURY
CONFLICT

ILLUSTRATED HISTORY OF 20th CENTURY CONFLICT

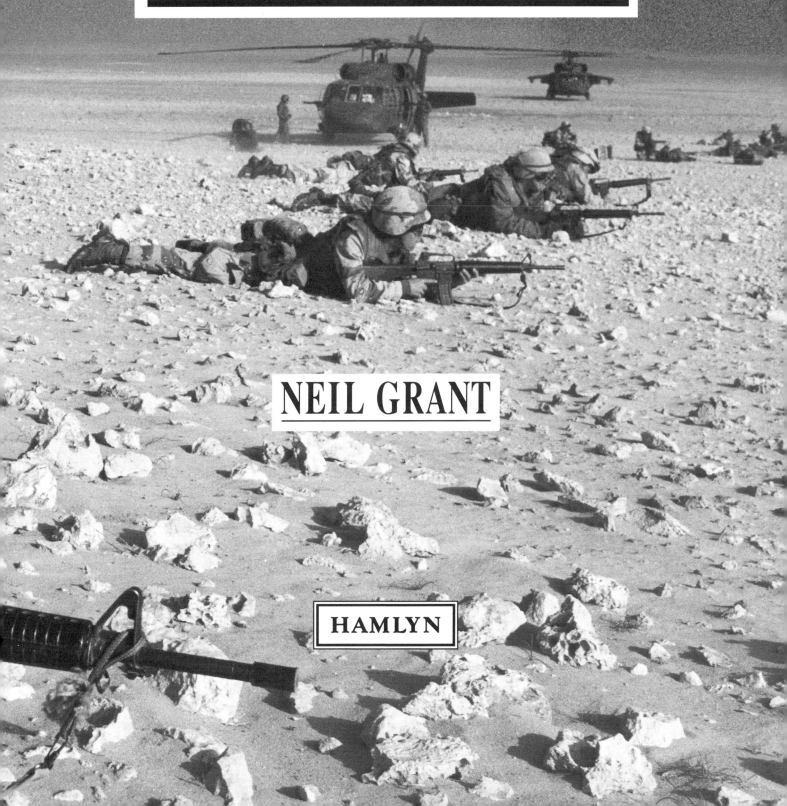

NEIL GRANT

HAMLYN

CONTENTS

Note Entries in capitals indicate feature spreads

Introduction page 9

Picture Militiamen embrace in front of the burning parliament building in Georgia, 1992

Endpaper picture
The Battle of Ypres, 1914. Sculpture by C.S. Jagger

Half title picture
An American marine on Okinawa, 1945

Title picture
Soldiers dropped by helicopter into combat positions during the Gulf War, 1991

Book design: Christopher Matthews

First published in 1992 by
Reed Consumer Books
Michelin House
81 Fulham Road
London SW3 6RB

Hamlyn is an imprint of
Reed Consumer Books
part of Reed International Books

A catalogue record for this book is available from the British Library

ISBN 0 600 57464 4

Produced by Mandarin Offset
Printed in China

UNCIVIL WARS   page 324

Picture Lebanese gunmen in Beirut behind a barricade, 1975

PHOTOGRAPHIC ACKNOWLEDGEMENTS

The publishers would like to thank all those who have supplied photographs for use in this book and apologise to any whose contribution may have been inadvertently omitted from these acknowledgements. We are particularly grateful to picture researchers Julia Ruxton and Anne Hobart, Dawn Wyman, Anna Calvert and the staff of the Hulton Picture Company, Julie Quiery of Paul Popper Limited, Judith Millidge of Bison Books, and Roy Segal of Leo Baeck College Library.

The majority of the photographs in this book are from the Hulton-Deutsch Collection, London, including material from the Bettmann Archive, the *Evening Standard* Collection, the Keystone Collection and UPI. Other sources are as follows: Argus Printing and Publishing Company, Durban/Laurie Bloomfield 270-1; Associated Press, London 286 top; Camera Press, London 146 bottom left; Mary Evans Picture Library, London 32 bottom, 38 left; The Trustees of the Imperial War Museum, London endpapers, 1, 48-9, 65 bottom, 66 right, 70-1, 71, 73 left, 74 left, 75 centre, 78 top, 84 bottom, 88 top, 96 bottom, 98-9, 101 centre, 103, 107 left and right, 111, 112 top and bottom right, 113 (all), 115 centre and bottom, 117 top, 120 top, 121 bottom left, 178 bottom, 181 right, 185 bottom, 186 top, 188 top, 190 top, 191 top and bottom, 199 top, 200 top and bottom, 203 top and bottom, 204, 205 bottom, 207 top and bottom, 209 bottom left and right, 214 bottom, 218 bottom, 219, 220 top and bottom, 222 bottom, 225 top right and centre, 228 bottom, 229 bottom, 233, 237 bottom, 240 bottom right, 242 top and bottom left, 243 bottom, 244 top, 245, 246 centre and bottom, 255 centre, 258 top, 259 bottom, 261 top, 268 bottom left; Kyodo Photo Service, Tokyo 208 bottom; Library of Congress, Washington 90; Marshall Cavendish Publishing, London/National Archives 266 top, Novosti 238 top left; National Archives, Washington/Navy Department 208 top, 215 top; National Army Museum, London 58 bottom left; National Maritime Museum, London 198 top; Novosti, London 238 top centre and right, 238-9, 239; Popperfoto, Northampton 176 bottom, 177, 178 top, 179 bottom left and right, 181 left and centre, 183 bottom left and right, 195 bottom, 197 bottom left, 206 centre, 212 top and bottom, 217 top and bottom, 223 right, 225 top left, 226 top right, 229 centre, 240 bottom left, 240-1, 242 bottom right, 247 top and bottom, 249 bottom, 252 right, 253, 256 bottom left, 258 bottom, 262 bottom left and right, 267, 269 bottom right, 278, 278-9, 279 top, 282 bottom, 288 top, 293 top, 294 right, 296 bottom, 298 bottom, 305 bottom, 306 (all), 307 top and bottom, 309 top and bottom, 310 left, 311 top and bottom, 313 top and bottom, 317 top and bottom, 323 top, 333 top, 341 top, 342 bottom left and right, 347, 350 top right, 352 top and bottom right, 355 top, 361 top, 364 top, 365, 366 top and bottom, 367 top, 368 centre and right, 369 bottom, 370, 371, 372 bottom, 374 top and bottom, 375 top and bottom, 376 left and right, 377 top and bottom, 378 bottom, 379 top, 380 (all), 382 top and bottom, 383, 385 bottom, 387 bottom, 388 right, 389 (all); Reed International Books Ltd 15 inset right, Victoria & Albert Museum 22 top; Rex Features, London 387 top left, Mike Moore/*Today* 386, 386-7, Leon Schadeberg 384 top, Sipa Press 384 bottom, Sipa Press/Chamussy 387 top right, Sipa Press/Bill Gentile 2-3, Sipa Press/Malcolm Linton 8, 388 left; Roger-Viollet, Paris 57 top, 79, 85; Society for Cultural Relations with the USSR, London 218 top; Syndication International, London 170-1; TRH Pictures, London 336 bottom, 337, 354 bottom; T. A. Davies 346 bottom right, Department of Defense 373, 379 bottom, 385 top, United Nations/Y. Nagata 343, US Air Force/Kai-uwe Heinrich 380-1, US Navy 360 top; US Air Force 265 top; US Army 230 top, 250 top, 255 bottom; US Navy 215 bottom, 216, 224-5; US Signal Corps 87 bottom, 89 bottom.

INTRODUCTION

IT HAS BEEN SUGGESTED THAT WAR, in the sense of violent and sustained conflict between different communities, was unknown during the Old Stone Age. It is hard to believe that there was no violence whatsoever, since conflict is characteristic of practically all human societies. One thing *is* certain: war, like many other human activities, gained significance with the advent of civilization. As society developed, the art of warfare became more and more sophisticated. Today it is possible to conceive of a future without war in the traditional sense of the word, but it is impossible to conceive of a future without some form of violent conflict.

In spite of the peaceful intentions of many individuals and organizations throughout history, the impetus of developing civilization has been predominantly towards waging war more effectively, not towards ending it. Many of the greatest advances in science and technology have been inspired either directly or indirectly by military motives.

Future generations may look back on the 20th century, the most violent century yet, as a watershed in the history of war and human conflict. For the first time, wars were fought on a worldwide scale, employing all the resources that had become available since the Industrial Revolution. War ceased to consist of limited engagements between professional soldiers and became a huge national enterprise involving the whole population. In the Second World War, casualties were greater among civilians than among the armed forces. Subsequently, weapons of such destructive power were developed that the employment of even a fraction of them would have been enough to destroy all life on Earth. Full-scale, international war became impractical: no one could win.

While nuclear weapons – or the capacity to make them – exist, it is highly likely that some day they will be put to use. Nevertheless, the experience of the Cold War, when the United States and the Soviet Union threatened each other with missiles capable of annihilation, but refrained from launching them, offered some hope that the ultimate holocaust may be avoided. The era of the Cold War, however, was by no means an era of peace. There were numerous local wars, in which the superpowers sometimes participated directly and sometimes by proxy, not to mention many other minor conflicts.

If anything, the scale of violence was escalating: a survey conducted in 1986 concluded that the number of people killed by bombs and bullets in the previous forty years was greater than the total number of military casualties in the Second World War. By 1992 the number of wars (involving regular armed forces) approached 200, and the incidence of such wars, about nine per year in the 1950s, rose to a peak of about 14 per year in the 1970s.

Comparatively few of these wars were waged between nations. More than half originated in attempts to overthrow a government in one particular country. However, in the 20th century, even civil wars cannot be fought in isolation and the interests of other powers usually affect the outcome of Third-World conflicts.

The localization of war, and the rising tide of ethnic hostility, demonstrates one way in which war and conflict have changed since the middle of the century. Another development is the rise of terrorism and guerrilla wafare, resulting partly from easy access to powerful weaponry but more importantly from the radicalization of disaffected groups and from the pervasiveness of the communications media, which encourages emulation and even co-operation among disparate groups, at the same time providing the publicity on which they thrive.

The existence of the United Nations (UN) was another factor which, though not new (it replaced the defunct League of Nations of 1918), acquired new significance in the second half of the century. Founded mainly to prevent international conflict, the UN holds a somewhat symbolic role. In practical terms its success has been limited, though less negligible than is often assumed. UN peacekeeping forces have performed thankless roles in many of the world's troublespots, where their presence has certainly helped to reduce the number of civilian casualties. The UN, of course, has proved ineffective in its attempts at arbitration in such bitter disputes as the Arab-Israeli conflict, nor was it able to contain the aggression of an unprincipled dictator like Saddam Hussein, although it did provide the sanction for the use of force against him by the United States. The almost unanimous opposition to the Iraqi invasion of Kuwait and the subsequent expulsion of the Iraqi forces was unprecedented and encouraging, though it gave no guarantees for the future.

Opposite. Militiamen embrace in front of the burning parliament building in Georgia, 1992

1900-1913
THE COMING
STORM

ALTHOUGH THE FIRST DECADE OF THE 20TH CENTURY was a period of relative stability, grave underlying problems threatened both the existing social order the world over and the peace of Europe in particular. Britain, isolated in its struggle with the Boers, sought an ally in France. German naval expansion alarmed its neighbours and the continuing Moroccan crisis exacerbated Franco-German enmity. In Russia, humiliated in a war with Japan, there was an attempt at revolution, and in China the Manchu Empire finally crumbled. Turkey was attacked in turn by Italy and the Balkan countries and lost most of its European possessions. At the end of 1913 the great powers, enmeshed in rival alliances, regarded one another with growing suspicion. There was, moreover, a particular conflict of interest between Russia and Austria-Hungary in the Balkans.

1900 Ladysmith relieved

The Boxer threat

On January 27 diplomatic representatives of the European powers in Peking requested the imperial government to take immediate action against rebellious elements known as the Boxers, who were responsible for threats and acts of violence against Europeans and other Christians in China.

The Chinese–Japanese war of 1894-95 had initiated a period of rapid change in China, one result of which was a rising tide of hostility towards the 'foreign devils' who appeared to be responsible for the looming destruction of Chinese culture. By early 1900 this hostility was taking an increasingly violent form. ▶ *page 17*

On February 28 the long ordeal of the people and garrison of Ladysmith was ended. British troops under General Sir Redvers Buller at last broke through the besieging Boers to relieve the town. It was the first occasion for real celebration in the British camp since the start of the South African War and especially satisfying for General Buller, whose earlier attempts to raise the siege had signally failed.

The South African War had begun four months earlier when Britain failed to respond to an ultimatum from President Kruger of the Transvaal republic which expired on October 12, 1899. It was a war which, all neutral observers agreed, the British could hardly lose in the long run, but at the beginning of 1900 they showed little sign of being able to win it.

The Boers, who were well prepared for war and had been collecting arms avidly for years, had invaded Natal on the outbreak of the war and, within about two weeks, the relatively small British forces in the region were all compelled to fall back to Ladysmith. In an ill-advised attempt to break up the investing forces, the British had lost about 1500 men in the battle of Lombard's Kop, and by the first week of November 1899 Ladysmith was cut off.

The initial appearance of complete British inadequacy was to some extent dissipated by Sir John French's resistance to a superior force at Colesberg and the continued resistance of Ladysmith, as well as Kimberley and Mafeking, which were also threatened by the Boers. However, in the west territory was lost as the British withdrew, while Buller's efforts to relieve Ladysmith were defeated at Spion Kop and, in a lesser engagement, at Vaal Krantz.

When Lord Roberts took over command of the British forces in February 1900, he set off from the Cape with 30,000 men on a sweeping advance northeast, aiming to clear out the Boers from the Orange Free State who had invaded Cape Colony. Cronje, commanding the Boer force at Kimberley, delayed his retreat too long and was captured with 4000 men at Paardeberg, 70 miles

General Sir Redvers Buller, the first British commander in the Boer War.

east of Kimberley. When the Boers withdrew from Cape Colony and Natal, the pressure on Ladysmith was reduced, and the town was at last relieved by the persevering Buller on February 28. The 22,000 inhabitants were in poor shape, half-starving and disease-ridden, though the garrison was prepared to set off after the retreating Boers if Buller had not forbidden this. ▶ *page 16*

Reform and reaction in China

The Japanese war had demonstrated dramatically the weakness of the Manchu government, the backwardness of China and the total failure of the 'self-strengthening' endeavours of the previous 30 years. It was followed by a 'scramble' on the part of the European powers for commercial and other privileges, including leases of territory (such as Kowloon, adjoining Hong Kong). The European countries delineated their own 'spheres of interest', and such was their influence that Britain, for example, as the largest trade partner, was able to insist on the appointment of a Briton as the chief maritime customs official. Although the situation was somewhat ameliorated by the

United States' insistence on an 'open-door' policy – a safety measure to ensure that U.S. businessmen and bankers were not excluded from the foreign spheres of interest – China appeared to be on the point of partition among the imperialist, capitalist powers.

The easy Japanese victory also encouraged the rise of various reform groups in China which argued that, since Japan had grown so strong by adopting Western customs and institutions, China should do likewise. They gained the ear of the young emperor, and a whole series of radical reforms were promulgated in education, law, the army – in fact in almost every aspect of society.

All this was carried out in a rather ham-fisted way by officials with little administrative experience. The new policies were far from universally popular, and in 1898 the Dowager-Empress Tzu Hsi, anticipating moves against herself and her conservative counsellors, staged a coup d'état. The leading reformers, or those who failed to make their escape in time, were executed, the emperor became a virtual prisoner and most of the recent reforms were annulled.

This successful counterstroke on behalf of conservative Chinese tradition encouraged more extreme views, in particular the desire to rid the country of alien influence and exploi-

tation. Unrest was widespread in 1898-99. The old village yeomanry or militia was extensively infiltrated by members of a secret society dedicated to ridding China of foreign aggressors. They adhered to some rather strange ideas, such as the belief that certain rites rendered them invulnerable to bullets. These people were known to Westerners by the name of Boxers, derived from the Chinese name meaning 'Fists of Righteous Harmony'. From late 1899, encouraged, or at least not discouraged, by the dowager-empress, they began to harrass and persecute Chinese Christians, and in December of that year a British missionary was brutally murdered.

1900

JANUARY
6 Boer attack on Ladysmith repulsed
24 British attempt to relieve Ladysmith checked at Spion Kop
27 European diplomats demand restriction of Boxers in Peking

FEBRUARY
28 Buller relieves Ladysmith

MARCH
13 Roberts captures Bloemfontein
27 Russian fleet arrives in Korea
31 Outbreak of fighting in Ashanti

MAY
17 Mafeking relieved
28 Britain annexes Orange Free State

JUNE
5 Roberts captures Pretoria
7 Boxers cut railway to Peking
17 Westerners seize Taku forts
U.S. troops ordered to China
20 German ambassador in Peking murdered
24 Boxers attack foreign embassies

JULY
26 Western forces capture Tientsin from Boxers
30 King Umberto I of Italy assassinated

AUGUST
5 Anti-Semitic violence in Odessa
14 Besieged Peking embassies relieved

SEPTEMBER
30 Ashanti defeated at Obassa

OCTOBER
19 President Kruger leaves South Africa
25 Britain annexes the Transvaal

NOVEMBER
9 Russia extends occupation of Manchuria
13 British colonial official killed in Somalia

DECEMBER
3 Philippine rebels surrender to U.S. troops
11 Roberts leaves South Africa
28 Last rebel chiefs in Ashanti captured

Top. British dead after the disastrous battle of Spion Kop, in which the Boers inflicted heavy casualties.

Left. Soldiers of the Royal Lancasters with fixed bayonets storm Boer positions before raising the siege of Ladysmith.

13

Paul Kruger, the president of the Transvaal.

Joseph Chamberlain, British colonial secretary 1895-1903.

THE BOERS AND THE BRITISH

Cecil Rhodes, financier, statesman and empire builder.

TROUBLE between the descendants of the Dutch settlers in Cape Colony and the British dated from Britain's takeover of the colony in 1814. Especially irritating to the Boers ('farmers') was the British government's protective policy towards the blacks. When slavery was abolished, for example, the Boers received what they considered inadequate compensation. It was to escape British restrictions that Boer families made the Great Trek across the Orange River in 1835.

Within a few years there were two Boer republics, the Orange Free State and Transvaal in the north. The Cape and Natal were British colonies. There also existed small black protectorates, such as Basutoland, where Boers to their disgust found themselves under black authority.

Existing frictions were exacerbated by the discovery of, first, diamonds and, later, gold. Meanwhile, high-handed action by the governor of the self-governing Cape Colony provoked, first, a brief war with the Zulu and, following the annexation of the Transvaal in 1877, a rebellion by the Boers. The British government restored independence to the Transvaal in 1881 but relations between Boer and British remained hostile.

When the European 'scramble' for African colonies got under way, the British became increasingly concerned for their strategic position in southern Africa. They made a series of territorial annexations, including Zululand, which had the result of denying Transvaal access to the Indian Ocean. The Boer republic, now seething with gold-hungry newcomers, or uitlanders, found itself surrounded – hemmed in like a kraal as President Kruger complained – by British territory.

The uitlanders, who far outnumbered the Boers, were denied the vote by Kruger and, although this did not prevent some of them growing very wealthy, it was ostensibly to assist them that the imperialist Cape governor, Cecil Rhodes, surreptitiously (but with the tacit assent of the British colonial secretary, Joseph Chamberlain) organized the Jameson Raid in 1895. This was an armed sortie into the Transvaal which was supposed to be in support of a (nonexistent) rising of the uitlanders. The raid fizzled out and Rhodes had to resign, but the Transvaal signed a military alliance with the Orange Free State. Chamberlain claimed to exercise powers over the Transvaal which were unacceptable to Kruger and, although Chamberlain gained judicial backing, these powers were unsupported by the agreement of 1881. Kruger refused to compromise over the question of political rights for uitlanders, the British government despatched 10,000 extra troops to South Africa and the South African, or Boer, War began on October 12, 1899.

THE AFRIKANERS AT WAR

THE BRITISH had only about 30,000 troops in Cape Colony at the start of the war, one-third of them colonial volunteers. The commander-in-chief, Sir Redvers Buller, arrived in Cape Town the day after Lombard's Kop, soon followed by the first troops from England.

The Boers, especially those of the Transvaal, were skilled and experienced fighters, organized in local commandos. Their main strength lay in their mounted riflemen (though they were also well supplied with artillery), who were armed with clip-loading German Mausers – superior to the British Lee-Metford rifles.

They fought well above their numerical strength; nevertheless, numbers were their fundamental weakness. Although, unlike the British, they did not have to allocate large numbers to logistical matters, their top fighting strength was only about 90,000, whereas the British ultimately deployed 448,000 men.

In view of the Boer threat to Ladysmith and, to a lesser extent, Mafeking and Kimberley, the British had to forego their initial plan of an invasion of the Orange Free State. Buller's force had therefore been split up into three immediately on arrival. In the west, a division under Lord Methuen was sent to Kimberley, but was held up by the Boers on the Modder River where it suffered 500 casualties. Methuen himself was wounded and encountered problems with supply.

This was the presage of near-total disaster. Methuen's advance was very decisively checked at Magersfontein, where a night attack by the Highland brigade was repulsed before it had begun with 750 casualties (including its general). In the same week (December 9-15) General Sir William Gatacre, advancing along the central line of the three Cape trunk railway lines, also essayed a night attack – on the Boers' position at Stormberg in the Great Kei valley – and, misled by guides, was ambushed and forced to retreat with heavy casualties. Buller himself advanced in the east along the third trunk line towards the relief of Ladysmith. At Colenso, on the Tugela River, he too was confounded by ignorance of the ground and defeated by the Boers, under Louis Botha, who were covering Ladysmith. He sent a message to Sir George White, in command at Ladysmith where conditions were deteriorating, suggesting that he should surrender the town, but White did not do so.

These disasters persuaded the British government that 'fifty thousand foot going to Table Bay' were not enough to defeat the Boers. The experienced Field Marshal Lord Roberts was sent out as commander-in-chief, with General Lord Kitchener as his chief-of-staff, and considerable reinforcements including volunteer militia and contingents from Canada and Australia.

Below. A naval gun bombards Boer defences around Magersfontein.

Boer artillery in action near Ladysmith.

The formidable clip-loading Mauser rifle.

Roberts invades Boer republics

On March 13 Roberts took Bloemfontein, capital of the Orange Free State. There was little resistance. However, the British advance was checked in part by outbreaks of disease, in particular enteric fever. Roberts was also forced to wait at Bloemfontein for supplies before continuing his advance towards the Transvaal.

The Boers made best use of the pause. On the death of the commandant-general, Piet Joubert, the more energetic Louis Botha took over, while the Orange Free Staters, whom Roberts had regarded as defeated, became active again under Christiaan de Wet, cutting off several of the flying columns which Roberts sent out to offer peace to the civilian population and ambushing a mounted brigade at Sannah's Post outside Bloemfontein.

In May Roberts moved off again. A flying column was sent to relieve Mafeking, where Colonel Robert Baden-Powell had commanded the long defence with the kind of determined cheerfulness that he was to bequeath to the Boy Scout movement. By the end of the month Roberts was in Johannesburg, securing the precious gold mines, and less than a week later he was in Pretoria. He had encountered little serious resistance, though De Wet harassed his communications and he was short of supplies. At this point the Boers had only about 15,000 men in the field and, not for the first time, there was talk of peace.

Above. Field Marshal Lord Roberts, the victorious British commander in South Africa.

Left. British infantry crossing a river with the aid of life-lines.

British governor trapped in Kumasi

The governor of the Gold Coast, Sir Frederic Hodgson, was trapped in Kumasi in March by a rising of the Ashanti against the British. Together with his wife and the other members of his party, he was forced to take refuge in the British fort, which was manned by less than 1000 troops, and with no immediate prospect of relief.

In 1896, when Ashanti (a region of modern Ghana) had shown some reluctance to accept British 'protection', a British force had occupied Kumasi, the capital. The young king, Prempeh, and members of his court were exiled to the Seychelles. The British wanted to protect the Gold Coast colony, not to occupy Ashanti, and the result was a power vacuum, with the old order destroyed but the British failing to offer a substitute. The golden stool of Kumasi, on which the ruler traditionally sat, was hidden away, and it was this action that provided the spark that set off war in 1900. The governor of the Gold Coast, while on a visit to Kumasi, demanded that the golden stool be produced for him to sit upon, whereupon the Ashanti rose in wrath against the British.

Reinforcements were sent, hastily despatched from the Gold Coast and Lagos, but by June 23, the date on which Hodgson had advised he would be forced to surrender, the relief forces were still far away. Nearly two weeks later, with help not yet in sight, the defenders broke out, their main force consisting of about 600 Hausa. They reached Cape Coast Castle on July 10. A relief force of mainly Yoruba troops, with four seven-pounders and several Maxim guns, relieved the skeleton garrison left in Kumasi five days later.

The Ashanti were at last defeated at Obassa on September 30, though a few rebel chiefs held out until the end of the year, when British control was finally re-established. The inevitable political result was the annexation of Ashanti in 1901.

Sir Frederick Hodgson, the governor of the Gold Coast.

Boxers besiege Peking embassies

On June 24 the Boxers laid siege to the foreign legation compound and the Roman Catholic cathedral in Peking. Besides European diplomatic staff, missionaries, Chinese Christians and others were taking refuge there. In other places Christian missionaries and thousands of their converts were killed, although some local authorities tried to protect foreigners.

During the first six months of 1900 attacks on foreigners and Christians in China had increased, the victims including Chinese workers on the foreign-owned railways. The European powers took steps to protect their own citizens and on June 17 they seized the Taku forts on the coast which guarded the route to Peking. That act provoked a full-scale rising by the Boxers. The empress, overriding more moder-ate counsels, demanded that all foreigners be killed. The German ambassador was murdered.

An international, six-nation force of about 10,000 men, under German command, was sent to rescue the besieged foreigners in Peking. It had to fight its way there, but completed the task on August 14 and, after looting the city, moved on to relieve pockets of Christians elsewhere and disperse the Boxers. ▶ page 18

Above. Senior European army officers entering Peking.

Left. A corner of the British Legation.

Boers defeated at Diamond Hill

On June 9 Louis Botha's men fought the last major battle of the South African War at Diamond Hill, 20 miles east of Pretoria, in order to protect the retreating Transvaal government. Part of Buller's army, already depleted by the need to replace Roberts' losses, joined up with Roberts, while the remainder marched west into the Orange Free State, forcing De Wet to flee and capturing 4000 men in the Brandwater Basin on the border of Basutoland. The last Transvaal force was defeated at Dalmanutha, and President Kruger of the Transvaal boarded a Dutch warship at Lourenço Marques in Mozambique, bound for Marseilles.
▶ page 18

A battalion of regular Chinese soldiers on the march.

1901

Christian De Wet, one of the ablest of the Boer commanders, showed himself to be a master of guerrilla warfare.

Protocol ends Boxer episode

Although in the previous year the European powers had insisted that they were not making war on China, only on the Boxers, a formal protocol was signed on September 7 1901. It imposed some severe conditions, including large financial reparations (secured against customs revenue) and the control of the route from Peking to the sea by Western troops. China was, even more obviously than before, in the grip of the 'foreign devils', who behaved like conquerors dealing with a defeated enemy. It was evident, even to the empress, that the West could not be excluded or ignored, while to informed outsiders the downfall of the Manchu dynasty appeared only a matter of time.

Boers launch guerrilla war

Roberts left South Africa in November 1900, having annexed the Orange Free State and the Transvaal and declared the South African War at an end. However, the Boers refused to stop fighting. Following the guerrilla tactics adopted so successfully by De Wet during 1901, they harassed the British at every turn. The fragile railway communications were constantly sabotaged, isolated outposts were captured and small detachments ambushed. Columns sent in pursuit of the perpetrators never managed to catch up with them. De Wet even surrounded a whole brigade at Frederickstad, though forced to retreat with the loss of guns and supplies. Botha was active in the northern Transvaal, De la Rey and Beyers in the west. De Wet's men spread disaffection and revolt in the Orange Free State and the Cape Colony, and the British were hard-pressed to keep the troubles localized.

Kitchener, who had succeeded Roberts as commander-in-chief, demanded reinforcements and evolved new strategies, most notoriously the depopulation of areas of conflict by moving the civilian families into concentration camps. (The imprisonment and, in the early days, frequent deaths of their wives and children did not incline the Boer fighters to sweet reason.) The railways were protected by chains of blockhouses linked with barbed wire, which proved so successful that Kitchener extended the plan to other areas.

The guerrilla leaders continued to evade the British, but they were running short of men and munitions. Botha opened negotiations with Kitchener on February 26, but they failed to reach agreement and the guerrilla war continued throughout the year, with De Wet securing a final Boer success at Tweefontein in the northern Orange Free State, where he captured a force of yeomanry in December.

Kitchener (seated), who succeeded Roberts as commander-in-chief in South Africa.

1902

THE BOER WAR

CRISIS IN VENEZUELA

Thousands die in Colombian clashes

Sporadic civil war in Colombia continued from 1899 to 1902, chiefly over religion and the control of education. Liberal rebels were finally defeated by government troops in 1902, and the revolt and eventual secession of Panama had, in the long run, a pacifying effect on the bitter partisan politics of Colombia. Future disturbances stemmed more from reasons of economic dissatisfaction.

Crowds at the Royal Exchange, London, celebrating peace in South Africa.

Venezuela blockaded

On December 19 1902 British and German ships captured the harbour of La Guaira, the port of the Venezuelan capital, Caracas. The Venezuelan navy, including several large if elderly warships, was effectively blockaded. British and German nationals in Venezuela were harassed and a few shots were fired at a harbour fortress, but no casualties were reported.

Apart from the 18-year-rule of Guzman Blanco (1870-88), Venezuela was in almost constant turmoil during the late 19th century. In the 1890s border conflicts with British Guiana almost ended in outright war before U.S. President Grover Cleveland compelled arbitration. In 1899 a rough veteran of the civil wars, Cipriano Castro, gained power. Moral principle was not a discernible feature of his rule and among those who suffered were foreign companies and individuals who had invested heavily in Venezuela in the 1890s.

It was to compel payment of these debts that British and German warships, joined by the Italians a few days later, blockaded the country. The dispute went to the International Court at the Hague, which eventually enforced payment to the blockading nations in a judgment given in 1907. Other European creditors remained unsatisfied, however. The French broke off diplomatic relations in 1906, and in 1908 Dutch gunboats destroyed the Venezuelan fleet and blockaded the coast. Venezuela's debts were not finally paid off until oil revenue began to flow in the 1920s.

South African peace agreed

A series of British drives wore down the last Boer resistance in the spring of 1902 and peace was signed at Vereeniging on May 31. The Boer republics lost their independence in return for reparations and a promise that self-government would be granted before the vote was given to blacks. Preparations began for the union of South Africa, which was formally established in 1910. In the course of the South African War, the Boers lost about 4000 killed, the British nearly 6000, with 23,000 wounded.

De Wet evades British

British forces appeared to have De Wet surrounded in the former Orange Free State in February, but the wily Boer leader once more evaded them. His son, however, was captured. Meanwhile a Boer commando managed to come within 50 miles of Cape Town before being pushed back. De Wet and other commando leaders, such as Steyn, remained at large until the war ended.

General Cipriano Castro, the despotic ruler of Venezuela.

19

British capture Kano

The old, mud-walled city of Kano, northern Nigeria, was captured on February 3 by 700 British-officered African troops under the orders of Colonel, later Lord Lugard. Sokoto fell a few weeks later.

By 1900 most of southern Nigeria, including Benin, had been brought into the British protectorate, authority having been transferred from the Royal Niger Company. Lugard was appointed to enforce British authority in northern Nigeria. The administration had to be formed under what was described as a 'somewhat acute military situation'; nevertheless, progress was rapid, though a few recalci-

trant emirs were replaced with more amenable successors.

In 1902 a British resident in Nasarawar was murdered and the murderer escaped north to Kano, then still an independent, Muslim state, the emir of which refused to surrender him to British justice. Kano was the chief commercial and military centre of the Fulani states of northern Nigeria, the leader of which was the sultan of Sokoto, a declared enemy of the British. It was evident that British control could not be imposed without the military defeat of the emirs (any one of whom could have put a much larger force in the field than Lugard commanded). A campaign aimed at

Sokoto and Kano began in January 1903. Sokoto fell, the sultan fled (before the battle) and he was replaced by an alternative who agreed to acknowledge British authority and abandon the slave trade. The various other emirs and chiefs of northern Nigeria rapidly fell into line. Apart from a minor rising against the new sultan of Sokoto in 1906, and one or two actions against non-Muslim tribal groups, no serious military resistance to Lugard's policy of 'indirect rule' was encountered.

A primitive foundry in northern Nigeria.

Pogrom in Kishinev

The bodies of victims of anti-Semitic outrages in Russia.

Beginning on April 8, savage attacks against Jews were perpetrated in the town of Kishinev in Bessarabia. The pogrom was said to have been instigated by Russian officials. About 50 people were killed, many more were wounded, women were raped and houses burned. In spite of the frequency of reports of social unrest in Russia – strikes, riots, assassinations, etc. – the Kishinev slaughter was especially shocking.

Anti-Semitism was rising everywhere in 19th-century Europe. It found its most violent expression in Russia where a special commission headed by a former minister of justice had in 1888 condemned the policy of Russification and remarked that 'the mass [of Jews]

lives in dread of pogroms, in dread of violence . . .' The commission's report was ignored, and violence became more frequent. The massacre at Kishinev marked a turning point for Eastern European Jewry – the beginning of self-defence. V. K. Pleve, the notorious interior minister responsible for numerous persecutions and probable organizer of pogroms carried out by the notorious Black Hundreds, was assassinated the following year. During the 1905 Revolution there were pogroms in numerous towns and cities, notably Odessa, where hundreds of people were killed before troops attempted to stop the massacre. Similar outbreaks occurred in Poland in 1905-06.
▶ *page 30*

Thousands of Bulgarians massacred

In a ferocious attack by Turkish troops on September 8 thousands of Bulgarians – men, women and children – were killed. One report (no doubt exaggerated) estimated the deaths at 50,000. Villagers who escaped into the forest were hunted down, flushed out and slaughtered. Further outbreaks of violence occurred later. A simultaneous revolt in Macedonia brought Turkey and Bulgaria, at this time an autonomous province, to the brink of war, but genocidal outbreaks in the Balkans had been going on for years.

It was a series of similar incidents that had brought the British prime minister, William Gladstone, out of political retirement in 1876 with his furious pamphlet denouncing the Turks for perpetrating *Bulgarian Horrors*. The massacre of 1903, though worse than most, was all too typical. The most publicized massacres were perpetrated on the former or current Christian subjects of Turkey by ill-disciplined and unpaid Turkish troops, but there were also many episodes of slaughter inflicted by one Christian nation on another. In this period, during the final stages of the Ottoman Empire's decline, the Balkans were a bloody cockpit of strife, where the value of human life was negligible.

Macedonian revolutionaries prepare to oppose Turkish rule.

Panama gains independence

Panamanian rebels declared their independence from Colombia on November 3 and launched a revolt. They acted in collusion with the French Panama Canal company and with the tacit encouragement of the United States, which promptly recognized Panamanian independence and prevented Colombian troops landing in Panama (despite a clause in the U.S.-Colombian treaty of 1846 recognizing Colombia's sovereignty in Panama).

Colombia, torn by civil war and facing economic ruin at the beginning of the century, looked for some relief from the proposal to cut a canal through the isthmus of Panama. The government had granted a concession to a French company for this purpose in 1878, but the project had foundered on human corruption and natural obstacles (especially disease). It was taken up again in 1899 by the United States, which had also considered an alternative route through Nicaragua. Difficulties then arose when the French company, which was hoping to recoup some of its losses, demanded a high price for its holdings. The U.S. Isthmian Canal Commission now recommended Nicaragua as a less expensive alternative. Political leaders in Panama were afraid the golden goose would lay its egg elsewhere, and, assured of powerful international support, declared independence. In 1921, on receipt of $25 million 'reparations' from the United States, Colombia recognized Panama's independence.

Locks on the Panama Canal under construction. Work on the canal actually began in 1904, but was not completed until ten years later.

1904

Yalu river defeat

The Japanese forces that invaded Korea defeated a larger Russian force on the Yalu River, forming the border between Korea and Manchuria, on April 30-May 1. The victorious Japanese continued their advance into southern Manchuria.

Dairen was captured on May 30, thus cutting off Port Arthur, which now came under attack from land as well as sea. In August the Russian Port Arthur fleet broke out, intending to join up with the Vladivostock squadron, but it was intercepted by Togo and scattered. Some ships returned to Port Arthur. Others escaped to neutral ports and were interned until the end of the war.

A Japanese officer on deck during a naval engagement.

British campaign in Somalia

The followers of the Somali religious leader, Sayyid Muhammad bin Abdullah Hassan, known to his enemies as the Mad Mullah, were said to have suffered 1000 casualties during an attack by a British military expedition on January 11.

The British Somaliland protectorate was regarded in London as one of the least significant constituents of the empire. It also proved one of the most troublesome. Rebellion had broken out there in 1899. Sayyid Muhammad was in fact a man of learning and political skill, as well as a zealous religious reformer. He had initially co-operated with the British authorities, but fell out with them in 1899 over various matters, notably the recent establishment of a Christian mission. A member of the reformist sect of the Salihiya, he was a fiery speaker inspired, no doubt, by the recent career of the Mahdi in the Sudan. His dervishes adopted guerrilla tactics against the cumbersome British troops who, restricted by logistical problems, were unable to crush the revolt.

The expedition of 1904 was one a series, and eventually the British almost completely abandoned the interior. They kept the dervishes in check by the use of a camel-riding police force, and finally routed them in 1920 in an operation that included the aerial bombing of the dervish stronghold of Taleh. Sayyid Muhammad died of flu a few months afterwards.

British-officered troops in action against dervishes in Somalia.

Japanese fleet attacks Russia

On the night of February 8 the main Japanese fleet, commanded by Vice-Admiral Heihachiro Togo, attacked the Russian squadron in Port Arthur – without declaring war. The Russians suffered serious losses, and some shore batteries were put out of action, but the Russian squadron, though depleted, remained intact. It was, however, confined to the harbour.

After weeks of stalemate, Japanese cruisers, sailing close to shore, tempted the Russians to put to sea, but they turned back when Togo's main battlefleet appeared. On the way home they encountered lines of electromagnetic mines laid by the Japanese (they had somehow missed them on the way out). The flagship *Petropavlovsk* was sunk and 600 men drowned, including the experienced and respected Admiral Stepan Makarov, and another battleship was badly damaged. Thereafter the Port Arthur squadron remained in harbour. Meanwhile, the Russian squadron at Vladivostock inflicted some damage on Japanese merchant ships while evading a squadron of Japanese cruisers under Vice-Admiral Kamimura.
► page 24

The Russian flagship *Petropavlovsk* goes down after striking a mine.

British expedition enters Lhasa

On August 3 the British military expedition accompanying the Younghusband mission entered Lhasa. Though fierce fighting had taken place before the expedition reached the Tibetan capital, there was only minor resistance – from unarmed peasants. The Dalai Lama sought sanctuary in a nearby monastery, whence he fled to Mongolia.

The British had been trying, with limited success, to open relations with the Tibetans since 1774. During the second half of the 19th century, with Manchu China too weak to intervene, dependants such as Burma, Sikkim, Nepal and Bhutan all became attached to the British raj. The Tibetans who, Chinese suzerainty notwithstanding, were virtually independent under their theocratic rulers, caused some trouble in this region, invading Sikkim in 1888, repudiating a treaty which the British had negotiated with the Chinese in 1890 and offering various other minor affronts to the dignity of the raj. However, what stirred the British into action was the sudden increase of Russian influence in the area, which, though opposed by the Chinese, was encouraged by the Dalai Lama. It was rumoured in the subcontinent that a draft treaty confirming Russian 'protection' over Tibet had already been drawn up.

The viceroy of India, Lord Curzon, favoured prompt and powerful military action, but the London government allowed only a small mission led by Colonel, later Sir Francis, Younghusband, a remarkable traveller, scholar and religious mystic, who in later life was to found the World Congress of (Religious) Faiths. The mission arrived at Kampa Dzong, more or less on the Tibetan frontier (its precise whereabouts was one of the subjects to be negotiated), on July 7, 1903. The Tibetans sent no authoritative representatives and no progress was made, so the British adopted more forceful measures. On October 3 the British government authorized an armed incursion, and on December 12 a military expedition, with troops under the command of General Ronald Macdonald, entered Tibet. The following spring, they advanced to Gyantse, after several minor brushes with the Tibetans. Thereafter, greater resistance was encountered. The chief problem for the British, besides human resistance, was transport in the mountainous terrain. On May 6 the troops protecting Younghusband's mission were ambushed by about 3000 Tibetans in the Karo Pass. Gurkha soldiers climbed sheer cliffs to attack the Tibetans from above, and about 400 Tibetans were killed in this engagement alone. Total Tibetan casualties were reported to run into thousands.

When he arrived at Lhasa Younghusband adopted a conciliatory tone, promising to go as soon as outstanding difficulties had been solved. The regent and national assembly proved relatively co-operative and a treaty was signed on September 7 which provided for two markets to be open to foreign trade, abolition of customs duties between Tibet and India, and no Tibetan territory to be ceded to any other foreign power (i.e., Russia). ▶ page 30

The 13th Dalai Lama, 1876-1933.

Followers of the Dalai Lama harassing the British expeditionary force.

1904

JANUARY
11 Herero massacre German settlers
British kill Somali rebels

FEBRUARY
5 U.S. troops leave Cuba
8 Surprise attack by Japanese on Port Arthur

MARCH
14 Extra German troops sent to South-West Africa
31 British clash with Tibetans near Guru

APRIL
5 Dutch suppress revolt in Sumatra
8 Anglo-French *Entente Cordiale* agreed
12 Russian battleship *Petropavlovsk* sunk

MAY
6 British defeat Tibetans in Karo Pass

JUNE
15 General Oku defeats Russians at Telissu
23 Russian governor of Finland assassinated

AUGUST
3 Younghusband mission enters Lhasa

SEPTEMBER
3 In South-West Africa Hottentot chief refuses to disarm his men
4 Japanese capture Liao-Yang
7 Anglo-Tibetan treaty signed

OCTOBER
22 Russians attack Hull trawlers

NOVEMBER
12 Von Trotha takes command in South-West Africa
13 50 die in Polish riots against Russian rule

The Russo-Japanese war

The Russian-Japanese war was the end result of the conflicting ambitions of the two chief imperial powers in the Far East. In 1895 Japan, having secured extensive gains from its successful war against China, was forced to give most of them up by the pressure of the European powers, which were not yet prepared to recognize Japan as a member of the imperialist club. Shortly thereafter, the Europeans took advantage of Manchu China's weakness by establishing themselves in various Chinese ports and coastal territories. Russia took over Port Arthur (Lu-shun) in 1898, after Japan had been forced to surrender it, and consolidated its position in Manchuria, which was developing into the most highly industrialized region of China. Japan's protests became more heated in 1903 when Russia was seen to be extending its interest to Korea. Intensive negotiations took place in St Petersburg from August 1903, but no agreement was reached and in February 1904 they were suddenly broken off.

Japan had harboured the strongest suspicions of Russia for much longer, certainly since the Sakhalin incident of 1875 (when Japan had been forced to cede that island to Russia). At that time it was comparatively weak militarily, but since then great changes had taken place. By 1903 Japan had a large and well-equipped army and navy, considerably stronger than the forces which had defeated China with such ease in 1894. It had also gained in confidence after securing an alliance with Britain in 1902.

Japan needed to strike a decisive blow before its vastly larger opponent could mobilize its massive resources – hence the naval strike at Port Arthur. The Russians needed to hold their position until they could bring up large reinforcements via the almost completed Trans-Siberian railway.

23

Russians kill British fishermen

Russian warships attacking British trawlers in the North Sea.

Japanese victory at Liao-yang

The Japanese forces in Manchuria, under Field Marshal Iwao Oyama, confronted a superior force of 500,000 Russians under General Alexei Kuropatkin at Liao-yang. The battle lasted from August 25 to September 4, with about 20,000 casualties on each side. Though Japanese casualties were probably higher, the battle was a victory for them, partly because of Kuropatkin's overestimate of their strength and his resulting defensive strategy.

The Russians retreated to Mukden but, with the Japanese, who had insufficient reserves, exhausted, and the railway bringing in 30,000 men a day, ultimate Russian victory still looked possible. Moreover, the initial Japanese attack on Port Arthur had been beaten off, though efforts to relieve the port failed.

Subsequent battles in Manchuria, though they involved large numbers of men, were indecisive. The Russians, with revolution simmering at home, lacked confidence; the Japanese lacked reserves. At sea, Japanese supremacy was unquestioned. The Vladivostock squadron, when Kamimura finally caught up with it, was defeated, and Port Arthur appeared doomed. ▶ *page 27*

On October 22 Russian ships of the Baltic fleet fired on British trawlers on the Dogger Bank. Several fishermen were killed, and the incident provoked furious indignation in Britain. The country was an ally of Japan, with whom Russia was at war, though the alliance required active intervention by Britain only if Japan were attacked by two powers simultaneously.

The Russian Baltic fleet, consisting of about 50 ships under Admiral Zinovi Rozhdestvenski, had been despatched to redress the balance in the Pacific, where Admiral Togo ruled the waves. The incident on the Dogger Bank sprang from Russian anxiety concerning torpedo attacks. Afterwards British ships shadowed Rozhdestvenski for some way but did not interfere.

Germans crush Herero revolt

A revolt in South-West Africa against German settlement, which began on January 11, was crushed by General Lothar von Trotha. The Germans thereafter pursued a campaign of vengeance against the Herero.

South-West Africa became a German protectorate in 1884, after Britain had ignored an implied invitation to take it over, and was effectively annexed by 1890. German settlers arrived in some numbers from 1892, and trouble with the various peoples of the region began almost at once. For example, over 100 Hottentots – men, women and children – were killed in 1893 after their chief had rebelled.

The appointment of Theodor Leutwein as governor in 1896 produced a more considerate policy, but did not assuage native African grievances. The most serious revolt occurred when the Herero, joined by some Hottentots and others, rose against the

German colonists in January 1904. As so often happened in areas of European settlement, the basic cause was land and misunderstanding of property rights. The settlers' land had been purchased legally, in European terms, but the Herero (and others) had no conception of private property in the European sense and were unaware that they were surrendering access to traditional grazing lands and waterholes. At the time of the outbreak most of the German soldiers in the area were away in the south dealing with trouble among the Namqua, and the Herero rapidly overran the forts. They killed over 100 German settlers, but not women or children (with one or two exceptions). Nor did they attack non-German Europeans, such as the British and Dutch missionaries in the region.

Von Trotha suppressed the rising, though a few Hottentots held out for several years, but his subsequent crusade reduced the Herero, who had numbered about 80,000 in 1904, to less than 20,000, mostly landless refugees.

Japanese troops on the march near Liao-yang.

1905

JANUARY

REVOLUTION IN RUSSIA

Count Sergei Witte, Russian statesman.

Bloody Sunday in St Petersburg

Several hundred unarmed workers were killed when the imperial guards at the Winter Palace opened fire on demonstrators on January 22. Some were shot and others trampled to death in the ensuing panic. One of the first to fall was Georgy Gapon, the priest leading the demonstration, though he proved to be unhurt.

The tsar, Nicholas II, a feeble character ill-suited to the role of autocrat yet determined to maintain this position, might have won over the moderate elements of the opposition when presented with a petition for civil rights organized by the Zemstvo Union in December 1904. Instead, he issued a conciliatory decree which was couched in general terms and passed over vital reforms in silence. The chance was lost, and the events of 'Bloody Sunday', January 22 (January 9 according to the Russian calendar then in use), heralded the outbreak of revolution.

One scheme employed by the police to smoke out revolutionaries was the organization of bogus trade unions which, by conducting strikes or demonstrations, revealed likely troublemakers. The trouble was that these police-licensed unions could turn out to be just as troublesome, especially to employers, as any others (trade unions were in any case illegal). When one such organization in St

Petersburg, led by Father Gapon, began to act like a genuine trade union, the employers requested its suppression. The request was refused, and the employers then enforced a lock-out. The workers decided to present a petition to the tsar, setting out their complaints against the employers. They carried icons and pictures of their 'little father' (the tsar) and sang religious and patriotic songs. The tsar was not present and the palace guard, panicked by the vast numbers, opened fire on the unarmed and relatively unaggressive crowd.

The immediate result was a wave of strikes and assassinations (especially of police officials), though one of the victims was the Grand Duke Sergei, son of Tsar Alexander II and military governor of Moscow. Disturbances spread to practically every region of the country and affected nearly all social classes. Dissident intellectuals shut down universities; Polish nationalists organized a boycott of the Russian language; Armenians and Tatars fought each other in the Caucasus; and peasants, demanding 'land for the people', attacked landlords and their property. Most dangerous of all, sporadic mutinies broke out in the armed forces. Poor conditions, not revolutionary zeal, were often the motive, but the crew of the battleship *Potemkin* demonstrated sympathy with striking workers by bombarding Odessa.

One of the main reasons for the surge of popular dissatisfaction with the government in 1904 had been the poor performance in the war against Japan. The defeats of early 1905 – Mukden in March, Tsushima in May – made matters worse. The constitutionalists (Zemstvo Union and the Union of Liberation) held a succession of congresses at which they drew up plans for reform, including an assembly elected by universal suffrage. In August the tsar conceded an imperial duma (parliament), but it was to be consultative only and membership was hedged about with restrictions (no Jews, for instance). This satisfied no one, though it did create some divisions among the constitutionalists between radicals and conservatives.

Besieged by his own subjects and humiliated by the Japanese, the tsar considered abdicating, but was saved by Count Witte, the one statesman who, if properly supported, might have circum-

vented the revolution but the tsar disliked his bourgeois origins. Witte was sent to lead the negotiations with the Japanese under the chairmanship of U.S. President Theodore Roosevelt, and it was largely thanks to him that the peace was successfully concluded in August. ▶ *page 28*

Officers of the battleship *Potemkin*, whose crew later mutinied.

REVOLUTION IN RUSSIA

AT THE beginning of the 20th century Russia remained an autocracy, with all power stemming from the tsar. Many reforms had been carried out (and more promised), but their effect had been largely cancelled out by subsequent restrictions and conditions. The State Council consisted of men appointed by the tsar himself and was, in any case, only an advisory body. The members of the executive Council of Ministers were individually appointed, and tended to run their own departments in competition, rather than in co-operation, with the others. The actual administration was conducted by a vast, hidebound bureaucracy, shot through with corruption. Representative bodies – the Zemstvos in the provinces and the dumas in the cities – had very limited powers locally and virtually none in state affairs.

For most of the previous 50 years Russians had asked one another not if revolution would occur but when. Opposition was widespread, but in spite of frequent violent outbreaks – strikes, riots, massacres and assassinations – it was less powerful than it seemed, partly because most of it

was forced to operate underground and partly because it comprised such a bewildering mass of different groups and interests with little in common.

Organized political opposition to the autocracy included: the Socialist Revolutionary Party, chiefly interested in the socialization of agricultural production; the Social Democratic Party, split since its congress held in London in 1903 into Bolsheviks ('majority men') and Mensheviks ('minority men'), who believed in immediate Marxist revolution or, in the case of the Bolsheviks, in Lenin's version of it; the Union of Liberation, organized in 1904, which broadly advocated constitutional democracy; and the Zemstvo Union, liberal in outlook and favouring democratic regional government. There was small prospect of these organizations co-operating with one other or with the dozens of other minor opposition groups. An additional weakness was that most opposition leaders, if not in prison or Siberia, were in exile.

Left. In Moscow a demonstrating crowd moves towards the city governor's palace.

Inset. Tsar Nicholas II and his son.   **Overturned trams and carts form street barricades in Odessa in November 1905.**

1905

RUSSO-JAPANESE WAR

REVOLUTION IN RUSSIA

Russian troops evacuating Port Arthur.

Port Arthur captured

The beleaguered port finally fell to General Maresuke Noge on January 2. Of the garrison of about 20,000 men, only about one-quarter were still fit to fight. The few remaining Russian warships in the harbour were scuttled before the surrender.

Noge's troops now became available for the Manchurian campaign, and the Japanese took Mukden in March. The battle lasted nearly two weeks, and virtually removed Kuropatkin's army as a fighting force. Casualties on both sides were very heavy, and General Oyama was unable to follow up the victory immediately despite the collapse of opposition.

Russian fleet destroyed

In one of the most one-sided naval engagements in history, the Russian Baltic fleet was shattered by Admiral Togo in Tsushima Strait on May 27. The complete superiority of Japan at sea was dramatically confirmed.

Rozhdestvenski's fleet was large, but of mixed quality, with many storeships and colliers. His voyage to the Far East, around South Africa, took over six months (reinforcements sent after him, which joined him off Indo-China, came via the Suez Canal), and he was not prepared for battle. Togo decided to wait for the Russians in home waters, calculating (correctly) that they would make for Vladivostock via the Tsushima Strait. With superior speed and manoeuvrability, Togo succeeded in effecting the tactic known as crossing the T, in which the fleet forming the bar of the T can bring all guns to bear while its opponent's fire power is confined to the guns of the ships at the head of the column only. By sunset of May 28 virtually the whole Russian fleet had been sunk or captured.

The Japanese fleet achieves a crushing victory at the Tsushima Strait.

Revolt in Crete

The Greek statesman, Alexandros Zaimis.

The union of the island of Crete with Greece was proclaimed in Theriso by opponents of the current regime led by Eleutherios Venizelos on March 30. Prompt support was voiced in the assembly at Canea. The European powers whose troops were stationed in Crete refused to concede constitutional change, and minor skirmishes occurred at Canae and elsewhere when the Greek flag was pulled down.

Resistance to Turkish rule had led to civil war in Crete in 1896. It was suppressed by Turkish forces. Subsequently, a new constitution was introduced and a Christian governor appointed, but the delay in carrying out the reforms which had been reluctantly promised by the Turkish government, together with the activities of Greek agents (eager to provoke war with Turkey for Macedonia), provoked revolt in 1897. A Greek force landed on the island and proclaimed it henceforth to be Greek, causing great enthusiasm among the Christian population and a massacre of Muslim peasants. The European powers then intervened, subdued the rebels and declared a compromise: Crete would have virtual self-government under Turkish suzerainty. Prince George of Greece was nominated as high commissioner and order was restored, though many Muslims, their livelihood destroyed by the disturbances, left the island.

The arbitrary government of Prince George was partly responsible for setting off further disturbances in 1904. Venizelos' proclamation of union with Greece received widespread popular support, but an armistice was eventually agreed. The European powers promised reforms (introduced in July 1906), which among other things provided for reorganization of the local police and militia under Greek command, to be followed by withdrawal of the international troops. Prince George was replaced as high commissioner by Alexandros Zaimis, a former (and later) prime minister of Greece. His skilful administration led to the withdrawal of foreign troops and, inevitably, to the union of Crete with Greece in 1913.

1905

Peace agreed by Russia and Japan

The U.S. president, Theodore Roosevelt, who had played some part as mediator, was present as Russian and Japanese representatives signed a treaty ending the Russo-Japanese War at Portsmouth, New Hampshire, on September 5.

Desultory fighting had continued until the peace, but neither side was able to contemplate a long war, and each accepted the offer of U.S. mediation. Among other gains, the Japanese were granted Port Arthur and Dairen as well as other cities in southern Manchuria, while the future of Korea was, in effect, left to them.

Some Japanese thought not enough had been gained and news of the peace terms provoked minor rioting in Tokyo.

Russian and Japanese plenipotentiaries in session at Portsmouth, New Hampshire, in August 1905.

St Petersburg Soviet directs general strike

The Soviet ('Council') of Workers' Deputies, founded in St Petersburg on October 13, directed the rapidly spreading general strike. It was perhaps the most successful general strike in history, since it included businessmen and professionals such as doctors and lawyers.

One effect of the strike was – temporarily – to strengthen the position of Count Witte in the tsarist government. His answer was the Manifesto of October 30 (October 17), which announced full civil liberties and declared that the state duma – which was to be elected on a much wider franchise – had to consent to all laws before they could be enforced.

On the face of things, victory had been won by the constitutionalists. However, no liberals joined Witte's ministry, and he had to deal with reactionaries on the right and revolutionary socialists on the left. The latter were more easily disposed of – for the time being. The St Petersburg Soviet, which was acting like an alternative government and, through Trotsky and Lenin, advocating 'permanent revolution', was arrested en masse on December 3. The armed rising that ensued was swiftly suppressed and revolutionaries were ruthlessly hunted down.

Witte's days were numbered, however, and his fate was sealed by the elections to the first duma, in which, despite a boycott by the Social Revolutionaries, parties of the left predominated. Witte resigned and, just before the duma met in April 1906, new laws were passed which in effect gave the tsar power to disregard it. The day of reckoning was yet to come.

Spectators on shore watch as a rebel warship is forced to surrender after the mutiny of November 1905 at Sebastopol.

HMS *Dreadnought* sailing out of harbour. Her launching marked the start of a race to build ever more powerful warships.

World's biggest battleship launched

The 18,000-ton battleship *Dreadnought* was launched at Portsmouth, England, on February 10. She was the first battleship in the world to be fitted with turbine engines and the first 'all big-gun' battleship, her 12-inch guns enabling her to fight out of torpedo range. Admiral Sir John Fisher, First Sea Lord, described her as 'a hard-boiled egg – because she can't be beat'. She was built in record speed, having only been laid down the previous October.

People soon became weary of hearing of the launching of ships described as 'the world's largest battleship', because the sensational speed and firepower of the *Dreadnought* signalled the beginning of an arms race in heavily armoured warships – the 'dreadnought race', which continued for some 15 years. In the same week the Japanese, who had made the 'biggest-battleship' claim for the (British-built) *Mikasa* in 1900 (and who had already laid down, but not completed, the first Dreadnought-type battleships, the *Aki* and the *Satsuma*), announced a projected doubling of their navy. However, it was naval expansion in Germany that gave the British most cause for concern. Other nations too began to build battleships of the Dreadnought type, and the *Dreadnought* herself was soon overhauled by 'super-Dreadnoughts', with 16-inch (rather than 12-inch) guns. The *Dreadnought* was the eighth ship of that name in the Royal Navy (the first had fought the Armada in 1588). She served throughout World War I and was sold for breaking up in 1920.

Moroccan problem defused at Algeciras

International conflict over Morocco was settled – temporarily – by an international conference which met in Algeciras on January 16. It was intended to solve the question of commercial control and of internal stability, and left France politically the dominant power.

In 1904, in response to the withdrawal of France from Egyptian affairs, Britain had agreed to refrain from pressing its own interests in Morocco and had acknowledged French pre-eminence. Spain had reluctantly acceded to the Anglo-French agreement, and in a secret treaty with France had acquired its own sphere of influence in the event – a probable one given the disturbed state of the country – that the authority of the sultan, Abd ul-Aziz IV, could not be maintained.

Germany remained dissatisfied, though German interests in Morocco were currently negligible, and in 1905 the German emperor made a spectacular state visit to the country, entering into negotiations with the sultan and his ministers. Concessions, such as the construction of the port of Tangier, which had been promised to France, were granted to Germany, and German pressure was partly responsible for forcing the pro-British French foreign minister, Théophile Delcassé, out of office. The Algeciras conference was intended to settle Moroccan affairs, and its result was, on the face of it, a modest victory for France (supported by Britain and other European powers).

The agreement provided for commercial equality, under the sovereignty of the sultan, with Germany recognizing France's special position, and also for various administrative and financial reforms. Morocco remained in a disturbed state, however, with sporadic violence and revolts directed against the sultan and against Europeans. The most effective revolt was that of a local sherif, Mulai Ahmed ar-Raisuli, in the Tangier area: a Frenchman was murdered in March and the British commander of the sultan's bodyguard, was later held for ransom (costing Britain £20,000). ▶ *page 31*

29

Dinizulu, the Zulu chieftain, with members of his council.

Guatemalan aggression repulsed

Guatemala suffered many casualties in a brief war with its immediate neighbours, which broke out in May. Defeat of the Guatemalan army plus pressure from the United States and Mexico brought about peace in July.

In their first century of independence, the Central American republics had been highly unstable, and wars between them had been frequent, often inciting U.S. intervention. Guatemala was traditionally favourable to Central American union (which had existed during the years 1825–39), and had attempted to bring it about by force in 1885. Its smaller neighbours, El Salvador and Honduras, resisted successfully, as in 1906, when peace rapidly followed a Guatemalan defeat. The whole region, however, remained unstable.

Natal revolt quelled

The leader of the revolt in Natal, Bambaata, was defeated and killed on June 10 in battle with a local force commanded by Colonel Sir Duncan Mackenzie. His head was cut off 'for identification purposes' but afterwards buried with his body. Other rebels, including chief Sigananda, reputed to be over 90 years old, subsequently surrendered.

The revolt, among people of mainly Zulu origin, had been sparked off by the imposition of a poll tax (£1 a head) on all male members of the population by the Natal legislature. There was already unrest among the Zulu, and the execution of leaders of the rising provoked a more serious rebellion. Bambaata had taken refuge in Zululand, apparently receiving sanctuary from Dinizulu, who was subsequently charged with harbouring him (though he had little choice). Dinizulu surrendered without further resistance and was subsequently sentenced to four years' imprisonment, being released on the day the Union of South Africa was officially established in 1910.

Britain controls access to Tibet

In an agreement with China signed on April 27, the terms of the Younghusband agreement with Tibet in 1904 were confirmed. No foreign power was to be permitted representation in Lhasa, and Britain was to control roads leading into Tibet.

China, which claimed suzerainty in Tibet, had not been party to the Anglo-Tibetan treaty of 1904, but shortly afterwards a Chinese representative had gone to India to negotiate with the British, and the agreement of 1906 was the result. The Dalai Lama, who had fled the country, was not involved in either agreement.

The main purpose, as far as the British were concerned, was to keep Russia out of Tibet, and in the following year Russia recognized Britain's 'special interest' there, with both countries agreeing not to negotiate with Tibet except through China and that neither was to send diplomatic representatives to the country. ▶ page 36

Jews massacred in Russia

On June 12 hundreds of people were said to have been killed, and many houses burned, in the city of Białystok, about 100 miles northeast of Warsaw (and then in Russia). It was widely believed that the pogrom, which began in June and continued for several days, had been encouraged, if not initiated, by the authorities. A Russian official admitted approval of the outbreak.

The pogrom in Białystok was merely a particularly savage example of the unrest and violence which were still endemic in Russia. Mutinies were reported in several garrison towns, and in July the Duma, Russia's first democratic national assembly, was dissolved by the prime minister, Stolypin, following an alleged plot against the tsar. Stolypin himself narrowly escaped assassination in August in a bomb attack that left 30 people dead. (He was to die at the hands of an assassin in 1911.)

The Russian authorities were also held to be responsible for a pogrom in Siedlce, Poland, in September.

1907

JANUARY–DECEMBER

FRENCH BOMBARDMENT OF CASABLANCA

Gandhi's 'passive resistance' in Transvaal

Following a declaration by the newly autonomous government of the Transvaal to enact a law requiring registration and finger-printing of Asians, on March 22 Mohandas Gandhi led a protest by the 10,000 Indian residents. Gandhi's method of opposition, *Satyagraha*, nonviolent force, involved civil disobedience and protest marches.

Gandhi had recently given up his prosperous legal practice for full-time politics, and was already in touch with the leaders of the widespread political agitation in India. He and many others courted imprisonment by their protests against the humiliating racist law in the Transvaal, but ultimately won their case.

Mohandas Gandhi photographed outside his office in the Transvaal with members of his staff.

French warships bombard Casablanca

On August 2 French warships shelled the Moroccan port of Casablanca following the murder of nine European workmen, six of them French, at the end of July. In heavy fighting, a section of the town was occupied. The many casualties ran into hundreds.

The French had found that maintaining peace and stability in Morocco was a harder task than they had bargained for. Violence against Europeans was common, and earlier in the year French troops had occupied Oudja after the murder of a French doctor. The killing of the nine Europeans, who were employed on harbour-construction works at Casablanca, had aroused indignation in France and compelled the French government to act. Some 15,000 French troops continued to garrison the port until the summer of 1908, when their numbers were reduced. ▶ *page 33*

French officers with native troops on duty in Morocco.

SHIFTING EUROPEAN ALLIANCES

The 1907 peace conference in session at The Hague. (Inset) An Italian cartoonist's impression of the *Entente Cordiale*.

THE Anglo-Russian Convention of August 31, 1907, marked a decisive stage in the diplomatic realignments, resulting in the division of Europe into two 'armed camps' which were to confront each other in World War I.

In 1894 a Franco-Russian alliance had been agreed. It was intended as a mutual safeguard against the members of the Triple Alliance – Germany, Austria-Hungary and Italy. Britain remained comparatively isolated but had traditionally taken a remote view of continental affairs, secure in its command of the seas. This was increasingly threatened, however, and Britain now sought allies. Germany seemed the likeliest candidate,

but Britain was not prepared to join the Triple Alliance. Increasing Russian activity in the Far East, challenging British interests, made a German alliance all the more attractive, but when this was not forthcoming, Britain secured an alliance with Japan in 1902. Moreover, the German decision to build a large navy – a threat to Britain – worsened relations between the two countries.

Since Britain was still keen to find a European ally, and France was anxious that its alliance with Russia should not draw it into a war in the Far East, the most sensational piece in this diplomatic/military jigsaw now fell into place – the Entente Cordiale of 1904. This was not a formal

treaty, but it proved to be the foundation of a longstanding alliance between the two nations whose previous history had been one of almost constant hostility.

Britain's relations with Russia, however, remained poor. The tsar's government was unpopular, the suppression of the 1905 revolution was deplored and the Dogger Bank incident almost provoked hostilities. Germany looked forward confidently to war between Britain and Russia, while doing its best to disrupt the Entente Cordiale by making trouble in Morocco. At the same time, the country opened negotiations with Russia.

However, German expectations were scotched. The Alge-

ciras conference represented a diplomatic defeat, and Russia decided to mend its fences with Britain, which was correspondingly anxious to prevent a Russo-German alliance. The Anglo-Russian convention of 1907, like the Entente Cordiale, was not a formal alliance but rather a settlement of various disputes, such as that over Tibet. Germany was now left facing the very situation that Bismarck, the founder of the Reich, had warned against – a combination of France, Britain and Russia. This combination was not hostile by intent, but to anxious Germans it seemed that they were encircled by enemies. The arms race gathered pace across Europe.

1908

JANUARY–DECEMBER

AUSTRIA ANNEXES BOSNIA AND HERCEGOVINA

YOUNG TURKS REVOLT

Bosnia and Hercegovina annexed

On October 5 the Austrian foreign minister, Count Alois von Aerenthal, announced the formal annexation of the Balkan states of Bosnia and Hercegovina. The declaration provoked instant protests from Serbia and other countries and opened a new round in the rivalry between Russia and Austria-Hungary in the Balkans.

Moroccan sultan overthrown

After a long struggle, Sultan Abd ul-Aziz was finally replaced by his brother, Mulai Hafid, on August 23. The disturbed state of the country, with constant anti-European outbreaks, had made Abd ul-Aziz unpopular, and his brother had been recognized as sultan in Marrakech the previous year. Mulai Hafid gained the support of France and Spain, and Abd ul-Aziz finally fled the country in August. In September France and Spain called for international recognition of Mulai Hafid.

Mulai Hafid promised the French a policy of moderation, thereby gaining a sizeable loan, and renounced the tribal *jihad* against Europeans. But his position proved to be no stronger than his predecessor's. In November Spain was forced to send 50,000 extra troops to quell a revolt of the Rif tribesmen in the north of the country.

Moroccan tribesmen raid Algeria

In the latest outbreak of anti-European violence in Morocco, a band of several hundred tribesmen crossed the ill-defined frontier with Algeria on April 15 and attacked French outposts. Over 100 Moroccans were reported killed and the French lost 28 dead before the raiders withdrew.

The Austrian takeover was largely a formality. Bosnia and Hercegovina, officially still within the Turkish empire, had been under Austrian military occupation since 1878, and Austria was therefore making a temporary situation permanent.

Opposition from Serbia was anticipated, since the Serbs had ambitions to absorb these provinces themselves – a prime reason for Austria's action. The assassination of King Alexander and Queen Draga of Serbia in 1903 had resulted in a reversal of Serbian foreign policy. Previously well-disposed towards Austria, Serbia had subsequently adopted a pro-Russian stance, while accepting military and financial help from France.

Aerenthal believed that Russian opposition had been defused because, during the course of a secret meeting with his Russian opposite number a few weeks earlier, Russia had agreed to the Austrian takeover; but the Russians were taken by surprise by Austria's precipitate announcement and supported the Serbian protest. Germany took Austria's side, stating that any mobilization of Russian forces would be followed by German mobilization. A crisis arose which, if international alliances had been as firm as they were in 1914, might have sparked off world war.

Russia eventually backed down, Turkey was brushed off with a cash payment and the crisis fizzled out in March 1909. The game had apparently been won by the Central Powers (Germany and Austria-Hungary), but Russian resentment of Germany had the effect of strengthening the British-French-Russian *entente* while Serbian hostility towards Austria was intensified.

Young Turks force restoration of constitution

Following revolts led by army officers in many cities, which began in Resna on July 3, the Turkish sultan, Abd ul-Hamid II, agreed to the restoration of constitutional government. The revolution was accomplished without bloodshed, and was welcomed by all the racial groups in the Turkish empire. Optimists suggested that these disparate and generally hostile groups might be able to unite amicably under a reformed regime.

The Young Turks, successors of an earlier movement known as the Young Ottomans, were the spearhead of liberal reform in the Turkish empire. The leaders of the 1908 revolution were army officers of progressive views, who formed a secret 'Committee of Union and Progress' in Constantinople headed by Enver (Pasha), Mehmed Talaat and Ahmed Jemal. A Turkish parliament met in December 1908, but thereafter serious divisions appeared within

1908

JANUARY
30 South African cabinet orders release of Gandhi

FEBRUARY
1 Portuguese king and crown prince assassinated
8 Russian troops defend Persian frontier against Turkish raiders

APRIL
15 French repel Moroccan raiders in western Algeria

JUNE
22 Shah's troops attack *majlis* building in Tehran

JULY
3 Outbreak of Young Turk's revolt
24 Turkish constitution restored

AUGUST
23 Flight of Moroccan sultan, Abd ul-Aziz

SEPTEMBER
15 France and Spain support legitimacy of Sultan Mulai Hafid

OCTOBER
5 Austria announces annexation of Bosnia and Hercegovina
5 Bulgaria declares complete independence from Turkey
12 Cretan parliament votes for union with Greece

NOVEMBER
Spain sends extra troops to Morocco

Sultan Abd ul-Hamid II.

the reform movement, as political exiles returned home and the leaders adopted a narrowly nationalistic policy.

33

Revolution in Persia

Nationalist forces gained control of Tehran on July 13 and forced the shah, Muhammad Ali, to seek safety in the Russian embassy. He was deposed by the victorious nationalists and subsequently left the country.

Shah Muzaffqar ed-Din had conceded a constitution with a national assembly (*majlis*) in 1906, the last year of his reign. His son and successor was an old-fashioned despot, who, though handicapped by an empty treasury, sought to overthrow the constitution by force. Despite a solemn oath to observe the constitution, six months later he sent in ruffian-like irregular forces, mainly Cossacks, who, behaving with savagery towards the ordinary inhabitants, bombarded the *majlis* building and captured some of the leading liberals. A rising broke out in Tabriz, while nationalist forces gathered in other cities. The siege of Tabriz by the shah's forces was broken up by the Russians early in 1909, for the sake of Russian inhabitants of the city, and the nationalists marched on Tehran. They encountered little opposition, and the revolution was accomplished with relatively little loss of life. Muhammad Ali's young son, Ahmed Shah, succeeded, and constitutional government was re-established.

The history of Persia for most of the previous century had been enacted against a background of Russo-British rivalry. An agreement (in the long run an unsatisfactory one) had, however, been reached as part of the Anglo-Russian convention of 1907, in which the two powers had bound themselves to respect the strict independence and integrity of Persia (as the country was called until 1935), while dividing the country into separate 'spheres of influence'.

Muhammad Ali, shah of Persia, who reigned briefly from 1907 to 1909.

Ahmed Shah, who succeeded his father, Muhammad Ali, on the Persian throne.

Spain on brink of civil war

Martial law was declared by the government of Antonio Maura in Spain on July 28 in the midst of street fighting in Barcelona, which raged for three days (July 27–29), and with violent unrest in other parts. The outbreak was preceded by a general strike in the north.

Anarchism was especially influential in Spain at the turn of the century, appealing both to the peasants and to the industrial working class. It was particularly strong in Catalonia, where regionalism was also a powerful force, especially since the various Catalan parties had formed a common front in the elections of 1907. The government was also weakened in 1909 by reverses in Morocco and the need to call out the reserves in order to strengthen Spanish forces there – a highly unpopular move which provided the immediate motive for the strike in Barcelona. It developed rapidly into a general political attack on Church and State.

The declaration of martial law was followed by a reign of terror, which lasted until October. Anyone whose opinions the government disliked was liable to be arrested. International consternation was aroused by the court martial and execution of Francisco Ferrer, a figure well-known throughout Europe for his anti-clerical views on education. In Paris troops were needed to defend the Spanish embassy, and when the Cortes (parliament) met in October, Maura was forced to resign.

Soldiers on the streets of Barcelona in July during a period of civil unrest.

1909

JANUARY
6 Communal rioting in Calcutta

FEBRUARY
9 France and Germany settle differences on Morocco

MARCH
31 Serbia accepts Austrian annexation of Bosnia and Hercegovina

APRIL
13 Military revolt against Sultan Abd ul-Hamid in Turkey
22 Massacres reported in Turkish Armenia and Anatolia
26 Sultan Abd ul-Hamid deposed

JULY
13 Persian nationalist forces capture Tehran
26 European troops withdrawn from Crete
28 Martial law declared in Spain

OCTOBER
13 Execution of Francisco Ferrer
26 Prince Ito, leading Japanese statesman, assassinated by a Korean

DECEMBER
16 U.S. forces resignation of President Zelaya of Nicaragua

Antonio Maura, Spanish prime minister.

U.S. intervention in Nicaragua

U.S. President Taft sent marines to Nicaragua on November 27 in response to the execution of hundreds of alleged rebels, who had risen against the government of President José Santos Zelaya. The U.S. troops acted in support of conservative opponents of the Zelaya regime. Zelaya had seized power in 1893 and, favouring a Central American union, had interfered in the affairs of his neighbours, El Salvador and Honduras. However, what angered the U.S. government was the inclusion of two U.S. citizens among those executed as rebels.

Zelaya was forced to resign a few weeks later. The United States refused to recognize his successor and held the business centre and revolutionary headquarters of Bluefields against government troops. U.S. support for Adolfo Díaz enabled him to hold power from 1911 to 1917 in the face of renewed civil war.

▶ *page 43*

1910

PORTUGUESE MONARCHY OVERTHROWN

MEXICAN REVOLUTION

Dalai Lama flees Tibet again

Following a quarrel with the Chinese authorities, on March 1 the Dalai Lama, who had only returned home from exile a few weeks earlier, again fled the country. He went to Darjeeling in India, while the Chinese tightened their hold on Tibet with the co-operation of the Panchen Lama, the rival theocratic leader whose base was the monastery at Zhikatse.

The Panchen Lama had taken advantage of his rival's flight from the British in 1904 to assert his own claims to control Tibet. He had signed a truce with the British and later visited Calcutta for negotiations. The British, however, had continued to deal with the representatives of the Dalai Lama in Lhasa.

Following the departure of the Dalai Lama the Panchen Lama attempted to curry favour with the Chinese, who sent troops into Lhasa. His success was short-lived, because after the Chinese Revolution the authority of the Dalai Lama was restored and the power of the Panchen Lama permanently curtailed.

Top. Manuel II, king of Portugal, who was deposed in October 1910.

Right. Soldiers and civilians manning the barricades in Lisbon.

Revolution in Portugal

Following the assassination on October 3 of a prominent republican leader, Miguel Bombarda, who was also a well-known physician, a rising against the monarchy began simultaneously among soldiers, civilians and the men on warships in the Tagus. It had long been expected and was well organized, being accomplished in little more than 24 hours. King Manuel II, who had reigned only since the assassination of King Carlos in 1908, escaped to Gibraltar and thence to England.

Republicanism in Portugal had been gaining ground since the reign of King Luis (1861-89), and there had been a republican rising in Oporto in 1891. The desperate financial state of the country had added to the government's difficulties, together with internal divisions among the monarchists themselves. In the elections of 1910 the republicans gained a majority in Lisbon and Oporto, and the murder of Bombarda, though apparently the act of a lunatic, served as a convenient excuse to start a revolution.

Madero calls for revolution in Mexico

Above. Porfirio Díaz, Mexican president.

Francisco Madero, who had recently emerged as opposition leader to the Mexican dictator Porfirio Díaz, called for a general insurrection to begin on November 20. He issued his challenge, while assuming the provisional presidency himself, from San Antonio in Texas, where he had fled while on bail from a charge of plotting against the government.

Madero, who stood only 5 ft 2 in tall, spoke in a high-pitched voice and was both a vegetarian and a teetotaller, seemed an unlikely opponent to the strong man Díaz, who had ruled the country by arbitrary means since 1876. But Díaz was old and so were the ruling clique known as the *científicos*, as were all the state governors, cabinet ministers and leading bureaucrats – in short the regime was on its last legs. Díaz still commanded some respect, but he was almost universally unpopular, and while he had increased the prosperity of the country by encouraging foreign investment, his agricultural policy in particular had been a disaster. By 1910, 97 per cent of all the agricultural land was held by an immensely rich group numbering little more than 1000. Madero's promise of agrarian reform enlisted the enthusiastic support of the peasants. (Madero himself came from a rich creole family with large industrial interests.)

The Revolution began, as it was to continue, with a mixture of tragedy and farce. When Madero returned from Texas to lead it, his forces consisted of less than 30 men, mostly unarmed. One of his leading supporters was besieged in his house and killed by the police, and Madero was on the point of fleeing to Europe when news arrived of more stirring events in the state of Chihuahua. Pascual Orozco, aided by a local bandit chief called Pancho Villa, had defeated federal soldiers and now controlled the southern part of the state. The Revolution was under way. ▶ *page 38*

Mexican government troops on their way to fight insurgents.

FEBRUARY
13 Troops mutiny in Canton

MARCH
1 Dalai Lama seeks sanctuary in India

APRIL
12 Turkish troops attack Albanian rebels

MAY
9 Cretan assembly demands union with Greece

JUNE
20 Francisco Madero arrested

AUGUST
28 Montenegro proclaims full independence
also this month
Republican gains in Portuguese elections

SEPTEMBER
11 Crowds stone Díaz's house

OCTOBER
3 Miguel Bombarda murdered
4 Portuguese revolution
7 Madero flees to Texas

NOVEMBER
27 Orozco and Villa defeat federal troops at Pedernales

DECEMBER
Turkish troops suppress Arab risings

Left. Francisco Madero (second left) and other leaders of the Mexican revolution.

37

U.S. troops sent to Mexican border

Some 20,000 U.S. troops were ordered to the Mexican border on March 27 in response to the growing revolutionary activity in the country's southern neighbour. They were there, it was said, to 'protect American interests'.

Supporters of the Díaz regime, especially his chief lieutenant, José Limantour, feared U.S. intervention, although the U.S. government had the previous month acceded to Díaz's repeated requests not to allow his political opponents (such as Madero) to cross the border.

French troops in Morocco

On April 23 the French government took the decision to send more troops to Morocco in April in view of the increasing threat to the city of Fez. Most of the troops were drawn from colonial forces elsewhere in Africa, though some were also sent from France. Disorder in Morocco was endemic, but the situation had been deteriorating for several months, as the sultan lost his grip – never a firm one – on events. France's action was prompted by the threat to European inhabitants of Fez, as well as Casablanca, but it carried with it the danger of international complications. The agreement reached between Germany and France in the wake of the Algeci-

Above. Moroccan warriors display the heads of executed rebels at Fez.

ras conference had not worked out very smoothly in practice. Germany had expressed no political interest in Moroccan affairs, but differed with France over precisely where the boundary lay between politician and economic matters – in particular over the construction and operation of railways. France had already made suggestions concerning a revised agreement before the deteriorating situation in Fez persuaded it to send in troops to occupy the area.

Mexican dictator overthrown

Outside Ciudad Juarez, at around midnight on May 21, the long-time dictator of Mexico, Porfirio Díaz, signed an agreement which provided for his resignation. The event took place in the open, and the table on which the document was laid was illuminated by the headlights of cars.

After the success of Orozco and Villa in Chihuahua, the rebellion in Mexico spread. Madero joined the rebels in February, and the whole country was soon ablaze. The Díaz administration was like an ancient oak tree, impressive in appearance but suddenly revealed to be rotten right through. An armistice was agreed in April, though it proved short-lived, and despite disagreements among the revolutionaries – in May Orozco and Villa attempted to arrest Madero – the old regime was clearly doomed. The leader of the peasants, Emiliano Zapata, took Cuautla, and state capitals began to fall to local guerrilla leaders.

Pending an election, a provisional president was installed who was associated with the Díaz regime, though he took some revolutionaries into his government. Revolutionary troops were disbanded and General Victoriano Huerta, known for his brutal suppression of the Maya, was sent to crush the followers of Zapata. There was no great disagreement on the candidate for the presidency, Madero, though rivalry over the potential vice-president did cause a split in the revolutionary movement. Madero was duly elected in October, in the freest election in Mexico's history, while people proclaiming sympathy with the Revolution were also elected to state governorships. Everyone prepared to welcome a glorious new era. They were to be disappointed. ▶ *page 45*

Emiliano Zapata, leader of the peasant rebels.

Italy declares war on the Turks

Italy declared war on Turkey on September 29, four days after publishing a list of grievances against the Turks. Constantinople's offer to negotiate was rejected out of hand. The declaration of war was made in defiance of several international agreements, and without consulting its allies.

A number of factors combined to hasten Italy's decision to make good its hold on Tripoli (Libya), the last available land in North Africa. The most immediate was the imminent French protectorate in Morocco (the French had already forestalled Italy in Tunisia), but Italy also feared German competition in Tripoli – all the more pressing since the Germans has been excluded from Morocco – and had become nervous at the prospect of the Young Turks putting more steel into the defence of the Turkish empire. Speed was essential to preclude the possibility of intervention by a third party and to present the world with a fait accompli. ▶ *page 40*

Turkish troops, with accompanying band, on their way to war with Italy.

German gunboat at Agadir

The ever-rumbling Moroccan problem suddenly reached a pitch of crisis at the beginning of July when a small German warship, the *Panther*, appeared off Agadir, a closed port within the French sphere of interest. Its purpose was said to be to 'protect German commercial interests', and the German government announced that the time had come for a new 'friendly exchange of views' on Morocco. Sending a warship, however, was not seen as a friendly act, and although one German firm claimed to have business there, German commercial interests in Agadir appeared to be negligible.

The Germans further asserted that the French occupation of Fez nullified the Algeciras agreement and was tantamount to permanent colonial control. There was no real disagreement over the German claim that the Moroccan settlement needed revision, but the despatch of the *Panther*, to persuade France to grant concessions, was a provocative act which cast suspicion on the nature of German intentions.

The French suggested that the British government should make some sort of gesture comparable to Germany's, which was refused, though the British were clear that no further Moroccan settlement should be made without their participation. But after increasing the tension by saying nothing, the German government accepted a French offer for an exchange of views and indicated that it was ready to relinquish all claims in Morocco if the French would hand over most of the French Congo. This was refused, and the British informed the Germans a few days later that its action in Morocco required explanation. It appeared that once again Germany's impetuous foreign policy had landed it in an impasse from which it could retreat only with loss of face. ▶ *page 41*

The German gunboat *Panther*.

1911 Revolution in China

An explosion in a house at Wuhan in October resulted in the discovery of a plot incriminating army officers. Their reaction was to lead their men in a rebellion against the Manchu dynasty, and the revolt, beginning on October 10, spread rapidly to south and central China.

Since the collapse of the Boxer rising, such authority as existed in China was mainly exercised by provincial governments. The central government, faced with widespread local autonomy, was further handicapped by financial strains and by the decayed state of the bureaucracy, not to mention the malign influence (until her death in 1908) of the Empress-dowager. She had been chiefly responsible for baulking the military reforms of Yuan Shih-k'ai, who had attempted to create a modern Chinese army. A constituent national assembly, convened to prepare a scheme of representative government in 1910, had demanded the right to make laws and had deluged the government with criticism.

A long-overdue scheme of modernization – to build a national railway system – was indirectly responsible for the fall of the Manchu. The Peking government took over a line in Szechwan but the terms failed to satisfy the shareholders, and the resulting discontent erupted into open revolt. Leadership fell to the mainly young men of radical ideas who had formed an organization devoted to turning China into a modern state. This would be headed by Sun Yat-sen, a Western-trained doctor of medicine who had been the leading reformer for 30 years. They were in touch with the leaders of the plot which provoked the mutiny in Hangchow the following month.

Left. Chinese revolutionaries on the march with national flags.

Below. Sun Yat-sen, Chinese statesman.

Italian troops land in Tripoli

Italian troops en route to Naples, where they embarked for Tripoli.

The first Italian troop transports reached Tripoli on October 11, two weeks after Italy's declaration of war on Turkey. Some naval action had taken place earlier, however, Tripoli itself having been occupied after a bombardment on October 5. Tobruk was also in Italian hands from October 4.

The Italian force, fully assembled by October 20, consisted of 9000 rifles with light artillery and two squadrons of cavalry. Very little transport had been provided, since the Italians had not anticipated a Turkish withdrawal to the interior or the willingness of many of the local tribesmen to fight in support of their masters.

In a battle at Shara Shat, near Tripoli, the Italians suffered heavy casualties and only just avoided a humiliating defeat. Reinforcements were sent from Italy, and by December General Caneva had defeated the Turks and their allies in the Tripoli oasis and established his headquarters some 30 miles to the south. Ordered not to risk heavy casualties, however, he was unable to pursue the Turks further. Meanwhile, Italian hopes of bringing the Turks to the point of surrender by naval action in the eastern Mediterranean was frustrated by warnings from Austria that in no circumstances would this be tolerated. ▶ *page 43*

An official with army escort makes his way through the streets of Tientsin during the Revolution.

Manchu authority crumbles in China

With rebellion spreading rapidly in China, the Manchu regent summoned Yuan Shih-k'ai from retirement to save the dynasty and lead the northern armies in October. In the following month he was made prime minister.

With city after city falling to the revolutionaries, Yuan was rather slow to act. By December, 14 provinces had declared against the Manchu and the regent had left Peking in secret. A pro-visional government was set up in Nanking and the revolutionary leader Sun Yat-sen, hastily returning from a trip abroad, was elected provisional president.

Yuan, despite having won mili-tary victory in the north, agreed to an armistice. He, however, turned out to be a less devoted servant of the dynasty than the Manchu had hoped.

Germany concedes French rights in Morocco

Following a financial panic in Germany which made the government more amenable, the French and Germans finally managed to reach an agreement on the Moroccan crisis on November 4. Germany withdrew all claims in Morocco and ack-nowledged, for the first time, France's right to establish a pro-tectorate there. In return it gained a thinnish slice of the French Congo adjoining the German colony of Kamerun.

It seemed a reasonable com-promise, but the agreement was not popular in either country and the surrender of West African territory was largely responsible for the fall of the French govern-ment in January 1912. Perhaps the most significant effect was the deterioration in Franco-German relations – the crisis had given rise to fierce chauvinistic feelings in both countries – and a similar worsening in Anglo-German rela-tions. Furthermore, the *Entente Cordiale* had been reinforced. When war had seemed possible, the French and British general staffs had decided on closer co-operation, and the problems of moving a British expeditionary force to France had been dis-cussed. The Agadir crisis was also largely responsible for Italy's move on Tripoli, which in turn created the conditions for the Bal-kan Wars of 1912-13. ► *page 42*

Establishment of French protectorate in Morocco

French control in Morocco was formally acknowledged in a treaty signed with the sultan on March 30. Negotiations had been going on since the Franco-German agreement of the previous year, which had implicitly acknowledged the French right to establish a protectorate, if necessary.

The terms allowed France to enact extensive internal reforms, while respecting the Muslim religion and the 'traditional prestige' of the sultan. In particular, France took over control of financial affairs and was permitted to occupy the whole country militarily. Foreign policy was to be conducted through the medium of the French resident-general (General Louis Lyautey).

Spain was unhappy with the settlement and refused to recognize the Franco-Moroccan treaty until urged to do so by the British government. A further agreement was then arranged between Spain and France. Spain retained a Moroccan protectorate, but one reduced in size, and administrative authority in the Spanish zone was ceded by France in its capacity as protector of the whole of the sultan's dominions, not directly by the sultan himself.

Left. A column of French troops on the move in a tented encampment in Morocco.

Below. French and Spanish officials signing an agreement over their respective administrative zones in Morocco.

Anti-Turkish alliance in the Balkans

A treaty of alliance was signed between Serbia and Bulgaria on March 13. Its purpose was said to be resistance to Austrian expansion in the Balkans, but a secret clause provided for the partition between the signatories of Macedonia, the last Slav territory still under Turkish rule. Russia was party to the treaty, whose terms were not known until later.

The treaty formed the basis of the 'Balkan League', which took shape between March and October. Among the incentives leading to this alliance were: the Italo-Turkish war, which kept Turkey preoccupied; an attempt by the Turks to impose a policy of disarmament in the Balkans; and discontent in all the Balkan countries with the situation in Macedonia, which contained substantial Serb, Bulgar and Greek minorities. Disturbances had broken out in Macedonia, and there was trouble, too, among the Albanians. In the past, the various peoples of Macedonia had been largely engaged in fighting each other, but the conditions of 1912 united them against Turkey.

In the case of Serbia, the ultimate enemy was, indeed, Austria, rather than Turkey. There was bitter resentment of Austria's annexation of Bosnia and Hercegovina in 1908. Moreover, Austria reserved the right, recognized by treaty, to occupy the little sanjak (administrative district) of Novi Pazar, which separated Montenegro from Serbia.

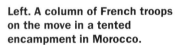

The Italians take over Libya

The Italo-Turkish War was brought officially to an end on October 15 with the signing of the Treaty of Ouchy, which bestowed Tripolitania and Cyrenaica on Italy. Negotiations had been continuing since August, and initially made little progress. The final settlement was accelerated by Italian successes in the field and by the threatening situation in the Balkans.

The slow progress of the Italian conquest of Tripolitania and Cyrenaica was due partly to unex-pected resistance from the Arabs and Berbers – some of whom were, incidentally, by no means willing to cease fighting when the peace was signed – but mainly to the delays and hesitancy of the Italian government. Between November 1911 and April 1912 a virtual stalemate existed. Enver Bey succeeded in creating near-unity among the Berber tribes of Cyrenaica and persuaded them to co-operate with the Turks, some-thing they had never done will-ingly in the past.

From April, the Italian con-quest of the interior proceeded with much greater vigour. In the same month, Italian warships appeared off the Dardanelles, and were fired on by the Turkish forts. Sharp protests from Austria pre-vented a repetition, although in May the Italians occupied Rhodes and certain islands of the Dodecanese.

An Italian cruiser in action in the Dardanelles.

Right. The king of Montenegro embraces a soldier.

U.S. Marines sent to Nicaragua

U.S. marines were ordered to Nicaragua on August 14 to sup-port the right-wing government of President Adolfo Díaz, follow-ing a renewal of civil war.

Direct U.S. involvement in Nicaragua had begun in 1909, helping to ensure the success of the revolutionaries. U.S. banks had subsequently taken a con-trolling interest in Nicaragua's railways and national bank, and the Knox-Castrillo Convention of 1911 had confirmed an official role for the United States in Nicaraguan affairs. The marines were sent in response to an appeal by President Díaz for help against his liberal opponents, whose revolt was marked by anti-Amer-ican propaganda. They were to remain, in smaller numbers, more or less indefinitely.

Montenegro declares war on Turkey

King Nicholas I of Montenegro, the smallest of the four Balkan states, declared war on Turkey on October 8. Geography rendered Montenegro safe from immediate attack, and the reason for the move appeared to be to divert attention from the three larger allies of the Balkan League.

Apart from Russia, which had virtually instigated the League, the European powers were ignor-ant of the offensive plans of the Balkan states until August, when the French were informed by the Russians. Aware that the pro-spect of a general European war loomed, the French were never-theless anxious not to antagonize their ally, Russia, and the various discussions which took place between the major powers in August and September led only to an agreement in favour of the status quo. No major diplomatic initiative was taken to prevent the Balkan war. ▶ *page 44*

Bulgars and Serbs defeat Turks

During October and November the Turks suffered a series of devastating defeats at the hands of the Balkan allies. Within six weeks of the outbreak of serious fighting the objectives of the Balkans allies had been achieved and the Turks were ready for an armistice.

Hostilities in the First Balkan War began on October 17, following Turkey's breaking off of relations with Bulgaria and Serbia and Greece's declaration of war. The growing weakness of the Turkish empire had been a major theme of European history for well over a century, and in 1912 the Turks were additionally vulnerable as a result of a recent purge of the army. Their first offensive against the Bulgars ended in total defeat, though they were able to hold their own after falling back on to their defensive lines a few miles west of Constantinople. The Serbs were equally successful and were able to penetrate deep into Macedonia. The Greeks reached Salonika on November 8, a few hours ahead of the Bulgars. The Turkish empire in Europe was all but annihilated, and an armistice was signed at the beginning of December.

Balkan peace conference

On December 16, two weeks after the armistice in the Balkan War, an international peace conference assembled in London under the chairmanship of the British foreign secretary, Sir Edward Grey. There was no question of restoring the Turkish empire to its former frontiers, but many awkward questions remained outstanding.

The representatives of the great powers had been busily trying to reach a settlement while the fighting in the Balkans was in progress. A key question was the attitude of Austria, in particular the Austrian determination to prevent Serbia gaining territory on the Adriatic. Austria had not exercised its option to occupy the sanjak of Novi Pazar, but instead proposed the creation of an independent Albania, blocking Serbian expansion to the sea. This was resented by Serbia, and resulted in a minor burst of sabre-rattling on the part of Austria and Russia (supporting Serbia). Other problems included the status of Adrianople and the Aegean islands, and the demands of Romania for territorial concessions. In the event, agreement on Albania was reached quickly, though Russia and Austria took different views of its proposed extent.

Top. Macedonian rebels in defensive positions, holding a highway north of Salonika.

Right. Bulgarian troops moving through the Balagradchiek Pass near the Serbian frontier.

1913

MEXICAN REVOLUTION

BALKAN WARS

Balkan War resumed

On February 3, while peace discussions were still under way in London, the Balkan allies renounced the recent armistice and resumed hostilities against Turkey.

A week earlier, the Turkish government had decided in favour of peace, but this had provoked a coup d'état by Young Turks led by Enver Pasha, who were unwilling to make the required concessions, in particular the surrender of Adrianople to Bulgaria. The Bulgars did not attack the Turks' defensive lines, where they had been repulsed in the previous October, but concentrated on the capture of Adrianople, which was eventually achieved in March.

Meanwhile, the Montenegrins had returned to the siege of Scutari, which fell in April. However, Austria had agreed to a compromise regarding the disputed northern border of the newly created Albania, which required the Montenegrins to surrender Scutari, something they did reluctantly and only after threat of Austrian military intervention. A persistent legend relates that the timing of the Montenegrin agreement was connected with bets placed by King Nicholas regarding the termination of the conflict.

Under pressure from other powers, particularly Britain, the

Madero government overthrown

The Mexican president was ousted on February 18 in a plot engineered by General Huerta aided by, among others, the U.S. ambassador, Henry Wilson. The ambassador had waged a largely personal campaign against Madero's government since its inception.

The popularity of the Madero government proved short-lived, and revolts had been frequent. Zapata, secure in his mountainous retreats, still demanded agrarian reform to restore the lands taken from the peons. By the beginning of 1913 another rebellion had become inevitable, and the coup d'état of February was anticipated by practically everyone with the possible exception of Madero himself.

The initial rebellion failed when an attempt to capture the palace met with unexpected resistance. Madero then made the disastrous mistake of appointing General Huerta to command the government troops. Huerta set out to ensure the success of the rebellion and to place himself at its head. He therefore betrayed his own soldiers while secretly negotiating with the rebel leader, Félix Díaz (nephew of the former dictator). On February 18 the president, and his one loyal general, were seized. Madero was killed – 'accidentally' – a few days later, after he had been persuaded to resign in exchange for a guarantee of immunity. By an agreement known as the Pact of the Embassy (i.e. the U.S. embassy), Huerta became provisional president. His rule, however, was to prove similarly short. ▶ *page 46*

Dead rebels in the Grand Plaza in Mexico City.

Balkan allies reluctantly agreed to discuss peace terms on the lines of the decisions of the London conference. This meant that the future Turkish frontier in Europe remained to be decided by the powers, while the destination of the Aegean islands was also left open. Peace was agreed at the end of May. ▶ *page 46*

Victorious Montenegrins entering Scutari after the end of the siege.

JANUARY
23 Coup d'état by Young Turks in Constantinople

FEBRUARY
3 Balkan War resumed
9 Rebellion in Mexico
18 Huerta engineers Mexican coup d'état
19 Carranza announces resistance to Huerta
23 Ex-President Madero killed

MARCH
13 Pancho Villa re-enters Mexico
18 King George of Greece assassinated in Salonika
26 Fall of Adrianople

APRIL
21 Balkan allies agree to peace talks
22 Montenegrins take Scutari

MAY
30 Treaty of London ends First Balkan War

JUNE
4 Emily Davison fatally injured by racehorse
11 Romanians invade Bulgaria

AUGUST
10 Treaty of Bucharest ends Second Balkan War

SEPTEMBER
29 Peace agreed between Bulgaria and Turkey

OCTOBER
18 Austrian ultimatum compels Serb withdrawal from Albania

NOVEMBER
6 Gandhi arrested in Johannesburg
14 Greece signs peace with Turkey
24 U.S. threatens action against Huerta
25 Riots in Natal
German general, Liman von Sanders, appointed to organize Turkish army

1913

Suffragette killed by king's horse

The running of the Derby, England's premier horse race, was disrupted on June 4 when a suffragette, Emily Davison, ran on to the track and attempted to seize the reins of a horse owned by the king. She died of her injuries some days later.

Emily Davison was one of the band of suffragettes led by Mrs Emmeline Pankhurst, who deliberately adopted militant tactics such as window-breaking and chaining themselves to railings in their campaign to obtain votes for women. Her funeral was the occasion for a massive, peaceful demonstration in London.

The movement for women's rights claimed its first martyr when Emily Davison fell under the king's horse at the Derby.

War breaks out again in the Balkans

A second Balkan War broke out on June 30 when the Bulgarian king, Ferdinand I, ordered an attack on Greek and Serbian forces in Macedonia. The order was countermanded by the Bulgarian cabinet three days later, but too late to prevent hostilities.

The Bulgar attack proved ill-advised. Help might have been expected from Austria, which supported Bulgaria as a counter-weight to Serbia, but Austria was inhibited by Bulgaria's resistance to territorial claims against it by Romania. Unaided, Bulgaria could not possibly win. The Serbs and Greeks were not defeated as quickly as had been planned. The Romanians were thus able to invade Bulgaria from the north almost unopposed, while the Turks took the opportunity to regain lost ground in Thrace. Bulgaria was consequently forced to seek a settlement.

Opposition builds up in Mexico

Following General Huerta's coup d'état, Venustiano Carranza, governor of Coahuila, rose in rebellion against him a few days later. He had once been a supporter of Madero and commanded a private army which, however, some people said had been raised to oppose Madero before Huerta overthrew him.

Carranza was not a major threat, but revolts against Huerta also broke out in Chihuahua and in Sonora, where the federal troops were driven out of the state by Alvaro Obregón in a few months. The Sonorans recognized Carranza as 'First Chief' (his own title), while the revolt in Chihuahua was led by Pancho Villa, who had entered the country in March by swimming his horse across the Rio Grande.

Villa defeated the federals in a succession of battles, captured Ciudad Juárez by a clever trick – a Trojan Horse scheme carried out by railway – and by the end of the year had taken Chihuahua City. Unfortunately, neither Carranza nor Villa appeared to be the man to carry out the true revolution that Mexico needed.

Victoriano Huerta, provisional president of Mexico in 1913-14.

Delegates at the International Peace Conference at Berne which was intended to establish a Franco-German rapprochement.

Peace treaty signed in Bucharest

A treaty between Bulgaria and its opponents – Serbia, Greece and Romania – in the recent, brief war was signed in Bucharest on August 10. The terms represented a diplomatic defeat for the unsuccessful aggressor in the so-called Second Balkan War.

Even though Bulgaria was granted a short stretch of Aegean coastline and a few other minor concessions, it was forced to surrender a substantial slice of territory in the north-east to Roma-nia, while Serbia and Greece both gained extra territory in Macedonia. In a later settlement with Turkey, Adrianople was retained by the Turks. Not all the territorial rearrangements had been concluded, however, by the time of the outbreak of World War I a year later

The Balkan wars had not provided permanent solutions to any of the problems and hostilities of the region. In particular, the relations between Serbia, ambitious to become the nation of all South Slavs, and Austria were even worse than before. Serbia had been denied its desired Adriatic coastline, and in October an Austrian ultimatum, backed by Germany, compelled the Serbs to remove their troops from north-ern Albania, where they had hoped to secure a more advantageous redrawing of the frontier.

Rioters protest jailing of Gandhi

On November 25 riots broke out in Natal after the arrest of Mohandas Gandhi, leader of the non-violent civil-rights campaign. Police opened fire on crowds, killing two and wounding others.

Gandhi's protest was aimed at new immigration laws, which restricted the freedom of movement of Asians. He led a protest march of some 2500 people and was arrested along with others. He was sentenced to a fine but, refusing to pay it, was sent to prison.

U.S. government opposes Huerta regime

On November 24 U.S. President Wilson declared his refusal to give 'aid or sympathy' to the Huerta regime in Mexico. Huerta had a bad reputation, and the killing of Madero was more than U.S. opinion could tolerate. The United States maintained a hostile attitude towards his government from the outset, and there were minor brushes with federalist troops on the Arizona border. Even without the rising tide of rebellion in Mexico, Huerta could hardly hope to survive in the face of U.S. hostility.

1914-1918
WORLD
WAR I

IF THERE IS EVER ANOTHER WAR IN EUROPE, IT WILL COME OUT OF SOME DAMNED SILLY THING IN THE BALKANS.

Otto von Bismarck

World War I had its origins in the rivalries of the European powers, but the immediate cause was a clash of interests in the Balkans. After Austria's declaration of war on Serbia a series of mutually entangling alliances brought all the great nations into conflict. On the Western Front early German successes ended in a bloody stalemate and the establishment of trenches running from the North Sea to the Swiss frontier. On the Eastern Front protracted fighting eventually destroyed the morale of the Russian army. At sea unrestricted submarine warfare posed an appalling threat to Allied and neutral shipping that finally compelled the United States to enter the war, thus ensuring Germany's ultimate defeat.

When the war ended nearly nine million men had lost their lives and the empires of Germany, Austria-Hungary and Russia had been destroyed. The peace treaties that followed sowed the seeds of future conflict.

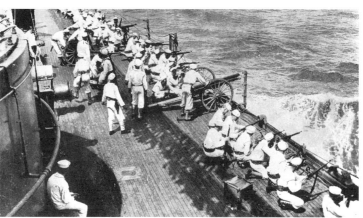

American sailors equipped with rifles and field artillery prepare for action during the landing at Vera Cruz.

U.S. marines seize Vera Cruz

U.S. forces took the Mexican city of Vera Cruz on April 21. Insults had been offered to U.S. personnel who allegedly trespassed on a military installation at Tampico and, although an apology was offered by the local commandant, a demand that the U.S. flag should be saluted brought no response, provoking the attack, in which 19 Americans and over 100 Mexicans were killed.

The U.S. government, under President Woodrow Wilson, objected strongly to the Huerta regime, described by one historian of Mexico as 'one of the most grotesque tyrannies in Mexican history', and had all but officially given its support to his chief opponent, the Constitutionalist, General Obregón. While Huerta patronized the bars of Mexico City and his cronies helped themselves to the Treasury, Obregón won a series of victories, emerging as the most statesmanlike of Huerta's opponents – certainly preferable to a bandit (albeit an idealistic bandit) like Villa or the more thoroughly idealistic Zapata, who was also capable of atrocities against opponents. Woodrow Wilson, having replaced Ambassador Henry Lane Wilson (Huerta's supporter), attempted to persuade Huerta to resign. An embargo on arms sales to Mexico had been lifted in February for the benefit of the Constitutionalists. The incident at Tampico was simply an excuse to pick a quarrel. ▶ *page 52*

Death comes for the archduke

In June 1914 the archduke Francis Ferdinand, heir to the throne of Austria-Hungary, had entertained Kaiser Wilhelm of Germany at his home in Bohemia, where they discussed the problems of the Balkans. The archduke favoured a federation of the various nationalities, with the Habsburg monarchy at the head of a happy coalition of equals.

Later that month, the archduke, accompanied by his morganatic wife, visited Bosnia. On June 28, while they were on their way to a reception at the town hall in Sarajevo, a bomb was thrown into their carriage. The archduke, with some presence of mind, threw it out again.

The carriage was supposed to make the return journey by a different route. For some reason it actually returned by the same route through the ill-guarded streets. By coincidence, it paused near the spot where the bomb had been thrown. A young man stepped out of the crowd and fired two shots. The archduke was shot in the neck, his wife in the stomach. Both died within minutes.

The perpetrator of the event which was to set off World War I was a South Slav nationalist, a Serb by birth, Gavrilo Princip. He was only 19, a fact which saved him from execution later. Nevertheless he was a figure in a well-laid plot, planned by the Serbian secret society known as the Black Hand, whose leader was the man best remembered by his code name, Apis. He was in an excellent position to organize such operations, since he also happened to be chief of

Police arrest a suspect at Sarajevo after the assassination.

military intelligence at the Serbian war ministry. The archduke, more friendly towards Slav nationalism than most people in Vienna, was the chosen victim because he represented Habsburg power and hostility to Serbian ambitions to form a greater South Slav kingdom.

How much the Serbian government knew of what was afoot is still uncertain. It certainly suspected something, since it had issued an advance warning to Vienna, but in terms so vague that it was ignored. The suspicion that Russia was also involved can be discounted (although the Black Hand certainly enjoyed Russian support).

Germany backs Austria

On July 5, following the assassination of Archduke Francis Ferdinand, the Austrian government received assurances of German support in its quarrel with Serbia. Kaiser Wilhelm II promised the Austrian emissary, Count Hoyos, that his country would receive Germany's backing even in the event that Austria's quarrel with Serbia should lead to war with Russia.

The Kaiser, about to leave for his annual tour with the German fleet, was in a hurry. But he was angry at the murder of the archduke, who had recently entertained him very pleasantly in Bohemia, and had been sympathetic to the outline of Austrian policy on the Balkans which Count Hoyos presented to him.

Austria hoped to win over Bulgaria as a counterweight to Romania, which had recently forsaken its pro-German stance in favour of closer relations with Russia, and Hoyos pointed out that Russian ambitions in the Balkans were levelled largely at German interests.

Germany calculated that Russia was not ready for war in 1914 but that it would be better prepared in three years' time, when, for example, its railway system would be more efficient. The Kaiser acknowledged that if Russia *did* become involved, this would be likely to bring in France as well. British intervention was not considered. In short, the German government did not envisage general war as a likely possibility.

Austria issues ultimatum to Serbia

On July 23 the Austrian government issued an ultimatum to Serbia. It was delivered at six p.m. and a favourable response was required within 48 hours. The terms of the ultimatum were harsh, and included several provisions which struck at the roots of pan-Slav ambitions.

The Austrians neither expected nor desired that the terms would be accepted. On July 7, following confirmation of Germany's support, the Austrian government had resolved to provoke the Serbs into war, and the ultimatum was designed to bring that about. Austria was also influenced by the assumption that Russia was not ready for war and considered that if there were to be war, the sooner it took place the better.

A number of factors resulted in the delay between the Austrian decision to push Serbia to the extreme and the actual issue of the ultimatum. The French president, Poincaré, was on a visit to Russia, and the Austrians did not want to issue the ultimatum while he was there, thereby facilitating discussions between their likely opponents. Another, homelier, reason was to get the harvest in before mobilizing the army.

Austria declares war on Serbia

The Serbian response to the Austrian ultimatum of July 23, since it fell short of the unconditional acceptance of all the terms, was rejected, and Austria accordingly declared war on July 28. Both sides had begun to mobilize before the reply was delivered.

In fact, the Serbian response had been remarkably conciliatory, especially since the Austrian police themselves had found no evidence of official Serbian involvement in the assassination of the Austrian archduke. Many of the terms had been accepted without argument, while the others had not so much been refuted as evaded. In Europe generally opinion coincided with that of the Kaiser, who remarked that Austria had won a moral victory and that cause for war had now disappeared. The British had already suggested an international conference, presumably similar to the London conference of 1913 which had attempted to sort out various Balkan problems. However, influence in decision-making was already moving away from the politicians and towards the generals who everywhere tended to believe that time was on the side of their opponents.

Horses being requisitioned by soldiers following the announcement of mobilization in Austria-Hungary. War with Serbia was now inevitable.

1914

Germany declares war

On August 1 Germany declared war on Russia and two days later on France. After a month of mounting tension, it had become clear that a major European war could not be avoided, although the position of Great Britain was still uncertain.

Chancellor Bethmann-Hollweg.

The first declaration of war – by Austria on Serbia – had not in itself made a general conflict inevitable, and talks between Russia and Austria continued after war had begun. However, if a war were to be fought, troops had to be mobilized – a long and cumbersome business, especially in Russia. On the day after the Austrian declaration, therefore, with the Serbian capital, Belgrade, already under Austrian bombardment, Russia had begun to mobilize. The original order for general mobilization – an act tantamount to a declaration of war – was almost immediately rescinded by the Tsar in favour of a partial mobilization – partly at least as a result of a message from Berlin, where the Kaiser was having second thoughts about his somewhat carefree assurance of support for Austria.

The situation was complicated by a lack of unity in European governments. In Germany, for instance, what the chancellor, Bethmann-Hollweg, said one minute was contradicted by what the chief of the general staff, Moltke, said the next. But the Russian decision, announced on July 31, to reinstate general mobilization, made it impossible to resist the German generals' demand for an equivalent response. Germany could mobilize much more quickly than Russia, and it was essential that it should do so, since German strategy called for a quick victory in the west, which would enable Germany to turn its attention to the Russian threat in the east.

The tremendous importance placed on mobilization was decisive in the outbreak of general war, yet, as events were soon to prove, it was misplaced. It was assumed that the war would be, like earlier European wars, relatively mobile. No one – at least, no one in a high position of command – foresaw that tactical mobility would be almost totally negated by the power of big guns, making speed of mobilization a much lesser advantage.

The German reaction to Russian mobilization was to declare a state-of-war emergency and to issue an ultimatum to Russia demanding an immediate halt to its military preparations. However, German strategy demanded that it fight France first, and accordingly a second ultimatum was issued, to France, requiring a statement of French neutrality. Naturally, that was not forthcoming, though France did not immediately declare war. Meanwhile, Germany had issued an equally unacceptable demand to Belgium, through whose territory its troops would have to move in furtherance of German strategy – the well-known Schlieffen Plan.

Huerta resigns

With the United States ranged against him and his opponents rapidly taking over the country, the Mexican president Huerta resigned on July 14. A decisive factor in this move was the flow of arms to the Constitutionalists following the lifting of the embargo by President Wilson in February. Villa and Obregón had become irresistible.

The success of the rebels evolved into a race for the capital, which Obregón won after Villa, having fallen out with his nominal chief, Carranza, was held up by lack of coal (arranged by Carranza). Obregón made his triumphal entry into Mexico City on August 15, after the surrender of the federal garrison five days earlier. Huerta had already left for Vera Cruz and exile in Europe and the United States.

The deposition of Huerta did not, however, bring peace to Mexico. Villa and Carranza now confronted each other, while Obregón made an attempt to mediate between them. A convention which assembled at Aguascalientes in October nominated Eulalio Gutierrez as president of Mexico, but Carranza and Villa had the armies, and the civil war was resumed, Obregón throwing in his lot with Carranza. ▶ page 81

Women helping German soldiers on their way to war.

Germany invades Belgium

On August 4 German forces invaded Belgium. Luxembourg had been invaded two days earlier. Both countries held international guarantees against attack, although only Belgium's guarantee demanded an individual reaction by the guaranteeing powers. The Germans published 'reasons' for their invasion, accusing Belgium of 'un-neutral conduct', but these were not taken seriously.

The invasion of Belgium brought Britain into the war. The British government issued the obligatory ultimatum, demanding immediate cessation of hostilities and German withdrawal. It was ignored, and thus all the major powers – Germany and Austria-Hungary, France and Russia and Britain – were at war.

Throughout the crisis that preceded the final collapse of the European concert, Britain had acted in a vaguely mediatory role. Historians differ as to whether, had Britain pursued a stronger line (the Germans still held out hopes of British neutrality at the beginning of August), war would have been less likely. The balance of opinion is that a stronger British policy would merely have accelerated the outbreak, which was the view of the British foreign secretary, Sir Edward Grey.

Nevertheless, Britain, like other countries but perhaps more strongly, needed a *casus belli* – a cause for war which would unite public opinion in support of the government and silence the considerable number of pacifists and isolationists. This was provided by the German invasion of Belgium, a small, neutral and inoffensive country, to whose defence Britain was in any case bound by treaty. Stories of German atrocities in Belgium, mainly fantasy, soon featured strongly in the British popular press.

The outbreak of war was greeted with jingoistic approval in Britain as in other countries. Sir Edward Grey remarked, in a memorable phrase, that the lamps were going out all over Europe, but neither he, nor his European counterparts, nor the chiefs of staff, nor almost anyone else, had the least idea of what the outbreak of the Great War implied for European civilization.

SEPTEMBER
19 South Africans take Luderitz
22 *Emden* bombards Madras

OCTOBER
10 Germans take Antwerp
14 Belgian government flees
16 Four German destroyers sunk off Belgian coast
19 Battle of Ypres begins
26 British battleship *Audacious* sunk by mine
27 Duala, Cameroon, captured by Anglo-French forces
31 Russian and Turkish fleets clash in Black Sea

NOVEMBER
1 British defeat off Coronel, Chile
2 German squadron raids Norfolk coast
4 Russians invade Armenia
4 German East Africa repels British Indian force landed at Tanga
5 Allies declare war on Turkey
8 Anglo-Japanese force takes German fort of Tsing-tau, China
9 *Emden* sunk off Cocos Island
12 Botha crushes rebellion in South Africa
24 Indian division captures Basra, commanding Persian Gulf
26 British batteship *Bulwark* explodes at Sheerness
29 Ex-President Roosevelt criticizes U.S. neutrality

DECEMBER
1 Admiral Peirse arrives at Suez to organize defence
5 Germans take Lodz
8 British victory off Falklands
16 British declare protectorate in Egypt
16 Germans bombard Yorkshire ports
25 Christmas truce in trenches

A column of Belgian cavalry near Ypres. In the face of infantry armed with machine-guns and quick-firing rifles the mounted soldier was fast becoming obsolete.

British foreign secretary, Sir Edward Grey.

THE RIVAL FORCES

ALTHOUGH the great powers had been preparing for war for years, they were not well equipped for the kind of war that began in 1914. For example, Britain and Germany had expended vast resources on building large battleships, but battleships were to play an insignificant part in the fighting, although they certainly affected strategy. Similarly, the nature of the land war, with the infantry (especially on the Western Front) rendered virtually immobile by the power of artillery and machine-guns, was not anticipated (though it had been forecast by Ivan Bloch, a Polish banker, in his work, The Future of War, in 1899).

In training and organization the Germany army was the best in Europe. Moreover, the Germans were inspired by a high degree of patriotism and a belief in a great destiny, as yet unfulfilled, for their country. The Germans also had the best understanding of the power in modern war of heavy artillery and machine-guns and of the significance of railway communications.

The Austro-Hungarian army was modelled on the German but was far inferior, above all because of its disparate mixture of nationalities and its indifferent record in recent wars – both features in marked contrast to the German army. France possessed an army only 20 per cent smaller than that of Germany, although its total manpower was little more than half. The main difference therefore lay in the reserves. Germany had plenty, France only very little. France depended on and – like most other countries – anticipated a short war. It was unprepared for a drawn-out conflict. Moreover, France was also geared to a mobile war, and was ill-equipped for the static warfare of the trenches.

Russia's chief advantage was its immense reserves of manpower, plus the well-proven courage of the Russian soldier. However, the Russian leadership was deplorable, corrupt and incompetent, and industrial backwardness made Russia ill-adapted to modern warfare. Communications were very poor, frontiers immense and the country was cut off geographically from its allies. It was suggested that Russia's engagement in what could be portrayed as a pan-Slavic crusade was a desperate attempt to restore national unity under the fast-disintegrating tsarist regime, but if so it failed.

Britain's position was quite different. Britain had never had a large army, depending on sea power since the 18th century, and harboured an even older tradition hostile to the concept of 'standing armies'. The British army was therefore extremely small and, although highly professional, was geared to maintaining peace in the empire overseas. Doubts existed as to whether British commanders were capable of conducting large-scale campaigns – doubts which events did little to dispel. Some were simply too old, though this drawback also affected Germany.

There is no better illustration of the failure of commanders on both sides to appreciate the characteristics of 20th-century scientific warfare than the widely held belief that the role of cavalry would be vital.

At sea, Britain's traditional supremacy was challenged by Germany. In 1914 Britain had 29 capital ships, Germany 18. The menace of the submarine was underestimated in Britain, which was vulnerable especially through its dependence on overseas food supplies and raw materials for its manufacturing industry. Britain was the main workshop of the Allied Powers just as Germany was for the Central Powers.

German machine-gunners protected against a gas attack.

German gunners with a cannon mounted on a railway truck. Developments in ballistics and other improvements made artillery a decisive weapon in the conduct of the war.

In Germany civilians join the colours in August 1914.

A batch of British recruits on their way to enlist.

1914

AUGUST

BEF IN FRANCE

EAST PRUSSIA INVADED

Germans take Liège

The advancing Germans captured the Belgian city of Liège on August 16. Belgian resistance was stiffer than expected, and the Germans were compelled to wait for the arrival of their heavy howitzers, which demolished the forts in a striking demonstration of the new power of modern artillery. The Belgian forces withdrew and fell back on Antwerp.

The purpose of the attack on Liège was to clear a route for the main German armies into the Belgian plain. These were already deployed after an exemplary operation, in which troop trains had crossed the Rhine at the rate of 550 a day. Seven German armies were massed on the frontier, ready to advance, and the 1st and 2nd Armies were already engaging with the main Belgian army protecting Brussels. The French gave the Belgians no support because they grossly misjudged German strength and were concentrating on their own offensive – chief of staff Joffre's Plan XVII against the German centre.

General Joffre in consultation with his senior officers.

BEF lands at Channel ports

The British Expeditionary Force disembarked quite successfully between August 12 and 17. The operation was carried out with notable despatch and excellent security. The Germans were unaware that the British had landed until they met them in combat.

The BEF, led by Sir John French, numbered 120,000 men, a minute force compared with the French, who had roughly one million in the field. Although independently commanded, it was seen strategically as an adjunct to the French armies and thus adapted to Marshal Joffre's ill-conceived offensive. The French had launched an attack into Lorraine, largely for political purposes, this being territory taken by Germany during the Franco-Prussian war of 1870. They were defeated on the Morhange-Sarrebourg line, east of Metz, though the Germans lacked the forces in that area to strike a decisive blow.

Meanwhile, in the northwest, the fall of Liège had prompted French reinforcement designed to catch the – vastly underestimated – German forces in a pincer movement. The reverse nearly occurred. Lanrezac's 5th army (ten divisions), with the British (four divisions) on their left, narrowly avoided entrapment by the German 1st, 2nd and 3rd armies (34 divisions). They fell back to the Marne. ▶ *page 58*

Russians invade East Prussia

The Russian forces under the overall command of the Grand Duke Nicholas took an unexpected initiative by invading East Prussia on August 17. The 1st Army (under Rennenkampf) and the 2nd Army (under Samsonov), acting to ease pressure on the French, had not yet concentrated their forces, but nevertheless commanded a numerical advantage of 2 to 1.

As the German commander showed momentary signs of panic, Moltke replaced him with the retired general Hindenburg, with Ludendorff (who had planned the Liège operation) as his chief of staff. Ludendorff took the daring step of concentrating most available forces against Samsonov in the south. His planning was assisted by the ineptitude of the Russians, who had got into a muddle with their codes and were resorting to radio communications in 'clear'. The Russians were resoundingly defeated in the battle subsequently known as Tannenberg (August 26–30). The Germans, reinforced with two divisions from the Western Front, then drove Rennenkampf out of East Prussia. Russian casualties in this campaign were put at 250,000.

These successes for the Central Powers were balanced by the failures of the Austrians who, having been checked in Serbia, were more disastrously defeated by the Russians at Lemberg (Lvov) when they invaded Russian Poland. They fell back towards Cracow, where, receiving reinforcement from the Germans in East Prussia, they renewed their offensive. However, Russian strength was building up, the offensive was checked and the Russian counter-attack threatened Silesia.

The Grand Duke Nicholas now had seven armies at his disposal, but though the Russians greatly outnumbered the enemy, they were handicapped by logistical and communications failures, not to mention the superior strategy of Hindenburg and Ludendorff, notably in their skilful employment of the railways. Superior mobility proved more than a match for numerical dominance and by December 15 the Russians had been pushed back to the Bzura-Ravka rivers, not far from Warsaw. The Russian commander-in-chief then decided to fall back on trenches along the Nida-Dunajec line, and the war settled into the kind of stalemate already established in the west, although the potential for breakout was somewhat less restricted. ▶ *page 67*

Hindenburg, German commander in East Prussia.

Ludendorff, who defeated the Russians at Tannenberg.

A Russian cavalryman on patrol exchanges greetings with the inhabitants of a village. Hopes of a quick victory for Russia were dashed by a disastrous defeat at the hands of the Germans.

Austrian prisoners of war trudging through the snow under Russian escort. The multi-national Austrian army proved no match for the Russian forces when it attempted to invade Russian-occupied Poland.

Retreat from Mons

The British fought a delaying battle at Mons on August 23, covering the French withdrawal. Vastly outnumbered, they retreated, fighting a similar type of engagement at Le Cateau three days later. The German assumption that the British were still based on the Channel ports lost them the chance to sever the British from the French 5th Army. The BEF, however, suffered heavy casualties.

As the Germans advanced into northeastern France, it was evident that neither side's plans were working effectively. Though the French and British had been driven back, their forces had not been destroyed and were falling back on good defensive positions. Plan XVII had been a total failure, but the Schlieffen Plan was not working either, and the German troops had advanced too far and too fast for their supplies to keep up. They missed a number of chances that might have led to the decisive result everyone expected. The blame for these mistakes is usually attributed mainly to Moltke, elderly, sick and unconfident, and shortly to be replaced as chief of staff by Falkenhayn.

General Erich von Falkenhayn.

Battle of the Marne

The Allies returned to the offensive in the west on September 6 with the largest battle so far, beginning on the line of the Marne. The opportunity for the new French offensive was presented by Moltke's virtual abandonment of the Schlieffen Plan in favour of a pincer movement centred on Verdun. This left his right wing open to attack, a situation clearly perceived by Gallieni, the military governor of Paris, who persuaded an initially reluctant Joffre to agree to the Marne offensive. Fresh troops were rushed to the front in Paris taxis.

A gap was opened up between the German 1st Army (under von Kluck) and 2nd army (von Bülow), and both were compelled to retreat. They fell back to the Aisne, and the French and British began to talk of invading Germany. They were unduly optimistic. The battle proved what was to be the preponderant feature of the war – the dominance of defence over attack.

The Germans still held a substantial portion of northeast France, a region which contained most of its coal and iron resources and many major industrial centres. The Germans were also in the fortunate position of being able to allow the enemy to do the attacking. For over three and a half years the battle zone was to remain more or less static.

Meanwhile, the Belgians had continued to put up stubborn resistance. They had launched an attack on the German right in support of the beleaguered French and British on August 24, which was broken off when the Allies retreated, and they attacked again on September 9, during the battle of the Marne. This resistance convinced the Germans of the necessity of securing Antwerp. Belated, small-scale British assistance failed to prevent the fall of the city, though it did enable the Belgian army to escape along the Flanders coast.

An artist's impression of a clash between British and German cavalry at the Marne.

General von Kluck, who commanded one of the three armies invading France.

Ypres

As both sides attempted to turn the flank of the enemy in the northwest, the main battleground shifted to Flanders. An Allied offensive on October 19 confronted the advancing Germans in the neighbourhood of Ypres ('Wipers' to the British Tommy). The ensuing battle, known as 'First Ypres', lasted five weeks.

It was notable for the stubborn defence of the British (outnumbered by more than 2 to 1), who were eventually saved by French reinforcements. It was also a strategic turning-point, since by the end of the battle the line of trenches – at first skimpy affairs but made increasingly impregnable – was completed along the whole of the Western Front. Thereafter, Falkenhayn was to rely on defence while attempting to crush Russia in the east, where greater mobility was possible.

First Ypres also seemed to confirm the decision of the minister of war, Lord Kitchener, memorably symbolized in a recruitment poster, that Britain had to raise a mass army. Recruitment flourished, with over one million men enlisted by December 1914. The total armed forces of the British Empire then numbered about two million.

Belgian soldiers on the Yser. Their stubborn defence deflected the German attack towards Ypres.

German infantry advancing over open country in November 1914 before the Western Front became stabilized.

Turkey enters the war

Russia, Britain and France declared war on Turkey on November 5. In the previous month the Turkish government had closed the Dardanelles and the Bosphorus to Allied shipping, virtually isolating Russia's Black Sea ports from the outside world and causing irreparable damage to that country's fragile economy.

In fact, this action by Turkey was almost certainly its single most useful contribution to the war effort of the Central Powers. Further provocation was provided when a squadron of Turkish naval vessels, including two recently acquired from Germany and still equipped with German crews, had bombarded Odessa and other ports in southern Russia at the end of October.

The ramshackle Ottoman empire had been gradually crumbling away for over half a century and had by this time lost the greater part of its European possessions. The army was exhausted after fighting unsuccessfully against the Italians in Tripoli, and the Balkan Wars had proved to be a further enormous drain on its resources. The leader of the Young Turks, Enver Pasha, who as minister of war was a dominant figure on the Turkish political scene, believed that an alliance with Germany would serve his country's interests best, and a secret treaty between the two nations had been signed on August 2. A German military mission had been active in Turkey since the end of 1913 charged with the task of reorganizing the Turkish army.

Despite the strong reservations expressed by his German advisers Enver Pasha decided upon an invasion of the Russian Caucasus and launched an attack in mid-December under appalling weather conditions. His soldiers fought well but suffered a severe defeat at the hands of their opponents. The Russian high command was nevertheless alarmed at the threat which Turkey represented to its southern borders and German strategic plans were well served by a move which forced the Russians to tie down troops who were badly needed elsewhere.

Emden sunk

The German light cruiser *Emden* was sunk off the Cocos Islands on November 9 by the Australian cruiser *Sydney*. The battle ended the short but highly successful career of the German raider, in which she destroyed a total of 15 ships.

The *Emden*, detached from Admiral Graf von Spee's squadron in the China Sea, entered the Indian Ocean from the Moluccas strait towards the end of August, evading a British cruiser that was searching for her. In the course of little more than two months she ranged the Indian Ocean, bombarding Madras, attacking merchant ships and refuelling at Diego Garcia.

On October 28 she was off Penang, where she succeeding in sinking a Russian cruiser and a French destroyer, then doubled back around the north of Sumatra. Meanwhile, her storeships had been found and sunk, and she was forced to make for the Cocos Islands, where the *Sydney* found her.

The Australian cruiser *Sydney* which ended the destructive career of the German warship *Emden*.

The Battle of the Falklands

In a major success for the Royal (British) Navy, the German squadron commanded by von Spee was defeated off the Falkland Islands on December 8. The squadron, which consisted of the battle cruisers *Scharnhorst* and *Gneisenau*, plus three light cruisers, was entirely destroyed with the exception of one ship, the *Dresden*.

Von Spee was forced to leave Chinese waters when Japan entered the war, and made for South America, bombarding Tahiti on the way. The British commander in the South Atlantic, Admiral Craddock, collected his forces near the Falklands and entered the Pacific. The two fleets met on November 1 off Coronel. Two British cruisers were sunk and Craddock retreated to the Falklands.

This German victory prompted a determined effort to destroy von Spee's squadron. Admiral Sturdee, with two battle cruisers, was despatched on this mission from Plymouth, while four other squadrons, including a Japanese one based on the Galapagos islands, were instructed to watch for the German ships. Sturdee was at Port Stanley when von Spee, unaware of his presence, arrived off the Falklands on December 8. The British 12-inch lyddite shells were too much for the German battle cruisers, which were sunk in a few hours with heavy casualties, including von Spee and the entire crew of the *Scharnhorst*.

Above. The German battle cruiser *Scharnhorst* which was sunk near the Falkland islands.

Admiral Sturdee, the victor at the Falklands.

Von Spee, who went down with his ship.

An unofficial Christmas truce

A remarkable incident occurred on the Western Front on Christmas Day. In an apparently spontaneous move, the troops on both sides left their trenches and came together in No Man's Land, exchanging cigarettes and sweets, and communicating mainly in basic French.

The enthusiasm, almost incomprehensible today, which had greeted the outbreak of war had quickly waned. Within three months it had become obvious that this was to be no short, sharp war. Though people at home, pounded daily by passionate propaganda, were shocked, on the battlefield there was a strange mood of tolerance. This too, however, was short-lived, as the terrible strain of war crushed more humane feelings and soldiers became conscious that they were involved in a cruel and atrocious struggle for survival.

NAVAL STRATEGY

THE WAR AT SEA boiled down to the question whether Germany could successfully challenge Britain's traditional command of the sea. As on land, the availability of new weapons – submarine, mine, torpedo, radio and aircraft – made defence easier than attack.

The Germans, with a smaller navy, assumed that the British would seek to destroy them in battle, which they therefore sought to avoid. The British strategy, however, was designed for rather different ends. Having moved the fleet to Scapa Flow in the Orkneys at the beginning of the war, thus gaining effective command of the North Sea, the British, wary of mines and torpedoes and the difficult German coast, opted for a long-range blockade, while remaining on the alert for any breakout by the German fleet. At the same time, dependent on seaborne supply, they had to maintain the security of the ocean routes.

The Germans had comparatively few warships in foreign stations in August 1914, though the cruisers Goeben and Breslau succeeded in reaching Constantinople at the beginning of the war, their presence helping to persuade Turkey to enter the conflict on the side of the Central Powers. The most formidable force, consisting of Admiral von Spee's battle cruisers Scharnhorst and Gneisenau, was destroyed in the battle of the Falklands, and by the end of 1914 the oceans were cleared – on the surface at least – of German raiders.

The chief threat to ocean commerce turned out to be not battle squadrons but submarines. As the war progressed, their inferiority in capital ships persuaded the Germans to concentrate increasingly on submarines, which the British, suffering severe losses in the Atlantic, regarded as an illegitimate means of warfare. In the end the policy of unrestricted submarine warfare, nearly disastrous to Britain, was to prove indirectly disastrous to Germany, since it was the immediate cause of the United States entering the war in 1917.

British – and imperial – command of the seas also facilitated the mopping up of German colonies around the world, mainly undertaken by Empire forces. General Louis Botha in South Africa, having learned his business fighting the British, proved a particularly effective ally in spite of anti-British feeling, momentarily breaking into actual revolt, among the Afrikaners.

British warships in Kiel harbour during a prewar courtesy visit.

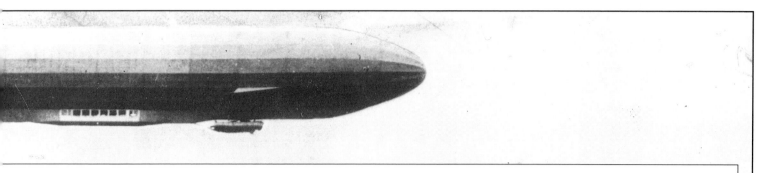

The German High Seas fleet in single line ahead.

The submarine U 15, sunk in August 1914.

BRITISH AND GERMAN NAVAL STRENGTH IN AUGUST 1914

British Grand Fleet		German High Seas Fleet	
Dreadnoughts	20	Dreadnoughts	9
Other battleships	40	Other battleships	22
Battle cruisers	8	Battle cruisers	5
Cruisers	58	Cruisers	7
Light cruisers	44	Light cruisers	34
Destroyers	301	Destroyers	144
Submarines	78	Submarines	28

(The figures include a number of obsolete ships of limited use, also ships on distant foreign stations.)

1915 Allied offensive on Western Front

JANUARY–MARCH

CHAMPAGNE

NEUVE CHAPELLE

THE DARDANELLES

On February 12 the French launched a new offensive in Champagne. Casualties were heavy, the French losing about 50,000 men while gaining about 500 yards. This was followed up by a British attack on Neuve Chapelle in March and a further French attack in April farther east, where the German line reached the Meuse valley.

The *Blücher* goes down

The German cruiser *Blücher* was sunk and two battle cruisers were damaged in a short, sharp naval action off the Dogger Bank in the North Sea on January 24. The British battle cruiser *Lion* was severely damaged but returned safely to Rosyth.

British battle cruisers commanded by Admiral Beatty lingered south of the Dogger Bank following the Zeppelin raids on the east coast. A German squadron was sighted on the morning of January 24 and engaged. Having lost the *Blücher*, the Germans retired to their base behind the minefields. The engagement encouraged a still more cautious policy in the command of the German High Seas Fleet, which thereafter endeavoured to evade action whenever the enemy was sighted.

In spite of the heavy losses and minimal gains, the French commander, Joffre, proclaimed his Champagne offensive worthwhile. The British attack on Neuve Chapelle in the Pas de Calais, carried out by Haig's 1st Army, was on a smaller scale but potentially more significant. A heavy but very brief barrage gained the advantage of surprise.

The initial advance was successful, but the attack was bogged down as the front was extended, partly because of insufficient artillery support. Shortage of munitions was a serious problem at this stage, not solved until a Ministry of Munitions was formed with the dynamic Lloyd George at its head. The battle also demonstrated that the British commanders had not yet grasped that the war was one of engineers and artillery, not cavalry and infantry – a notion that continued to elude many of them throughout the war. The battle was broken off on the third day, following German counter-attacks and shortage of ammunition. British casualties were about 13,000.

The French offensive of April, conducted on a broad front between the Meuse and Moselle, attained no significant object and cost over 60,000 casualties.

German artillery in action on the Western Front.

German airships attack English coast

Signifying a sinister new extension of the means of warfare, German Zeppelins began to raid the eastern coast of England on January 19. Several people were killed in Norfolk ports and some bombs fell near the royal home at Sandringham.

Rigid airships played a small but significant role in the First World War. Most were used on naval and surveillance duties, not on bombing missions, causing considerable panic initially but creating comparatively little damage. They represented an admission that war was no longer a matter of winning battles but of all-out attack on an entire nation – children were among the earliest casualties – though to begin with it was asserted that only military targets were selected.

Zeppelins were used in raids throughout 1915–16, until they were superseded by aeroplanes. The great drawback of the Zeppelin was that it was a 'soft' target, its vast bag of hydrogen making it especially vulnerable to incendiary devices.

The gondola of the German airship L 6.

Allied fleet bombards Dardanelles

British and French warships began a bombardment of the Turkish defences of the Dardanelles on February 16. With intervals, caused partly by bad weather, the naval action continued for two months.

The Dardanelles campaign originated in a request from the Russians for a diversionary attack on Turkey which would relieve pressure on the Russians fighting the Turks in the Crimea. In January the Dardanelles, a strait nearly 40 miles long and from one to four miles wide, which joins the Aegean and the Sea of Marmara, was selected as the objective.

The forcing of the Dardanelles, opening the way for an attack on Constantinople, had figured in Allied military planning before the war, but had been rejected as too difficult. With the entry of Turkey into the war, the plan was reclassified as possible though hazardous. Originally, a purely naval expedition was planned, but it was swiftly realized that a combined naval and military operation would be necessary. This plan was enthusiastically supported by the British first lord of the admiralty, Winston Churchill.

The outcome of the operation which, if successful, would have opened a 'back door' to Russia, was hazarded by the Allies' disinclination to send a sufficiently large force at the outset and by the choice of largely obsolete warships. Moreover, the essential element of surprise was lost in the course of the lengthy and largely ineffective bombardment. At the beginning the Turks had only two divisions guarding the strait. By the time the Allied landings took place, they had six divisions and thus outnumbered the five Allied divisions, besides possessing formidable natural defences.

▶ page 66

The Anglo-French fleet at the entrance to the Dardanelles in February 1915.

The French battleship *Bouvet* sinking after striking a mine at the Dardanelles.

1915

GALLIPOLI LANDINGS

2nd BATTLE OF YPRES

GALICIAN CAMPAIGN

Below. Russian soldiers in their trenches seek protection against the cold.

Bottom. A Russian battery in action during the assault upon Przemysl.

Russians capture Przemysl

The fortress of Przemysl, which commanded a bridgehead on the River San in Galicia, was captured by the Russians on March 22 after a siege. Over 100,000 Austrian prisoners were taken, besides the heavy casualties suffered by Austria during vain efforts to lift the siege.

Russian strategy early in 1915 was to hold the flanks secure while striking towards Silesia and Hungary, a campaign in which the capture of Przemysl was the Russian army's main success (although it was only to hold the fortress for a couple of months). The Russians made little further progress, while in northern Poland they were surprised by Ludendorff's offensive of February, losing four divisions in the Augustovo forests, which sapped the strength of their own advance.

The events tended to confirm the evidence that the Russians were a match for the Austrians but not for the far better organized Germans.

Allied forces land in Gallipoli

Allied forces landed at two places on the Gallipoli peninsula in the early hours of April 25. The British disembarked at Cape Helles, near the southern tip of the peninsula, while ANZAC (Australian and New Zealand) troops fought their way ashore some 15 miles farther north on the Aegean coast. At the same time a French brigade made a diversionary attack on Kum Kale, on the Anatolian coast.

The invading force, consisting of one French and four British divisions, had been assembled in Egypt under the command of General Ian Hamilton, and the transports gathered at the Greek Island of Lemnos before the landings. Despite barbed wire and heavy machine-gun fire, both groups were able to establish a beachhead. However, the Turks commanded the heights above, and the British and ANZAC forces could not advance. Stalemate, not unlike that on the Western Front, set in. ▶ page 73

Germans wage war with poison gas

On the evening of April 22 men in the Allied front lines in the Ypres sector observed a strange, greenish-yellow cloud drifting towards their trenches. Minutes later the members of a French territorial division and an Algerian division, which the cloud reached first, were running from their trenches, coughing and gasping. The Germans had attacked with chlorine gas.

Although the release of gas was followed by an intensive bombardment and a substantial section of the Allied defences was left almost totally unmanned, the Germans advanced only a few miles and failed to take Ypres, which for a short time was virtually undefended. The Allies had warning, through the statements of prisoners of war, of the presence of gas cylinders in the German trenches, yet were taken by surprise by this new weapon. Like all new weapons, from the crossbow to the atomic bomb, it was passionately denounced as inhumane and vile, though its effects were not discernibly more dreadful than an artillery bombardment or even a bayonet thrust.

This was not in fact the first use of gas by the Germans. They had fired some in shells the previous November, though this was so ineffective that its intended victims never noticed it. A form of tear gas had also been used against the Russians in Poland at the end of January. ▶ page 72

British soldiers under a gas attack.

Central Powers launch major offensive in the east

On May 2 crack troops of Field Marshal Mackensen's 11th Army, augmented by the Austro-Hungarian 4th army, attacked along a 20-mile front in western Galicia. After an artillery bombardment at dawn had destroyed the initial Russian defences, the troops poured through, achieving complete surprise. In less than two weeks they reached the River San, an advance of nearly 100 miles.

A very youthful Russian prisoner of war among the hundreds of thousands captured during the great Austro-German offensive.

Lack of German reserves prevented a total rout. The Austrians were anxious to withdraw troops to deal with the new threat from Italy in the south, but were dissuaded by Falkenhayn in the (justified) conviction that they could hold the mountainous frontier against the Italians with comparatively small forces. Falkenhayn himself still adhered to at least the basic principles of the Schlieffen Plan, which called for a decision in the west and a holding action in the east, but in view of the failure of Anglo-French spring offensives on the Western Front he was prepared to withdraw troops from that sector temporarily in the hope of returning them in larger numbers following success against the Russians.

Thus reinforced, Mackensen advanced once again, recapturing Przemysl and Lemberg. The attack then turned north towards the main Russian forces between the Bug and the Vistula, while at the same time Hindenburg advanced southeast from East Prussia, creating the beginning of a gigantic scissors movement. However, the Russians were able to withdraw before they were cut off, and by the end of August Falkenhayn decided to call a halt. Apart from his disinclination to get too deeply committed in the east, he was anxious to stiffen the coming attack on Serbia and also to restore troops to the Western Front before another French offensive began. In the four-months campaign, the whole of Poland had been conquered and about 800,000 Russian prisoners taken. ► *page 86*

German troops on the march in Galicia during their victorious campaign.

An artist's impression of the sinking *Lusitania*. The huge loss of life included many Americans, and did much to ensure that the United States would enter the war.

Lusitania sunk

At lunchtime on May 7 the big Cunard liner *Lusitania*, sailing from New York to Liverpool, was struck by a torpedo from a German U-boat off the coast of Ireland. She sank rapidly and about 1200 people, nearly three-quarters of the total on board, were drowned.

The German submarine campaign had effectively begun in February, when the waters around Britain had been declared a war zone in which all ships, including neutrals, would be sunk on sight. The British had similarly claimed the right to intercept all ships suspected of carrying cargo for Germany and to bring them into British ports for search. In international law it was accepted that goods directly linked to the war effort – arms, machines, raw materials – were subject to confiscation by a blockading belligerent. The British, however, extended this to all cargo, including food (much more important to Germany, of course). These policies had given great offence to neutrals. The United States had some sharp exchanges with Britain, but the German submarines proved the more offensive. One or two U.S. and other neutral ships had already been attacked and a few U.S. citizens killed on British ships, but the German government had apologized for these incidents. The sinking of the *Lusitania*, whose speed had been thought to make her invulnerable

to torpedoes, brought matters to a head. The fact that the Germans had issued a guarded warning to Americans not to sail on her merely confirmed that the attack was the result of advance planning rather than an impulsive decision by a U-boat commander, and the striking of a commemorative medal hardly suggested that the Germans regretted the incident.

A more counterproductive act

could scarcely be imagined, for it provoked fierce anti-German protests in many countries, notbably in the United States. Nearly 200 U.S. citizens were among the dead passengers, including famous figures like the millionaire Alfred Vanderbilt. The disaster, condemned by former President Theodore Roosevelt as an act of piracy and murder, placed a great strain upon President Woodrow Wilson's declared policy of strict neutrality, and from this time U.S. involvement in the war became a potent possibility.

French launch new offensive near Arras

On May 9 a French offensive directed by Foch was begun by General d'Urbal's army on a four-mile front between Lens and Arras. It made little territorial progress despite a brief, three-mile breakthrough achieved by Pétain. Simultaneously, Haig's 1st (British) Army directed a two-pronged attack on the lines near Neuve Chapelle.

This was one of a series of indeterminate offensives founded on the optimism of the French commander-in-chief, Joffre, and on an exaggerated estimate of German losses. The attack was maintained until mid-June, the French achieving no significant advance and losing about 100,000 men, compared with fewer than 50,000 German casualties. The British, still handicapped by a shortage of shells, made a series of unavailing sorties against the German lines before breaking off on May 27.

Dazed survivors from the *Lusitania* being escorted through the streets of Queenstown (now Cobh) in Ireland.

Italy enters the war

On May 23 Italy declared war on Austria, having signed the secret Treaty of London with the Allies the previous month. The Triple Alliance, which linked Italy with the Central Powers, was denounced, although Italy for the time being declined to declare war on Germany.

At the outbreak of the war Italy had declared its neutrality, on the grounds that the Triple Alliance did not oblige it to take part in an aggressive war. What largely guided Italy's actions, however, was its desire for territorial acquisitions from Austria, and a policy of neutrality threatened to leave it with no bargaining position at the end of the hostilities. Austria was unwilling to make the concessions requested by Italy – for instance to surrender Trieste, for Austria a vital port on the Mediterranean. Moreover, by 1915 Italian public opinion was turning in favour of the Allies, and former pacifists like the Revolutionary Socialists, led by Mussolini among others, saw opportunity for revolution in the instability of a society at war. In March the Austrian government did make a move to meet Italian desires, but by then it was too late. The Italians got what they wanted – or most of it – by the Treaty of London, which promised Italy the Trentino, the southern Tyrol, Trieste, Istria and other largely Italian-speaking areas.

Left. Italian soldiers making their way up a mountain during the winter of 1915.

Below. General Cadorna, commander of the Italian forces.

1915

OCTOBER
5 Venizelos government falls in Greece
6 Austro-German invasion of Serbia
8 Russia attacks Bulgaria
12 Nurse Cavell executed
15 Plans announced to expand U.S. army
21 Austrians bombard Dede Agatch (Alexandroupolis), Thrace
30 Gallieni becomes French minister of war
31 Famine reported in parts of Russia

NOVEMBER
10 Austrians prevent Italian advance at River Isonzo
11 Churchill resigns as British naval supremo
14 Masaryk calls for Czech independence from Austria
17 Italian liner *Ancona* sunk with 27 U.S. citizens among the dead
21 Serbia under Austro-German control

DECEMBER
3 German diplomats expelled from Washington
3 Joffre obtains supreme command of all French armies
8 Turks lay siege to Kut
15 Haig replaces French as British commander-in-chief in France
18 British and ANZAC forces withdraw from northern Gallipoli
18 Joffre asserts impregnability of Verdun defences
30 Liner *Persia* sunk in Mediterranean
31 British cruiser *Natal* explodes at Cromarty
31 Total of British ships sunk by U-boats reaches 259

Italians advance against Austria

On May 30 the Italians opened their campaign against Austria with the advance of the 2nd and 3rd Armies, under the overall command of General Cadorna, in the northeast.

The Italian potential for damaging the cause of the Central Powers was, in the short term at least, limited. Italy was handicapped by lack of military preparedness (the army had scarcely recovered from the Libyan campaign and only seven divisions out of Cadorna's 24 were fully operational) and by an awkward strategic position, with an advance to the east leaving an opportunity for a counter-attack from the Trentino into the Po valley. Bad weather causing floods in the Isonzo valley helped to halt the advance, but in June Cadorna launched an attack which lasted two weeks. It achieved little and the Isonzo front settled into stalemate, with Cadorna planning to renew his attack, with greatly superior numbers, in the autumn. ▶ *page 88*

THE HOME FRONT

IN THE COURSE of 1915 it became evident that the war was not, like all previous wars, simply a military conflict, but a struggle for national survival. The 'enemy' was not a fleet or an army but a nation, and all citizens of a participating state were involved. The formation of a national government in Britain, with its long tradition of government by a political party, was symptomatic of the political changes taking place and reflected the mood of grim determination which had replaced the superficial enthusiasm of August 1914, when trench warfare had hardly been heard of.

Wars often bring, or hasten, important social changes, and the First World War was no exception. One of the most obvious was the changing role of women. The demand for military manpower resulted in an acute labour shortage, and finding new resources of manpower became a growing problem for governments. Women were employed in jobs previously reserved for men, including factories – munitions factories above all (see below). It was found that in many ways women were better industrial workers than men. For example, they were less inclined to get drunk – a severe problem among male workers in the war years (King George V even volunteered

Women in an engineering factory.

Land girls undergoing training.

to become an abstainer as an example to his subjects).

An allied problem for governments at war was maintenance of the food supply, threatened not only by military action but also by a shortage of farm workers. Ultimately, all such governments were forced to impose rationing. This was merely one example of the way the war took over the government, or more accurately, of the way the government took over everything – manpower, raw materials, the food supply, transport, consumer goods, industrial relations, etc. In effect government became totalitarian, though on the whole with the consent of the governed, and this was no less characteristic of Britain and France than of Russia or Austria-Hungary, if only because bureaucracy was more efficient in the former countries.

In a total, national war, the morale of the civilian population was all-important, and the expression 'home front' was no idle, sentimental phrase. All governments made good use of censorship and propaganda, the purpose of which was to make people hate the enemy and to convince them that their side was in the right. Propaganda in Britain against 'the Huns' was particularly effective, partly no doubt because it usually had at least some basis in truth: the Germans did commit atrocities in Belgium, though less frightful than some they were accused of. Innocent people who happened to have German ancestors and therefore German names were physically attacked. Housewives discarded kitchen knives that were inscribed 'Solingen', people stopped listening to Bach and Beethoven. These and other absurdities were legion.

Women ratings of the WRNS.

1915

Ypres battle ends

The second battle of Ypres ended on May 25. The Germans had advanced three or four miles but failed to reach the town. The new weapon, gas, proved to have only limited effect once the enemy was forewarned.

The battle had begun with the gas attack of April 22, but the Germans had failed to take advantage of the initial hole it created in the Allied defences, and Canadian troops in particular resisted strenuously. When gas was released against the Canadians on April 24, they were able to reduce its effects somewhat by covering their faces with wet rags. Nevertheless, the Allied lines were pushed back, and a series of counterattacks proved costly and ineffective. The British position was exposed, while the French failed to regain the ground they had lost, partly because of Joffre's unwillingness to allow more troops to Foch in the Ypres sector in view of his offensive planned for May 9. A further two-mile zone was relinquished by the British and ferocious fighting took place in the area known as Hill 60. German bombardment forced a further retreat, but with General Plumer's II Corps strongly entrenched in its new position, the Germans called off the assault.

Rhodesian troops during the campaign in South-West Africa.

Italian cruiser sunk in Mediterranean

On July 18 the Italian cruiser *Giuseppe Garibaldi* was torpedoed by an Austrian submarine and sank. The British cruiser *Dublin* had been similarly attacked a few days earlier but escaped with serious damage.

The task of blockading the Adriatic fell to the French fleet based on Malta. Austrian submarines were active and, after the loss of the battleship *Jean Bart* in December 1914, the French were wary of releasing their heavy ships, relying on cruisers and destroyers. After Italy's entry into the war, the Italian fleet, reinforced by French and British warships, took over the Adriatic blockade, with the French admiral nominally in overall command. German submarines also entered the Mediterranean in the summer, and the task of protecting the numerous transports and supply ships making their way to and from Gallipoli, and later Salonika, placed some strain on the Allies' resources. An attempt was made in September to blockade the Strait of Otranto with nets but the submarines proved able to sail underneath. Dede Agatch (Alexandroupolis) in Thrace was bombarded in October and, after the defeat of Serbia, the Austrians launched a naval raid on Durazzo. The raiders were beaten off by Italian and British vessels and lost a destroyer, as well as suffering severe damage to the cruiser *Helgoland*. Austrian and German submarines found many safe refuges among the Greek islands.

Botha conquers South-West Africa

The main German force in South-West Africa (about 3500 men) surrendered to General Louis Botha on July 9. The war, unpopular with many Afrikaners, had been fought with restraint. Although the Germans had poisoned wells and laid mines, they usually gave notice of these hazards. They could muster only about 6000 able-bodied men altogether and their small numbers made Botha's victory inevitable.

After crushing rebellion at home – interpreted without serious evidence at the time as being German-instigated – Botha acted with his accustomed vigour in completing the conquest of the German colony. The main problem was the terrain: marching across the Kalahari Desert in midsummer was no picnic.

German naval operations checked in the Baltic

In separate engagements in the Baltic in July the Russians disabled a German minelayer and a British submarine torpedoed the cruiser *Prinz Adalbert*.

There was considerable activity in the Baltic in the late summer of 1915. The Russian fleet, newly augmented by a few British submarines, was generally successful in frustrating the Germans, forestalling an attempt to land troops in Courland and disrupting minelaying. In general German warships in the Baltic were elderly vessels, though a battle cruiser of the High Seas Fleet, the *Moltke*, was badly damaged by submarine attack in August during an attempt to force the Gulf of Riga. Thereafter the Germans abstained from serious operations in the Baltic.

British submarines also endeavoured to disrupt the German supplies of Swedish iron and steel, sinking 14 ships involved in the trade later in the year as well as the *Prinz Adalbert* and a couple of other escorting warships.

The campaign began in April. One column advanced from the Orange River via Warmbad and Keetmanshoop, two others from the South African-held ports. Windhoek fell in May and the campaign was concluded two months later. The South Africans suffered minimal casualties and Botha offered the Germans generous terms. The colonists mostly returned to their farms.

British troops land at Suvla Bay

In the Gallipoli campaign General Hamilton took a new initiative on August 6. While renewing the offensive in the south, he despatched troops to Suvla Bay in an attempt to seize the centre of the peninsula opposite the Narrows.

The British government had authorized reinforcements in July, and Hamilton now commanded 12 divisions. The Turks, however, still holding the heights above the Narrows, now had 16 divisions. Although the Suvla Bay landing achieved surprise, command was poor, the troops were inexperienced, and the chance to break through was lost. The southern offensive was also unsuccessful.

Hamilton was getting the more vigorous subordinates he had asked for, and advocated conti- nuance of the campaign, but the British government was by this time thoroughly disillusioned. Only its fear of the effect on public opinion had prevented an earlier decision to withdraw. In September Hamilton was replaced by General Sir Charles Monro who, having inspected all three zones in a single morning, pronounced in favour of evacuation. 'He came, he saw, he capitulated,' remarked Churchill, who was later to resign as first lord of the admiralty over the Dardanelles debacle. The minister of war, Lord Kitchener, arrived in November and reluc- tantly confirmed Monro's advice. Probably the best-executed British operation throughout the campaign was the withdrawal, which was accomplished in Dec- ember–January, virtually with- out a casualty.

A charge by Australian troops during the Gallipoli campaign.

Artillerymen firing a 60-pounder gun at Gallipoli.

Allies launch major offensive on Western Front

On September 25 the Allies launched their anticipated autumn offensive in the west. The main thrust came from the French in Champagne, while the British attacked in Artois.

The offensive was another pro- duct of Joffre's belief in the princi- ple of continual attack. The aim was to break through the German lines at two points as a prelude to a general offensive which would hurl the Germans back to the Meuse (if not farther), but the prolonged artillery bombard- ment which preceded the advance gave the Germans plenty of warn- ing, while the British com- manders, French and Haig, were dubious about the plan from the first. Regarding the ground as unfavourable, they were forced to agree to the idea by Kitchener, the British war minister – strangely since Kitchener had previously recorded his (correct) opinion that Joffre's attacks were a waste of lives. The British forces were also still short of heavy artillery and ammunition. In June (when Lloyd George became minister for munitions) British factories were turning out 22,000 shells a day, while the French managed 100,000 and the Germans and Austrians nearly three times as many.

Like all large battles the battle of Loos (the name given to the British part in the offensive) was marked by muddle and confu- sion, besides errors in strategy and tactics. At one point the British gas (in insufficient supply to outlast the oxygen supplies of the German machine gunners) affected their own men, not the Germans. At another a reserve brigade was halted by a military policeman because its com- mander could not produce a pass to enter the area.

Initially the attack was moder- ately successful, the German line being overrun and the village of Loos captured. However, the Germans had built a second line, more strongly defended than the first, while the arrival of the essen- tial British reserves was delayed through the fault of the High Command (causing a row between French and Haig and the eventual replacement of the former, as commander-in-chief, by the latter). By the time they reached the battlefield, on Sep- tember 26, the reserves, which included New Army troops fresh out from Britain, were tired as a result of night marches, the need to evade German aircraft and delays caused by poor logistics. The attack on the second German line was a failure.

The larger French attack to the south was also ineffective. Some subordinate commanders may have – sensibly – failed to press as hard as they might when they saw the futility of the operation. In the section south of Lens Joffre him- self ordered Foch to push the 10th Army only as hard as was necess- ary to convince the British that they were not being left to fight alone. At first greater success had been achieved in Champagne, but there too the attack, which as in Artois had dwindled to ragged trench warfare, was called off on September 30 to allow prep- arations for a later assault.
▶ *page 76*

The French armoured cruiser *Bruix* at Salonika in December 1915.

Kut defeat for Turks

While British and French forces were hurling themselves unavailingly at the German lines on the Western Front, on September 28, a small British force scored a small but significant victory to the south of Kut-al-Amara on the River Tigris. British cavalry subsequently pursued the fleeing Turks halfway to Baghdad.

The Mesopotamian campaign originated in the British need to protect its fuel supply. Immediately prior to the entry of Turkey into the war, a division was despatched from India to guard the oil wells in the vicinity of the Persian Gulf. Basra, at the head of the Gulf, was taken in November 1914 in order to protect the approaches and, as Turkish forces built up, a second division was added. The Turks made a series of unsuccessful attacks early in 1915, but the British commander, General Sir John Nixon, considered his position vulnerable in view of the small area he held. He therefore sent General Townshend's division up river to Kut, the strategic importance of which lay in its position on a waterway linking the Tigris to the Euphrates.

The British government, exhilarated by a victory, though a small one, amidst the disasters of Gallipoli and the Western Front, gave permission for Townshend to advance on Baghdad. But the British force, though it had performed so well at Kut, was vastly outnumbered. It was operating with tenuous communications in the middle of enemy territory and was short of equipment and supplies. After fighting an indecisive battle at Ctesiphon, Townshend was forced to fall back on Kut. There, on December 8, he was besieged by the Turks, and the vessels of the Royal Indian Marine which had supported his campaign, retreated down river. ▶ *page 84*

Troops of the 14th Hussars being transported up the Tigris during the Mesopotamian campaign.

Allied forces land in Salonika

British and French divisions, transferred from Gallipoli, disembarked in Salonika, in Greek Macedonia on October 5. Their purpose was to bring aid to the Serbs, in imminent danger from Austro-German invasion.

From Salonika a railway ran north to Uskub (Skopje) in southern Serbia, but the Allied effort came too late. Advancing into southern Serbia the advance guard of the Allied force, commanded by General Sarrail, who had previously headed the French 3rd army on the Western Front, found itself cut off from the Serbian armies by the invading Bulgarians and was chased back to Salonika. The fall of the pro-Allies Venizelos government in Greece created complications, and the Serbian army was retreating westward, not south to join the Allies as had been planned before the Bulgarians intervened.

Nevertheless, the decision was taken to continue occupation of Salonika rather than withdraw altogether, whatever the attitude of the, at that time, pro-German Greek government. This decision was eventually to pay off. In the meantime the Germans referred to Salonika as their largest internment camp. ▶ *page 88*

Austro-German attack on Serbia

On October 6 Austro-German armies crossed the Danube and invaded Serbia. They were commanded by Field Marshal Mackensen, fresh from his successes on the Eastern Front. At the same time Bulgarian troops invaded Serbia from the east.

The Serbs showed themselves to be fine fighters in their mountainous country, as they had proved when repelling the Austrian attacks of 1914, but they lacked the equipment necessary for sustained modern warfare. King Peter might take his place with a rifle in the front line, but rifles alone could not stop the Germans. Failure to supply the necessary equipment was a bad error on the part of the Allies, for Serbia represented, at the very least, an important irritant in Austria's backyard.

Austria, having failed in 1914, had long been anxious to suppress Serbia. With the offensive on the Eastern Front successfully concluded and the Italians held on the Isonzo, the time was ripe. Germany was equally eager to

conquer Serbia, which would open up communications with Turkey (currently fighting to defend the Dardanelles) and create a broad swathe of territory under the control of the Central Powers, stretching from the North Sea to the Black Sea.

The Serbs fought a gallant delaying action, but their position was made hopeless by the failure of Greece to come to their aid (as a result of the fall of the Venizelos government) and the failure of the Allies to supply support in time. Serbia was conquered before the end of November, and the Serbian forces then withdrew through the Albanian mountains, where weather and terrain claimed more casualties. Ultimately they joined the Allied forces in Salonika.

Serbian soldiers lying dead in their trenches.

Serbian cavalry crossing a river in Albania.

Serbian soldiers in retreat. They fought bravely but were no match for the combined Austro-German armies.

1915

Allies renew the attack on the Western Front

In October the Allies returned to the attack in Artois and Champagne. They suffered very heavy casualties and made no impression on the German defences.

Renewal of the offensive, originally scheduled for October 2, was constantly delayed by bad weather, German counterattacks and other factors. In the event, all three attacks – the British and the French in Artois, the French in Champagne – took place on different dates. Haig was preparing yet another pointless bloodbath in November when the weather worsened and both sides settled down for another miserable winter in the trenches.

British casualties sustained in the autumn offensive between September 25 and November 7 were approximately 60,000 officers and men killed; the Germans lost about one-third of that number. The French, in both sectors, lost nearly 200,000 and their German opponents about 120,000. Once again, in the conditions prevailing on the Western Front, defence had proved by far the better option.

British nurse shot

In the early hours of October 12 Edith Cavell, a British nurse, was shot by a German firing squad in Brussels. She had been found guilty of actions aiding the enemy, and strong diplomatic pressure from the United States and others had failed to prevent the death sentence being carried out.

Edith Cavell was the daughter of a Norfolk rector. She was not, as British propaganda tended to portray her, an innocent young girl, being 50 years old at the time of her death. She had been in Belgium, running a school of nursing, since 1906, and had elected to remain there when the Germans invaded. She had nursed the wounded on both sides, Germans as well as Belgians, French and British, but she had also helped a number of Allied soldiers to escape across the border into neutral Holland.

Among so many unjust deaths, this was a minor incident, but nonetheless a typical German failure in public relations and a propaganda gift to the Allies. After the war Edith Cavell's body was returned to England. Her grave forms a small shrine close to the ancient walls of Norwich cathedral. It was recently vandalized.

Bulgaria enters war

Following a secret convention with the Central Powers in September, Bulgaria launched an attack on Serbia on September 24. It was timed to coincide with the Austro-German assault on the Serbs from the north. Though the Bulgarians had confined their declaration of war to Serbia, the Allies promptly declared war on Bulgaria.

The Bulgarians had abandoned their pro-Russian policy in 1913 in favour of a rapprochement with Austria-Hungary. Shortly before the outbreak of war the Bulgarian government had negotiated a large loan from a German financial group and discussions concerning a German treaty were conducted at the same time. The king's sympathies were pro-German, and he was also convinced that Germany could not be defeated.

However, the prime consideration of the Bulgarian government was to regain territory lost in the Second Balkan War (1913), when Romania had acquired the province of Dobruja and Macedonian territory promised to Bulgaria in the Treaty of London (1913) had been divided between Serbia and Greece. During the summer of 1915 efforts had been made by the Allies to entice Bulgaria into declaring war on Turkey with talk of cessions in Macedonia, but Greece and Serbia had proved unwilling to agree. Bulgaria's best option was thus alliance with the Central Powers, who were anxious for Bulgarian assistance in the planned attack on Serbia and had no objection to handing over land held by their enemy, notwithstanding vociferous opposition from the many sections of the populace who favoured neutrality.

King Ferdinand of Bulgaria in army uniform.

British losses to U-boats exceed 250

By the end of the year a total of about 250 British merchant ships had been lost to German U-boats. This followed the German declaration in February of their intention to wage unrestricted submarine warfare in British waters. Some 50 ships were sunk by mines in the same period.

Essential to British strategy was command of the seas to ensure free passage of merchant ships, and by the end of 1914 this had been largely achieved – on the surface. The British were quite unprepared for the submarine campaign – and for the German minefields – and they lacked sufficient coastal patrols and minesweepers to deal with this new form of warfare. Ships and boats of all kinds, including yachts and pleasure steamers, were hastily armed to reinforce the patrols, and fishermen and other sailors were enrolled in the naval reserves. By the end of the summer of 1915 the auxiliary patrol was a coherent organization performing a wide variety of duties besides submarine hunting.

Although in terms of numbers or tonnage losses of merchant ships were severe, they formed a relatively small proportion of the total, and by the end of 1915 the submarine campaign could be regarded as only a moderate success. Against the Grand Fleet itself the U-boats achieved little. This was due to strenuous patrolling by destroyers, whose crews were seriously overworked until new destroyers began to appear towards the end of the year.
▶ page 94

A German U-boat comes to the surface in order to open fire on a merchant ship.

The stalemate: easterners and westerners

During 1915 about 2 million young Frenchmen and Britons (including subjects of their empires) died on the Western Front. The largest territorial gain in all the offensives of that year was about three miles.

Attacks tended to follow a pattern. (1) Reconnaissance of the enemy position by means of balloon and/or aircraft. (2) Prolonged artillery bombardment, designed to destroy the barbed wire, trenches and machine-gun posts of the front line. (3) Assault by the infantry (going 'over the top') in a series of waves. (4) Successful conquest of the first line of defences. (5) A check at the second – or third, or fourth – line. (6) Retreat in the face of enemy counter-attack. As this pattern had become established since the Battle of the Marne, there seemed little point in continuing with it. Yet the high command appeared to have no other solution.

Although some generals displayed a remarkable equanimity when confronted with casualties far exceeding those of any previous war, it would be wrong to suppose that no one suggested any way out of the savage impasse of trench warfare. Gas appeared to be one possibility, but once it became familiar, counter measures were fairly easy. Otherwise there were few tactical innovations; aircraft and tanks were to play some part later. Sir John French

German soldiers in a heavily fortified trench.

complained, justly, of shortage of shells, but a major drawback of the huge artillery bombardments considered necessary to enable the infantry to advance was that they gave the enemy ample and precise advice about where to place its reserves.

In Britain there was a division between 'westerners', who were committed to the defence of France, and 'easterners', who believed a decisive outcome could be achieved by striking in a completely separate theatre of war. Unfortunately, the Dardanelles expedition, the fruit of this doctrine, was a failure. (Historians still argue about its viability, but the general opinion is that it was a good idea poorly executed.) One effect of the failure in Gallipoli was to reinforce the authority of the generals, although they had even fewer ideas on how to break the deadlock than the politicians. But in the new conditions of total war, political leadership was vital, and eventually this was to be demonstrated by Lloyd George in Britain and Clemenceau in France.

The Germans, even more dominated by military opinion, were also torn between east and west. Falkenhayn believed that it would be necessary, sooner or later, to win in France and strongly doubted the possibility of conquering Russia. He was persuaded in 1915 to concentrate on the east because of the success of Hindenburg and Ludendorff, who indeed went on to secure further victories on that front. However, the passive campaign in the west in 1915 arguably gave the Allies time to build up their strength to a point where they were unbeatable.

Britain introduces conscription

Britain's most famous recruiting poster.

The Military Service Act, introducing compulsory military service, was approved by parliament on January 6. Conscription had been an emotive subject for some months, furiously opposed by some, including the Labour party and the trade unions, angrily demanded by others, including Lloyd George though not other Liberals.

The original measure was a compromise, requiring men of military age to 'attest' their willingness to serve and promising that single men would be called up before married men. This had proved unworkable, but the act of January 1916 was also a compromise. It prescribed compulsory service for all unmarried men between 18 and 41. The act aroused less opposition than the government expected, partly because it provided for conscientious objectors to be excused if their request was agreed to by a tribunal. In fact there was more trouble inside the cabinet than outside and, following the Easter

Rising and Townshend's surrender at Kut in April, conscription was widened to include all able-bodied men up to the age of 41.

The introduction of conscription was more a political than a practical measure. Men had been volunteering in large numbers, and the chief difficulty had so far been not shortage of men but shortage of the equipment to turn them into soldiers. The need to provide a variety of exemptions actually led to a fall in the numbers enlisted in the early months of conscription. There was, however, widespread resentment of alleged 'slackers' and 'shirkers' – men who did not

volunteer though apparently eligible. One aspect of this was the custom adopted by a few 'patriotic' ladies of presenting a white feather to those whom they assumed to be guilty of such a failure of duty. (They were sometimes embarrassed by the discovery that the supposed 'slacker' was a veteran in civilian dress of the Western Front, who had been gassed, shot or shelled.) A figure of 650,000 was often quoted as the number of those shirking military service, though how this was arrived at was not explained. However, the number claiming exemption under the new act was larger – about 750,000.

Russians take Erzurum

In a brilliant feat of arms the Russians captured Erzurum, in northeastern Turkey, on February 16. The town, which had been an important fortress in Byzantine times and was the scene of successful resistance by the Turks in the Russo-Turkish war of 1877, was vital to the defences of eastern Turkey.

Enver Pasha, Turkey's war minister, was blinded to strategic realities by his grandiose dreams of uniting the Turks with the Turkic people of southern Russia. Increasingly, however, he was challenged by the dynamic genius of Mustafa Kemal (Atatürk), who was largely responsible for the successes against the Allies in Gallipoli. In March Enver Pasha appointed Kemal to command in eastern Anatolia (largely because he wanted him away from the capital). The Russian advance proceeded no farther than Erzurum and Erzincan. Later in the year Kemal conducted a successful campaign against the Russians, though without regaining the lost territory.

Turkey's war effort was handicapped, not only by the number of different fronts on which its soldiers had to fight, but also by the activities of subject peoples such as the Armenians, who suffered yet another brutal massacre in 1915 and, encouraged by the Russians, responded by carrying out sabotage behind the Turkish lines on the Caucasian front.

Volunteers looking remarkably cheerful queuing up at a recruiting office in London in 1915.

German attack on Verdun

At dawn on February 21 the German artillery opened up on the French lines opposite the famous fortress of Verdun. Within a few hours the area looked like the surface of the moon – a mass of shell holes and flattened trenches with mangled barbed wire poking out of the tumbled earth here and there. The German infantry began to advance, on a narrow front, shortly before dusk.

The Verdun offensive signified Falkenhayn's desire to strike a decisive blow on the Western Front, postponed in 1915 following the successes in the east. Falkenhayn considered that Germany's chief enemy was Britain, but he recognized that Britain could not be conquered on the Western Front, partly because the British sector offered little advantage to an offensive campaign, partly because a military defeat in Europe would not knock Britain out of the war. The submarine campaign was the chief hope of this eventuality, and Falkenhayn saw his task as the destruction of Britain's allies in Europe. Russia appeared as good as beaten, and the Austrians had shown they could handle the Italians. That left France. In view of the proven strength of the defence in the conditions of trench warfare, Falkenhayn dismissed the option of an all-out attempt to break the French line. The strategy he adopted at Verdun was one of attrition. He planned a series of short advances to draw in the French reserves, which would then be destroyed by the German artillery. France would slowly bleed to death. Verdun was chosen as the objective partly because it was on a salient and hindered German communications, partly because of the historical significance of that great fortress. Once battle was joined, moreover, the Germans were as determined to take Verdun as the French were to hold it.

Falkenhayn was right to suppose that the French would not surrender Verdun easily. However, their task was made harder by the fact that Verdun was not currently a great fortress, having been largely denuded of guns. Nevertheless, the French, though forced to retreat, held the forts, while reinforcements were rushed in along the very narrow line left open by the German artillery bombardment. By the time General Pétain, commanding the 2nd Army, was sent in to command the defence of Verdun at the end of the month, the immediate danger was over. The German crown prince, who commanded an army corps, called for a supreme effort on March 4. After two days' bombardment, the assault was launched, but by March 9 it had been checked. Falkenhayn's strategy, however, was still intact. ▶ *page 86*

French soldiers in a captured German trench at Verdun.

THE POWER OF THE GENERALS

IN 1914 the German Social Democratic party was the largest and most powerful socialist group in Europe, and most people would have agreed with Karl Marx that Germany was the most likely place for the outbreak of the working-class revolution. Although a revolutionary outbreak did occur in Germany at the end of the war, there, as in other countries, nationalism proved a stronger force than socialism or the international brotherhood of the working class. In 1914 the German Social Democrats abandoned the cause of revolutionary socialism and concentrated on the defence of the fatherland, voting without demur for the government's war measures although still excluded from power.

As time went on the real power became increasingly concentrated in the hands of the military high command. To some extent this is inevitable in wartime, and it happened in other countries besides Germany. In Britain, for example, Haig remained as commander-in-chief of the forces on the Western Front in spite of the fact that the prime minister, Lloyd George, had no faith in him.

In August 1916 Falkenhayn, who had been in charge of German strategy as chief of staff since 1914 (for a time he was also minister of war), resigned. The immediate cause was the German failure at Verdun, but Falkenhayn, for all his intelligence, had not been very successful (one of his last acts, ironically, was to engineer the dismissal of his Austrian opposite number, Conrad). He was replaced by Hindenburg with his perennial sidekick, Ludendorff – who provided the brains in the partnership. These two had been popular heroes since their victories over the Russians in the early months of the war, at Tannenberg and the Masurian Lakes, although the foundation for those victories had been laid by their predecessors. (Hindenburg was close to 70 and had retired in 1911.) Their later successes owed as much to the inadequacies of the Russian army as to Ludendorff's undoubted ability.

For two years Hindenburg and Ludendorff exercised what was, in effect, a military dictatorship. The Kaiser, for all his bravado, was fundamentally a weak leader, and was frightened of them, and in 1917 they were strong enough to bring down the chancellor, Bethmann-Hollweg, and have him replaced by their own puppet. They formed a natural alliance with the conservative bureaucracy which still, as in peacetime, administered the country, and with the leaders of industry supported the aim of total victory to ensure the retention of what had been won in the way of Belgian and French industrial wealth and, in the east, rich agricultural land.

Increasingly, these grandiose and unrealistic aims aroused opposition, and the internal conflicts of prewar Germany were exacerbated by the argument over war aims in 1916–18. This in turn made the conversion of Germany into a democratic republic a difficult undertaking and contributed to the outbreak of civil war at the end of 1918.

Field Marshal Hindenburg (left) and General Ludendorff.

Field Marshal August von Mackensen.

1916

Germans surrender Cameroon to Allies

Although fighting went on sporadically in the interior, the German colony of Cameroon finally surrendered to Anglo-French forces on February 18. With this defeat, the Germans retained a colonial foothold in Africa only in the eastern part of the continent.

The first attack on the German colony had occurred in August 1914, when the seaport of Douala was attacked by a British cruiser supported by a small Anglo-French force. A military base was established in the Cameroon estuary, the river was cleared of mines and Douala surrendered.

River warfare · continued throughout 1915, while a naval blockade was established to prevent supplies reaching the colony from the neutral Spanish island of Fernando Po. The coast was soon in Allied hands, but the rainforest of the interior proved to be more difficult terrain, protecting the resisters until surrender became inevitable early the following year.

A motorized convoy of U.S. Troops passing through New Mexico. They formed part of an expedition sent into Mexican territory under the command of General Pershing.

Germany declares war on Portugal

On March 9 Germany declared war on Portugal. The declaration followed the seizure of four German ships lying in ports of Portuguese East Africa (Mozambique).

Soon after the outbreak of war in August 1914, Portugal, England's oldest ally, had declared its allegiance to the British cause. Additional forces were sent out to the Portuguese colonies in southern Africa, and clashes occurred on the frontiers of Mozambique with Tanganyika and Angola with German South-West Africa. After Germany's formal declaration of war, a small Portuguese expeditionary force commanded by General Tamagnini de Abreu was sent to the Western Front.

Villa's men raid New Mexico

Soldiers from Pancho Villa's Army of the North crossed the U.S. border on March 9 and attacked the small town of Columbus, New Mexico. About 20 Americans were killed in the raid. It was not the first anti-American outrage perpetrated by Villa's men and it provoked the despatch of a U.S. military expedition to Mexico the following week, led by General Pershing.

Villa was antagonized by U.S. support for Carranza and consequent opposition to his own forces as well as those of Zapata. Villa, however, was hard-pressed by Carranza's lieutenant, Obregón, who had been studying war reports from Europe and employed barbed wire and machine-guns to deadly effect. After a series of battles in the spring, Villa was forced to retreat to the north. His army dwindled away and, by the autumn had ceased to

exist as a threat to the Carranza government.

Simultaneously, Pablo Gonzalez led the campaign against the *Zapatistas*, employing means far more brutal than those of Zapata himself. Zapata was forced to retreat to the mountains, where, like Villa, he was for the time being safe among his own people.

General Pershing's expedition, meanwhile, failed in its object of running down Villa, and evoked wrathful protests from the Carranza government. At one point there was even a minor clash with government troops and full-scale war seemed possible. It was perhaps only avoided by the character of President Wilson himself, who eventually agreed to Carranza's demand that Pershing should be withdrawn. In February 1917 Pershing returned to the United States, ready to lead a much larger military expedition.

1916

JUNE
4 Brusilov launches offensive in Galicia
5 Sherif of Mecca raises Arab revolt in the Hejaz
7 British war minister Kitchener drowned in HMS *Hampshire*
7 Germans take Fort Vaux (Verdun)
10 Russians cross River Dniester
15 German troops in transit from Western to Eastern Front
17 Austria breaks off Trentino offensive
20 Germans fire diphosgene gas shells in Verdun battle
21 Turkish offensive against Persia checked by Russians
21 Allied ultimatum to Greece
23 Brusilov defeats Austrians at Sokal (River Styr)
24 Renewed German offensive at Verdun

JULY
1 Battle of the Somme begins
6 Lloyd George becomes British war minister
14 Renewal of Somme offensive
27 Russians defeat Turks at Erzinjan
31 Exploding ammunition freight cars kill 26 in New York

AUGUST
2 Peace demonstrations in German cities
8 Italians take Gorizia
17 Romania signs treaty with Allies
18 Much of Salonika destroyed by fire
21 Massacre of Armenians by Turks reported
22 Romania declares war on Austria
24 Venizelos calls for overthrow of King Constantine in Greece
26 Italy declares war on Germany
27 Romanians invade Transylvania
29 Hindenburg becomes German chief of staff

SEPTEMBER
3 Last German attack at Verdun
4 British occupy Dar-es-Salaam
5 Mackensen invades Dobruja
11 Allied offensive begins in Macedonia
15 Italian offensive checked by Austrians
15 Tanks used in new British Somme offensive
16 Britain and France recognize Czech provisional government
25 British take Thiepval (Somme)
29 Germany protests at U.S. citizens enlisting in British air force

1916

THE EASTER RISING

James Connolly, a leader of the Easter Rising.

Revolt in Dublin

At midday on Easter Monday, April 24, Patrick Henry Pearse, dressed in a green uniform, stood on the steps of the General Post Office in Dublin and read out to a small and bewildered crowd the proclamation of the Irish republic. His words signalled the beginning of a nationalist rebellion against British rule.

The authorities were taken by surprise, but the rebellion, postponed at the eleventh hour and believed by some participants to have been cancelled, went off at half-cock, scarcely spreading beyond Dublin. The British were able to find enough soldiers and guns to crush the Easter Rising within a week. About 460 people were killed and the leaders were shot as traitors a few days later.

Although the rising appeared on the face of things to have been a disastrous failure, its leaders' purpose – to kindle the sparks of militant Irish nationalism into an unquenchable blaze – was achieved. It destroyed the basis on which, in the past, the Irish had negotiated with Britain for a degree of independence and it heralded the end of seven centuries of British dominance.

For most of the second half of the 19th century, 'home rule' for Ireland had been the dominant political issue in the British parliament. It had split the Liberal party and had brought down Gladstone. Irish nationalists like Parnell did not demand a fully independent republic and were not in sympathy with the Irish Republican Brotherhood (ancestor of the IRA), which had launched an unsuccessful revolt in 1867, or later with the militantly nationalist Sinn Fein. Home rule had finally been conceded and a bill passed in 1912, but it never went into effect because the outbreak of the war caused its postponement. The ultimate effect of the Easter Rising was to render it redundant.

The largest obstacle to Irish independence was the adamant hostility of the Protestant majority in most of Ulster. Its leaders had threatened civil war rather than submit. Both sides had formed volunteer militia, and a breakaway group of the nationalist Irish Volunteers led by Eoin MacNeill formed the main force of the Easter Rising (along with the Irish Citizen Army, a militant, nationalist workers' organization led by James Larkin and James Connolly).

The leaders of the Rising sought help from Germany, but the *Aud*, carrying arms from Lübeck, was intercepted by the British, and was scuttled two days before the rising to prevent the weapons being captured.

AT THE GPO

*S*HORTLY before Pearse read out the proclamation on behalf of 'the Provisional Government of the Irish Republic' at noon on Easter Monday, James Connolly, commandant of the Dublin forces, led his men down Abbey Street and halted them opposite the distinguished classical façade of the Dublin General Post Office. Some wore the dark green uniform of the Citizen Army, some the lighter green of the Irish Volunteers; a greater number wore no uniform at all. Some had rifles, some shotguns, some no guns whatever. Yet they drilled with precision; they had been practising a long time.

Pearse read his proclamation, the Post Office was occupied peacefully and the green and gold flag of republican Ireland was soon flying proudly above it. The counterattack then began. Within 48 hours British reinforcements outnumbered the insurgents by nearly 20 to 1. The street barricades were smashed to matchwood by artillery, and the armed steamer Helga sailed up the Liffey to bring her guns to bear on the insurgents' strongholds.

By Friday the GPO, under a heavy barrage, had become a smoking, burning hell. Inside, Connolly lay on a stretcher, his leg smashed by a stray bullet. Joseph Plunkett, who had planned the Dublin strategy and was already suffering from glandular fever, could hardly stand. No one had slept more than an hour or two at a time since Sunday night. Even Sean MacDermott (Mac Diarmada), leader of the Irish Republican Brotherhood, had stopped cracking jokes. One insurgent led a forlorn charge against the British and was shot dead within a few yards.

The GPO had to be evacuated and the next day Pearse advised surrender 'to prevent further slaughter'. The other leaders agreed, believing they had 'redeemed Dublin from many shames and made her name splendid among cities'. In some places the insurgents held out longer. At Boland's Mills, Commandant Eamon de Valera, later president of Ireland, would not give up until the surrender order had been countersigned by his superior officer.

About 3500 people were arrested after the Rising, although only 171 were tried by court martial. Pearse, Plunkett, Connolly, MacDermott and seven others were executed – martyrs to a cause, the success of which was now, paradoxically, assured. When five by-elections were held in Irish districts in 1917, Sinn Fein, which had not bothered to put up candidates since its poor showing in the general election of 1908, won every seat. The old, moderate, Home Rule party was discredited, and was in effect finished off by the introduction of conscription to Ireland in 1918. It had opposed that measure, but it had become too closely identified with the British establishment to survive this hugely unpopular move.

British soldiers in the ruins of the GPO.

Eamon de Valera.

The aftermath of the Rising.

1916

Above. Jellicoe, commander of the British Grand Fleet.

Below. Admiral Sir David Beatty.

British surrender at Kut

On April 29 General Townshend, commanding the British-Indian force in Kut-al-Amara, was forced to surrender to the Turks. The siege of Kut had lasted nearly five months.

During that time several efforts had been made to relieve the town, efforts doomed by poor command, faulty communications and difficult conditions. Relieving forces had failed to penetrate the Turkish lines on either side of the River Tigris. Townshend's unit, of less than 9000 men, had made no serious effort to break out of Kut in the early weeks of the siege since help was confidently expected. By April, with some Hindu and Muslim soldiers starving to death rather than eat horsemeat, his position was hopeless. Partly because of their poor condition, but rather more because of ill treatment by the Turks, two-thirds of Townshend's men failed to survive imprisonment.

A British warship opens fire during what proved to be an inconclusive contest.

British and German fleets clash at Jutland

In the afternoon of May 31 the British light cruiser *Galatea*, attached to Admiral Beatty's squadron of battle cruisers based at Rosyth, sighted a German warship attached to Admiral Hipper's force of cruisers. Beatty moved to intercept and battle was joined. Both Beatty and Hipper were, in effect, acting as scouts ahead of their respective main fleets, the British Grand Fleet, commanded by Admiral Jellicoe, and the German High Seas Fleet, commanded by Admiral Scheer. Within hours the two fleets, which had avoided any agreement with each other since the beginning of the war, were locked together in battle.

The naval strategy of both powers was cautious. The British considered that command of the sea was of primary importance, defeat of the German fleet secondary. As Winston Churchill remarked, Jellicoe was 'the only man on either side who could lose the war in an afternoon'. The Germans were equally unwilling to risk open battle with a fleet which was considerably stronger than their own. It was therefore surprising that the battle of Jutland, the only major naval battle of the war, took place at all.

Early in 1916 Scheer was appointed to command the High Seas Fleet. He was somewhat more inclined to aggressive action and he was encouraged in this by rumours of the division of the Grand Fleet to cover the English coast. He planned to entice out part of the British fleet by a cruiser raid on the coast, with his own fleet lying in wait nearby. Since bad weather prevented air reconnaissance, he was forced to modify this plan, but sent Hipper's squadron north, towards Norway, with the same purpose – luring part of the Grand Fleet within range of his battleships, following 50 miles behind. British naval intelligence was excellent, and Scheer's departure was already known. Jellicoe sailed

east from Scapa Flow, while Beatty searched for the enemy farther south.

Beatty was supported by a battleship squadron, under the command of Admiral Evan-Thomas, but by the time he made contact with Hipper, Evan-Thomas was ten miles away, as a result of a failure in communications – a running theme of the battle, especially on the British side. Two of Beatty's battle cruisers were blown up, provoking his famous comment, 'There's something wrong with our bloody ships today', but when Evan-Thomas caught up the odds were readjusted in favour of the British, and Scheer, who had been hoping to lure Beatty into his trap, was forced to speed to Hipper's aid. It was now Beatty's turn to act as bait, attempting to lure Scheer north towards Jellicoe's battle fleet.

Jellicoe knew of Scheer's presence, but not his position or his course, while Scheer was altogether ignorant of the proximity of the Grand Fleet. However, when Scheer sighted a cruiser squadron (Admiral Hood) des-

A German artist's impression of the battle at its height.

patched by Jellicoe to support Beatty, he mistook it for battleships and beat a hasty retreat.

The battle lasted only a few hours, but it was an extremely complicated affair of manoeuvre and counter-manoeuvre compounded by tactical error, poor visibility and many other factors, the largest being, perhaps, sheer chance. Although Jellicoe had failed to engage the main German fleet, he had got between it and its home ports, and all depended on whether Scheer could evade the British in the night. During the hours of darkness there were numerous clashes, false alarms and lost opportunities, one notable incident being the ramming of the German battleship *Nassau* by a British destroyer, but, thanks partly to luck and partly to Jellicoe's ultra-cautious tactics, Scheer succeeded in making his escape by sailing around the stern of Jellicoe. To the chagrin of the British sunrise on June 1 revealed a North Sea empty of German ships.

The battle demonstrated that Beatty was right. There was something wrong with the British ships. Their gunnery was inferior to the Germans' and an alarmingly high percentage of their shells failed to explode. They were

also extremely vulnerable to a hit amidships setting off the magazine – the immediate cause of Beatty's remark. In the longer term it raised doubts about the efficacy of battleships in the era of mines, submarines and torpedoes.

In the battle of Jutland, or the Skagerrak, the British Grand Fleet had failed to do much damage to the enemy. The only German battleship lost, an antique vessel, was sunk by a torpedo from a destroyer. Total British losses were three battle cruisers, three cruisers and eight destroyers, with 6000 men killed. German losses were one battleship, one battle cruiser, four light cruisers and five destroyers, with 2500 killed.

Strategically the battle changed nothing. Britain retained command of the sea and the blockade of Germany continued. The Germans were compelled to fall back on submarine warfare, the restriction of which (in response to U.S. protests) had been one reason for Scheer's sally. While the unimpressive British performance lowered the high prestige of the Royal Navy, the German experience contributed to the dissatisfaction in the fleet which led eventually to mutiny.

Arab revolt in the Hejaz

The sherif of Mecca, Husain ibn Ali, raised the standard of revolt against the Turkish rulers of the Hejaz on June 5. The revolt was encouraged by the British, who had been in negotiation with him.

The British had maintained a military presence in Egypt since the unsuccessful Turkish advance on Suez in 1915 and, after the evacuation of Gallipoli, which released Turkish as well as Allied troops, an assault was planned on the Syrian coast to forestall the Turks, but aborted by French objections. Meanwhile the Turks had stirred up trouble among the tribes in both Sinai and the Western Desert, which also spread to Egypt. The revolt of the sherif of Mecca – from October acknowledged as king of the Hejaz – encouraged the British to greater aggression. ▶ *page 90*

1916

JUNE–JULY

RUSSIAN ATTACK IN GALICIA

THE SOMME CAMPAIGN

Germans capture Fort Vaux

Fort Vaux, which covered the right of the French line at Verdun, was captured by the Germans on June 7. The next day they took Thiaumont farm, (though not the strongpoint behind it that commanded the French left), which had changed hands twice already since the current offensive began on June 1. It appeared that Verdun was in imminent danger.

In March the Germans had failed to gain an immediate victory at Verdun, but they continued the attack with great ferocity, interrupted by occasional pauses. The French had held them off and had mounted a series

of counterattacks. An additional motive for the renewed assault in June was the Germans' knowledge of an impending Allied attack on the Somme, and their determination to prevent the French contributing to it.

By June 23 the French position was so precarious that Pétain suggested withdrawing from the east bank of the Meuse, but Joffre ordered that it must held at all costs. Although the battle of the Somme was now imminent, German attacks on Verdun continued, in what was to become the longest single 'battle' of the war. ▶ *page 90*

The remains of Fort Vaux.

Brusilov launches offensive in Galicia

On June 4 the Russian 8th Army (General Kaledin) advanced in the region of Luck (Lutsk), in what was intended as an exploratory probe. To the Russians' surprise the Austrian line crumbled before them, and General Aleksei Brusilov, in overall command of the southern sector of the front, at once widened his attack, bringing in the 11th army (Sakharov), the 7th Army (Shcherbachev) and the 9th army (Lechitski). Although Sakharov was checked near Tarnopol, elsewhere the Austrians were soon in headlong retreat. The Russians took 200,000 prisoners in three days.

The extraordinary success of the Brusilov offensive was to have important effects elsewhere, frustrating German plans at Verdun and the Somme, and relieving the Italians under pressure from the Trentino.

The Russians had already made one gallant effort on behalf of their allies in March, when they fought a long and inconclusive battle near Lake Narocz in Belo-

russia in an effort to relieve the pressure on Verdun. Soon afterwards the tsar and his senior commanders held a conference on strategy for the summer offensive. They agreed that the main attack should be made in the centre (General Evert) while the northern armies (Kuropatkin) wheeled inwards to meet them, and the south (Brusilov) remained on the defensive. The ground

in the southern sector was less suitable for attack, but Brusilov argued that this was all the more reason to make one there. He believed that earlier Russian failures had been due to a failure to launch a broad enough attack. Accordingly, he was given a free hand to act as a diversion to the main offensive farther north. Recognizing the importance of surprise, especially difficult to achieve in an army increasingly plagued by desertion, he prepared for an attack in many widely scattered places, and kept his reserves strung out.

Appeals from the west made the Russian high command anxious to begin the attack earlier than planned. Brusilov was ready by June 1, but Evert complained that was too soon for him. It was

agreed that Brusilov should move on June 4 and Evert ten days later.

The Austrians were taken completely by surprise by Brusilov's bold plan, and he rapidly overran eastern Galicia and the Bukovina (now in Romania; then a province of the Austrian empire). In the centre, however, Evert was still delaying; neither was Kuropatkin much more energetic in the north. Alekseiev, the Russian chief of staff and in effect commander-in-chief (given the character of the tsar), attempted to shift reserves to Brusilov, but poor Russian communications again ensured that they failed to arrive in time, i.e. before the Germans were able to move reinforcements from the Western Front.

The Russians continued to press on towards the Carpathians for the rest of the year, but without comparable success. In the end the Brusilov offensive must be accounted a Pyrrhic victory since, short of adequate artillery, Russia lost about one million men, a factor not without influence in the collapse of the country in 1917. ▶ *page 93*

Austrian troops prepared for gas warfare.

An Austrian heavy howitzer in action.

Allies launch Somme offensive

After a bombardment lasting a week the Allies' offensive on the Somme began on July 1. As a result of the drain on the French at Verdun, the British took the major part in the offensive and became henceforth the leading Allied power on the Western Front.

Sir Douglas Haig in London just before the Somme offensive.

The Somme campaign had been planned in December 1915. It was originally intended to take place in the spring, but the German offensive at Verdun intervened and the later date was agreed. The initial attack was carried out on a 15-mile front by 11 divisions of General Rawlinson's 4th Army. Five French divisions (all that were available, although before Verdun Joffre had planned to commit 40 divisions) attacked farther south. The Germans had only six divisions facing the British.

The artillery was more thickly concentrated than in previous battles. However, the long bombardment not only alerted the Germans but also failed to flatten their front line. When the infantry reported that, contrary to assurances, the German machine-gunners were still firing, they were told by the divisional staffs, situated well behind the battlefield, not to be frightened. The men of Kitchener's volunteer army confirmed the truth of their report by leaving their bodies strewn in thousands among the barbed wire and shell holes. On the first day of the battle the British lost more men than in any previous engagement in their history.

Except in the south of the sector, where the German line was overrun, the attack was a failure. The French, attacking a less well-defended sector and enjoying the advantage of surprise, succeeded in taking their objectives.

The breakthrough having failed, Haig, the British commander, settled for a war of attrition. The British advance was described as 'methodical'. This meant in effect an extremely small and immensely costly advance. A young Australian subaltern, shortly before his death, wrote a letter condemning the 'murder' of his comrades through the 'incompetence, callousness, and personal vanity of those high in authority'. Haig's persistence with what had already proved a desperate exercise is hard to explain less damningly. ▶ *page 90*

British dead in a devastated landscape. German artillery shells explode in the distance.

Italians capture Gorizia

At the beginning of August, the Italian 3rd Army, under the Duke of Aosta, attacked in the Isonzo valley after a diversionary move towards the Adriatic. The Italians, who enjoyed a numerical superiority of nearly three to one, overcame the rugged natural defences of Monte Sabotino and crossed the river, whereupon the town was theirs.

The Isonzo valley sector had been General Cadorna's chosen battlefield since Italy's entry into the war, but the Austrians, despite smaller numbers, held such secure positions that a whole series of attacks had failed to make progress. In May 1916 the Austrians opened an attack from the Trentino, designed to cut the Italians' communications (withdrawing troops from Galicia for this purpose and thus facilitating Brusilov's offensive). Though they suffered a series of tactical defeats, the Italians held on and, when the Austrian offensive was broken off, Cadorna returned to the attack on the Isonzo.

The capture of Gorizia, however, failed to break the deadlock. Three efforts were made in the next three months to advance eastward, but each was stopped by Austrian resistance, which was more determined against the Italians than it was against the Russians. ▶ *page 102*

General von Falkenhayn (fourth from the right) in Romania with members of his staff.

Romania declares war

Romania declared war on Austria-Hungary on August 22. Romanian troops invaded Transylvania, anticipating that Austro-German reserves were fully occupied on the Somme, in stiffening resistance to Brusilov beyond the Carpathians and in holding the Allies in Salonika.

On the outbreak of war in 1914 the Romanian government had mixed sympathies. Both the Central Powers and the Allies tried to woo Romania with promises of territorial cessions, but as time went on German successes gave grounds for alarm while the influence of the strong-minded Marie of Edinburgh, granddaughter of Britain's Queen Victoria and wife of King Ferdinand, together with the success of the Brusilov offensive, helped tilt the balance in favour of the Allies. By a treaty of August 17 the Allies promised Transylvania and other areas to Romania, which accordingly declared war.

Romania's army was relatively primitive – bayonets were more numerous than machine guns – while the country's strategic position, with a long frontier relative to area, was weak and communications were poor. Moreover, Serbia having been conquered, Romania had few friends in the area, though the Russians promised two divisions. The advance was slow, allowing time to reinforce the weak Austrian defences. In September the invasion of the Dobruja by Mackensen, whose army possessed the sort of equipment the Romanians had scarcely heard of, brought the Romanian advance to a halt. In spite of determined resistance in the mountains, the Germans broke through the passes in November. With Mackensen advancing across the Danube from northern Bulgaria, Bucharest was caught in a pincer movement. The city was compelled to surrender on December 6.

Most of the Romanian forces escaped and reorganized, under Russian supervision, in Moldavia, but the Germans had gained a great strategic advantage, including the large Romanian production of oil and wheat.

Allied offensive starts in Salonika

On September 11 the Allied forces in Salonika launched an offensive against the largely Bulgarian troops confronting them. British detachments began with scattered raids across the River Struma, which were swiftly followed by the main attack, west of the River Vardar, by French, Serbian and Russian troops under the command of General Cordonnier.

Since the Allied expeditionary force to Salonika under the overall command of General Sarrail had been forced to fall back on Salonika, after its unavailing support of the Serbs in December 1915, the front had been relatively inactive. The Allied forces there had been reinforced and by July 1916 consisted of five British and four French divisions besides the Serbian army and other troops. Their purpose was to launch an offensive in support of Romania when Romania entered the war – a decision that was delayed until the end of August.

There had meanwhile been some activity: first as a result of Joffre's request that Sarrail pin down the opposing troops to prevent Falkenhayn sending reinforcements to Verdun, secondly as a result of the handover (in May) of Fort Rupel to the Bulgarians by the – neutral – Greeks. This opened the way for a Bulgarian advance into eastern Macedonia and resulted in the British reinforcing their position on the Struma while Allied diplomatic pressure compelled the demobilization of the Greek army and the resignation of the government. In the event, however, no Bulgarian offensive took place.

The Salonika force also had internal problems. General Sarrail was a 'political' general and a difficult character, whose leftist sympathies had prompted his removal from the Western Front. He quarrelled fiercely with his own subordinate, Cordonnier, and there were obvious difficulties in commanding a force made up of such ethnically disparate elements. At the same time the British remained aloof under their own commander, General

Serbian refugees find shelter in Salonika.

Milne. This had certain advantages but also meant that they were sometimes unaware of what orders Sarrail had issued.

In the September offensive the Serbs made good progress, fighting towards their own frontier, but Cordonnier was held up by poor transport and the Bulgarians were able to slip out of the net before it closed. A British force under General Briggs also achieved its immediate objective, but a Franco-Russian attack failed and when Sarrail ordered its renewal his decision was opposed (justifiably, as things turned out) by Cordonnier, who was shortly after removed from his command. The Serbs were left unsupported, until Sarrail appointed the Serbian general, Michich, to command the whole attack. He launched a successful assault in November, advancing into Serbian territory east of Lake Prespa. ▶ *page 90*

Bulgarian troops in action against the Allies in the mountains of Monastir.

British tanks arrive on the Somme

The battlefield of the Somme was the scene of the introduction on September 15 of a new weapon: the tank. The effects of the British machines, first called 'landships' because they seemed to reproduce the characteristics of naval warfare on land, were indecisive, but then very few were actually involved in battle. They had a dramatic psychological effect. The Germans 'felt quite powerless against these monsters which crawled along the top of the trench enfilading it with continuous machine-gun fire, and closely followed by small parties of infantry who threw hand grenades on the survivors'.

The destructive stalemate of trench warfare was largely the result of the machine-gun. The antidote to the machine-gun and the means of breaking the deadlock was the tank – originally, like the machine-gun, partly a U.S. invention. However, only a small number of tanks were available in September 1916 (the number that accompanied the infantry advance was just nine!), and they were not mechanically reliable. Their employment was premature – only 60 of the 150 tanks built had arrived in France – but Haig was desperate for new expedients.

Senior commanders, with a few notable exceptions, had always been unenthusiastic about the tank (a design for a tank submitted to the War Office by a Nottingham inventor in 1911 had been consigned to the dead files with the comment 'the man's mad'). They considered that its first deployment proved them correct – an example of the conservatism that was so marked a feature of World War I generalship. By the end of the war tanks were being used on a much larger scale (a German general ascribed the final defeat not to Marshal Foch but to 'General Tank'), but, like aircraft, they were still a long way short of their full potential.

A British tank lumbers out of the dust and smoke on its way to the German lines.

French counter-attack at Verdun

On October 24 General Nivelle, who had taken over the 2nd Army in April after Pétain assumed overall command, launched a counter-offensive at Verdun. The initial attack, by three divisions, was preceded by three days' artillery bombardment.

With the opening of the Somme offensive at the beginning of July, German reserves had ceased to flow to Verdun. Further attacks were made in July and August, and a last one on September 3, but they got nowhere.

The French counterattack was covered by a 'creeping barrage', a new development in which the infantry advanced behind the gradually extending range of the artillery according to a fixed timetable, and the immediate objectives were taken, along with 6000 prisoners. A further assault in late November was frustrated by bad weather, but it was resumed in December in what is known as the battle of Louvement. Nearly 10,000 prisoners and over 100 guns were captured.

Salonika offensive ends

In December Sarrail was ordered to return to the defensive. The Allied line now stretched from Lake Prespa to Lake Doiran and (roughly) the Struma valley.

Despite appalling weather and difficult terrain, the Serbs had fought their way back into their own country and the Bulgarians were momentarily in retreat. In November Sarrail stopped the advance following the collapse of Romania, in whose support the offensive had been undertaken, though for a while the Serbs, poorly supplied and unsupported, pressed ahead. Sarrail's decision was confirmed by Joffre on December 11 and the position remained unchanged for over a year. The British held the line of the River Struma. Sarrail's forces – deliberately mixed up to avoid large national blocs – held the western sector. Total Allied troops numbered about 6000, not counting the Venizelist Greek army. ▶ page 116

Somme offensive bogged down

On November 13 the British scored another small success on the Somme when two villages were captured and 7000 German prisoners taken. With the autumn rains turning the battlefield into a sea of mud knee-deep and more, the long and expensive offensive was then brought to an end.

The Somme was in reality a series of battles and the final attacks were particularly pointless because even Haig had given up hope of a real breakthrough that would 'roll up' the German front. The result was that the British, having gained an advantageous position on the high ground beyond the original German front in mid-September, had to fight their way down to the lowlands, at the usual huge cost, in order to spend the winter in trenches swimming in mud and permitting only poor visibility.

The battle of the Somme imposed huge strains on the British, but 'Kitchener's army', despite such casualties that some battalions were reduced to about 100 men, had not broken. The Germans too had suffered, thanks (like the British) largely to the pig-headed attitude of their high command. General von Bülow, who commanded the 1st Army, at one stage ordered that any officer who retreated a foot would be court-martialled.

British take El Arish

British forces from Egypt, commanded by General Sir Archibald Murray, captured El Arish, a strategic port on the coast of Sinai, on December 20. The Turkish outposts of Magdhaba and Rafah were overrun and the British obtained strategic control of the Sinai Desert.

The attack had been planned to coincide with the Arab revolt in the Hejaz, but the advance had been delayed by the need to lay a railway and a water pipeline across the desert. The success of the operation meant that the British were now well placed to mount an attack on Palestine, but meanwhile the Arab revolt had languished somewhat. It was soon revived through the initiative of a young British intelligence officer, who before the war had been an archaeologist in Palestine, Captain T. E. Lawrence. He formed a close association with the Amir Faisal, son of Husain of the Hejaz, and his forces, whom the Turks had driven back from Medina. Under Lawrence's influence Faisal moved north to threaten the Hejaz railway and thus the communications of Medina. ▶ page 102

British artillerymen struggling to extricate a field gun from the grip of the mud.

Above and left. A common sight in German streets during 1916–17 – waiting to be fed from mobile soup kitchens.

TURNIP TIME

THE GERMAN people referred to the winter of 1916–17 as the 'turnip winter' because turnips were the only food in plentiful supply. Turnips, they were assured, were extremely nourishing – an excellent substitute for potatoes, vegetables and indeed any other kind of food, all of which was very scarce. Fortunately, too, they were easy to cook. Coal, too, was in short supply and people were cold that winter as well as hungry. Even cinemas were forced to close intermittently to conserve fuel for heating.

The severe shortages delivered a salutary shock to the authorities, and for the rest of the war, although the situation hardly improved, supplies were better organized so that the shortages seemed less severe. People also grew accustomed to them. As many officials noted, men and women were prepared to endure considerable deprivation; what made them angry was the knowledge, or suspicion, that others were doing better. 'It is strange', reported the Regional Army Command in Münster, 'that the people will put up with any privation, but that they cannot stand it if others have a bit more than themselves'. A reduction in the bread ration was at least partly responsible for strikes among munition workers in Berlin in April 1917. As in other countries, there was great resentment of war profiteers, real or suspected.

In Austria, too, food and other everyday supplies were in desperately short supply. Transport was a major problem – the railways were busy carrying troops from one front to another – and Hungarian producers were unwilling to sell to Austrian cities at the government's fixed price.

Shortages contributed to the growing war-weariness in the Central Powers. In France and Britain such shortages were not so acute and they caused less civil unrest than in Germany. War-weariness was just as prevalent, but brought about more by heavy casualties and lack of military success. In Britain the harvest of 1917 was the best for years and meat was in good supply, too. Shortages and queues resulted not so much from genuine scarcity but from people's fear of it, which led to panic buying. Rationing was introduced not to reduce consumption but to reassure the populace that food would be available.

United States breaks off relations with Germany

On February 3, following the German decision, at a conference in January, to resume submarine warfare against neutral shipping in the war zone, a U.S. passenger ship, the *Housatonic*, was torpedoed and sunk in the Mediterranean. President Wilson responded by breaking off diplomatic relations with Germany.

The German decision was taken in full awareness of the likely intervention of the United States when attacks were resumed on its shipping, but the Germans believed (or hoped) that the submarine campaign would bring the Allies to the point of collapse before U.S. intervention could become effective.

Wilson, still expressing hopes for 'a peace without victory', called for the arming of U.S. merchant vessels. This measure was passed in the face of obstructive tactics in the Senate, but as U.S. ships continued to fall victims to the U-boats, preparations for war accelerated. ▶ *page 94*

German plot against United States published

The text of a telegram from the German foreign minister, Arthur Zimmermann, to the German ambassadors in Washington and Mexico City was published in the press on March 1. It revealed a plan to persuade Mexico to declare war on the United States, if possible in conjunction with Japan. The Germans promised restoration of lost Mexican territory in the southwest of the United States.

The Zimmermann telegram provided the evidence of German hostility towards the United States which President Wilson had often said was necessary before he was prepared to contemplate war. Behind the incident was a smart piece of work by British naval intelligence. The telegram had been intercepted in January in 'Room 40', Whitehall, the subsequently famous seat of operations of naval intelligence. The men of Room 40 had learnt something about German codes, and recognized the coded signature as signifying 'Zimmermann' and the classification as 'most secret'. By a mixture of careful elimination, elaborate cross-checking and inspired guesswork of the kind that makes a good code-breaker, two members of Captain 'Blinker' Hall's staff (in private life respectively a publisher and a clergyman) succeeded in decoding enough of the telegram to reveal its explosive message. To protect security the original message was taken to the U.S. embassy and decoded a second time by a U.S. officer, with one of the British decoders leaning helpfully over his shoulder. This enabled President Wilson to announce that the telegram had been decoded by U.S. officers on U.S. soil.

President Woodrow Wilson.

British capture Baghdad

On March 11 the British flag was hoisted over the ancient and much-conquered city of Baghdad, the capital of Mesopotamia. The Turks, outnumbered and outflanked, had withdrawn from the city the previous night. In Britain, starved of victories, news of General Maude's success was greeted ecstatically.

After the loss of Kut, the British chief of staff, Sir William Robertson, favoured a defensive posture in Mesopotamia. He was reluctant to supply more troops, since he considered that the main object was merely to protect the Persian oilfields and to guard the Tigris-Euphrates waterway. However, General Maude, Robertson's own appointment, by slow and imperceptible steps converted a policy of defence into one of attack. Most of 1916 was devoted to preparation for this move, building up supplies and improving morale, and from December Maude began gradually to extend his front up the Tigris. By the middle of February the Turks were in a weak position between Sanniyat and Aziziya, facing two converging forces. Moving rather slowly (partly, perhaps, to prevent a command from London to stop the advance), Maude failed to cut off the Turks and, in a situation where cavalry, for once, could have played a vital role, Maude's cavalry provided only a desultory pursuit, though the retreating Turks were harassed by the British gunboats on the Tigris. The victory nevertheless encouraged Robertson to give the go-ahead for an advance on Baghdad, which, after a few checks on the way, was entered without resistance.

General Maude, who commanded the British forces in Mesopotamia.

Russian state collapses

Within the space of about four days in March (February in the old calendar then in use) tsarist Russia collapsed as a viable state. There was no planned revolution, despite the disaffection with the government that spread to nearly every section of the community. Disorder reached such a pitch that the government was shown to be completely powerless; willy-nilly, a revolution had taken place.

At the outbreak of war most classes of Russian society had supported the government. The peasants, who were to make up 80 per cent of Russia's armies, did not enjoy the prospect of war, but they offered no opposition. Among politically active groups, even some on the extreme left (though not Lenin) asserted that defence of the motherland was more vital than revolution.

This support did not last long. The government made no effort to cash in on the public mood by making concessions, and the shattering defeat of the Russian armies in 1914 provoked criticism of the country's leadership. In 1915 the so-called Progressive bloc in the Duma (parliament) proposed a coalition government and a programme of reform. The tsar's answer was to prorogue the Duma. Critical ministers received a sympathetic audience – and shortly afterwards found themselves sacked. When the tsar took command of the armies in person,

the tsarina and her gang of advisers ruled the roost in Petrograd (St Petersburg). The murder of the worst of them, Rasputin, changed nothing.

By the end of 1916 it was evident that constitutional reform was impossible, and both political and military leaders openly agreed on the desirability of a coup d'etat. But no one was willing to take the initial risk. General Krymov, a fighting general, did attempt to organize a court revolution, but the plot was overtaken by other events.

Strikes for higher wages had been increasing for some time, and by March some 130,000 were said to be on strike in the capital. On March 8 a crowd queuing for bread turned violent on being told none was available. Rioting spread rapidly. Two days later the tsar ordered the army to suppress the disorders, but the soldiers, for the most part raw recruits accustomed to drilling with broomsticks, failed to respond.

Many simply disappeared from their barracks. Troops summoned from the front failed to reach Petrograd because the railways were not functioning. The failure of martial force marked a decisive difference from events in the revolution of 1905, when the government had been able to use troops to crush revolt.

By March 12 the entire city was in the hands of the strikers and deserters. Revolutionary workers set up a Petrograd soviet. While the tsar prevaricated, a committee of the Duma decided to form themselves into a government, largely to forestall any action by the soviet. In the event their decision was welcomed by the soviet (in which Bolsheviks had little influence), thanks largely to Alexander Kerensky, a member of both the soviet and the Duma. The new government speedily issued a grandiose programme of reform which, even if it had not been so heavily dependent on the soviet, would have been impracticable in the circumstances.

Meanwhile, the tsar had been persuaded to abdicate in favour of his brother, Michael. His brother refused this – in the circumstances – doubtful honour, and the Romanov dynasty thus came to an end. Tsar Nicholas requested that he and his family be allowed to go to Britain, but they were arrested and sent into Siberian exile. ▶ *page 97*

A patriotic pro-war demonstration in Petrograd led by blinded ex-soldiers.

1917 The United States enters the war

MARCH–APRIL

UNITED STATES AT WAR

BATTLE OF ARRAS

BATTLE OF THE AISNE

On April 6 the United States formally declared war on Germany. In his speech requesting Congressional approval of such a declaration, President Wilson had denied any U.S. territorial ambitions and had asserted that the world must be made safe for democracy. His policy was overwhelmingly approved, with only six votes against in the Senate and 50 (out of 423) in the House of Representatives.

The immediate causes of Wilson's change in policy were Germany's resumption of unrestricted submarine warfare against neutral as well as Allied shipping at the end of January, and the discovery of the German attempt to persuade Mexico to make war on the United States.

Hitherto the official U.S. policy had been strict neutrality. There was a considerable amount of pro-Allied, and some pro-German, feeling in the United States, but the great majority of citizens had supported non-intervention. Difficulties had arisen with both sides as a result of operations at sea, but the sinking of the *Lusitania* had tilted public opinion generally against Germany. Increasingly, U.S. policy had favoured the Allies, who were supplied with food, raw materials and even munitions, and were even allowed to raise war loans in the United States. The German complaint that U.S. neutrality was bogus was not unjustified.

The resumption of unrestricted submarine warfare led to the sinking of a number of U.S. ships, making war inevitable. Although it was obvious that U.S. forces could have no effect in France for some time, a more immediate result was the tightening of the naval blockade of Germany.

Over 1 million British troops in France

By the beginning of 1917 the British had about 1.25 million soldiers in France, including Australians, Canadians and others. The number was growing almost daily. The total French strength was about 2.3 million, including troops from the French colonies. The Belgians boosted Allied forces to a total of almost 4 million, while the Germans had about 2.5 million.

Numbers alone meant little. The Russians, for example, still had the largest army of any of the combatants, but it was a spent force. The French were practically at the end of their reserves; in November 1916 Joffre had stated that the French army could mount one more great battle. After that its strength was bound to decline because, at the current rate of casualties, France did not have the manpower to replace its losses. The Germans were also beginning to run short of reserves. By September the German government was calling on 15-year-old boys to volunteer.

U-boats sink a million tons a month

In April Allied losses to German submarines were 852,000 tons, more than half the total being British. Roughly one-quarter of British ships leaving home ports never regained them. Coming on top of similar losses in the previous two months, it was apparent that the German forecast that Britain would be brought economically to its knees by April was not far short of the mark.

Members of the crew of a U-boat.

Britain had food supplies for about another six weeks. The various means employed to combat the submarine success – building more ships, increasing patrols and mine-laying activities, imposing rationing by indirect means – were obviously ineffective. A U.S. officer, shown the figures for shipping losses, remarked in horror, 'Then we're losing the war!' His British informant agreed, and added, 'And there's nothing we can do about it.' ▶ *page 96*

German attack on Dover Patrol

Under cover of darkness on March 17 German destroyers attacked the British monitors of the Dover Patrol in the English Channel. One destroyer was sunk and another badly damaged.

The Dover Patrol was active in attacking German naval bases in the Belgian ports, although without putting them out of action for long. The mine and net barrage in the Channel was also patrolled, and the Germans made numerous attempts to disable the British naval units in order to clear the way through the Channel for submarines. After the successful attack of March 17 a German flotilla made another raid on April 20, but this time came off worse, losing two destroyers in close fighting. One or two minor attacks were made in the next few weeks but thereafter the Dover Patrol was left largely undisturbed until 1918.

Allies launch the spring offensive on the Western Front

On April 9 the planned offensive began when the British 3rd Army (General Allenby) attacked near Arras in Artois. The attack brought initial success, with most of the Vimy Ridge – an old objective – taken. The British gas had a paralysing effect on the German artillery, killing the horses that brought up the ammunition.

The Allied offensive, of which Allenby's attack represented the first move, had its genesis in the military discussions held toward the end of 1916, but plans had not gone smoothly. This was the offensive that, it was hoped, would win the war, since it was the last, according to Joffre, that the French army could mount at this level. Subsequently Joffre, whose reputation had never been as high since the weakness of the Verdun defences was revealed, was replaced by Nivelle, who owed his advancement, paradoxically, to his performance at Verdun.

Nivelle changed the plan, giving the French the main role in the attack, in Champagne, which necessitated the British taking over more of the French front south of the River Somme. Haig was not happy with the new arrangement and resented being placed in a subordinate position to Nivelle at a conference in Calais in February. The new plan also caused a postponement of the date of the offensive, originally set for that month, while further disruption was effected by German moves.

The cause this time was not a German offensive, as in 1916, but a German withdrawal. As a result of a major overhaul of the German war machine initiated by Hindenburg and Ludendorff, the decision was taken to adopt a defensive posture on the Western Front. In view of the likelihood of a renewed Allied attack on the Somme, a new line of defence was created behind the current front line. Very strong and deep, it became known subsequently as the Hindenburg, or Siegfried, Line. The land in front of the new defences was systematically devastated – houses were flattened, trees cut down and wells poisoned. Numerous and varied booby traps were then placed

Nivelle, who became French commander-in-chief.

amid the wreckage. By the middle of March the Germans, voluntarily conceding as much territory as the Anglo-French forces had sacrificed thousands of lives to gain, had completed their withdrawal to the Hindenburg Line, and a potential Allied advance was confronted by up to two miles of dangerous wasteland.

French offensive fails

The main, French-led attack in the Allies' spring offensive (battle of the Aisne) began on April 16 in the region of Reims. It was preceded by a long artillery bombardment. The Germans were thoroughly prepared, and the French troops threw themselves unavailingly against barbed wire and a hail of machine-gun fire.

Nivelle, who was now in the militarily dubious position of being both the director of the whole campaign and the commander of the French assault, had promised a great breakthrough, in marked contrast to Joffre's tired and costly strategy of attrition. Some of his subordinate commanders, however, were less sanguine. By May 7 the

French had advanced only four miles – hardly a breakthrough – while suffering heavy casualties.

A dramatic moment as French troops raid a German trench in the Champagne region.

British introduce convoy system

In April the British Admiralty decided to adopt the convoy system for shipping in the North Sea and the Channel. Losses inflicted by U-boats were immediately reduced and the system was extended to the Atlantic.

The convoy system was not a new idea, and the long resistance to it by the Admiralty, despite the urging of more progressive elements, ultimately backed by Lloyd George, is one of the more inexplicable features of the war.

The difficulty was finding sufficient destroyers to provide the escorts, but the arrival of U.S. flotillas eased that problem. Within a few weeks losses to shipping sailing in convoy were reduced to a comparatively trivial 1 per cent.

The convoy system was not the only reason for the final failure of the U-boat campaign. Germany did not have sufficient vessels (only 150 at the beginning of February) or crews to fulfil so large a task. The strain on the crews was dreadful and some loss of efficiency was an inevitable result. Mines, especially the horned mines introduced in 1917, which made the lives of submarine crews as dangerous as those of merchant seamen, also contributed. So did the new submarine chasers and aircraft. ▶ *page 118*

The U-boat base and harbour at Heligoland.

Mutiny in the French army

Mutiny broke out in a regiment of the French 2nd Colonial Division on May 3. Although it was swiftly put down, similar outbreaks spread, ultimately affecting 16 corps, so that, according to official sources, only two divisions in the Champagne sector were reliable.

Although subversive propaganda was predictably blamed for the mutinies, the true cause was the sacrifice of lives for little discernible gain. The mutinous troops were generally willing to defend their lines but refused to advance across open ground against machine-guns situated in impregnable concrete pillboxes. Dissatisfaction had been growing steadily; the ravages of Verdun had taken a terrible toll, and the number of deserters in the French army rose from about 500 in 1914 to about 21,000 in 1917.

Pétain replaces Nivelle

On May 15 General Pétain replaced Nivelle as supreme commander in France. He acted swiftly to restore discipline to the French army, which appeared to be on the point of moral collapse.

The government, wary of Nivelle's policy which combined recklessness with rigidity, had made Pétain chief of the general staff at the end of April in order to enable him to exercise some control over Nivelle, and two weeks later he took over Nivelle's command. He spent four weeks visiting the soldiers at the front – a place where generals were not often seen – listening to the complaints of the officers and men, while maintaining a firm but fair attitude which did much to restore the confidence of the French fighting men in their high command. He initiated important reforms, setting up more rest camps, providing more leave and limiting tours of duty in the trenches.

Pétain also introduced important tactical changes, placing the emphasis on firepower rather than manpower and ensuring that in the immediate future his troops were not committed to major offensive action.

King George V decorates General Pétain.

Second provisional government formed in Russia

Kerensky (left) taking the salute at a parade.

On May 18 the soviet agreed to form part of the revolutionary government in Russia. This ended an impossible situation in which the government had attempted to govern while power resided largely with the soviet.

Civil war had been narrowly avoided a month earlier when the foreign minister, Milyukov, reluctantly obeying the soviet's insistence that he communicate to the Allies Russia's desire for peace based on the self-determination, had accompanied that statement with a private reassurance that Russia's position regarding the war was unchanged.

In the second provisional government, Kerensky was minister of war, while Milyukov lost his place to Tereshchenko. Although the government now included representatives of the workers as well as of the bourgeoisie, it was still faced with the difficult problem of how to resolve differences over peace and war, as well as demands for national autonomy in various parts of the Russian empire.

People scatter in panic as shots are fired during rioting in Petrograd in July 1917.

THE GROWING IMPORTANCE OF THE AEROPLANE

THE HEIGHT of the submarine campaign against Allied shipping coincided with increasing attacks from the air. By 1917 Zeppelins had been largely ruled out as offensive weapons – they were too vulnerable to explosive bullets – but aircraft took their place. German aircraft began bombing raids on London in January, and the seriousness of the threat, despite the small number of aircraft (less than 20 on the first raid), was emphasized by the death of ten children in a school that received a direct hit.

At the beginning of the war aircraft were hardly considered as a potential weapon. Germany had only about 200 aeroplanes, France and Britain about half that number. They were employed solely for reconnaissance, and pilots on opposing sides allegedly waved to one another, although they were soon taking pot shots with a hand gun or dropping grenades. Rapid aeronautical developments brought changes. Aircraft remained, nevertheless, largely a support weapon for the army or navy.

Genuine fighter aircraft were first developed to knock out reconnaissance planes and gain control of the air over a battlefield. The German Fokker monoplane, introduced in 1915, which had a synchronized machine-gun firing though the blades of the propeller, was the first really successful fighter, and it stimulated developments among the Allies, who were forced to protect their reconnaissance planes with up to 12 escorting fighters. Aerial 'dog fights' followed the introduction of Allied fighters that matched the Fokker, and relatively serious bombing raids were carried out during the battles of Verdun and the Somme, in conjunction with the movements of troops on the ground. Towards the end of the war, commanders had come to recognize the advantages of bombing strategic areas, such as railway centres or factories, behind the lines. Faster and more heavily armed fighters were rapidly developed on both sides, and formations became larger. Over 100 aircraft were sometimes involved in air battles in 1917. Fighter pilots on both sides became folk heroes, the most notable being, perhaps, von Richthofen (the 'Red Baron') and the U.S. 'ace', Eddie Rickenbacker, a former racing driver.

German raids on London in May, carried out by Gotha G.IV aircraft, bore witness to the effectiveness of long-range bombardment, althought that effectiveness stemmed more from indirect effects – disrupting production, creating panic, drawing enemy aircraft away from the front – than direct damage. By that time, however, air defences had been organized properly in London, and the Germans switched their primary target to Paris. The raids also provided support for General (later Air Marshal) Trenchard's endeavours to form a British long-range bomber force.

Aircraft under construction at a Birmingham factory.

A motorized air-raid warning in London.

A German airman sets off on a reconnaissance flight.

A machine-gun mounted on board a German plane.

A French fighter ace.

Manfred von Richthofen.

1917

Kerensky's new Russian offensive

On July 1 the Russian army, under Brusilov's supreme command, began a new offensive. Morale had improved slightly since the revolution in March, in spite of Bolshevik propaganda, but this offensive was motivated by political considerations. Success would encourage the Germans to agree to peace. Failure might force the German revolutionary socialists to support Russia.

The operation opened auspiciously. The Austrian line was broken near Stanislau and a large number of prisoners and guns were captured. The picture changed dramatically when the Russians were counterattacked by the Germans under General Hoffmann. Within a month the Russians had been driven out of Galicia and the Bukovina. The Germans halted at the Russian frontier, not because of the resistance they met but because an invasion of Russia threatened to bring about severe political complications.

Meanwhile, an abortive rising against the provisional government in July led to the suppression of the Bolsheviks and the formation of a new government in which Kerensky was prime minister as well as minister for war.

▶ page 104

Russian soldiers in Galicia surrendering after the failure of Kerensky's new (and final) offensive.

British success in Flanders

The British 2nd Army (General Plumer) was in June given the task of straightening out the Ypres salient by an attack on the Messines ridge. Massive explosions at 3 a.m. on June 7 were the signal for the attack, which was a notable success although, as on other occasions, the initial advantage was lost when the main attack, coming six weeks later, became bogged down.

General Plumer was one of the few commanders who enhanced his reputation on the Western Front, thanks to his well-planned and well-executed assault on Messines, which to some extent alleviated the disappointing failure to make progress at Arras.

The temporary collapse of the French army in May naturally placed more responsibility on the British, who carried the weight of the campaign on the Western Front for the remainder of 1917. Despite the failure of their allies – Russia was also on the point of disintegration – the British were in a better position to take on the extra burden, since they now had over 60 divisions in France and the shortage of munitions had been overcome. General Haig decided on an attack in Flanders, his preferred field of battle, similar to that planned before Nivelle took over. The attack on the Messines ridge was the opening move of this campaign, designed to secure the flank of the main assault at Ypres.

Plumer's success involved the preliminary digging of thousands of yards of tunnel and the planting of 19 large mines, containing 600 tons of explosives. The simultaneous explosion of the mines, combined with artillery fire from over 2000 guns, resulted in the objective being attained in a few hours, with 16,000 casualties and 7000 prisoners taken. A German counterattack the next day was repulsed.

British attack at Ypres

The main attack in Field Marshal Haig's new Flanders offensive, following the 2nd Army's capture of the Messines ridge, was launched on July 31. It began in heavy rain which, following the prolonged artillery bombardment which preceded the attack, soon turned the battlefield into a sea of mud.

One purpose of the attack in this particular sector was to capture the Belgian ports (assuming the troops could break through), but the strategic advantages of this were not obvious. The German submarines operated mainly from German, not Belgian, ports; neither did the direction of the attack serve to relieve pressure on France. General Haig was optimistic that he could defeat Germany, with or without the French, but his optimism was not widely shared.

The battle – like most of the so-called 'battles' on the Western Front it was really a campaign including numerous engagements – rapidly assumed a familiar pattern. The first attack, which involved mainly General Gough's 5th Army, scored some initial successes; the line was pushed forward over a mile in some parts on the first day, although in other places it remained stationary. Thereafter the advance was minimal. The rain continued to pour down in torrents, so that tanks could make no progress. The infantry, too, were soon struggling. Their predicament was worsened by the type of defence shrewdly adopted by the Germans. This consisted of machine-gun posts in concrete pillboxes, capable of withstanding a direct hit from heavy artillery, which were arranged in depth rather than in line. Gough advised that the offensive should be called off, but Haig, misled by optimistic intelligence reports and motivated by religious faith in victory, continued to suppose that the Germans were approaching collapse.

The attack was renewed two weeks later when the weather had improved a little. Again, little progress was made on the most important part of the front. Haig then replaced the 5th Army with the 2nd (General Plumer), which had performed so well in taking the Messines ridge. Plumer's superior staff work and strategic grasp resulted in some progress being made during September-October where none had been made before, and counterattacks were beaten off thanks to good spotting by the Royal Flying Corps and prompt and accurate fire by the artillery. Nevertheless, the strategic effect of the campaign was virtually nil and hopes of a substantial break-through faded. ▶ *page 103*

British stretcher-bearers in Belgium in August 1917.

Troops on the march in Belgium pass a scene of devastation.

NOVEMBER
9 Trotsky issues call for peace
10 Italians retreat to the River Piave
11 Bolsheviks defeat attempted counter-coup in Petrograd
12 Krasnov's Cossacks defeated near Petrograd
16 Bolsheviks control Moscow
17 British cruisers attack German minesweepers off Heligoland
17 Clemenceau becomes French premier
18 British take Jaffa
20 Tanks lead assault at Cambrai
21 Flight of the airship L-59 to Africa
22 Six French and five British divisions transported to Italy
23 Bolsheviks publish secret Allied treaties
25 Lettow-Vorbeck leaves German East Africa
29 Allied conference in Paris
30 U.S. 'rainbow division' arrives in France
30 Germans counterattack at Cambrai

DECEMBER
5 Germans and Russians agree a ten-day truce
6 Romania signs armistice
9 United States declares war on Austria-Hungary
9 Allenby enters Jerusalem
12 General Paes leads coup in Portugal
12 German destroyers sink escort ships in Scandinavian convoy
19 Austro-German Caporetto offensive ceases
22 Russo-German peace talks begin at Brest-Litovsk
23 Conscription defeated in Australian referendum

Ypres in 1917 showing the utter destruction of the town centre.

British troops moving up to trenches near Ypres.

1917

ITALIAN ARMY DEFEATED

3rd BATTLE OF YPRES

Lawrence rides to Aqaba

In a totally unexpected coup rebel Arab forces captured the port of Aqaba on August 25, on behalf of the emir (later King) Faisal. The attackers were led by the British guerrilla officer, T. E. Lawrence, in co-operation with the bandit chief, Auda Abu Tayyi.

Leaving Faisal to attack the Hejaz railway, Lawrence travelled north on his own initiative to further the Arab revolt against the Turks in Syria. Returning, he joined up with the Huweitat (a small Bedouin tribe with a rough reputation) of Auda Abu Tayyi.

Together they defeated a Turkish battalion at Ma'an. Then, apparently acting on impulse, they made the sudden dash to Aqaba.

Subsequently, with the benign approval of Allenby, British commander in Palestine, Lawrence and the Arabs continued guerrilla warfare, especially against railways. The Turks offered a reward for the capture of 'El Orens, destroyer of engines'.
▶ page 107

T.E. Lawrence in Arab dress.

Germans capture Riga

On September 17 the Germans under General Hutier captured Riga, with little opposition from the increasingly disorganized and demoralized Russian army. By occupying the island of Oesel the following month they gained command of the Baltic.

However, possession of the Baltic was disputed by the British. Damage to several German battleships by mines as well as submarines persuaded the High Seas fleet to withdraw, though Oesel Island remained under German occupation.

Scandinavian convoy destroyed

Two German light cruisers made a surprise attack on a British-Scandinavian convoy on October 17. They sank two destroyers escorting the convoy and destroyed all nine merchant ships before making their getaway.

The Scandinavian convoy, though safe from submarines and escorted by ships of the Grand Fleet, was vulnerable to attack by fast-moving surface vessels. Further evidence of this vulnerability came two months later when the Germans made another successful assault, although this time most of the merchant vessels escaped. Thereafter the British changed the convoy route and strengthened the escorts.

Italians defeated at Caporetto

The long campaign of attrition on the Isonzo front was suddenly transformed on October 24 when Italy suffered a shattering defeat near Caporetto. The Italian forces, in full retreat, were pushed back to the River Piave, less than 20 miles from Venice, before they managed to make a firm defensive stand.

The Italo-Austrian campaign on the Isonzo had long before resolved itself into a costly stalemate like that on the Western Front. General Cadorna had launched a seemingly endless series of attacks (ten so far), sacrificing many lives but achieving only minor gains. These efforts had sapped Italian morale, but they had also weakened the Austrians, and in September Ludendorff succumbed to Austrian appeals for assistance because the likely alternative seemed to be total Austrian collapse.

Much earlier Cadorna had also appealed to his allies. At the

Italian soldiers in retreat after Caporetto.

Chantilly conference in November 1916 he had requested British and French co-operation in order to knock Austria out of the war. This had been rejected, but the suggestion came up again later and, though vigorously opposed by Haig, had been supported by Lloyd George. The Allied obsession with victory on the Western Front had again won the day, and in May Cadorna's 2nd Army had launched yet another assault on its own. This made some progress, but eventually petered out.

Ludendorff was able to supply only six divisions, but he chose a weak point to make a breakthrough. The Italians were subjected to a particularly fierce artillery bombardment (the Germans had moved in the guns unnoticed) and, as the attack was launched, their centre broke. By the end of the month the Italians were staggering back over the River Tagliamento. Cadorna was forced to pull in his flanks and make a stand on the Piave.

The startling success of the offensive, led by General von Bülow but masterminded by the mountain-warfare expert Krafft von Delmensingen, surprised Ludendorff as much as anyone, and he was unable to move in the reinforcements that might have turned victory into conquest owing to faulty railway communications (and to the pauses by the advancing German troops to enjoy the well-stocked Italian supply depots). British and French reserves were hurriedly conveyed to the Italian front and, despite a vigorous Austrian assault from the Trentino, the line held at the Piave. Shortly before Christmas the offensive was brought to an end by the winter snow. The Italians had lost 250,000 prisoners and Cadorna, who was in poor health, had lost his command. He was replaced by General Diaz.

The Rapallo conference in November marked the beginning of the process leading to a united Allied command. ▶ *page 119*

Canadians occupy Passchendaele

On November 4 troops of the Canadian Corps occupied the village of Passchendaele. The strategic ridge had become an almost obsessional object for Field Marshal Haig in the Flanders campaign and its conquest brought the so-called 3rd battle of Ypres to a close.

The minor gains achieved in the attacks by the 2nd Army in late September and early October had the unfortunate effect of encouraging continuation of an offensive that no longer had any realistic chance of significant success. Early October brought more heavy rains, and the infantry were compelled to attack through mud that often came up to their thighs and, among other inconveniences, rendered their weapons nonfunctional. Besides machine-gun fire and fresh German reserves, they also had to contend with mustard gas. After several attacks had completely failed, Haig called up the Canadians in support and it was Canadian troops who eventually took the ruined village.

The whole campaign is sometimes known as '3rd Ypres' and sometimes as the battle of Passchendaele – a name likely to stand for ever as a symbol of the futile and horrific warfare of the Western Front. The Germans were not exhausted, though certainly severely strained. The British suffered more. They lost 245,000 men (possibly a considerable underestimate). German losses were probably under 200,000.

Canadian machine-gunners manning shell holes in appalling conditions on Passchendaele ridge in November 1917.

1917
NOVEMBER

BOLSHEVIK
COUP IN RUSSIA

BATTLE OF
CAMBRAI

Women soldiers were recruited in a desperate attempt to save Russia from defeat.

Bolsheviks seize power in Russia

On November 7 (mid-October, in the old calendar), the Bolsheviks took over the Russian government virtually without a shot being fired. Lenin reappeared from hiding and congratulated the Petrograd soviet on launching a new historical era. Members of the government congregated in the Winter Palace, without Kerensky, who was trying to get troops from the front to crush the revolt. Before he could return, however, the government surrendered.

Red Guards outside Lenin's office in Petrograd.

The failure of a Bolshevik rising in July had seemed to end that particular threat to Kerensky's provisional government. However, an attempted coup from the right in September, which was led by General Kornilov, forced Kerensky to appeal for support from the left, and the Bolsheviks rapidly re-established their position. They began to work openly for the overthrow of Kerensky's 'bourgeois' government. They held a majority in many of the soviets, which represented the real seat of power in most cities and towns. Meanwhile, national minorities of all kinds announced their secession from the Russian empire, bread riots broke out in towns and in the country peasants tried to solve the land problem by the most basic means (e.g., burning down landlords' houses). The government was entirely helpless. Since the failure of the Kornilov coup not even Cossack regiments

could be relied on for support.

Following the German occupation of Oesel in October, which offered an obvious threat to the capital, the government attempted to reinforce the Petrograd garrison with troops from the front. The order was countermanded by Trotsky, now leader of the Petrograd soviet. On October 23 the Bolshevik central committee declared support for an armed uprising and Trotsky began to organize his forces.

Events hinged on the forthcoming congress of soviets, due to assemble on November 7 (October 20 in the old calendar). A Bolshevik majority was anticipated and a consequent vote in favour of a soviet government. While others waited, Trotsky (perhaps recalling Lenin's remark to the effect that bayonets are more reliable than votes) acted first. His Red Guards (workers' militia) took over

Russian soldiers with revolutionary banners.

government offices and communications. Kerensky left for the front. The government caved in when threatened with force.

The congress of soviets met on November 7. Those opposed to the Bolshevik coup resigned and joined the committee of public defence, which ordered the cadets from the military schools to arrest Trotsky's military revolutionary committee and attack soviet strongholds. This took place in conjunction with the march on

Petrograd by General Krasnov, a Cossack general who had agreed to Kerensky's request for troops.

The Bolsheviks in Petrograd, supported by cruisers on the River Neva, held out and the advancing Cossacks were defeated on November 12. Kerensky fled. The Bolsheviks had made good their grip on power and the revolution, proclaiming 'land, bread and peace', swept the country, although civil war now appeared inevitable. ▶ page 106

British attack minesweepers

A long-range naval action took place in the Heligoland Bight on November 17, following the attack of two British cruiser squadrons on German minesweepers. The result was indecisive, since the Germans retreated behind a smokescreen to the cover of their own minefields and, when two German battleships appeared, the British withdrew.

The German minesweepers were forced to become more active in the autumn of 1917 because increase in the production of mines had enabled the British to begin intensive mining of the approaches to German ports. They were sometimes forced to operate well over 100 miles from safety, covered by warships of the High Seas Fleet and they attracted frequent raids from cruisers of the Grand Fleet.

German East Africa occupied

Early in the morning of November 25 the force commanded by General Paul von Lettow-Vorbeck waded across the Rovuma River into Portuguese East Africa, thus surrendering German East Africa to the British. Lettow-Vorbeck had trimmed his *Schutztruppe* to 200 Europeans and 2000 Askaris (African troops). They confronted a Portuguese force sent to prevent the crossing and massacred it, capturing a large amount of – mostly British – supplies.

The East African campaign, though certainly no more than a relatively insignificant sideshow, was one of the most remarkable of the war. After the British expeditionary force had been repulsed at Tanga in November 1914, nothing much was done to disturb the Germans in their last surviving colony until the South African soldier Smuts took command in February 1916. The vastly outnumbered Germans, taking advantage of mountains, bush and forest, consistently eluded all efforts to bring them to a decisive battle. Lettow-Vorbeck's force, about 5000 strong at the start (and 95 per cent black Africans) was opposed by a maximum of 130,000 men, mainly African and Indian but including a huge variety of nations and individuals.

Having reached Portuguese territory successfully and enjoying considerable local support because of the hostility of the inhabitants to their colonial masters, the extraordinary Lettow-Vorbeck embarked on a highly effective guerrilla campaign. The *Shutztruppe* were still going strong at the time of the armistice in 1918. Lettow-Vorbeck later became a good friend of Smuts; he died in 1964 aged 94.

Tanks break through at Cambrai

On November 20, two weeks after the British offensive in Flanders had squelched to a halt in mud and blood, a completely different attack was made by the British near Cambrai in Artois. With no preliminary bombardment, the attack – by 380 tanks – began in the misty pre-dawn light and took the Germans completely by surprise. The Siegfried Line was swiftly breached with the aid of vast bundles of brushwood which carried the tanks over the trenches.

This was the first mass attack by tanks of the war. The ground had been carefully chosen by the British Tank Corps to suit their vehicles (which were useless in the Flanders mud). Within a few hours the tanks had advanced much farther, and with far fewer casualties, than any previous offensive on the Western Front.

The sequel was less successful. The only back-up, in view of the concentration of all reserves in Flanders, was provided by the cavalry, which as usual proved almost completely useless. Ten days after the initial attack, which had produced a salient extending five miles beyond the original front line, the Germans counterattacked from both sides of the salient – against troops who had been in almost continuous action for ten days – and regained most of the lost ground.

British tanks carrying bundles of brushwood in preparation for the battle of Cambrai.

The 'rainbow division' arrives

On November 30 the U.S. 'rainbow division', later commanded by Douglas MacArthur, arrived in France. It was so called because it contained U.S. National Guard units from every, or almost every, state (not because it was of mixed colour).

The first troops of the American Expeditionary Force, commanded by General 'Black Jack' Pershing, had seen action over a month earlier. President Wilson

American troops in a mainly horse-drawn convoy in France towards the end of 1917.

had hoped that the U.S. contribution to the war effort might be largely confined to subsidies, ships and loans, but the Allied losses made a U.S. expeditionary force vital. Volunteers were

plentiful, although Congress passed a Selective Service act in May and nearly 5 million men were eventually called up for military service of some kind. The first soldiers of Pershing's force

arrived in June, and by the end of the year there were about 200,000 U.S. troops in France. They did not begin to arrive there in really large numbers, however, until March 1918.

Trotsky calls for peace

After brief negotiations at the front the Germans agreed to a ten-day truce with Russia on December 5. As part of the agreement, the Germans promised not to transfer troops from the Eastern to the Western Front, although this promise was not kept.

Trotsky had issued a call to all belligerents for an armistice a month earlier. This had brought protests from the Allies, disturbed by the prospect of German reinforcements reaching France and Italy, although it was clear that the Russian army was in no way able to continue the fight. The former commander-in-chief, General Dukhonin, was murdered by his troops because he was alleged to favour the Allies'

protest, and counter-revolutionaries were engaged in a damaging campaign of sabotage.

Formal peace negotiations began at Brest-Litovsk on December 22. Trotsky, now commissar for foreign affairs, put forward proposals based on no indemnity, no annexation and self-determination for subject peoples. The Germans stated their reservations and submitted counter-proposals. ▶ *page 108*

German and Russian peace delegates meeting.

British capture Jerusalem

On December 9 General Allenby rode into Jerusalem – on a horse. The decisive incident in the conquest was probably Allenby's seizure of the passes through the hills at the end of November, a manoeuvre that had taken the Turks by surprise.

The British Palestine campaign had originally made rather slow progress. General Sir Archibald Murray's failure to take Gaza in two attempts in the spring had resulted in his replacement by Allenby in July. After spending some time reorganizing his command Allenby took Beersheba and Gaza early in November. Falkenhayn, now in command in Syria, was forced to call off a counter-offensive. With the Turks in retreat, Allenby advanced up the coast, taking Jaffa, then wheeled his main force inland towards Jerusalem. ▶ *page 116*

Right. The interior of the mosque at Gaza, which was badly damaged by British gunfire.

Below. Turkish cavalry near Gaza in April 1917. The town was captured by the British towards the end of the year.

The flight of the L-59

The most curious incidents in war are not always the most important. Certainly, the flight of the L-59 had, as things turned out, no military significance whatever.

L-59 was a German airship, built in the autumn of 1917. By that time zeppelins were of little use for either bombing or reconnaissance, but they still had certain unique qualities. They could, for example, fly a long way. L-59's estimated range was 10,000 miles. Someone at the German admiralty, puzzling over what to do with the L-59, had the bright if improbable idea that it might be used to send supplies to East Africa, where General von Lettow-Vorbeck was fighting his remarkable guerrilla campaign with no hope of support.

The zeppelin was loaded with 15 tons of useful supplies, from machine guns to sewing machines. Its parts were adapted for use after landing: gas bags convertible into sleeping bags, the balloon body into tents, etc. A pilot was appointed, Lt Commander Ludwig Bockholt. He had rather few flying hours in zeppelins, but he had accomplished a remarkable feat in one – he had captured a ship. (She was a Norwegian timber vessel sailing to England; he lowered a boarding party from the zeppelin). His crew of 21 were all volunteers.

The zeppelin flew first to Yambol in Bulgaria. From there it began its flight to East Africa on September 21. The course was over friendly Turkey, across the Mediterranean between Crete and Rhodes, then over British-controlled Egypt and on to the south, steering by the stars. The worst part was flying over the desert, where the sudden changes in air temperature caused the L-59 to droop dangerously at night, once almost hitting a mountain, and to float sharply up during the day. It rolled so much that many of the crew were airsick and, interestingly, some experienced mirage-like hallucinations at even as low as 3000 feet.

As night fell on November 22 the L-59 was over Aswan. A message, faint and hard to decipher, came through on the wireless telling the airship to turn back. There was some doubt if the message were genuine or a ploy by British intelligence – a question to which neither British nor German archives have provided an answer, though Bockholt was probably correct in deciding it was genuine. The L-59 swung cumbersomely about and the following day returned to land at Yambol after travelling over 4000 miles in 95 hours – at that time far the longest sustained flight ever achieved.

What the intended beneficiary, Lettow-Vorbeck, thought of all this is not recorded. Probably he was untroubled by the non-arrival of the supplies. A month later he was eating his Christmas dinner in Portuguese East Africa: roast pork, Portuguese wine, coffee and cigars – a pleasant change from the usual meal of hippopotamus fat smeared on bread.

1918

TREATY OF BREST-LITOVSK

FINNISH WAR

GERMAN SPRING OFFENSIVE

Wilson publishes peace conditions

On January 8 President Wilson published his 'Fourteen Points' in a speech to Congress. Designed to raise Allied morale and reassure the Central Powers of a just peace, they defined how peace was to be maintained in the post-war world.

The Fourteen Points covered such matters as restoration of conquered territory, independence for nations such as Poland and the nationalities of the Austro-Hungarian empire, freedom of the seas and removal of trade barriers, and finally (Point 14) an international association to arbitrate future disputes.

Bolsheviks and Germans agree peace terms

The Treaty of Brest-Litovsk was signed on March 3, ending hostilities between Germany and Russia. Three weeks earlier, the German terms had been rejected by Trotsky, whereupon the Germans had renewed the fighting. Lenin then decided on immediate peace at almost any price and forced his opinion through the Soviet central committee by threatening to resign.

The treaty left Poland and the Baltic states – and in effect the Ukraine and Finland also – in German hands. In addition, the Soviet government agreed to pay a large indemnity, or its equivalent in raw materials. The Germans thus gained valuable resources (80 per cent of Russian iron and coal production), besides the freedom to concentrate troops on the Western Front.

Facing domestic difficulties, including the sabotage campaign by anti-revolutionaries and growing troubles for the Bolshevik Revolution in various parts of the country, Lenin nevertheless believed that the Revolution would spread rapidly all over Europe. He was therefore intent on gaining, as he said, a breathing space.

The Allies regarded the Treaty of Brest-Litovsk as a betrayal and they resented the transport of raw materials and supplies from Russia to Germany. They also believed that the Bolsheviks would eventually be overthrown. The new Soviet regime thus had few friends in Europe.

There was widespread resistance to the peace treaty inside Russia itself. Boris Savinkov, who had been war minister under Kerensky, led the Right Socialist Revolutionaries, who were anti-Bolshevik and opposed to the treaty. They were responsible for acts of sabotage, and for the murder (in July) of the German ambassador, by which they hoped to provoke renewed German hostilities. Savinkov briefly held Yaroslavl, less than 200 miles from Moscow.

Civil war in Finland

Finland's independence was recognized by Russia and the Central Powers on January 4. However, 40,000 Russian troops remained in the country, and they generally supported the Red Guards. The government raised a force (there was no Finnish army) commanded by General Mannerheim to maintain order and expel the Russians.

The conflict resolved itself into a civil war (aggravating the country's intense economic hardship), for the Red Guards controlled the south of the country. Mannerheim was aided by the return from Germany of the Finnish 'Jägers' (Finns trained as soldiers in Germany for the purpose of starting a Finnish rebellion against Russia), and by a German expeditionary force some 12,000 strong under General Rudiger von der Goltz. The Treaty of Brest-Litovsk (March) also provided for Russian evacuation of Finland. By May 16 Mannerheim had carried hostilities to a successful conclusion and at the end of the year, pending a constitution, he was elected regent.

German troops in Helsinki firing on Red Guards.

German and Austrian delegates at Brest-Litovsk.

Germans break through on the Somme

Ludendorff's carefully planned offensive on the Western Front began on March 21 with an attack in the region of the Somme. It covered a front of about 50 miles and involved 62 divisions. The 18th Army broke through easily in the south, while the 17th and 2nd Armies made slower progress north of the river, around Arras.

This was the beginning of the most successful offensive since 1914. The German breakthrough, after over three years of virtual stalemate, can be explained partly by their numerical superiority, since the collapse of Russia had permitted the transfer of troops from the east. However, it was obvious that this advantage would not last long as U.S. troops began to reach France in ever growing numbers. Ludendorff saw this offensive as Germany's last chance. It almost succeeded.

His plan was to split the Allied armies, then turn against the British and drive them back to the Belgian coast. The attack involved significant novelties in tactics. It was carried out not by a wall of infantry following a long artillery bombardment but by small groups of stormtroopers who penetrated the enemy lines, bypassing strong points and attempting to reach the artillery. It was helped by fog, augmented by smokescreens, and by newly developed mustard gas.

The British 5th Army was broken and Pétain warned Haig he might have to withdraw his troops to cover Paris. The crisis had the effect of spurring the Allies into at last appointing a single commander-in-chief, General (later Marshal) Foch.

By March 28 the British 3rd Army was holding off the Germans east of Arras, and Ludendorff switched his main effort to the advance on Amiens. By March 30 the Germans had advanced over 40 miles, capturing 80,000 prisoners and 1000 guns. ▶ *page 110*

British prisoners dig a mass grave for dead comrades killed during the German breakthrough.

German troops advancing rapidly during the March offensive which brought them close to Amiens.

1918

APRIL–JULY

GERMANS REACH
MARNE

ALLIED
COUNTERATTACK

CZECH LEGION IN
RUSSIA

Germans advance in Flanders

On April 9 Ludendorff launched a secondary German attack on the Allied lines in Flanders. By chance the front was held by exhausted Portuguese troops, due for relief, and the Germans broke through. The narrow breach was rapidly widened.

Though intended mainly as a distraction, the battle of the Lys (as the engagement is called) turned into a major effort. All the gains made at such cost by the British during 1917 were lost within a few hours. However, aided by French reinforcements, the British managed to stem the advance when pressed dangerously close to the sea (or, as Haig put it with characteristic lack of originality, 'with our backs to the wall').

Ludendorff had won great tactical victories – inflicting over 300,000 casualties – but he had not won the strategic success he had aimed for and, time was running out.

A German machine-gun unit in action in open country during the battle of the Lys.

British submarines scuttled

On April 13 the seven British submarines which had been stationed in the Baltic under Russian command sailed out to sea through the ice and were scuttled to prevent them falling into the hands of the Germans, following the peace treaty between Russia and Germany.

German attack near Reims

The third stage of Ludendorff's huge spring offensive began – rather belatedly – on May 27, when 15 divisions launched a diversionary attack on the Allied front west of Reims, along the Chemin-des-Dames. After a ferocious bombardment, the Germans, with more than two to one superiority, advanced 12 miles the first day. In three days they reached the Marne.

The attack on the Chemin-des-Dames, like the two that had preceded it, had the advantage of surprise. This section was not considered by the Allied high command to be a likely battle site, and as a result troops who needed a rest were often sent there.

When the Germans swung to the west, in the direction of Paris, they ran into a defensive ring hastily constructed by Pétain, and were subjected to a fierce attack by the U.S. 2nd Division at the vital strategic point of Château-Thierry. The advance was also held up by the discovery of the vast stocks of supplies left behind by the French troops. In some places officers were unable to control their drunken men.

In June the Germans made an effort to straighten out their line between the 'bulges' made by their advances at Amiens and the Marne, but it was not successful. Ludendorff was forced to wait another month before he could resume the offensive against the British in Flanders.

British prisoners, some of them wounded, captured during the final stage of the German spring offensive.

Germans renew attack on the Marne

On July 15 Ludendorff ordered a new German attack on the Marne front. Some progress was made west of Reims (the River Marne being crossed) but very little to the east, where Pétain's new, less rigid form of defence proved effective. The main objective, Reims itself, was not taken.

This time, the Germans did not have the advantage of surprise. Insofar as they gained territory, it weakened their position in the forthcoming Allied counter-attack. Although, like the attack in the same sector in May, this was a minor offensive designed to draw off reserves from the Flanders front where an attack was planned for July 20, it proved to be Ludendorff's last throw.

Allies counterattack on the Marne

Three days after the Germans had renewed their offensive on the Marne sector, the Allies' counter-attack began on March 18. Planned by Foch, it was commanded by Pétain. The attack was launched toward Soissons, against the west flank of the 'bulge' in the German line created by the German advance earlier in the year and extended slightly on July 15–16. Pétain's object was to turn the 'bulge' into a 'bag' and by closing the neck to cut off the German 7th and 1st Armies on the Marne.

Foch and Pétain had several advantages denied to Ludendorff. First, they had tanks – nearly 500 of them. Second, they had a steadily increasing supply of fresh and effective troops from the United States, whose importance was not merely material. Their presence, with the promise of millions more to come, boosted Allied morale and correspondingly depressed the Germans.

The Allied breakthrough forced Ludendorff to call off his attack in Flanders, planned for July 20, although the Germans did manage to extricate most of their troops from the rapidly tightening 'bag'. Nevertheless, they lost 25,000 prisoners and a great deal of equipment.

Czechs fight the Soviets

After fighting between local soviets and Czech troops being evacuated from Russia, the Moscow government demanded that the Czechs surrender their weapons. They refused, and when an attempt was made on May 29 to enforce the demand, they resisted forcibly.

About 30,000 Czechs, who had deserted from the Austro-Hungarian forces, had been formed into an army to fight with the Russians on the Austrian front. After the Treaty of Brest-Litovsk Moscow had agreed that the Czechs should be evacuated via the Pacific coast to take part in fighting on the Western Front. The arrangement had broken down, with resulting violence.

The Czechs then openly joined the 'White' (anti-Bolshevik) Russians. As a trained force, they were more than a match for the local soviets. They set up an anti-Bolshevik regime – with Allied support – in Vladivostok and moved west to attack the Soviet state, which by the end of July had lost control of most of Siberia.

Heavily armed Czech troops, who lent their support to the White Russians, prepare for action.

PROPAGANDA

Together with the tank and the aeroplane, propaganda became established, in 1918, as a modern instrument of war. The Germans had been the first to make significant use of it, although all combatants came to recognize its importance. In the last year of the war Germany was subjected to the first really high-powered propaganda campaign, organized in particular by the British press baron Northcliffe under the minister of information, Beaverbrook, which had some effect – how much it is impossible to tell – on the disillusionment of the German people in the last months of the war.

The campaign, although, like all propaganda, dishonest, gave German civilians a more realistic account of the war's progress (it included maps of the Allies' advance) than they received from the German authorities, who continued to forecast a glorious victory until suddenly forced to admit imminent defeat.

Government-sponsored propaganda, the use of the press and the deliberate encouragement of nationalistic hatreds were among the most ominous cultural aspects of the war. Austria-Hungary was an easy target. Vast quantities of leaflets were dropped from balloons on the starving civilians and tired soldiers which aimed to exacerbate the national antagonisms of the various components of the old Habsburg empire. Germany could not be attacked in the same manner, and there Allied propaganda concentrated on the evils of Prussian militarism (which it held to be sole cause of the war), on the significance of U.S. involvement and on the possibilities of a fair and prosperous peace when the war ended. Northcliffe's propaganda came close to deciding government policy – for example, in supporting Polish and Czech independence. It was much more exhilarating than the reasoned tones of British Foreign Office reports.

One effect of propaganda was that it made a compromise peace almost impossible. It painted the Allied cause as one of selfless righteousness and the enemy as the very incarnation of evil. In such an atmosphere, reasoned discussion became difficult and moderation appeared almost treasonable. Propaganda portrayed a new world order that would emerge after the war, when the world had been 'made safe for democracy'. It raised expectations impossible to fulfil. It sowed the seeds of future bitterness.

No one can foresee the future, and the manufacturers of World War I propaganda cannot be blamed for the staggeringly successful and morally appalling use that was to be made of it by future totalitarian regimes in the Soviet Union and Nazi Germany.

The aftermath of anti-German riots in London's East End.

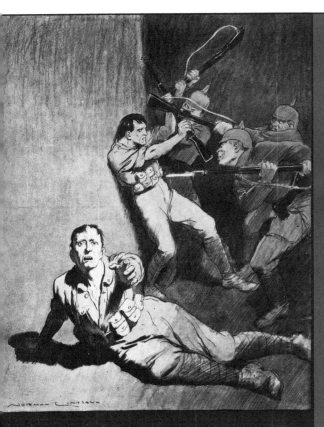

Quick!

RED CROSS OR IRON CROSS?

WOUNDED AND A PRISONER
OUR SOLDIER CRIES FOR WATER.

THE GERMAN "SISTER"
POURS IT ON THE GROUND BEFORE HIS EYES.

THERE IS NO WOMAN IN BRITAIN
WHO WOULD DO IT.

THERE IS NO WOMAN IN BRITAIN
WHO WILL FORGET IT.

On les aura!

2^E EMPRUNT
DE
LA DÉFENSE NATIONALE

Souscrivez

VATERLAND
≈FAMILIE ≈ ZUKUNFT≈

K·K·PRIVIL·LEBENS-
VERSICHERUNGS≈GESEL
OESTERR·PHÖNIX
IN·WIEN ≈ ZEICHNET
KRIEGS≈ANLEIHE!
SORGET·FÜR·EUCH
UND·EURE·LIEBEN!

K·K·PRIVIL·LEBENS
VERSICHERUNGS≈GESEL
OESTERR·PHÖNIX
IN·WIEN
TRETET≈DER≈
KRIEGS≈ANLEIHE
VERSICHERUNG·BE

≈8·KRIEGSANLEIHE≈

1918

ALLIED TROOPS AT ARCHANGEL

BATTLE OF AMIENS

Allied forces land at Archangel

On August 2 some 9000 Allied troops disembarked at Archangel. The British had already landed at Murmansk, where several warships had been sent after the Russian collapse.

The original purpose of the landings in Russia was to prevent Russian supplies going to the Germans. At Archangel, the local soviet was overthrown and a provisional government set up. Within a few days further Allied landings took place at Vladivostok: British and French troops, soon followed by Japanese and U.S. forces. The Czechs already controlled western Siberia and anti-Soviet groups held power in various places. By early September Soviet government east of the Urals had been swept away.

At the end of the month, however, the tide turned in favour of the Bolsheviks. The advance, first of the Czechs, then of White Russian forces from the Don, was checked, while the disintegration of Germany and Turkey, and particularly the outbreak of revolution in Germany, seemed to bear out Lenin's prophecy that events would soon sweep away both the Treaty of Brest-Litovsk and the capitalist system in Europe. However the Allies remained, and in greater force. By the end of 1918 British and French forces, holding a large section of the north, numbered about 15,000. The Japanese in the east had about 70,000, the French held Odessa, and smaller Allied groups protected the Siberian railway and supported Admiral Kolchak, who had established an 'all-Russian' (White) government at Omsk.

Lenin wounded in assassination attempt

The attempted assassination of Lenin on August 30 by a woman member of the Social Revolutionary terrorist group led by Boris Savinkov, followed by the killing of the head of the Petrograd Cheka (secret police) the next day, provoked a reign of terror in Soviet Russia.

Hundreds of innocent opponents of the Bolsheviks were executed in revenge for the terrorist acts of the Social Revolutionaries. The system of 'War Communism' was introduced: all free-enterprise activities were banned; cards, instead of money (being rapidly devalued by inflation), were introduced to pay for food, clothing, etc., and wide powers were given to the Cheka. One result of this policy was to increase the hostility between the Soviet government and the rest of the world.

Lenin leaving a meeting of the All-Russian Congress on Education in August 1918.

Germans defeated near Amiens

British and French forces launched an offensive on August 8 in order to relieve the German pressure on Amiens. The plan, apparently conceived by Field Marshal Haig, was not particularly ambitious but, enlarged by Foch, commander-in-chief of the Allied forces, it resulted in a major German defeat.

Tremendous efforts were made to achieve surprise; not even the British war cabinet was informed.

General Rawlinson's 4th Army was doubled in size without the Germans becoming aware of it, and some Canadian troops, regarded by the Germans as Britain's stormtroopers – their presence signifying imminent attack – were ostentatiously despatched towards Flanders. The remainder of the Canadian Corps, together with the Australians, took part in Rawlinson's assault.

The attack, shrouded in convenient mist, was led by tanks. The Canadians and Australians swept over the German lines and advanced about seven miles on the first day. Thereafter the advance continued at a slower pace, but on August 10 the French 3rd Army attacked further south and on August 17 the French 10th Army south of the 3rd. On August 21 the British 3rd Army, and on August 28 the 1st Army, struck to the north. In a memorable engagement on September 12–13 Pershing's army, which after unfortunate experiences he had refused to split up, nipped off the long-surviving German St Mihiel salient near Verdun. The strategy of successive attacks at different but connected points paid off handsomely. The Germans were unable to deploy the diminishing reserves where most needed. By the second week of September the Allies were across the Somme and within sight of St Quentin. The Germans were back on the Siegfried Line, where their spring offensive had begun.

This was the most successful Allied offensive on the Western Front since the beginning of the war. Measured in terms of miles gained or prisoners taken, it was not startling, but its effect was decisive. August 8, as Ludendorff said, was a black day for the German army. The German high command was demoralized. Ludendorff declared the need for an armistice, so did the Kaiser. There was no longer any hope of victory. ▶ *page 118*

General Pershing (left) in France.

New Zealand tanks and infantry with captured German field guns.

SEPTEMBER
24 British take Haifa
26 Major Allied offensive begins on the Western Front
29 Bulgaria surrenders

OCTOBER
1 Faisal and Lawrence enter Damascus
3 Germans offer armistice
3 Prince Max of Baden becomes German chancellor
4 U.S. 1st and 2nd Armies renew drive towards Metz
5 British break through Siegfried Line
6 430 killed in U.S. troopship collision
17 Hungary declares independence
20 Germans abandon submarine warfare
23 President Wilson announces terms for German surrender
24 Italians seize crossings on the River Piave
25 Arabs take Aleppo
26 Ludendorff resigns
29 Mutiny in German fleet
30 Italians defeat Austrians at Vittorio Veneto
31 Austria withdraws forces from Italy
31 Turkey surrenders
31 Italians sink Austrian battleship at Pola

NOVEMBER
1 British drop 140,000 propaganda leaflets a day on Germany
1 U.S. advance resumed
3 Austria signs armistice
7 Socialist republic proclaimed in Bavaria
9 German emperor abdicates
9 Republic proclaimed in Berlin
10 British battleship *Britannia* torpedoed off Cape Trafalgar
11 Germany surrenders
11 Austrian emperor abdicates
13 Soviet government denounces Brest-Litovsk treaty
18 Latvia declares independence
18 Admiral Kolchak establishes White Russian government at Omsk
21 German High Seas Fleet surrenders to Britain

DECEMBER
2 Pogrom in Lvov (Lemberg)
7 Spartacists call for German revolution
14 President Wilson arrives in Paris
15 Portuguese President Paes assassinated
23 German chancellor captured by revolutionaries

British cavalry on the move following the Allied offensive in August.

1918

TURKEY
SURRENDERS

BULGARIA SIGNS
ARMISTICE

Turkey defeated

As the September sun rose over the desert General Allenby launched his attack on the Turks in Palestine. Within a short time he had secured one of the most decisive victories of the war, in the battle (so called) of Megiddo (September 19). Yet there was relatively little hard fighting: the battle was won by superior strategy, plus superiority in men and weapons, and by speedy mobility of comparatively lightweight forces.

Allenby had planned his offensive for the spring, but the forces under his command had been largely denuded of British troops, hastily withdrawn to help stem the German advance in France. By September, however reinforced from other theatres, he was ready. His plan, which unlike most battle plans worked almost perfectly in practice, was to cut the Turkish army's communications and to block completely its line of retreat.

An important part was played by Faisal, Lawrence and their Arab irregulars, who constituted almost an informal right wing to Allenby's army and blew up the vital railway links of Deraa. Allenby also enjoyed command of the air, so effectively that the

Turkish fighters were not able to take off, while the successful bombing of the telegraph and telephone exchange at El Afule seriously disrupted Turkish communications. Among other ruses, 15,000 dummy horses were placed on the Jordan so as to mislead the Turks' concerning the whereabouts of the cavalry. Lawrence sent agents to buy vast quantities of forage in Amman in order to strengthen the illusion.

After a feint towards the Jordan, Allenby's main attack was launched in the west, along the coast. Vastly outnumbering the defenders, the infantry overran the trenches and opened a 'door' along the coastal corridor as the Turks swung back in a north-easterly arc. The cavalry swept

through the 'door' and on to Nazareth, the Turkish HQ, from which Liman von Sanders, the able German commander (who had first arrived in Turkey as military adviser in 1913), narrowly escaped. Other cavalry divisions cut off the Turks' line of retreat to the north, leaving only the eastward route, across the fast-flowing Jordan, which was effectively sealed by air force bombing. The Turkish 7th and 8th Armies disintegrated. The remaining 4th Army, already east of the Jordan, began to retreat towards Damascus, but the railway line had been cut and the Arabs were in between. They, and Allenby's cavalry, reached Damascus first.

In the course of the battle – or campaign – Allenby's forces advanced some 350 miles and took 75,000 prisoners, while their casualties were less than 5000. The Turkish army had ceased to exist and on October 31 Turkey surrendered.

Bulgaria surrenders

On the Salonika front the French commander, General Franchet d'Esperey, launched a decisive attack on the Bulgarians on September 15. The main assault, by Franco-Serbian troops under General Michich, was directed at the sector west of the River Vardar, where Bulgarian defences were comparatively weak. The mountainous terrain was regarded as a powerful defence in itself. The British attacked on the Doiran front three days later.

The Bulgarian forces, already weary of the war, rapidly crumbled under Michich's determined assault. The retreat turned into a rout, panic ensuing as British aircraft attacked the retreating columns in the Kosturino Pass. Two weeks after the attack began, Bulgaria signed an armistice, ending its participation in the war, fracturing the Central Powers' Quadruple Alliance and leaving Austria's back door wide open.

General Franchet d'Esperey.

The Turkish commander-in-chief in Palestine, Dyonal Pasha, seated centre.

Indian lancers passing through the streets of Haifa shortly after its capture.

General Allenby and King Faisal of Iraq.

Liman von Sanders, commander of Turkish Middle Eastern forces.

Foch launches all-out attack on the Western Front

On September 26 a major Allied offensive began with the U.S. attack on the Meuse-Argonne sector, northwest of Verdun. Encouraged by the success of the August offensive, Marshal Foch and his subordinates decided to mount a major effort to defeat Germany in the autumn of 1918 instead of waiting until the following year.

For the planned objectives of the Meuse-Argonne offensives to be achieved, the U.S. troops would have to make extraordinary progress. By the time they had reached the Siegfried Line, their attack was faltering, partly owing to difficulties with logistics. Meanwhile, the British on their left, with not so far to go, were also attacking the German defences. Haig had long been convinced that he could break the Siegfried Line and the demoralized state of the German troops made his task easier. In the centre the French advanced with deliberate caution, so that the attack on the flanks outpaced the advance in the centre, creating another potential 'bag' in which to entrap the Germans.

Early in October the British broke through the Siegfried Line and emerged into open country with little to stop their further advance. The U.S. 1st Army resumed its advance at the beginning of November, but a few days later the armistice brought all fighting to an end. The lines were then drawn roughly where they were in August 1914. ▶ *page 120*

German submarine campaign ends

The German submarine campaign was formally abandoned on October 20. Though for a time it had promised to win the war for Germany, the threat it presented had been largely overcome during the previous year. In the first three months of 1918 the British were still losing an average of 17 merchant ships a week, but by September the number was down to 11. A far higher proportion of ships attacked by U-boats escaped – a sign of the greater efficacy of anti-submarine defence, while the number of Allied ships lost to mines also fell dramatically. Allied naval forces managed to sink about 60 German submarines between January and September.

Marshal Ferdinand Foch.

U.S. troops, here manning a machine-gun, were the spearhead of the Allied September offensive.

Germany becomes a republic

The German Kaiser, Wilhelm II, abdicated on November 9. Pressed by the Social Democrats in the government, he had shown great reluctance to do so, but once it became obvious that he would get no support from the army, he agreed.

Germany had already, at the order of the high command, become a constitutional monarchy in October practically overnight, the main purpose being not to draw the teeth of revolutionaries like the Spartacists but to aid the peace approach to the Allies.

The German princes, including Prince Max, the chancellor, resigned along with the emperor. A Social Democrat, Friedrich Ebert, who became chancellor, was also the chosen leader of the Berlin 'soviet'. Although this was helpful, it was more important to gain the support of the high command, which was still a powerful body in spite of current disillusionment. It was agreed that Hindenburg should retain his command and that revolution should be resisted by force, i.e. with the help of the army. The signing of the armistice reduced popular support for revolution and, although revolutionary activities were not over, Ebert was able to organize elections for a constituent assembly. Revolutionary sailors then occupied the chancellery and made Ebert a prisoner, but he was rescued the next day (Christmas Eve) by soldiers of the Potsdam garrison.

The Italian general Diaz.

Italian victory at Vittorio Veneto

General Diaz opened his main atttack on the Austrians at Vittorio Veneto on October 27, after seizing the crossings on the River Piave. By the evening of the following day an extensive bridgehead was established beyond the river, and the Austrian 5th and 6th Armies had been split. The first Italian troops entered the town on October 29.

The Austrians had launched their last offensive in Italy to coincide with the German attacks in France in the spring. They had been repulsed, and Diaz made his plans for an all-out assault, to include British and French troops, on October 16. Bad weather caused a postponement.

In less than three days, over 30,000 prisoners were taken and the Austrian position had become untenable. The order to withdraw turned into a rout, and even in sectors where the Austrians had initially put up a stern defence, all resistance collapsed.

The order was given for all Austrian troops to withdraw from Italy, and on the same day the commander of the Austrian 6th Corps requested an armistice – in the knowledge that negotiations for an armistice were also taking place on the Western Front. While the Italian armies continued to advance, penetrating deep into the Trentino, passing the old frontier on the Isonzo and occupying Trieste from the sea, negotiations continued. Hostilities officially ceased on November 4.

Right. Friedrich Ebert (second from right), the chancellor of the German republic.
Below. The proclamation of the republic outside the Reichstag in Berlin.

1918

GERMANY SURRENDERS

Vessels of the German fleet at Scapa Flow.

Germany surrenders

At 5 a.m. on November 11 German delegates signed the terms of surrender in Marshal Foch's railway carriage in the Forest of Compiègne. The surrender came into effect six hours later. The Great War, as it was then called, thus ended at 11 a.m. on November 11.

President Wilson's reply to the German request for an armistice, delivered on October 23, had been severe. The terms demanded amounted virtually to unconditional surrender. Strategically, the German position, though certainly very bad, was not entirely hopeless. The Allies would have a long, hard job ahead if called upon to conquer Germany. What made the German acceptance of the terms inevitable was not so much defeat on the battlefield as defeat on the home front.

Already the sailors of the High Seas Fleet at Kiel and Wilhelmshaven had mutinied when ordered out on a last, clearly futile, mission against the British. Soldiers sent in to subdue them merely joined them. Economic anarchy and social disorder were spreading. Revolutionaries known as Spartacists (after the leader of a slave revolt in imperial Rome) took the lead in instigating revolution in the towns. Even Munich, Catholic and conservative, was involved. Workers' and soldiers' soviets were set up in many places.

Armed revolutionaries, including soldiers, sailors and civilians, in the streets of Berlin.

---

*T**HE COST** of the war, in lives and material, was enormous – far beyond anything conceived of in 1914. As with most wars, the cost was hard to justify for, although it brought desirable changes, these could not reasonably be held to balance the losses. Moreover, far from being a war that made the world safe for democracy, it played some part in encouraging the growth of barbaric totalitarianism which was such a marked feature of later 20th-century politics.*

CASUALTIES

(killed and wounded)	
Germany	1,770,000
Russia	1,700,000
France	1,360,000
Austria-Hungary	1,200,000
British Empire	910,000
Italy	460,000
Romania	450,000
Turkey	330,000
Bulgaria	240,000
Serbia	190,000
Belgium	60,000
United States	50,000
Portugal	13,000
Montenegro	13,000

[Note: casualty figures are notoriously unreliable. Figures for those killed include persons dying on active service from other causes.]

TOTAL CASUALTIES

(including prisoners and those posted missing) as a percentage of the total number mobilized		
Austria-Hungary	7.8 m	90%
Russia	12.0 m	76%
France	8.4 m	73%
Romania	0.75 m	71%
Germany	11.0 m	65%
Serbia	0.7 m	47%
Italy	5.6 m	39%
British Empire	8.9 m	36%
Belgium	0.27 m	35%
Turkey	2.8 m	34%
Bulgaria	1.2 m	22%

Above right. A military cemetery at Ypres, Belgium.

Right. A British hospital train.

Far right. Last post for a New Zealand soldier.

THE COST OF THE GREAT WAR

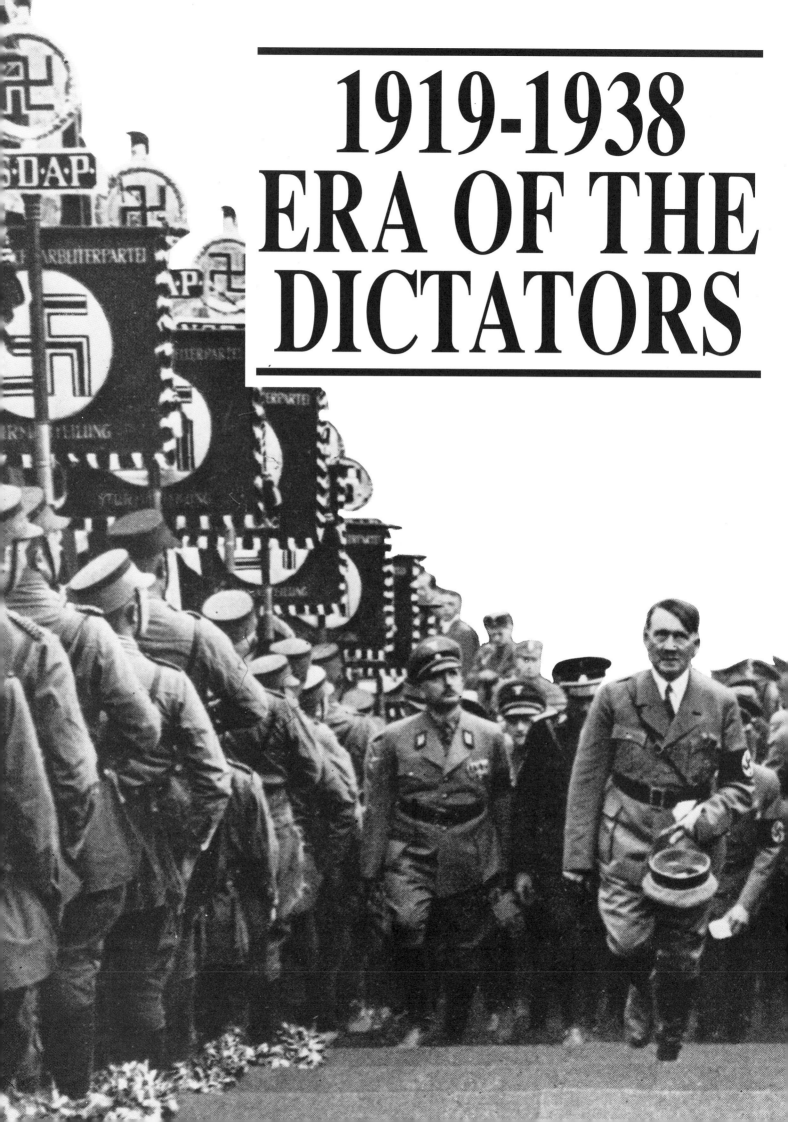

1919-1938
ERA OF THE DICTATORS

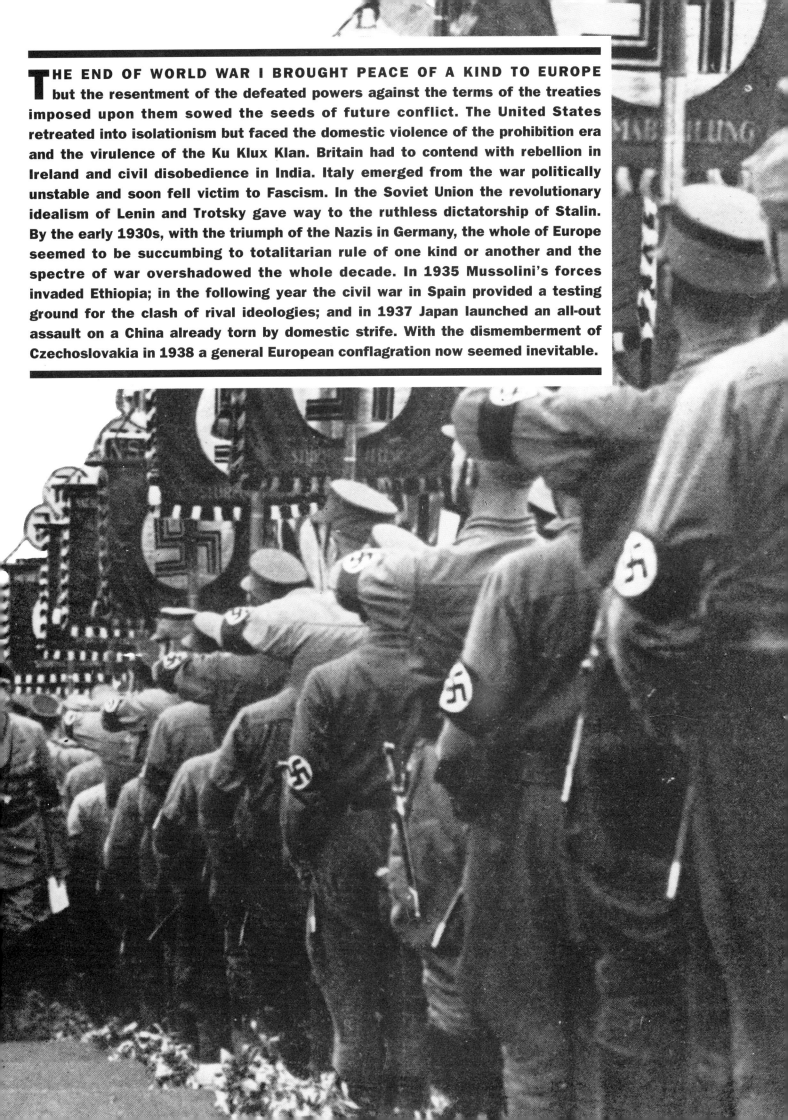

THE END OF WORLD WAR I BROUGHT PEACE OF A KIND TO EUROPE but the resentment of the defeated powers against the terms of the treaties imposed upon them sowed the seeds of future conflict. The United States retreated into isolationism but faced the domestic violence of the prohibition era and the virulence of the Ku Klux Klan. Britain had to contend with rebellion in Ireland and civil disobedience in India. Italy emerged from the war politically unstable and soon fell victim to Fascism. In the Soviet Union the revolutionary idealism of Lenin and Trotsky gave way to the ruthless dictatorship of Stalin. By the early 1930s, with the triumph of the Nazis in Germany, the whole of Europe seemed to be succumbing to totalitarian rule of one kind or another and the spectre of war overshadowed the whole decade. In 1935 Mussolini's forces invaded Ethiopia; in the following year the civil war in Spain provided a testing ground for the clash of rival ideologies; and in 1937 Japan launched an all-out assault on a China already torn by domestic strife. With the dismemberment of Czechoslovakia in 1938 a general European conflagration now seemed inevitable.

1919

Sparticists and government troops discuss truce terms in Berlin.

Spartacist revolt crushed in Berlin

Street fighting began in Berlin on January 6 between the Spartacists (Communists) and government forces. The Spartacist revolt was finally suppressed by the *Freikorps*, volunteer units organized by the military high command and led by veterans of the war. The Spartacist leaders, Rosa Luxemburg and Karl Liebknecht, were arrested and murdered on their way to jail.

The majority of German Socialists were opposed to radical change because they believed that it would destroy Germany unity. Separatist movements had arisen in Bavaria, where a soviet-type republic was proclaimed, and in the Rhineland. Risings also took place in Hamburg, the Ruhr and other areas. The alliance of the Socialist government with the military high command resulted in the suppression of most revolutionary outbreaks by the end of January, and in February the newly elected delegates to a constituent assembly met at Weimar to establish a democratic, republican government.

Below. The scene at Rosa Luxemburg's funeral.

Anti-British violence in Egypt

Following the arrest of Zaghlul Pasha Saad and three other nationalist leaders in Egypt on March 8, widespread agitation broke out directed against foreigners, and in particular the British as the protecting power. Communications were sabotaged and several British subjects were murdered.

The Egyptians had endured a considerable burden on Britain's behalf during the war. They had, however, been influenced by President Woodrow Wilson's principles of self-determination and democracy and especially by the promise of independence to the former provinces of Turkey. Nevertheless, Zaghlul had been refused permission to go to London to lobby for Egyptian independence and his arrest and deportation (to Malta) provoked the violence. The Egyptian police and army were largely unaffected, though British troops were required to restore order.

Field Marshal Allenby was sent out as special high commissioner and he adopted a policy of conciliation, ordering the release of Zaghlul and his associates in April.

Above. Zaghlul Pasha, the Egyptian nationalist leader.

The Karolyi government falls in Hungary

The pro-Western Hungarian president, Count Karolyi, resigned on March 20 in protest against the demands made by the Allies regarding the future frontiers of Hungary.

Hungarian troops had been largely disbanded at the armistice, but hopes of being accepted by the Allies as one of the new nations, rather than as part of an old enemy, were disappointed. Hungary had been unable to prevent incursions by Czechs, Serbs and Romanians.

Led by Bela Kun, a Soviet agent, a Communist regime took over in Hungary. Kun promised Soviet assistance in expelling the invaders and at first enjoyed support from most classes. He attacked the Czechs, but was forced to withdraw from Slovakia by the Allies, while his increasingly dictatorial rule forfeited support at home. In August Kun fled to Russia. The old ruling class, led by Admiral Miklós von Horthy, took over, and began a purge of suspected revolutionaries, especially Jews (Kun was Jewish). ▶ *page 127*

British soldiers on duty at the Khyber Pass during the conflict with Afghanistan.

Massacre in Amritsar

The British general, Reginald Dyer, ordered his Gurkha and Baluchi troops to fire on an unarmed crowd at Amritsar in the Punjab, India, on April 13. Nearly 400 people were killed and 1000 wounded, including women and children, by rifle fire or in the ensuing panic.

Rioting had occurred throughout India after Gandhi's call for a strike by business people against proposed new security regulations, and the arrest of two well-known nationalist leaders in Amritsar resulted in violence on a large scale. Reinforcements were called in under Dyer, whose small force was confronted by a very large, hostile crowd. Nevertheless, he appears to have given the order to fire when the safety of his men was not threatened and after blocking the crowd's only escape route with armoured cars. He later justified his action as producing a 'necessary moral and widespread effect'.

The Amritsar massacre marked a turning point in the Raj. The great majority of Indians were henceforth hostile to British rule, and Gandhi's campaign of civil disobedience commanded wide support.

British-Afghan war erupts

The reluctance of the British Indian government to recognize the independence of Afghanistan resulted in the outbreak of the third British-Afghan war on May 3. Fighting was not very heavy and results were inconclusive.

Under the enlightened rule of Habibullah Khan, Afghanistan had preserved a policy of strict neutrality in the Great War. In February 1919 Habibullah wrote to the Indian viceroy demanding recognition of Afghan independence at the Paris peace conference. A few days later he was assassinated. His third son, Amanullah Khan, seized power after displacing his uncle and immediately declared Afghanistan's independence in both internal and external affairs. Hostilities between the British and Afghans continued until peace was agreed in August, with Afghan independence acknowledged.

1919

TREATY OF VERSAILLES

CIVIL WAR IN RUSSIA

Admiral Kolchak at the centre of a group of White Russian and Allied soldiers.

White Russian offensive in the east

In May the forces of Admiral Aleksandr Kolchak, which had begun an offensive towards the Volga in March, threatened Kazan and Samara. A diversion by the British in the north was planned to assist him, but no effective co-ordination was achieved with other White Russian forces.

Trotsky meanwhile had forged the Red Army into a highly efficient organization, while the Allied powers, having intervened against the Bolsheviks at too late a stage, were anxious to extricate themselves, and in some areas had already withdrawn. Kolchak's sanguine assurance that he would reach Moscow by June proved badly misplaced.

Germans sign treaty

On June 28 the First World War was officially concluded, when German delegates signed the Treaty of Versailles in the famous Hall of Mirrors. They emerged grim-faced, perhaps aware that they had also signed away their political lives. Crowds outside the palace cheered. More far-sighted observers shook their heads in dismay.

The Germans had anticipated, or hoped for, a peace based on Wilson's Fourteen Points. But any concept of a just peace had foundered on the desire of the victors to make Germany pay for their own losses and in particular the French desire to prevent Germany from ever becoming a military threat to France again.

Germany lost about 13 per cent of its territory, including all its overseas colonies. Its army was reduced to 100,000 men and all its weapons, including the navy, were confiscated. The Rhineland was occupied and permanently demilitarized, and France was granted temporary control of the industrially rich Saar. The treaty, which adopted a strong moral tone, permitted no negotiation of the terms and denied Germany membership of the League of Nations.

The trickiest problem was presented by reparations. The sort of sums the Allies spoke of were far beyond Germany's capability to pay. To bridge the gap between public expectations and economic reality was impossible, and in the end the precise amount was left open.

The Treaty of Versailles was deeply resented in Germany and the severity of its terms was later to be blamed for the rise of Nazism and for the Second World War. Other historians have remarked that if the terms have been rigorously enforced, many of Hitler's activities would have been impossible and Germany would never have been in a position to wage war in 1939.

The Treaty of Versailles concluded peace between the Allies and Germany. A series of additional treaties in 1919–20 settled affairs between other combatants.

Race hatred ablaze in Chicago

The drowning of a black youth off a segregated white beach in Lake Michigan in July sparked off racial violence in Chicago which began on July 20 and lasted for about two weeks. Nearly 40 people, mainly black youths, died and hundreds were injured as rival gangs burned buildings and looted stores.

The Chicago riots were a particularly noteworthy example of widespread social violence in the United States in 1919, which continued into the early 1920s. The Ku Klux Klan was active in the South, and approximately 70 blacks were lynched in the course of the year. There were serious race riots in 23 cities, as well as a series of national strikes – even (in Boston) a police strike. Distrust of 'foreigners' and a fear of mysterious subversives, usually dubbed anarchists, were other features of this disturbed era. The arrest, conviction and eventual execution of Nicola Sacco and Bartolomeo Vanzetti for murder – largely, it seemed, on the grounds that they were Italian – were symptoms of the current malaise.

Lloyd George, Orlando, Clemenceau and Wilson.

Romanians invade Hungary

As the Communist regime of Bela Kun fell from power in Hungary in August, Romanian troops took possession of Budapest on August 3. In spite of international protests they remained in occupation of the Hungarian capital for three months.

The conflict arose from frontier disputes during the peace settlement. In March a neutral zone had been delineated by the negotiators at Versailles, and Romania was given the right to occupy this zone. Reacting to Hungarian resistance, Romanian forces advanced farther, to the River Tisza, where they were stopped by the Allies. Bela Kun ordered another offensive against them in July, but was defeated, whereupon the Romanians, disregarding Allied protests, crossed the river and marched into Budapest.

D'Annunzio occupies Fiume

The Italian buccaneer-poet, Gabriele d'Annunzio, at the head of a group of volunteers, seized the port of Fiume (Rijeka) on the Adriatic on September 12. The city was currently the subject of international negotiations, and d'Annunzio's purpose was to establish a fait accompli.

Italy, in common with other countries, was dissatisfied with the peace settlement, which failed to fulfil all the promises that Britain, France and Russia had made in 1915 in order to entice Italy into the war on their side. The territorial acquisitions promised then had been designed to protect Italy from future Austrian aggression but, with the break-up of the old Habsburg empire, this threat no longer existed. The 1915 agreement would also have breached the principle of national self-determination by placing one million Yugoslavs under Italian rule. Italy was prepared to accept less than promised in Dalmatia if it received

Gabriele d'Annunzio in conversation with Mussolini.

Fiume, but this was resisted by Yugoslavia. The peace conference made no final decision.

Dissatisfaction with the results of the war, together with Italy's older domestic problems (such as the failure to deal with the intense social and economic distress in the south) tended to encourage extremism, and d'Annunzio's seizure of Fiume exposed the fee-

ble character of the government. It also encouraged chauvinism of the kind shown by Benito Mussolini's new Fascist party, which appealed to many people, both middle and working class, whose prosperity had been eroded by inflation and other economic difficulties. ▶ *page 133*

White Russians on the retreat

The White Russian forces advancing on both Russia's capital cities – old (Petrograd) and new (Moscow) – were checked on October 20. The Red Army, which had come near defeat, gained the upper hand.

The Allied intervention had ceased to have much effect, and foreign forces would have been withdrawn sooner but for unwillingness to leave the White Russians, who had been largely supplied by the Allies, in the lurch.

Of the three White Russian armies Kolchak's had failed first. Confronted with the full force of the Red Army on the Volga, he had been defeated. In November Omsk was lost and Kolchak re-

signed soon afterwards. Denikin made rapid progress from the south during the summer, and by October he was less than 200 miles from Moscow. At the same time Yudenich was approaching Petrograd. However, he got no farther, while Denikin, who posed the greatest threat and was now accordingly confronted with the main force of the Red Army, was resoundingly defeated at Orel. The rapid collapse of the

anti-Bolshevik forces was due as much to their failure to arouse support among the local people as to military events.

By the end of the year nearly all Allied forces had been withdrawn from Russia, although the Japanese still occupied Vladivostok and parts of the Pacific coast. Denikin's army, or what remained of it, had retired to the Crimea, where it was reorganized by Denikin's former subordinate, General Wrangel.

The White Russian general, Pyotr Wrangel.

1919

JULY
20 Chicago torn by race riots
22 Hungarians attack Romanians

AUGUST
1 Kun flees Hungary
3 Romanians occupy Budapest
8 Anglo-Afghan Treaty of Rawalpindi signed
19 Anglo-Persian treaty agreed
23 Denikin occupies Odessa
28 German troops crush revolt in Silesia
31 Denikin occupies Kiev

SEPTEMBER
10 Treaty of Saint Germain between Allies and Austria
11 British close down Irish Sinn Fein parliament
12 D'Annunzio seizes Fiume
15 Anglo-French agreement on Syria concluded
19 Allies evacuate Archangel
22 President Wilson suffers collapse

OCTOBER
20 Denikin begins retreat
23 Police fire on nationalist demonstrators in Egypt

NOVEMBER
14 Romanians evacuate Budapest
14 Red Army occupies Omsk
16 British troops clash with Cairo demonstrators
19 U.S. Senate rejects Versailles treaty
19 Mussolini arrested after riots following Fascist election failure
27 Treaty of Neuilly between the Allies and Bulgaria

DECEMBER
12 Red Army occupies Kharkov
16 Red Army retakes Kiev
22 Partition of Ireland proposed

1920

Violence in the Holy City

On April 26 violent riots among the Arab population broke out in Jerusalem and other parts of Palestine. They were contained by the British military administration, which was sanctioned by the (currently unconfirmed) mandate of the League of Nations.

Arab leaders in Palestine had publicized demands for independence. They were wary of the British as authors of the Balfour Declaration, which was represented by Zionists as supporting the principle of a Jewish national home in Palestine. In July a civil administration took over, but unrest continued. ▶ page 137

British armoured car on patrol in Palestine.

Poles invade the Ukraine

Following the outbreak of war between Soviet Russia and Poland on April 24, the Poles invaded the Ukraine. On May 6 they captured Kiev.

The Versailles conference had established an independent Poland but, since Russia was not represented, it had been unable to fix the country's eastern frontier. Once the White Russians had been defeated, the Poles somewhat ambitiously advanced into the Ukraine and secured considerable initial success. The Red Army counter-attack then drove them back almost to Warsaw, where the Polish commander-in-chief, Józef Piłsudski, organized a successful defence of the capital and, by attacking the Soviet lines of communication, compelled a rapid retreat. Peace was then provisionally agreed.

Józef Piłsudski, Polish general and statesman.

French occupy Damascus

King Faisal at the time of the Paris peace conference.

On July 24 the French entered Damascus in accordance with the League of Nations award of a French mandate in Syria. King Faisal left the country.

The French and the British, themselves rivals for power and influence in the Middle East, had made contradictory promises to the Arabs. In March Faisal, recently an ally of the British, had been elected king by a national congress in Syria, where the French mandate was unpopular.

The French sent an ultimatum demanding acceptance of the mandate, which was rejected and, the League having officially confirmed the mandate, the French marched in.

In September the French created Lebanon, consisting largely of a former Christian, autonomous province, but including predominantly Muslim areas. Periodic demonstrations, often violent, took place in both Lebanon and Syria. ▶ page 138

Turkey truncated

The last of the treaties arranged at the Versailles conference, the Treaty of Sèvres with Turkey, was signed on August 10. It reduced the country to about one-quarter of its former size and was fiercely resented by the Turks.

The country was on the brink of civil war. Mustafa Kemal led nationalist resistance to the Allies and their 'puppet', the sultan, and set up a rival government in Ankara. The Greeks, already occupying Smyrna, advanced inland and war broke out between Greece and Turkey. The former Allies were divided in their attitude to this conflict (though increasingly aware that the Sèvres treaty was untenable), and the Turks had some help from Soviet Russia, now the leader of the growing anti-Western movement in a world shaken up by the political and social effects of the Great War.

Mustafa Kemal (centre) with supporters.

Armenia, engaged in frontier warfare with the Turks and still enduring murderous Turkish assaults, was another problem.

The United States and Britain both declined the offer of a League of Nations mandate for the country. ▶ *page 130*

Bloody Sunday massacre in Dublin

The increasing civil violence in Ireland reached a new pitch on November 21 when, in three separate incidents, 28 people were killed in Dublin. IRA hit men murdered 14 British officers and agents in their beds in the early hours, and 12 people died, shot or trampled upon, when British irregulars fired on a crowd in Croke Park.

British soldiers search a suspected IRA member at gunpoint. By the end of the 1920 independence for Ireland appeared inevitable.

Early in 1919 Sinn Fein members of parliament, who declined to take their seats in the British House of Commons in Westminster, set up their own parliament of Ireland (Dáil Eireann). They declared Irish independence and elected Eamon de Valera as president. The British authorities eventually closed this assembly down, but as they tried to maintain their grip on the country, more and more Sinn Feiners went to prison, where several died on hunger strike, and Ireland slid steadily towards civil war. It began with isolated acts of violence but soon developed into more general guerrilla war, aggravated by the use of British irregulars, known as the Black and Tans (from their uniform). Many atrocities were committed by both sides. ▶ *page 131*

Moplah rebellion in India

Hundreds of deaths were reported following the rebellion of the Moplahs of Malabar, which broke out on August 25. The revolt seriously damaged communal relations in India, which had improved as a result of Gandhi's co-operation with the Khilafat movement.

The movement, which had its origins in Muslim attempts to protect the integrity of Islam, had hoped to preserve the Turkish empire and the authority of the Turkish sultan as caliph. The Allied occupation of Constantinople was consequently resented. Two of the leading members of the movement had been chiefly responsible for encouraging the flight (*hijrat*) of thousands of Indian Muslims to Afghanistan in 1920–21, in which many people had died of privation.

The Moplahs were zealous Muslims who hoped to establish an independent Khilafat kingdom in Malabar. Thousands of Hindus were killed or forcibly converted to Islam in this endeavour, and successful guerrilla warfare was maintained against government forces for six months. Thereafter, with the collapse of the *hijrat* and the establishment of a secular state in Turkey, the Khilafat movement gradually faded away.

Greek artillery in action against the Turks.

Reza Khan takes over in Persia

Early in the morning of February 22 Reza Khan, commanding 4000 mainly Cossack troops, arrived in Tehran. He had made a rapid move from Tazvin, destroying communications as he went and overthrowing the government almost without firing a shot.

Reza Khan's intervention was welcomed by nationalists exasperated by the weakness and corruption of the current government, a symptom of which was the Anglo-Persian treaty of 1919. While officially acknowledging Persian independence, this treaty, its acceptance eased by fat British bribes, would in effect have made Persia virtually a British protectorate. The treaty was denounced by Reza Khan's government (which he controlled, though holding only minor office himself), while a treaty with Soviet Russia, renouncing Russian influence in Persia, was signed the same week. ▶ *page 138*

Reza Khan, the new ruler of Persia.

Greeks defeated at Sakarya river

The Greek advance towards Ankara was checked on August 24 by Kemal Pasha on the Sakarya river. The Greeks were compelled to retreat.

The Greek attack, with a poorly equipped army, was, in the words of the British prime minister Lloyd George, himself a fervent philhellene, a mad enterprise. The Greeks had some success early in the year, taking Afyon and Eskiskehr in April, but were then forced to withdraw towards Smyrna (Izmir). They renewed their offensive in July, largely to forestall a Turkish attack, recovered lost ground and appeared to be threatening Ankara before they were decisively defeated. ▶ *page 133*

Abd-el-Krim routs Spaniards in Morocco

In September Abd-el-Krim inflicted a comprehensive defeat on a force of 20,000 soldiers in Spanish Morocco. The survivors were chased back to Melilla.

This setback for the Spaniards forced them to withdraw from the interior, allowing Abd-el-Krim, who was an Arabic scholar as well as a dynamic Berber leader, to organize a rudimentary republic among the Rif tribes, based on his capital, Ajdir. ▶ *page 140*

Attempted monarchist coup fails in Hungary

On October 25 the former Austrian emperor and Hungarian king, Karl von Habsburg, attempted to regain the throne. He marched on Budapest with 12,000 men, but was defeated by the forces of the regent, Miklós von Horthy.

Hungary was riven by the confiscations of the Versailles settlement, by the 'Red Terror' of Bela Kun followed by the 'White Terror' of the reaction, by conflicting social grievances, by runaway inflation and by the presence of thousands of refugees from the forfeited territories. The ex-emperor Karl had made one unsuccessful attempt to return to Hungary in March. His second attempt also failed. Under pressure from the great powers the Hungarian parliament subsequently passed a law declaring that the Habsburgs had permanently forfeited the throne.

Irish Free State gains independence

On December 6 a treaty was signed providing for an autonomous republic in Ireland – the Irish Free State. Six counties of Ulster (Northern Ireland) opted for continued union with Britain, an expedient accepted by Irish republicans as a necessary but temporary arrangement.

A truce in the summer had ended the guerrilla warfare in Ireland, in which about 700 people had died, and the Free State treaty followed months of intense and often acrimonious negotiations. The precise border between north and south was left to the decision of a commission. The agreement represented the best compromise that could be attained at the time without full-scale war but proved to be burdened with future trouble – imminently for the Irish signatories (such as the IRA leader Michael Collins, who remarked that he was also signing his death warrant), in the longer term for Britain and the people of Northern Ireland. ▶ *page 132*

Regular Irish troops firing on rebels.

1922

Soviets and Germans sign surprise treaty

Soviet delegates in Berlin before the Rapallo conference.

Western representatives at an economic conference in Genoa in April found the headlines had suddenly been stolen from them by an unexpected deal made on the side. Russian and German representatives had taken the opportunity to sign an agreement at Rapallo on April 16.

On the German side the chief reason for this unexpected alliance was desperation at the prospect of reparations, impossible to pay (especially with the German mark made practically valueless by hyperinflation), yet constantly insisted on – especially by France. One hidden result of the Rapallo agreement was that Germany was enabled to build armaments in Russia, forbidden by the Versailles treaty.

The agreement was signed for Germany by the foreign minister, Walter Rathenau, a moderate (and a Jew), who was murdered two months later by an extreme group dedicated to eliminating people (like Rathenau) who were determined to re-establish Germany's status as a respectable great power by a co-operative policy on reparations. Rathenau, like Liebknecht and Luxemburg in 1919, was a victim of an epidemic of political assassinations in Germany after the war.

General Wu victorious in Chinese civil wars

On May 5 the northern leader, General Wu P'ei-fu, defeated his chief rival, Chang Tso-lin, and drove him back to Manchuria. The victory was so complete that Wu was left practically unchallenged in the north of China and was able to make an effort to unify the country. A separate government, mainly Kuomintang (Nationalist), existed in Canton under Sun Yat-sen.

The collapse of authority in China dated from the death of President Yuan Shih-k'ai in 1916. Conditions deteriorated further after the end of the First World War. Much of the country, north and south, was dominated by quarrelsome war lords, who fought one another, raised private armies by means of conscription, levied destructive taxes and generally devastated the economy. General Wu's efforts to reunite the country soon faltered, partly owing to lack of funds. However, two powerful centralizing forces were at work: nationalism, currently represented by Sun Yat-sen's precarious hold on Canton, and communism. The Communist party was founded in 1921 with a handful of members, many of them associated with the 'May 4' movement (the popular protest against the peace settlement of 1919). It sought a solution for China's chronic instability in Marxism and received advice from agents of the Comintern. ▶ *page 140*

Above. General Wu, virtual ruler of northern China.

Right. Armed IRA men patrolling the streets of Dublin.

Michael Collins assassinated

The Irish leader Michael Collins, currently a government minister as well as commander-in-chief, was killed in an ambush in Cork on August 2. His death was one of many in the civil strife which re-engulfed Ireland after the creation of the Irish Free State.

The Irish delegates had signed the Free State agreement as the only alternative to 'immediate and terrible war'. The treaty came within a few votes of defeat in Dáil Eireann, and the new state was riven by civil war between those who supported the treaty (which left Ireland's constitutional position somewhat vague) and those Sinn Feiners, like Eamon de Valera, who opposed it for surrendering too much – not least the six counties of Northern Ireland. The complete independence of the Irish republic was not achieved until 1937, while the division of the country into north and south proved permanent.

Turks confront British at Chanak

A new international crisis arose when the Turkish troops of Mustafa Kemal, continuing their successful offensive against the Greeks, confronted a small British force at Chanak on the Dardanelles on September 16. Briefly, the British government of Lloyd George seemed prepared to contemplate war.

Earlier in the month the Turks had completed their rout of the Greeks by taking Smyrna (which in an excess of enthusiasm they largely burned down). Kemal now decided to make good the Turkish claim to eastern Thrace, currently occupied by the Greeks. A small Allied force was stationed on the eastern shore of the Darda-nelles, but the French and Italians had recently withdrawn their contingents since they favoured the Turkish nationalists and distrusted British policy. Britain found no support among the great powers nor, significantly enough, among the dominions (the Canadians in particular showed that their foreign policy would no longer be dictated by London). Kemal was not anxious to attack the British either, especially since the armistice arranged at Mudania conceded Turkish sovereignty on the European side of the straits.

Kemal's success enabled him to establish the Ankara government as the unchallenged ruler of Turkey. The ancient Ottoman sultanate was ended, though the sultan retained his spiritual position as caliph (an arrangement contrary to all Islamic tradition). ▶ *page 134*

The city of Smyrna ablaze after its capture by Turkish forces.

The Fascists march to power

On October 28, 25,000 of Mussolini's Fascists began a concerted march on Rome from four different directions. King Vittorio Emanuele III summoned Mussolini (who did not take part in the march) to the Quirinal palace and invited him to form a government.

Negotiations about a role for the Fascists in government had been continuing for some time. The March on Rome was designed as a show of strength, but such was its success that it amounted to a bloodless revolution and Mussolini was able to demand not just a cabinet post but the post of prime minister. ▶ *page 134*

King Vittorio Emanuele.

French troops occupy the Ruhr

On January 11 French and Belgian troops marched into the German industrial region of the Ruhr. Their action, prompted by frustration at Germany's failure to pay war reparations, was deplored by Britain, the United States and other friendly nations.

The threat of occupation had been used before in order to compel Germany's compliance. In 1921 Allied troops had occupied certain Rhineland cities after Germany rejected Allied proposals, and they were still there. The occupation of 1923, intended to divert all production to France, was a much more serious affair.

The German government pro-tested and immediately ceased all reparations payments to France and Belgium. Officials in the Ruhr were instructed not to obey French orders, while the miners and steel workers mounted a campaign of passive resistance. The French expelled, fined or imprisoned recalcitrant German officials and erected a customs barrier around the region.

The cost of what amounted to strike pay for the workers in the Ruhr delivered the final blow to German finances. The mark became worthless (about 20 billion to the pound), thus providing further stimulation to civil unrest and political revolt. In September the new German government of Gustav Stresemann declared a national emergency and ended passive resistance. The French, while making little profit from the occupation themselves, continued supporting separatist movements in the Rhineland.

Turkey reaps fruits of victory at Lausanne

The Treaty of Lausanne was signed on July 24. The Turkish delegation, led by Ismet Inönü, gained more or less all it wanted. It did not attempt to claim the former Arab provinces, conceded Cyprus to Britain, the Dodecanese to Italy and some Aegean islands to Greece, but all genuinely Turkish territory of 1914 was restored.

The Treaty of Lausanne replaced the Treaty of Sèvres (1920), which had been signed by the sultan's government in Istanbul, then already being superseded by the nationalist government in Ankara. Following their victory over the Greeks, the Turks had signed an armistice agreement at Mudania. The Lausanne treaty confirmed it, while withdrawing the Greco-Turkish frontier some distance into Thrace.

French soldiers on guard outside the general post office in Düsseldorf.

Ismet Inönü at Lausanne.

Italians seize Corfu

On August 31 Italian forces captured the Greek island of Corfu, after a preliminary bombardment. The action followed an Italian ultimatum to Greece two days earlier, to which the Greek government had been slow to respond.

The ultimatum was provoked by the assassination, on Greek soil, of a group of Italian officers who were part of an Allied delegation arbitrating the Greek-Albanian frontier. Mussolini's ultimatum, characteristically high-flown, demanded among other compensations a large indemnity, and the attack on Corfu illustrated the Fascist determination to raise Italy to the status of a great power, no longer subservient to France or Britain.

The Corfu incident also presented the League of Nations with its first opportunity for international arbitration. Its decision, though favourable to Italy, was accepted by Greece, and the Italians withdrew from Corfu at the end of September. ▶ page 136

Hitler makes a move in Munich

On November 8 Gustav von Kahr who, with the chief of police and the local army commander, was virtual dictator of Bavaria, was addressing a large meeting in the Burgerbrau Keller in Munich. The door burst open and a group of armed men in brown shirts burst in led by Adolf Hitler, waving a revolver and screaming in excitement, 'The national revolution has begun!'

Hitler had originally planned to stage his putsch in co-operation with Kahr and his associates, though their aims were different: Kahr wanted Bavarian secession while Hitler and the National Socialists (Nazis) wanted a Greater Germany. The attempted putsch collapsed next day when police dispersed a Nazi march through the city. Hitler, having reneged on his promise to commit suicide if the putsch failed, was arrested along with his most notable supporter, General Ludendorff. It looked like a comic-opera affair in a country hovering on the brink of political chaos, with civil war threatened from Saxony (which was increasingly under Communist influence), from Hamburg and other industrial centres, from the separatists in the Rhineland and the nationalists in the extreme north.

However, the situation in Germany was soon to improve, thanks to the Dawes Plan and other factors, and Hitler's beer-hall putsch was soon forgotten by most people. Hitler himself, in prison, began writing *Mein Kampf*. ▶ *page 153*

An artist's impression of Adolf Hitler addressing a meeting in the early 1920s.

Hitler with Ludendorff (centre) at the time of the Munich putsch.

Anglo-Iraqi treaty ratified

After a stormy special session of the Iraqi assembly the treaty with Britain was ratified on June 10, minutes before the deadline which the British had set as indication of the treaty's rejection.

The treaty, intended to clarify Britain's relationship with Iraq, had been discussed even before the coronation of King Faisal in 1921. There was a good deal of nationalist agitation and opposition from groups such as the Shi'ite clergy, and in 1922 the British commissioner had, during Faisal's illness, taken measures to suppress the opposition. Unrest caused repeated postponements of elections to the assembly, which did not meet until March 1924, and it soon appeared that in the current atmosphere the treaty was unlikely to command a majority. The British gave assurances that the more burdensome financial provisions would be revised after the treaty was ratified, and named June 10 as the deadline – the day before a scheduled League of Nations debate on Iraq. Having been (narrowly) passed, the treaty was then approved by the League of Nations in September as the basis for Anglo-Iraqi relations under the mandate.

Military takeover in Chile

Chronic instability combined with the fact of unpaid army salaries resulted in the takeover of the government in Chile by a military junta on September 5. Chile had experienced over 100 changes of government in the previous 30 years, and the military takeover marked the failure of the efforts of Alessandri Palma, the 'Lion of Tarapaca', to end the stalemate and enforce political and economic reforms.

The army was no more successful, and Alessandri Palma was invited back the following year. He made the condition that the constitution should be revised to end the dominance of the executive by the legislature, but was nevertheless forced out of office by yet another coup in October 1925.

Demonstrations in Sudan

On August 9 disturbances broke out in Khartoum and other places arising out of the Egyptian claim to the Sudan and the British insistence that their governor-general had sole authority. Meetings took place in London the following month but without agreement, and Zaghlul Pasha Saad, the Egyptian prime minister, thereafter adopted a more strongly nationalist line. The assassination of the British governor-general in November provoked fierce indignation in Britain, and what amounted to an ultimatum was delivered to the Egyptian government. Zaghlul resigned and was replaced by a more moderate ministry.

President Alessandri Palma of Chile who was forced out of office after a military coup.

THE LAST WORD.

ZAGHLUL PASHA. "BY THE WAY, WHAT'S THAT BIRD DOING HERE?"
MR. RAMSAY MACDONALD. "OH, THAT'S THOMAS'S. I BORROWED IT TO MAKE YOU FEEL AT HOME. IT COMES FROM AFRICA, LIKE YOU."
ZAGHLUL PASHA. "WELL, AS I WAS SAYING, I DESIRE THE COMPLETE SEPARATION OF THE SOUDAN FROM BRITISH CONTROL."
THE BIRD. "NO SEPARATION!" [*Exit* ZAGHLUL.
[Mr. J. H. THOMAS asserts that in South Africa (from which he has brought home a parrot or two) "Separation is a very old corpse."]

A comment by *Punch* on the Sudan crisis.

The Matteotti crisis

The kidnapping and murder of the Italian Socialist leader Giacomo Matteotti on June 10 by Fascists led to a confrontation between Mussolini's government and the parliamentary opposition. Matteotti's death came as a great shock to world opinion and actually threatened to bring down the fascist regime in Italy.

Having first entered the Italian Chamber of Deputies in 1919, Matteotti had subsequently become general secretary of the Italian Socialist party and was a vigorous opponent of fascism. Only a few days before his disappearance he had delivered an outspoken denunciation of the use of violence by Fascists during election campaigns.

When the news of Matteotti's kidnapping became known the anti-Fascist deputies withdrew from parliament in protest. However, their attempts to organize concerted efforts in order to bring about the overthrow of Mussolini proved completely ineffective. Mussolini himself subsequently took the offensive and gradually eliminated all democratic opposition to his regime, establishing a virtual dictatorship.

Wahhabis take Mecca

On October 13 the forces of ibn-Saud gained possession of Mecca. Coming soon after their victory at At Ta'if, their action met little opposition. Ibn-Saud himself entered the holy city in December.

In the early years of the century Abdul-Aziz II ibn-Saud, founder of the modern kingdom of Saudi Arabia, had already made considerable progress in re-establishing Wahhabi control of Arabia. By his policy of forming military and agricultural colonies with Bedouin groups he had laid the basis for a powerful army. During the First World War, surrounded by enemies, he was forced to lie low, while Sherif Husain, in alliance with the British, built up a strong position in the Hejaz.

In 1919 ibn-Saud moved against King (as he had now become) Husain. His son captured the province of Asir – between the Hejaz and the Yemen – in 1920, and the following year ibn-Saud took over northern Arabia after defeating his dynastic rival, ibn-Rashid (who had sided with the Turks in the war). Meanwhile, with British support, Husain's sons, Faisal and Abdullah, had become kings of Iraq and Transjordan respectively, so that the Wahhabi kingdom was surrounded by British-supported states. Border incidents were common, and in 1923 the British called the concerned parties together at a conference in Kuwait. In early 1924 the conference collapsed without any agreement, and in September the Wahhabis renewed the attack on the Hejaz. After the capture of Mecca King Husain abdicated, leaving his son to face what, by the end of the year, had become a very doubtful inheritance. ▶ *page 140*

Ibn-Saud, ruler of the kingdom of Saudi Arabia.

New wave of Jewish immigrants to Palestine

Allenby Street, Jerusalem, in 1924 at the time of the fourth *aliyah*.

In the course of 1924 Jewish immigrants to Palestine totalled about 14,000. This was the beginning of the fourth *aliyah*, which continued for about two years. About half the new arrivals came from Poland.

The migration was sparked off by anti-Semitic legislation in Poland, and consisted principally of people from a higher social class than manual labourers. One result was a mushrooming of small shops in Tel Aviv and Haifa. The fourth *aliyah* caused disquiet within the Zionist movement and also in Palestine, where the British authorities were becoming less sympathetic and the Arab population was by now thoroughly hostile. ▶ *page 145*

1924

JANUARY
9 Secessionist Rhineland leader Heinz assassinated
21 Death of Lenin
27 Italo-Yugoslav pact cedes Fiume to Italy

FEBRUARY
4 Gandhi released from prison

MARCH
3 Caliphate abolished as Turkish republic is secularized
25 Greece proclaimed a republic

APRIL
1 Hitler sentenced in Munich
6 Fascists win Italian election by intimidation and fraud
13 Referendum confirms republic in Greece
16 Germany accepts Dawes Plan for reparations

MAY
7 Haya de la Torre founds Aprista party

JUNE
10 Italian Socialist leader Matteotti murdered by Fascists
10 Anglo-Iraqi treaty ratified

JULY
6 Anti-government revolt in São Paulo leaves 300 dead

AUGUST
9 Nationalist disorders in Khartoum

SEPTEMBER
5 Military junta takes over in Chile
8 British reinforcements sent to Shanghai amid rising unrest
13 Wahhabi victory in the Hejaz
16 Revolt in Georgia crushed by Red Army
18 Gandhi begins fast in protest against Hindu–Muslim conflict

OCTOBER
2 League of Nations adopts Geneva protocol
13 Lu Yung-s'ang surrenders in Chinese civil war
13 Ibn-Saud takes Mecca

NOVEMBER
19 British governor-general of Sudan assassinated in Cairo
24 Zaghlul Pasha Saad resigns as Egyptian prime minister
26 Trotsky denounced in Soviet Union
30 Franco-Belgian forces complete withdrawal from Ruhr

DECEMBER
1 Calles inaugurated as Mexican president after Obregón crushes revolt
5 Press censorship in Italy
20 Hitler released from prison
24 Albania declared a republic

1925

Kurdish rebellion against Turkey

On February 25 a rebellion among the Kurds broke out in the Taurus mountain region, led by tribal chiefs such as Sheikh Said. The Turkish government was taken by surprise and at first the Kurds had considerable success.

The Kurds had suffered heavy casualties in the Caucasus and Mesopotamian fronts during the First World War, and they sent a representative to the Paris peace conference demanding independence for Kurdistan. The Treaty of Sèvres had delineated provisional boundaries of Kurdistan, but in the Treaty of Lausanne Kurdish nationalism was ignored, and the northern boundary of Iraq was left to be settled by agreement between Turkey and Britain, with League of Nations arbitration if necessary.

Once the Turks were able to put regular troops into the field, the Kurds were swiftly defeated and their leaders captured. Nearly 50 of them were executed after court martial in August; others were subjected to internal exile.

The Druse rise against the French

A rebellion broke out against French rule in the Jabal Druse in Syria on July 20. It was led by Sultan el-Altrash, and spread rapidly to other parts of the country.

The French mandate in Syria was unpopular from the first, having been imposed by force after the creation of a Syrian kingdom with an independent government. The French divided the country into four states, each with its own constitution which, however, was worth little more than the paper it was written on, since real power remained firmly in French hands. There were violent protests, most notably in Damascus, but the Druse rising was more serious. Within a few weeks the rebels invaded Damascus and formed common cause with the nationalists, setting up a revolutionary government in the Jabal Druse.

Kurdish tribesmen. Resurgent Kurdish nationalism was one of the legacies of the First World War.

Reza Khan Pahlavi seated on his golden throne.

Reza Khan becomes shah of Persia

A constituent assembly elected Reza Khan Pahlavi shah of Persia on December 16. Scenes of vast public enthusiasm greeted the official proclamation. The new shah later declared his eldest son, Shahpur Muhammad Reza Pahlavi, to be the Crown Prince.

Reza Khan, having already appointed himself prime minister, was granted supreme military powers by the Persian parliament in February. Six months later he asked for the crown, and Sultan Ahmed Shah who, bereft of support, had left the country two years earlier, was deposed by a vote of parliament.

Mosul question resolved

A long-running dispute between Iraq and Turkey over the northern frontier of Iraq, including the Mosul area, was finally settled on December 16 following a visit to the region by a League of Nations mission. The city of Mosul, a historic communications centre, had lost much of its commercial significance after World War I when Iraq achieved independence from Turkey. However, the growing importance of the surrounding oil fields had become a potential source of conflict between the two countries and Turkey continued to lay claim to the territory. The Permanent Court of International Justice delivered its verdict in favour of Iraq, this award being subsequently confirmed by the Treaty of Ankara.

***Punch* reviews the Iraqi-Turkish dispute.**

ONE GOOD "TERM" SUGGESTS ANOTHER.

Mr. Amery. "WHY SHOULDN'T THIS OTHER BOUNDARY QUESTION BE SETTLED OVER A GLASS OF THE 'SPIRIT OF LOCARNO'?"
The Turk. "THANK YOU—MOSUL FOR ME."

League of Nations keeps the peace

An informal gathering of signatories of the Locarno Pact and their wives.

The League of Nations, in spite of the non-membership of powerful countries, notably the United States, had considerable success in arbitrating minor international disputes in the 1920s. In 1925 Chile and Peru accepted the League's decision in a boundary dispute, while the Greek occupation of Bulgarian territory in October was also settled by the League. Whether it would be equally successful when great powers were involved remained to be seen.

However, the international scene appeared far more promising in this respect at the end of 1925 thanks to the series of European treaties known as the Locarno Pact. Broadly, their effect was to guarantee the maintenance of peace in western Europe. They involved mutual guarantees between the main European powers (but excluding the Soviet Union) and, more specifically, treaties between France and Poland and France and Czechoslovakia assuring military support in case of attack. Germany renounced the use of force in order to change its western frontiers and accepted arbitration regarding its eastern ones.

1926

JANUARY–DECEMBER

**IBN SAUD
VICTORIOUS**

**CHINESE
NATIONALISTS IN
HANKOW**

Ibn-Saud conquers Arabia

The Wahhabi invasion of the Hejaz was led to a successful conclusion in January when ibn-Saud was proclaimed king of the Hejaz in the splendour of the great mosque of Mecca.

The other cities of the Hejaz had been overrun at the end of the previous year, while differences with the British over Transjordan and Iraq had been amicably resolved. Having become king of the Hejaz, ibn-Saud converted his title as sultan of Nejd into that of king. His possessions were renamed as the Kingdom of Saudi Arabia in 1932. ▶ *page 143*

U.S. troops return to Nicaragua

U.S. marines, who had been withdrawn from Nicaragua in 1925, returned on May 10. Civil conflict appeared to threaten foreign investments and, with U.S. support, Adolfo Díaz was restored to the presidency as a compromise candidate. The most notable of the opponents of Díaz and his U.S. supporters was General Augusto César Sandino, hero of the peasants.

**The Nationalist leader Chiang
Kai-shek (centre) with two of his
generals.**

Abd-el-Krim surrenders

After a conclusive defeat inflicted by overwhelming French and Spanish forces, Abd-el-Krim surrendered to Marshal Pétain on May 23. The Rif republic came to an end, though many years passed before Morocco could be said to be entirely under European control, and Abd-el-Krim was sent into exile on the island of Réunion, where he remained for over 20 years.

**The French and Spanish prime
ministers and Marshal Pétain
(seated left to right) at the
signing of the joint agreement
on Morocco.**

Chinese Nationalists take Hankow

In December the Chinese Nationalist army, led by Chiang Kai-shek, took Hankow (Wuhan), which became the Nationalist capital at the end of the year. The Nationalists had made rapid progress since the summer when Chiang Kai-shek launched the 'northern expedition' in an effort to unify the country.

The advance of the Nationalists was the result of skilful propaganda as much as military force. Since 1923 the Kuomintang had been advised by agents of the Comintern, who had turned it into a strong, centralized organization and had persuaded the Nationalists to co-operate with the Communists, at least on an individual level.

Chiang Kai-shek took over the leadership in 1925, after the sudden death of Sun Yat-sen, who assumed the status of a national hero: his 'three principles' – nationalism, democracy and livelihood (or, as some said, socialism) – were the rallying cry of the Nationalists.

Chiang Kai-shek, Sun's former lieutenant, threatened the authority of Sun Chu'ang-fang and Wu P'ei-fu, the chief powers in the north, by taking Hankow and its sister cities. The more radical elements of the Kuomintang, aroused the people by attacking foreign imperialists and local landlords, which led to the despatch of Western forces to protect the concessions. Meanwhile Chiang prepared to carry his advance into the lower Yangtse basin. ▶ *page 142*

Sun Yat-sen, who remained a hero to Nationalists and Communists alike after his death.

A cavalry patrol of Chiang Kai-shek's troops riding through the streets of Canton.

JANUARY

3 General Pangalos becomes dictator in Greece
8 Ibn-Saud proclaimed king of the Hejaz

FEBRUARY

2 Military revolt in Portugal suppressed

APRIL

4 Severe Hindu-Muslim riots in Calcutta
24 Russo-German treaty reaffirms Rapallo agreement

MAY

4 General strike in Britain
10 U.S. troops sent to Nicaragua
14 Piłsudski takes over Warsaw by force
18 International conference on disarmament opens in Geneva
23 Abd-el-Krim surrenders to French army
28 Gomes da Costa controls Portuguese government

JUNE

1 Piłsudski elected president but installs his nominee Moscicki
5 Britain, Iraq and Turkey reach agreement on Mosul

JULY

9 Da Costa ousted by Fragoso Carmona in Portugal
10 Chiang Kai-shek organizes northern expedition into Kiangsi

AUGUST

2 Piłsudski makes constitutional changes to increase president's powers
22 Pangalos government overthrown in Greece
29 Nazi rally in Nuremberg

SEPTEMBER

7 Chiang Kai-shek takes Hankow
8 Germany admitted to League of Nations
11 Spanish referendum supports Rivera regime

OCTOBER

23 Trotsky expelled from central committee of Communist party

NOVEMBER

6 Ban on all opposition parties gives Mussolini absolute power
12 Nationalist revolt against Dutch rule in Java
20 Dominions gain complete autonomy at London conference
27 Italo-Albanian treaty gives Italy economic concessions
30 U.S. warships sent to China ports

DECEMBER

16 Military-backed Nationalist coup in Lithuania
25 Hirohito succeeds as Japanese emperor

1927

JANUARY–DECEMBER

ANTI-COMMUNIST
COUP IN SHANGHAI

VIOLENCE IN
VIENNA

Chiang Kai-shek breaks with the Communists

At dawn on April 12 the Chinese Nationalist leader, Chiang Kai-shek, made a decisive break with the Chinese Communist party by ordering a series of dawn raids in Shanghai. The main target was the labour unions and their organizers. Many leading Communists were killed; others went hastily underground.

Bloodshed in Vienna

The elegant city of Vienna, ancient capital of the old Habsburg empire, was plunged into violence for several days in mid-July as police and soldiers fired on rioting crowds, who burnt down the Palace of Justice. The riots were sparked off by the acquittal of extreme rightists for the murder of two Communists. The fear of communism was as strong in Austria as it was in Germany, and the authorities were inclined to anti-communist bias, as was suspected in this case. A number of people were killed during the worst of the violence in Vienna, and there was trouble in other parts of Austria throughout the summer.

The Kuomintang government had moved to Wuhan at the beginning of the year, where it became more radical in tenor. Meanwhile, Chiang Kai-shek set up his own headquarters at Nanchang, to the southeast, from which he gained control of the lower Yangtse valley by the end of March. The capture of Shanghai was facilitated by a Communist-led rising in the city, which had been in turmoil for most of the previous two years – especially since foreign troops had opened fire on demonstrators.

Chiang, formerly known as a progressive, thus opted for the right wing of the Kuomintang, and set up a separate Nationalist government in Nanking. This caused a split with the Wuhan government, but Chiang not only had the armies, he also had the money (thanks to his Shanghai business contacts). Moreover, he retained Soviet support in spite of the war waged sporadically on Communists in the cities. In June the Wuhan regime also turned against the Communists after the discovery of subversive plotting.

A number of Communist risings against the Kuomintang took place in August, notably the 'Autumn Harvest' revolt among the peasants in Hunan organized by Mao Tse-tung, the failure of which resulted in Mao's removal from the central committee and his flight to the mountains of Kiangsi. Some 6000 people were said to have been killed in a last-ditch Communist rising in Canton in December.

Chiang, having temporarily resigned office and removed himself from the scene (a ploy he had used before), was recalled by the reunited Kuomintang to undertake the campaign against the Japanese-supported warlord, Chang Tso-lin, in Shantung.

The bodies of Communists killed in mass-executions.

Mao Tse-tung (third from left) in 1927 at the time of the Nationalist-Communist rupture.

1928
JANUARY–DECEMBER

NATIONALISTS SEIZE PEKING

SAUDI ARABIAN REVOLT

Nationalists capture Peking

On June 7 the forces of Chiang Kai-shek occupied Peking. They met little opposition. The Manchurian warlord, Chang Tso-lin, had left the city four days earlier.

On their advance through Shantung, the Nationalists had clashed with Japanese troops. However, the Japanese government, foreseeing the inevitable fall of Peking, suggested that Chang Tso-lin should be allowed to withdraw to Manchuria and that the Nationalists should not advance into that province. (Chang never arrived: Japanese officers blew up his train, hoping to provoke their government into extending military control of Manchuria.)

With the capture of Peking, the Nationalists could claim to have unified China under their control and to have brought to an end the political disorder that had prevailed since 1916. The Western powers, especially the United States, were on the whole sym-pathetic and ready to end 'extra-territoriality' (though not so promptly as the Nationalist government desired). However, serious difficulties remained. Chiang Kai-shek's position was not challenged but Nationalist leaders were still divided among themselves on matters of policy, and their authority in the provinces was tenuous. Private armies still existed and taxes could not be gathered.

The trickiest problem was Manchuria. By the end of the year Manchuria was reunited with China, despite Japanese opposition, but the Japanese were still there and with a large degree of autonomy. Moreover, for Chiang the Communists presented a threat which had to be eliminated. ▶ *page 147*

Wahhabi revolt in the desert

In March raiding Wahhabi tribesmen of Arabia, out of Ibn Saud's control, threatened the (ill-defined) borders of Kuwait and Iraq.

Ibn Saud realized that the progress and stability of his regime depended on maintaining amicable relations with the West, and his conquest of the Hejaz, a much more cosmopolitan kingdom than the historically isolated deserts of inner Arabia, had not been followed by the Islamic puritanism widely expected. The tolerance of the Saudi regime was resented by the hard-core Wahhabis, with their tradition of religious xenophobia. Leaders of the desert brotherhood (*Ikhwan*) such as Faisal al-Dawish and Sultan ibn Bijad launched attacks on Iraq and its British protectors. British air attacks on the camel-riding Wahhabis were reinforced by gunships on the Euphrates and a patrolling armoured train.

The *Ikhwan* were finally defeated in 1930 and their leaders imprisoned in Riyadh, where they later died.

Chang Tso-lin, who was murdered by the Japanese.

The powers renounce war

On August 27 a dozen nations agreed to sign the Kellogg–Briand pact. Eventually 64 nations were to sign. The Kellogg–Briand pact originated in the proposal of Aristide Briand, the French foreign minister, that France and the United States should sign a treaty renouncing war as an instrument of national policy. The U.S. secretary of state, Frank B. Kellogg, suggested in response a multilateral pact to which all nations should have the opportunity of acceding.

1929

ROYAL DICTATOR IN YUGOSLAVIA

VIOLENCE IN PALESTINE

Yugoslav king assumes dictatorial powers

King Alexander of Yugoslavia as crown prince of Serbia.

Afghan king overthrown

On January 17, following the outbreak of civil war the Afghan capital of Kabul was seized by a usurper, Habibullah. King Amanullah abdicated and sought refuge in Kandahar.

Having secured the full independence of Afghanistan and international recognition of the kingdom in 1919–21, King Amanullah introduced a series of reforms intended to 'westernize'

On January 4 King Alexander of Yugoslavia (hitherto the Kingdom of Serbs, Croats and Slovenes) suspended the constitution and declared himself dictator. The royal pronouncement recognized parliamentary democracy as the most desirable system but stated that in current circumstances it was unworkable.

There was much to be said for the king's point of view. The major opposing forces in Yugoslavia were Serbian centralism and Croatian separatism, but the situation was complicated by numerous other conflicts, both political and personal. The king, who had led the Serbian forces in the Great War, was opposed to Serbian as well as Croatian nationalism and was exasperated with Serbian politicians. An administrative reorganization, which was intended to create a greater sense of union, only perpetuated Serbian dominance. The king, while trying to pick politicians from all parties, was in practice unable to gain the co-operation of leading Croats, and Croatian nationalism grew stronger. In short, the king's abandonment of parliamentary government failed to reduce – and perhaps exacerbated – the divisions among the South Slavs.

the country. His policy was fiercely resented by reactionary tribal elements, resulting in the loss of his capital and his throne. An attempt to regain both from Kandahar in the spring was unsuccessful. Habibullah, by nature and by upbringing a brigand, declared himself king and instigated a reign of terror which ended with his overthrow in October and the subsequent election as king of the enlightened Nadir Khan, Amanullah's cousin.

South American boundary dispute settled

A long-running boundary dispute was finally settled on February 21. U.S. arbitration had been unsuccessful in earlier attempts to find a solution to the argument between Chile and Peru over Tacna and Arica.

The Tacna–Arica dispute dated right back to 1883 when the treaty concluding the War of the Pacific had left the matter to be decided by a future referendum. Numerous attempts to effect this had been frustrated by the failure of the respective governments to agree to the terms under which the referendum should be conducted. In 1922 the U.S. president had stepped in as arbitrator, and in 1925 General Pershing had headed a commission to look into the matter. When this too failed, the secretary of state, Frank Kellogg, suggested ceding the area to Bolivia, which Chile accepted but Peru did not. The two governments resumed direct negotiations in 1928 and six months later agreed that Tacna should go to Peru and Arica to Chile.

King Amanullah visiting the British fleet at Portsmouth.

Incident at Wailing Wall

Vladimir Jabotinski, a prominent British Zionist.

In 1929 Palestine was peaceful. There had been no serious outbreaks of violence since 1921 and the British security forces had been reduced to a few aeroplanes and a squadron of armoured cars. Jewish immigration had fallen sharply during the previous three or four years. In fact, as a result of rising unemployment in the *Yishuv* (the Jewish community in Palestine), some Jews had left Palestine and returned to Europe. However, no one but the most incurable optimist could foresee a peaceful conclusion, satisfactory to all parties, to the simmering hostilities in Palestine. The violence that broke out on August 4 nevertheless took the British by surprise.

The economic situation was brighter in 1929, encouraging an increase in Jewish immigration. Arab resentment was further stimulated by the proceedings of the 16th Zionist Congress, meeting in Zurich. There, the bullish speeches of the Revisionists, the party led by Vladimir Jabotinsky, advocated massive Jewish immigration and the formation of a Jewish state spanning the River Jordan. Though the Revisionists had not secured acceptance of their policy, they frightened and infuriated the Palestine Arabs.

The small spark that was needed to set off a general outbreak was provided by a quarrel over access to the Wailing Wall (the Jewish shrine in Jerusalem alleged to be the remains of the Temple of Solomon), which was aggravated by the bellicose attitude shown by young Revisionist hotheads.

Violence rapidly swept the country. No one could deny that the Arabs were the aggressors, and the chief victims were inoffensive Orthodox Jews who had no interest in politics or a Jewish state. Massacres occurred at Safed and Hebron, where casualties would have been higher but for the single British officer present in the town who, armed with a revolver, diverted an angry crowd from the Jewish ghetto. There were exaggerated reports of large numbers of Arabs advancing over the border from Syria, and the British rushed in reinforcements from other parts of the Middle East.

By the end of the month order had been restored, and the British set up the usual commission of inquiry which reported, not unpredictably, that the root of the trouble was the Arabs' 'disappointment of their political and national aspirations and fear for their economic future'.

The Simpson Report, the work of a more searching, follow-up inquiry, resulted in a new statement of British policy in 1930 which voiced the need to restrict Jewish immigration and Jewish purchase of land. It thus appeared to contradict of the Balfour Declaration and was anathema to all Zionists. So powerful was the opposition that the British, in a further 'clarification', virtually scrapped this new policy, leaving the situation no nearer resolution. ▶ *page 161*

The interior of the Jewish hospital at Hebron, after it had been pillaged by rioting Arabs.

1930

JANUARY–DECEMBER

UNREST IN
SOUTH AMERICA

ANTI-COMMUNIST
ONSLAUGHT IN
CHINA

Mr Gandhi takes a pinch of salt

A new campaign of civil disobedience began in India in March, when Gandhi led a widely publicized 'March to the Sea', in protest against the hated salt monopoly. Starting out on March 12, with about 80 followers (the numbers increased as the march progressed), he walked about 250 miles to the sea at Dandi and symbolically broke the law by collecting salt on the shore.

The march caught the public's imagination and became something of a triumphal progress, while demonstrations in sympathy took place in many parts of India. Simultaneously other form of opposition began, including a boycott of imported cloth, another longstanding source of grievance.

A determined-looking Gandhi, accompanied by his supporters, takes part in the 'March to the Sea'.

Peruvian president ousted

After rebellion broke out in Arequipa, southern Peru, on August 25 President Augusto Leguía was forced to resign. The leader of the revolt was General Luis Sánchez Cerro, and its immediate purpose was to prevent the autocratic Leguía, who had secured previous re-election by changing the constitution, from running for yet another term. The radical Aprista movement, founded by Haya de la Torre, which encouraged increasing opposition to Leguía, also inspired the harshest criticism of Sánchez Cerro after he became president in 1931 and adopted emergency powers to deal with opponents. Leguía died in prison in 1932. ▶ *page 160*

Haya de la Torre, Peruvian political leader.

Irigoyen overthrown in Argentina

President Hipólito Irigoyen was forced to resign by General José Uriburu, who took over the government after a huge but orderly demonstration in Buenos Aires on September 4 clearly indicated that the elderly president had lost virtually all popular support.

Anti-democratic feelings had increased in recent years, largely due to the influence of Mussolini, while Irigoyen's government, increasingly hidebound and unable to solve the severe economic crisis, had lost the vital support of organized labour by taking a hard line against strikes during the previous months.

Revolt in Brazil

On October 14, only six weeks after the revolution in Argentina, the 'old republic' fell in Brazil. Rebellion broke out after elections in which (as usual) the candidate of the administration was declared the winner. Its successful leader was Getulio Vargas.

Economic difficulties had been exacerbated by the collapse of the scheme in which the government controlled the coffee industry, Brazil's main export earner. Speedy industrialization and the spread of cities, combined with a high proportion of unassimilated immigrants, contributed to urban unrest. Rivalry among the individual states was also a crucial factor. Vargas came from the rapidly growing state of Rio Grande do Sul, which felt unjustly excluded from a government traditionally dominated by the central states, and he was supported by the state of Minas Gerais, which also objected to the declared result of the recent election. Vargas became president with enhanced powers: he was to remain in office until 1945.

Getulio Vargas, the new president of Brazil.

Polish elections represent Piłsudski victory

Following the arrest and persecution of opposition leaders in the *Sejm* (Polish parliament), new elections were held on November 23. The government scored an unsurprising victory, which Piłsudski interpreted as a mandate for a new constitution.

In his coup d'état of 1926 Piłsudski had left the parliamentary system more or less intact, though the powerlessness of the members resulted in the disintegration of the major parties and reduced domestic politics to the simple alternative of support for or opposition to Piłsudski. There was sufficient opposition in the parliament elected in 1928 to make co-operation with Piłsudski practically impossible and, as tension increased in 1930, Piłsudski moved against his chief opponents.

Latin American revolution

During 1930 and 1931 more than half the republics in South and Central American underwent some sort of revolution, or at least an irregular change of government. In general, these non-constitutional changes took place with very little violence – in contrast with the savage events of the Mexican Revolution. Typically, the standard of revolt was raised, an unpopular incumbent recognized the writing on the wall – and resigned.

There were ample reasons for social and political dissatisfaction in Latin America and, though they varied from state to state, corruption, administrative incompetence and arbitrary rule were fairly common phenomena. However, the reason for the overthrow of so many governments at this specific time must be sought in the effects of the world-wide economic depression that followed the business slump of 1929. When times are bad governments, even worthy ones, take the blame. Democratic governments are especially vulnerable and, although many of the revolutions of 1930–31 included dislike of dictatorship among their motives, the ultimate result was, as in Europe, an increase in dictatorial rule.

Chiang Kai-shek begins campaign against Communists

On December 15 the Nationalist Chinese government launched a campaign against the Communists. It was aimed at the destruction of both the Communist armed forces and of the 'soviets' established in southern Kiangsi, in parts of Fukien and Hunan, and elsewhere.

Although the Nationalist government claimed that it had united China under its control, large areas, especially in the south and west, remained unruly. From 1927 the Communists presented the greatest threat, having created a substantial military force from landless peasants and deserting soldiers. As Mao Tse-tung, on the verge of proclaiming a 'soviet republic' in Kiangsi, recognized (though his Russian advisers did not), the revolutionary force in China had to be generated among the peasants, not among the (rather small) class of industrial workers – the mainspring of Marxist revolution in Europe.

The campaign of December 1930 was the first of five military efforts against the Communists within three years. The Nationalist government, among whose leaders Chiang Kai-shek remained dominant, steadily gained the upper hand, but the Communist party was far from extinguished and a greater menace, from Japan, introduced a complicating factor. ▶ *page 150*

Mao Tse-tung with companions, including Chu Teh (second right), the Communist army commander.

JANUARY
26 Jawaharlal Nehru demands independence on behalf of the Indian National Congress
28 Spanish dictator Primo de Rivera resigns
31 Naval conference meets in London

FEBRUARY
12 Indian National Congress calls for new civil disobedience campaign
24 Reports of killing of Russian kulaks

MARCH
2 Stalin pronounces success of collectivization
12 Gandhi begins 'March to the Sea'

APRIL
21 London conference agrees limit on warships

MAY
5 Riots in India after the arrest of Gandhi
17 Young Plan comes into force
22 Syrian constitution promulgated

JUNE
8 Romanian king, Ferdinand, ousted by vote of parliament
30 Last French troops leave the Rhineland
30 Britain acknowledges Iraqi independence

JULY
10 Chinese Communists attack Hankow
20 Riots in Egypt against Britain and the monarchy
30 Fascist National Union party founded in Portugal

AUGUST
4 Red Army fires on strikers in Odessa
25 Peruvian revolution

SEPTEMBER
4 Argentine revolution
15 Nazis become second largest party in Germany

OCTOBER
14 Revolution in Brazil

NOVEMBER
23 Polish elections produce a pro-Piłsudski majority
14 Assassination attempt on Japanese prime minister Hamaguchi

DECEMBER
15 Nationalists launch campaign against Communists in China
16 Abortive revolution in Spain

PERSECUTION OF THE KULAKS

REPORTS of the murder and exile of kulaks in Soviet Russia reached the west in February. It appeared that in many places the Communist party's announced aim to 'liquidate the kulaks' as a social class was applied literally to individuals.

The name 'kulak', meaning 'tight-fisted', was the opprobrious nickname of the better-off peasants – those who produced surplus crops and employed paid labourers. (Later, it meant simply all peasants who opposed the collectivization of agriculture.) The kulaks were blamed for the persistent failures of Russian agriculture, which resulted in serious famines during the 1920s and 1930s (the famine of 1931–32 was responsible for an estimated three million deaths), chiefly because this class of 'peasant capitalists' was seen as a potential threat to the Soviet system. In May 1918, during the period of 'war communism', a decree of the central executive committee of the Soviets had summoned 'all toiling and propertyless peasants to immediate union for a merciless fight against the kulaks'. Trotsky had endeavoured to split each village 'into two irreconcilably hostile camps' and to 'rouse the village poor against the village bourgeoisie'. Lenin had declaimed against the kulaks as 'criminals torturing the population with the hunger from which tens of millions are suffering'.

By the late 1920s agriculture was still the worst domestic problem in Russia, just as it had been before the Revolution. Despite the persecution of the kulaks in the phase of 'war communism', they continued to be the most productive farmers, and under the 'New Economic Policy' (1921) their numbers rose. The Soviet leaders' fear of 'peasant capitalism' increased proportionately and, after a spectacularly good harvest in 1925 had assuaged anxieties, a new progressive taxation system was introduced designed to fall heavily on the most prosperous peasants. Yields promptly decreased, as the better-off peasants began to refuse to sell their grain to the state at a fixed price. The government then returned to earlier, more direct policies, with committees of the poorer peasants in each community empowered to seize hoarded grain and to seek out places where it might be hidden. The kulaks then reduced production.

In 1929 it was decided to embark on large-scale collectivization of peasant smallholdings: peasants were not to be allowed to rent land or hire labour; local soviets were given authority to confiscate the property of kulaks and turn it over to the collective. Subsistence peasant farmers and wage labourers took this as an invitation to seize all the property of such people, often murdering them as well. An additional side-effect was that the harvest of 1929 was the smallest for five years.

Collectivization aroused such fierce and widespread hostility that the Soviet government was forced to moderate it. In the spring of 1930 Stalin announced that the party was 'dizzy with success' over collectivization and that therefore the programme should be relaxed in some respects.

The idealized portrayal of workers of a collective farm (right) stands in grim contrast to the mass starvation (opposite) which was the lot of many Russians both during the civil war and later when Stalin (above) ruthlessly enforced large-scale collectivization.

Destitute peasants in the Volga region.

Children near starvation quietly await their fate.

1931 Spanish king abdicates

Alfonso XIII, king of Spain.

In the wake of a sweeping republican election victory, King Alfonso of Spain abdicated on April 14. The monarchy had looked highly precarious since the resignation a year earlier of the dictator, Primo de Rivera, whose regime had been supported by the king.

The failure of the old regime to deal with the economic crisis and the inability of the army to crush opposition in Morocco brought Spain to the brink of rebellion. However, the victory of republicanism, though widely celebrated, looked unlikely to ensure stability. Long-established problems – the struggle between church and state, the separatism of Catalonia – combined with newer ones, notably the radicalization of the working class and the emergence of extreme nationalism and reaction, together with continuing economic distress, presented the republic with formidable difficulties. ▶ *page 162*

Japanese forces seize Mukden

Troops of the Japanese Kwantung army, whose main purpose was to patrol the South Manchurian railway zone, seized the city of Mukden on September 18. The pretext, convincing to no one, was that Chinese soldiers had tried to blow up a South Manchurian train.

The occupation of Mukden signalled the full occupation of Manchuria and a turning point in Japanese foreign policy. The invasion, though sanctioned by military chiefs in Tokyo, contradicted the policy of the Japanese government and marked the ascendancy of the military over the civilian power. The government had, in broad terms, sought amicable relations with the western nations, which were currently involved in negotiations with the Chinese Nationalist government to reduce foreign privileges in China, and with the Chinese Nationalists. This policy – and the credibility of the government – had been undermined by events, in particular the economic depression, which had drastic effects on the Japanese economy. The deepening unpopularity of the government weakened it in its dealings with the military. A planned coup, involving officers in both Tokyo and Manchuria, fizzled out in May; the 'Mukden incident' forced the government's hand.

Japanese troops enter Manchuria following the seizure of the city of Mukden in the so-called 'Mukden Incident'.

1932

Independent republic of Manchukuo proclaimed

On February 18 the independent republic of Manchukuo was proclaimed, covering the whole of Manchuria. Although under Japanese control, it was given an air of legitimacy by installing the ex-emperor P'u-Yi as head of state.

After their surprise seizure of Mukden, the Japanese rapidly secured other strategic centres. The Chinese, who never broke off diplomatic relations with Japan, appealed to the League of Nations, which condemned the Japanese takeover. The League was unable to make Japan withdraw from Manchuria, though Japan did withdraw from the League. The puppet state of Manchukuo was not recognized internationally except by Japan's Axis allies and by El Salvador.

P'u-Yi, puppet ruler.

War over the Chaco

The long-simmering dispute between Bolivia and Paraguay over the Gran Chaco ('big hunting ground') erupted into full-scale war in May. The dispute was sharpened by expectations of oil in the region, by economic decline connected with the world depression and by the Bolivian coup of 1931 which brought the bellicose Daniel Salamanca to the presidency. The war did not go well for Bolivia, however. Its invasion of Paraguay and seizure of Pitiantuta were swiftly reversed with heavy casualties. The conflict led to a series of further coups and severe economic distress in Bolivia and to heightened military prestige in Paraguay. A truce was arranged in 1935 and a settlement was finally reached in 1938 which gave most of the disputed region to Paraguay.

Peruvian force seizes Leticia

The Amazon border town of Leticia was seized by the Peruvians on September 1, precipitating a two-year war with Colombia. The crisis arguably prevented a conservative coup in Colombia by restoring national unity.

Both states had claimed the region, with its oil, until it was ceded to Colombia by treaty in 1922. The League of Nations restored it to Colombia again in 1933, and the decision was eventually accepted by Peru, which withdrew the following year.

Japanese attack Shanghai

Defending Chinese soldiers in trenches near Shanghai.

In a move that demonstrated that their territorial ambitions were not confined to the Manchurian provinces, the Japanese attacked Shanghai on March 28. Some fighting had taken place earlier, and foreign troops had been reinforced.

Chiang Kai-shek ordered the local Nationalist commander not to resist, since he regarded the Chinese Communists as a more immediate threat than the Japanese, but this order was disregarded. International protests and Chinese resistance induced the Japanese to withdraw about six weeks later. ▶ *page 152*

1933

HITLER BECOMES CHANCELLOR

SINO-JAPANESE TRUCE

U.S. marines leave Nicaragua

The inauguration of Juan Sacasa as president in Nicaragua on January 1 was followed by the withdrawal of the last U.S. marines, whose presence had been a dominating influence in Nicaragua since 1910, and the conclusion of the revolt of the Sandinistas. The real power in Nicaragua, however, now lay with the National Guard, trained by the U.S. marines, and its commander, Anastasio Somoza, the nephew of the president. Two years later Somoza was to depose his uncle and establish the rule of himself and his family, which lasted until 1979.

Anastasio Somoza, who became dictator of Nicaragua.

Japanese forces approach Peking

Beginning on January 30 Japanese and Manchurian forces rapidly occupied the northern Chinese province of Jehol (Ch'eng-te). The Nationalist Chinese leader in the north, Chang Hsueh-liang, resigned.

In retaliation for raids launched from Peking, the Japanese advanced farther, beyond the Great Wall, in April. Fighting was brought to an end by a truce in June which established a neutral zone south of the Great Wall. The Japanese takeover of Manchuria was thus implicitly acknowledged by China.

Chinese cavalry moving through rugged terrain on their way to the Jehol front.

Chinese troops use camels to carry supplies of arms and ammunition in their struggle with the ever-advancing Japanese

A convenient conflagration in Berlin

On the night of February 27 the Reichstag (imperial parliament) building in Berlin was burned down. A young Dutchman was caught in the building but clearly he had not acted alone. The Nazis, whose leader, Adolf Hitler, had been appointed chancellor a month earlier, promptly asserted that the fire had been caused by the Communists, preparatory to an intended coup.

Although it has never been proved, the most likely instigators of the Reichstag fire were the Nazis themselves. By saddling the Communists with the blame, Hitler was able to pass a series of 'emergency decrees' (never rescinded) which in effect destroyed civil liberties in Germany.

The elections, insisted on by Hitler as a condition of becoming chancellor, took place a week later. The National Socialist party gained 44 per cent of the votes which, with the 8 per cent of the conservative Nationalists, gave them a majority. Hitler then proposed the Enabling Laws which transferred all powers from the Reichstag to the government headed by himself. Although Hitler did not yet have complete control of the country, he had the legal framework for totalitarian rule. Within little more than a year his absolute dictatorship was established and all opposition silenced. ▶ *page 156*

The Reichstag building in flames. The incident came at a fortunate moment for Hitler.

RISE OF THE NAZIS

O N THE EVENING of January 30, 1933, a huge torchlight parade took place in Berlin. It was a celebration, organized by the National Socialist, or Nazi, party and among those taking part, such as military veterans' organizations, the most prominent were the brown-shirted SA (Sturmabteilung), the Nazis' private army. The parade signified the beginning of a new era, in which the glory of the German Reich would be restored. The event it celebrated was the appointment of the National Socialists' leader, Adolf Hitler, as chancellor of Germany.

The Weimar Republic in Germany had failed to overcome the huge difficulties – some old, some new – which faced it in the 1920s. Besides being saddled with responsibility for the hated Versailles settlement, with an anti-democratic officer corps, a pro-monarchist civil service and a powerful Communist revolutionary movement, it failed to solve the devastating economic problems presented first by runaway inflation, then by intense economic depression, in which unemployment exceeded five million. (Additionally, it lost the one statesman who might have preserved moderate constitutionalism, Gustav Stresemann, who died aged 51 in 1929.)

In these circumstances extremism flourished. The National Socialist party, which in the early 1920s had seemed to belong to the lunatic fringe, attracted enormous support, especially from the lower middle class of shopkeepers, white-collar workers, small farmers and the like, who had suffered most from inflation and recession. In the elections of September 1930 the party increased its seats in the Reichstag from 15 to 107. The Nazis could no longer be ignored. The question now was whether, or how, they would gain office.

The current chancellor, Heinrich Brüning, adopted the policy later exploited by Hitler of ruling by emergency presidential decree. He had no solutions, however, and after the International Court of Justice outlawed the 1931 customs union with Austria, provoking a severe financial crisis, his support crumbled and he was dismissed (March 1931) by President Hindenburg.

With nationalism gaining ground, conservative and military leaders were inclined towards co-operation with the Nazis, in spite of the fact that Hitler's total lack of morality or respect for law were known, as well as his virulent anti-Semitism and belief in violence. The Nazis, however, refused to co-operate with any government in which Hitler was not the chancellor. Brüning's replacement, Franz von Papen, believed that he could control Hitler, even as chancellor, in a government in which he was vice-chancellor. Few other Nazis would be admitted to the cabinet and Hitler would thus be outnumbered by the conservatives. His hands would in effect be tied. This erroneous belief was shared by Hindenburg, or those who advised him, and as a result Hitler was appointed chancellor in January 1933.

Hitler takes the salute at a march-past of SA men at Weimar in 1930.

Hitler with the aging President Hindenburg.

Mass arrests of their opponents by the Nazis.

Bonfire of 'anti-German' literature in Berlin in May 1933.

Hitler (with Goering) after his election as chancellor.

1934 Hitler's Night of the Long Knives

NAZI PURGE

LONG MARCH BEGINS

On June 30 Hitler struck against unwanted friends and hated foes alike when some hundreds of people were dragged from their beds and shot. The most surprising victims were Ernst Roehm, head of the SA (*Sturmabteilung*), and his colleagues. Others included former Chancellor Kurt von Schleicher and his wife.

Roehm was an old associate. He was also homosexual, which had become a rather obvious attribute of the SA generally, and he believed that the 'socialist' in the National Socialist party label meant just that. However, the reason for his assassination, which took place in a Bavarian resort hotel with Hitler himself present, was that he and the SA were profoundly disliked by the German military, with whom Hitler was keen to remain on good terms.

The purge of one Nazi paramilitary force left the way clear for the ascendancy of another, still more sinister one – the SS (*Schutzstaffel*), commanded by Heinrich Himmler.

Kurt von Schleicher, another of Hitler's victims.

Ernst Roehm, SA leader, murdered on Hitler's orders.

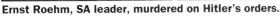

Nazi coup fails in Austria

In an attempted coup by Austrian Nazis on July 25, the chancellery in Vienna was seized and the chancellor, Engelbert Dollfuss, murdered. Nazi risings elsewhere were quickly snuffed out, however, and the group in the chancellery were forced to surrender.

In the face of German propaganda for *Anschluss* ('union'), the Austrian chancellor had sought support from Mussolini, who was not eager to acquire Hitler as a neighbour, and he purchased that support by allowing the Austrian military to proceed against the Social Democratic party. The harassed Austrian socialists rebelled in February, an action which resulted in their rapid destruction. The savagery of the army provoked international protests.

Dollfuss then took steps to increase his own dictatorial powers, but that did not prevent the attempted Nazi coup. Mussolini's reaction to this incident was to move Italian forces rapidly to the Austrian border, which discouraged Hitler from supporting the Austrian Nazis. Dollfuss was replaced by Schuschnigg, who maintained the dictatorial regime of his predecessor but exercised it more moderately. ▶ *page 166*

Kurt von Schuschnigg, the successor to Dollfuss.

Mao sets off on the Long March

On October 16 the Chinese Communist forces besieged in the mountains in Kiangsi decided to break out. About 100,000 men in five groups escaped from the trap and joined up again later, having evaded the surrounding troops of the Kuomintang.

Chiang Kai-shek had launched a series of attacks against the Communist stronghold since 1930. At first he had little success, but the fifth campaign, begun in October 1933, was the most serious effort so far, with some 700,000 troops (against the Red Army's 150,000), and the valuable assistance of the able German general, Hans von Seeckt.

After a year in which the noose was gradually tightened, the Communist command decided to break out. The original purpose was simply to escape, but after three months Mao Tse-tung's policy – to go north and fight the Japanese – was adopted.

The ensuing Long March, which took just over a year from the original breakout, became an almost mythic event in modern Chinese history. Of approximately 100,000 who set out, about one-third survived the journey (some of the missing were left behind to organize revolution in places they passed through). Those who completed the trek marched about 6000 miles, crossed 24 rivers, 18 mountain ranges (some under permanent snow) and occupied 62 cities. Fighting took place almost daily and conditions were generally appalling. Incidents of superhuman courage and endurance were numerous.

They eventually reached relative security in the remote northwest, around Yenan, where the future guidelines of party policy were hammered out in ideological debate and guerrilla training.

Above. Mao Tse-tung with Chou En-lai during the Long March.

Right. Hans von Seeckt, who assisted Chiang Kai-shek.

1934

JANUARY
7 Lutheran ministers in Germany denounce Nazi control of Church

FEBRUARY
9 Balkan entente (Greece, Romania, Turkey, Yugoslavia)
16 Austrian socialists crushed with extreme violence

MARCH
1 P'u-yi enthroned as 'emperor of Manchukuo'
16 French campaign against Berber insurgents in Morocco concluded

APRIL
7 Soviet–Finnish non-aggression pact
30 Dollfuss granted dictatorial powers in Austria

MAY
13 Truce agreed at Jeddah in Saudi–Yemeni 'Desert War'
15 Ulmanis assumes autocratic powers in Latvia
19 Military coup in Bulgaria
24 Colombia and Peru conclude Leticia dispute

JUNE
14 Hitler meets Mussolini in Venice
30 Nazi SA purged in Night of the Long Knives

JULY
3 Von Papen resigns as German vice-chancellor
25 Austrian chancellor Dollfuss assassinated
27 Italian troops sent to Austrian border

AUGUST
2 Hitler becomes head of state on death of Hindenburg

SEPTEMBER
18 Soviet Union becomes a member of League of Nations

OCTOBER
5 Moroccan troops crush Catalan rebels
6 Leftist revolt in Asturias
9 King of Yugoslavia and French foreign minister assassinated
16 Long March begins in Kiangsi
24 Gandhi leaves Congress party

NOVEMBER
30 Italian troops from Somaliland infiltrate Abyssinia

DECEMBER
1 Murder of Kirov sparks off repression in Soviet Union
16 Mussolini rejects League of Nations arbitration in Abyssinia
29 Japan renounces Washington naval treaty of 1922

1935

The Saar goes back to Germany

In a referendum supervised by the League of Nations the people of the Saarland voted on January 13 to resume German citizenship. Over 90 per cent of the votes were in favour of reunion with Germany. Most of the remainder were for independence.

The Saar was one acquisition made by the Hitler government using legal, if not fair, means (the voting was neither as free nor as secret as it was supposed to be). Under the Treaty of Versailles the coal-rich industrial region of the Saar was to be governed by a League commission, with the product of the mines going to

France as part of war reparations for 15 years, when its future was to be decided by referendum.

Nazi supporters in Saarbrücken noisily celebrate the reunion of the Saarland with Germany.

Venizelos plays his last card

On March 12 an attempted coup d'etat on behalf of the Liberals led by the veteran statesman Eleutherios Venizelos was crushed. Venizelos left for Crete, announcing his retirement from the political arena.

Politics in Greece had reached a state of deadlock in 1935, with the Populists controlling the lower chamber and the Liberals the senate. Crisis loomed with the declared intention of the Populists to restore the monarchy, anathema to Venizelos's party. The failure of the coup made the Populists' goal easier. A referendum in November approved the restoration of the monarchy; King George II returned to Athens a few days later.

The Greek statesman Venizelos.

Italian forces launch invasion of Abyssinia

On October 3 a full-scale invasion of Abyssinia (Ethiopia) by Italian forces began. The attack was hardly unexpected, since Mussolini had been publicly gearing up for it for nearly a year and less publicly for much longer. Within three days the Italians captured Adowa (Adua), the scene of their humiliating defeat in 1896.

Italian troops in Abyssinia. Their vastly superior military equipment ensured victory after a relatively easy campaign.

The first armed clash had taken place towards the end of 1934 at the oasis of Wal Wal, near the undefined border between Abyssinia and Italian Somaliland. The Italians demanded compensation and Abyssinia appealed to the League of Nations. By the time the League was in a position to arbitrate, however, it was obvious that Mussolini was bent on war. His aims were to demonstrate fascist Italy's status as a great imperial power, while gaining more colonial territory for the country's increasing population.

The Italians put 250,000 men into the field, backed by the weapons of modern military science, including poison gas. The original commander, a fascist, soon had to be replaced by the experienced and capable Marshal Pietro Badoglio, but there was comparatively little large-scale fighting, since the Abyssinians were hopelessly outgunned. The campaign was concluded in seven months with Badoglio's entry into Addis Ababa and the flight of the emperor, Haile Selassie. Guerrilla resistance continued after the conquest.

Italian aggression was condemned by the League, which imposed economic sanctions in November. These excluded oil, were not enforced by some countries, such as Germany, and proved totally ineffective. The episode demonstrated the inability of the League to deal with a determined aggressor and provided a valuable lesson for Hitler, soon to become Mussolini's ally.

Smoke from burning huts screens Italian soldiers during an attack.

British foreign secretary resigns over Abyssinian crisis

The British foreign secretary, Sir Samuel Hoare, resigned on December 18, following an outcry over the agreement made with France (the Hoare–Laval pact) ten days earlier. In effect, he had been made a scapegoat, since the agreement had received cabinet approval.

Mussolini had prepared the way for his invasion of Abyssinia by obtaining tacit French approval for the extension of Italian influence in northeast Africa early in 1935 during talks with the French prime minister, Pierre Laval, in return for Italian support for Austrian independence. He anticipated a similar attitude from Britain, but revelation of the Hoare–Laval pact, which seemed to condone the Italian aggression, roused a public storm in Britain. Hoare was replaced by Anthony Eden, known as an opponent of Italy. Nevertheless, the British government failed to take a strong line against Mussolini, hesitating (for example) to press for oil to be included in the League's economic sanctions. It did just enough to antagonize Italy, making nonsense of the Stresa pact of 1934 and helping to drive Mussolini into alliance with Hitler.

Sir Samuel Hoare arriving at the Foreign Office.

1936

GERMANY TAKES RHINELAND

REVOLT IN PALESTINE

Tokyo revolt

The intense factionalism and plotting that had become endemic in Japanese military and political circles came to a peak on February 26 when a regiment about to leave for Manchuria mutinied. The incident sparked off a revolt among junior officers.

Rebel units held much of Tokyo for three days, and many prominent politicians were assassinated, including the finance minister, Takahashi Korekiyo, who had been chiefly responsible for bringing Japan out of the depression but had angered the military by his opposition to further large-scale expenditure. The prime minister, Okada Kei-suke, escaped because the rebels failed to identify him and shot his brother in error.

The suppression of the rebellion and the execution of its leaders resulted in the ascendancy of what was called the Control (*Tsoei ha*) faction, older, less radical with regard to internal change, but sharing the same expansionist foreign-policy aims.

Prime minister Okada Keisuke.

Hitler sends German troops into the Rhineland

On March 7 German troops marched without warning into the Rhineland. The next 24 hours, Hitler was to say, were the most exciting in his life, as he waited to see if the French would retaliate.

The French had been reluctant to allow the Rhineland, which guarded the industrial region of the Ruhr, to remain German in 1919. By the terms of the Treaty of Versailles it was made a permanently demilitarized zone (occupied temporarily by Allied troops). Hitler was thus acting in undisguised violation of the treaty, not to mention the Locarno pact of 1925.

Hitler had great difficulty persuading his generals to countenance his gamble and had agreed that, if the French did respond, German forces would at once withdraw to the east bank of the Rhine. The troops entered the forbidden territory, not like an army in a blaze of defiance, but as a small garrison force, which kept well clear of the frontier.

A French invasion of the Rhineland would have been justified, and on past performance likely, but times had changed since the French sent their soldiers into the Ruhr in 1923. France received no support from its allies, other than the Czechs and Romanians, and its military chiefs, obsessed with a strategy of defence, were not eager to launch an invasion. There was therefore no military response. Hitler's gamble paid off.

Peru denied democracy

The electoral success of an Aprista-backed candidate for president in Peru caused the conservative-dominated congress to deny the legality of the elections held on October 11. It awarded a further mandate, with autocratic powers, to General Oscar Benavides, who had been appointed president in 1933 after the murder of Sánchez Cerro.

A German military band provides a triumphant accompaniment to the entry into the Rhineland.

Arab revolt in Palestine

Arab discontent in Palestine, fanned by growing Jewish immigration and by the advance to independence of other Arab states, burst into open rebellion on April 19. A general strike was declared by the Arab Higher Committee (AHC), and armed bands fought pitched battles with British troops.

The British adopted emergency powers and arrested all the Arab leaders they could lay their hands on, but they failed to nip the revolt in the bud. They were forced to send in reinforcements, as well as conduct the inevitable commission of inquiry.

A further complication was the increasing interest of Arab nations such as Iraq and Egypt in Palestinian affairs. The Arabs never managed to form quite as solid a front as did the Jews, but the foundation of the AHC, dominated by the mufti of Jerusalem, Haj Amin al-Husseini, was a sign of the powerful current of nationalism now running through the whole community.

The general strike was called off in October after the British had made what appeared to be faint concessions to the Arabs. One effect of this was to break down the fragile unity achieved by the AHC. Extremist groups, led by the mufti, continued to wage guerrilla warfare, but to some extent the revolt lost its national character. ▶ *page 167*

A violent confrontation between soldiers and demonstrators during the rebellion in Palestine.

JANUARY
15 Japan withdraws from naval conference with Britain, France and the United States
21 Bolivia and Paraguay sign Chaco peace treaty

FEBRUARY
16 Popular Front wins Spanish elections
17 Military revolt in Paraguay installs quasi-fascist regime
26 Military rebellion in Japan

MARCH
7 German troops occupy the Rhineland
31 Abyssinians defeated at Mai Chio

APRIL
25 Arab Higher Committee formed to organize Arab resistance in Palestine

MAY
2 Emperor Haile Selassie flees Abyssinia
5 Italians occupy Addis Ababa
10 Azaña elected president by Spanish Cortes

JUNE
3 Popular Front wins elections in France

JULY
12 Leading Spanish rightist, Calvo Sotelo, assassinated
15 League of Nations sanctions against Italy abandoned
17 Military rising against Republican government in Spain
19 Franco lands in Cadiz
30 Britain, France and United States sign naval treaty limiting armaments

AUGUST
7 European powers agree non-intervention in Spanish Civil War
14 Massacre in Badajoz after capture by Nationalists
24 Compulsory two-year military service introduced in Germany
25 Zinoviev, Kamenev and other old Bolsheviks executed in Moscow after show trials
26 British protectorate of Egypt ended except for Suez

SEPTEMBER
9 First meeting of international committee on non-intervention in Spain
27 Franco's forces capture Toledo

OCTOBER
1 Spanish Nationalists declare Franco head of state in Burgos
19 Hindu–Muslim riots in Bombay over siting of Hindu temple near mosque

General Franco, head of the rebel Nationalist government, addresses a crowd in Burgos.

Attempted military coup brings civil war to Spain

On July 17 there was a military rising against the Spanish Republican government. Though already planned to take place at this time, the revolt directly followed the assassination, a few days earlier, of a right-wing politician, José Calvo Sotelo, by an officer of the Republican police force, an event that seemed to emphasize the claim that the government was incapable of enforcing law and order.

Civil disorder had indeed marked the short history of the Spanish republic and had encouraged the growth of extremism. The forces of the right were sympathetic to the Falange, a political movement of the fascist type. In view of the mounting threat of counter-revolution, the forces of the left combined to form a Popular Front. In the elections of February 1936 the Popular Front was victorious.

The new government considered it had a mandate to press ahead with reforms, such as the splitting up of large estates and the granting of the right of striking workers to keep their jobs. The failure of previous governments to undertake such measures had caused much dissatisfaction and violence on the left, exacerbated by deliberate incitement on the part of the right. The efforts of the Popular Front government to enforce radical reforms provoked fierce resistance on the right. This led to the attempted coup, which began as an entirely military affair but swiftly turned into full-scale war.

The Spanish Civil War was not a simple conflict. Although it could be seen, internationally, as a clash between the two dominant ideologies – a rehearsal for the greater clash which would begin three years later – it was also a uniquely Spanish struggle, incorporating ancient quarrels, such as Catalan separatism and the position of the Roman Catholic Church. The Popular Front included many groups with different ideas and aims which were later to result in a civil war within a civil war.

The immediate result of the coup was, perhaps, the worst possible. It failed to bring down the government but gained control of about half the country – a large part of the northwest and a section of the south – besides Spanish Morocco, which was the source of the best troops, commanded by General Franco. Naturally, the strategic situation did not reflect individual sympathies. The expression 'fifth column' originated with the Nationalist general Emilio Mola, who advanced on Madrid with four columns but said he had 'a fifth column' in the city.

European powers agree on policy of nonintervention in Spain

Following an agreement by the European powers not to intervene in the Spanish Civil War, an international committee to supervise this arrangement met in London on September 9. It was already apparent that the agreement was being ignored.

Both sides had appealed for military aid on the outbreak of the war. France, where a Popular Front government was also in power, was divided on the question but in Britain, where Republican excesses against the Church and reports of massacres of Nationalists in Republican-held territory had caused great indignation, official opinion was opposed to supporting the Republicans.

Despite the agreement on non-intervention, Germany, Italy and Portugal poured arms and supplies, including fighting units disguised as 'volunteers', into Spain to lend support to the Nationalists, while the Soviet Union sent arms and advisers to the Republicans.

Particularly influential was the German air force. Since the Spanish navy remained loyal to the Republican government, Franco would not have been able to transport troops from Morocco without the assistance of German aircraft. The German aircrews also gained valuable experience, and the opportunity was taken to try out the *Blitzkrieg* type of warfare which had been evolved by German military strategists in recent years.

Nationalists advance on Madrid

On September 28 the Nationalist forces began to advance on Madrid, the capital of Spain and seat of the Republican government. At this early stage of the war, commanding the best of the Spanish military forces, they appeared to be unstoppable.

The capture of Madrid was clearly the key to Nationalist success. Following the capture of Badajoz in August, the Nationalist forces in the south were able to link up with those in the north. A rapid move towards Madrid followed, but a delay ensued when it became necessary for Franco to march to the relief of Toledo, where the Nationalist garrison was besieged in the Alcázar. This interval enabled reinforcements to be brought to Madrid, including the International Brigade, consisting of volunteers, anti-Fascists and Communist sympathizers from many countries. Instead of the triumphal entry expected, in early November the Nationalist forces were checked near the Escorial – the 16th-century palace-monastery of the Habsburg kings – by a fierce counter-attack supported by artillery and aircraft. While the Republican government withdrew to Valencia, the defenders of Madrid held out for two and a half years. ▶ *page 164*

Above. Franco's Foreign Legionaries in action in Mérida. Right. Nationalist troops in position outside Madrid.

1936

OCTOBER
24 Italy and Germany sign 'Axis' pact

NOVEMBER
6 Nationalist advance checked near Madrid
7 Spanish government withdraws to Valencia
18 Axis powers recognize Franco's government in Burgos
24 Germany and Japan sign Anti-Comintern pact

DECEMBER
8 Nicaragua strong man Somoza elected president
25 Chiang Kai-shek released from brief captivity in Sian

Chinese Nationalist leader kidnapped

The Chinese Nationalist general Chang Hsueh-liang.

Chiang Kai-shek arrived in Sian on December 12 to co-ordinate a new campaign against the Communists. To his surprise he was made a prisoner by his own commander in the region, Chang Hsueh-liang.

Chiang Kai-shek was no doubt unaware how much effect Communist propaganda had achieved among Chang Hsueh-liang's mainly Manchurian troops. The Communists had called for an end to the civil war and a united front against the Japanese. These requests appealed to the patriotism of Chinese of all persuasions, including Nationalists restive at Chiang Kai-shek's policy of defeating the Communists before resisting the Japanese.

The precise nature of the 'Sian incident' remains mysterious. Chiang Kai-shek was soon released, apparently without having renounced his policy. He then travelled with Chang Hsueh-liang to Nanking, where the latter was imprisoned, though not for long. Thereafter, the pressure was taken off the Communists, and events moved towards the united front that Chang Hsueh-liang himself had demanded.

1937

JANUARY–DECEMBER

GUERNICA
DESTROYED

RED ARMY
PURGE

WAR IN CHINA

Victorious Japanese troops marching through Shanghai.

Guernica destroyed

During Franco's campaign in the Basque country in April, the town of Guernica was subjected to two days of bombing and strafing by German aircraft of the so-called Condor Legion, beginning on April 26. At least 1000 inhabitants were killed.

Guernica was not a target of much military significance. The reason for the attack was, as the Germans later admitted, to test the effects of the strategy of concentrated 'terror-bombing'. The episode became celebrated as an example of the barbarity of modern war partly through the painting, *Guernica*, by Pablo Picasso. ▶ *page 166*

Stalin purges his high command

On June 12 several Soviet generals, including the Red Army chief of staff, Mikhail Tukhachevsky, were shot after secret trials. Forged documents incriminating Tukhachevsky seem to have originated with Nazi agents hoping to inflict moral damage on the Red Army.

Earlier in the year a second spate of show trials had resulted in the execution or imprisonment of a number of leading Communists, including Karl Radek, once a close associate of Lenin. The judicial assassination of military chiefs marked another, unexpected development in Stalin's paranoia, though no doubt there were grounds for his fears that the power of the army had grown dangerously independent. The decimation of the upper ranks of the military on the eve of a major conflict was nevertheless a remarkable example of the crass brutality of Stalin's rule. About half of the senior staff officers of the Red Army were purged during 1937–38.

Karl Radek, one of Stalin's victims, was sentenced to ten years' imprisonment and is thought to have died in 1939.

War in China

On July 7 Japanese troops carrying out manoeuvres near Peking demanded to search some houses. A brief exchange of fire took place at the Marco Polo Bridge and, before mutual indignation could be soothed, further clashes occurred elsewhere. The Japanese then launched a full-scale attack on China.

Japanese actions were hard to understand, largely because there was no such thing as a single Japanese policy, and the army, navy and foreign ministry often operated in ignorance of one another's plans. Certainly the Japanese had further designs on China, but probably not even the hot-headed younger generation of officers contemplated taking over the whole country. They aimed to lop off another province in the north, continuing a policy which had so far been rather successful.

Japanese troops invaded from Manchuria. Japanese aircraft bombed the cities and ships bombarded the ports. The Chinese put up unexpectedly determined resistance, but the Japanese were far better provided with equipment and military know-how. Chiang Kai-shek's policy was therefore to use the vastness of the country to evade a pitched battle until the Japanese overstretched themselves. The government withdrew, first to Hankow, then to the mountains of Szechwan. Much industrial equipment, including even the books from university libraries, was carried away in carts and boats to safety. The Japanese steadily captured the main cities and transport routes in the east, though they could not control the countryside in between, where Communist guerrilla units embarked on an often ingenious campaign.

Smoke arising from the burning ruins of the Chapei district of Shanghai during a Japanese attack.

The Duce visits the Fuehrer

On September 25 Hitler welcomed his ally Mussolini on a visit to Germany. The visit was intended to cement the Axis of October 1936 and to impress Mussolini with German might.

Carefully orchestrated parades and public demonstrations were the lifeblood of Fascist parties. The highlight of Mussolini's visit, after he had saluted a ceremonial parade of the SS in Munich, witnessed army manoeuvres in Mecklenburg and inspected the vast Krupp factories in Essen, was a torchlit rally in Berlin, where a crowd of 800,000 was addressed by the two dictators. A terrific thunderstorm rather ruined the speeches and stampeded the audience. Mussolini had to make his own way back to the capital, soaking wet but nevertheless vastly impressed.

Although no serious discussions took place, Mussolini was eager to oblige when invited to join Germany and Japan in the Anti-Comintern pact shortly after.

During a visit to Hitler Mussolini takes the salute at a march-past in Munich.

The Japanese take Nanking

On December 13 the Japanese occupied Nanking, the former capital of Nationalist China. The undeclared war, which the Japanese persisted in referring to as the 'China incident', had been fought with unbridled savagery. In an effort to break down the Chinese will to resist, the Japanese troops were given their head. In Nanking murder, rape and pillage reached such a pitch that even the Japanese army high command became seriously alarmed at the collapse of discipline.

1937

FEBRUARY
1 'Trotskyites' executed after show trials in Moscow
8 Spanish Nationalist and Italian troops take Málaga
22 Abyssinian revolt against Italian conquerors suppressed
27 France extends Maginot Line
28 Congress party wins all but four provinces in first Indian elections

MARCH
23 Italians defeated by Spanish Republicans at Guadalajara

APRIL
26 German air attack on Guernica

MAY
15 Spanish prime minister Largo Caballero resigns under Communist pressure

JUNE
6 Munich students attack Nazis
12 Eight Soviet generals shot
19 Nationalists take Basque capital, Bilbao

JULY
7 Peel Commission recommends partition of Palestine
7 Japan attacks China

AUGUST
8 Japanese occupy Peking
14 Japanese bomb Shanghai
19 Poet and dramatist García Lorca executed by Spanish Nationalists
25 Nationalists capture Santander

SEPTEMBER
13 China appeals to the League of Nations against Japan
28 League of Nations condemns Japanese attack on China
29 Chiang Kai-shek and Mao Tse-tung form joint command

OCTOBER
17 Nazis in Sudetenland provoke riots
20 British impose curb on Jewish immigration to Palestine
31 Spanish government moves to Barcelona

NOVEMBER
6 Italy joins Anti-Comintern pact
8 Japanese take Shanghai

DECEMBER
11 Italy leaves League of Nations
12 Japanese attack U.S. and British ships in Yangtse River
13 Japanese occupy Nanking
15 Spanish Republican offensive at Teruel

The Germans take over Austria

Following intensive Nazi propaganda, Hitler's troops moved into Austria on March 11 and effected the *Anschluss* ('union') of Austria with the German Reich. Such a move was expressly forbidden by the Treaty of Versailles and was resisted until almost the last moment by the Austrian government.

Hitler's foreign policy became steadily more aggressive after the successful occupation of the Rhineland, which the western democracies, Britain and France, had not resisted. He got rid of conservative generals who demurred at his plans and appointed himself commander-in-chief of the armed forces. Ribbentrop, an enthusiastic Nazi, became foreign minister. All potential dissent was thus quelled.

Although Hitler's expansionist agenda depended on changing circumstances, it contained certain crucial objectives, including the subjugation of Czechoslovakia and Poland as well as the *Anschluss*, the first of these objectives to be achieved.

Nazi propaganda in Austria had led the Austrian government to suppress the movement. In February Schuschnigg, the Austrian chancellor, was summoned to Berchtesgaden where, thoroughly intimidated by Hitler's hectoring and by German troop movements on the border, he consented to release imprisoned Nazis, remove restrictions and accept Nazis in the government. This was tantamount to a Nazi takeover, but Schuschnigg then hit upon the device of holding a referendum on Austrian independence. A favourable vote would have ruined the case for *Anschluss*, but Schuschnigg allowed three days' notice – long enough for Hitler to act. He sent an ultimatum demanding, among other things, the postponement of the referendum. Schuschnigg found little support, either in Europe or in his own cabinet. He resigned and the next day, the day before the scheduled referendum, German troops moved in, having been summoned (on Hitler's instructions) by the Nazi interior minister, Artur von Seyss-Inquart, in order to 'keep the peace'. Britain and France naturally protested but, as Hitler had calculated, took no action.

General Franco studying maps before the battle of Teruel.

Franco reaches the sea

The Nationalist forces in the Spanish Civil War broke through to the Mediterranean coast between Valencia and Barcelona on April 15. The area held by the Republican government was thus split in two.

In spite of one or two setbacks, such as the heroic defence of Madrid and the Republican holding operation on the River Ebro from July to November 1938, the Francoist forces steadily extended their control westward during 1937–38. They continued to obtain support from the Axis powers, while the Republicans received less from the Soviet Union which, as the eventual outcome became obvious, was losing interest. Franco refused to consider peace negotiations, insisting on unconditional surrender. What was to be the last major campaign of the war began in December, as Franco's forces closed in on Catalonia. ▶ *page 172*

Truce agreed on the Manchurian frontier

Following a full-scale battle between Soviet and Japanese forces on the Mongolian border, a truce was arranged on August 10. The fighting had no very specific purpose, being essentially a mutual test of strength.

Though the Soviet Union had given up its holdings in the South Manchurian railway in 1935, thus strengthening the Japanese puppet state of Manchukuo, relations between the two powers were frosty. The Anti-Comintern pact hardly improved matters, and in 1937 the Soviet Union had agreed upon a non-aggression pact with China, joining in the condemnation of the Japanese invasion.

In Vienna Hitler makes a triumphant progress through streets lined with troops and supporters. His enthusiastic reception made him determined to annex Austria outright.

Munich agreement

After a hastily arranged four-power conference in Munich, on September 30 an agreement was signed in the early hours concerning the crisis over Czechoslovakia. Returning to Britain the same day, the elderly prime minister, Neville Chamberlain, waved a paper signed by Hitler which, Chamberlain said, meant 'peace in our time'.

The Munich agreement reached jointly by Hitler, Mussolini, Chamberlain and the French prime minister, Edouard Daladier, signed over to Germany the border region of the Sudetenland where there was a large German population. Led by Konrad Henlein and subsidized from Berlin, the Nazis among the German inhabitants became increasingly vociferous in their demand to be reunited with Germany. The position of Czechoslovakia was vulnerable. Its chief guarantor was France. Britain was under obligation to act in the Czechs' defence only if France did. As the crisis loomed, and Hitler threatened to 'smash Czechoslovakia by military force', the Soviet Union offered assistance – if Poland and Romania would grant permission for Soviet troops to cross their territory.

By September 1938 the British government had come to the conclusion that war could be avoided only if the Sudetenland was handed over. Daladier's objection that giving in to Hitler would only encourage further aggression was brushed aside.

At the Munich meeting the terms were suggested by Mussolini, though Hitler had dictated them to him beforehand. The 'German' areas (which incidentally contained the substantial Czech military defences) were to be handed over. Claims by Hungary and Poland to other portions of Czechoslovakia were put aside, but later made good by Hitler. Czech representatives were not admitted to the meeting, and President Eduard Beneš resigned a few days later. ▶ *page 173*

British troops invade the Old City in Jerusalem

After the declaration of martial law in Jerusalem British troops cleared the Old City on October 18. It had been held by Arab insurgents.

In spite of the steps taken to suppress it in 1937, the Arab revolt in Palestine grew even more vigorous in 1938. Notwithstanding the use of aircraft, the British writ did not run beyond the cities, as the Arab insurgents controlled most of the countryside, apart from Jewish areas. There was a rise also in retaliatory attacks on Arabs by Jewish terrorist groups. Normal activities were several times brought to a standstill in much of the country, and the British moved in more reinforcements. A government commission seeking a solution reported in November that any scheme of partition was open to overwhelming objections, and that policy was subsequently abandoned.

British soldiers lead Arab prisoners away following the outbreak of serious rioting in Palestine.

The sound of breaking glass

On the night of November 9 a pogrom was carried out against German Jews. Such was the noise of plate glass shattering as Jewish shops were attacked and looted that the incident was known as *Kristallnacht* (literally 'crystal night').

According to the propaganda minister, Joseph Goebbels, the terror was a spontaneous reaction to the murder of a German diplomat in Paris by a Polish Jew a few days earlier. If not actually instigated, it was certainly encouraged by the Nazi authorities. Jewish property was vandalized, hundreds of synagogues were burnt down and unknown numbers of people were murdered or beaten up.

APPEASEMENT

T HE WORD *appeasement, applied to the policy of Britain and France towards Hitler's Germany in the late 1930s, suggests weakness and lack of courage. However, appeasement is basically the usual manner of approaching international disputes – seeking compromise as a way of avoiding greater calamity – and it was originally supported by most people. Appeasement in the end was taken too far: the surrender at Munich was the point at which many rebelled against it. Even then, some historians maintain, Britain and France were in no state to declare war on Germany and, by awarding Hitler a slice of Czechoslovakia, purchased valuable time to prepare for the inevitable conflict.*

The exemplar of appeasement was Neville Chamberlain, British prime minister from 1937. Chamberlain was not blind to the viciousness of the Nazi regime. He may have supposed, along with many others, that reports from Germany were exaggerated, but the brutalities of the SS were no secret. Nor was Chamberlain ignorant of Hitler's ambitions in eastern Europe. In 1934 he had said that only force would keep Hitler in his place, but he also acknowledged that many German objections to the Versailles settlement were just and reasonable.

Chamberlain was also aware – more than most of his countrymen – of Britain's economic weakness, of which the continuing depression was only one among several causes. He believed that Britain could not fight in 1938 and, like many others who had lived through the First World War, he had a profound horror of war.

Altogether, Chamberlain's view of European affairs was not unrealistic, but he was guilty of several errors and omissions. On the diplomatic front he made no serious effort to engage the Soviet Union in an alliance, since he distrusted the Communists. At home Chamberlain recognized the necessity of increasing armaments, but his hatred of war and his belief that an arms race would make war more likely, meant that he did not pursue a sufficiently energetic rearmament policy.

Chamberlain made a fundamental mistake in supposing that he could deal with Hitler by normal diplomatic means. He assumed that there was some point at which Hitler's demands would be satisfied and that by conciliating Hitler he would be able to co-opt him in the effort to maintain peace in Europe.

The piece of paper that Chamberlain waved triumphantly in front of the press cameras on his return from Munich was a brief statement signed by Hitler which agreed that future quarrels in Europe would be decided by negotiation not force. Chamberlain thought he had secured something of a coup in getting Hitler, more or less on the spur of the moment, to sign such a document. In spite of mounting evidence, he failed to realize that statements from Hitler were not worth the paper they were written on.

Above left. Hitler addressing a vast parade of German troops at Nuremberg in September 1938.
From left to right. Neville Chamberlain at the window of 10 Downing Street receiving an enthusiastic greeting. President Beneš of Czechoslovakia. The French prime minister Edouard Daladier (left) with members of his cabinet. Chamberlain addressing the crowds at Heston Airport after his return from Munich.

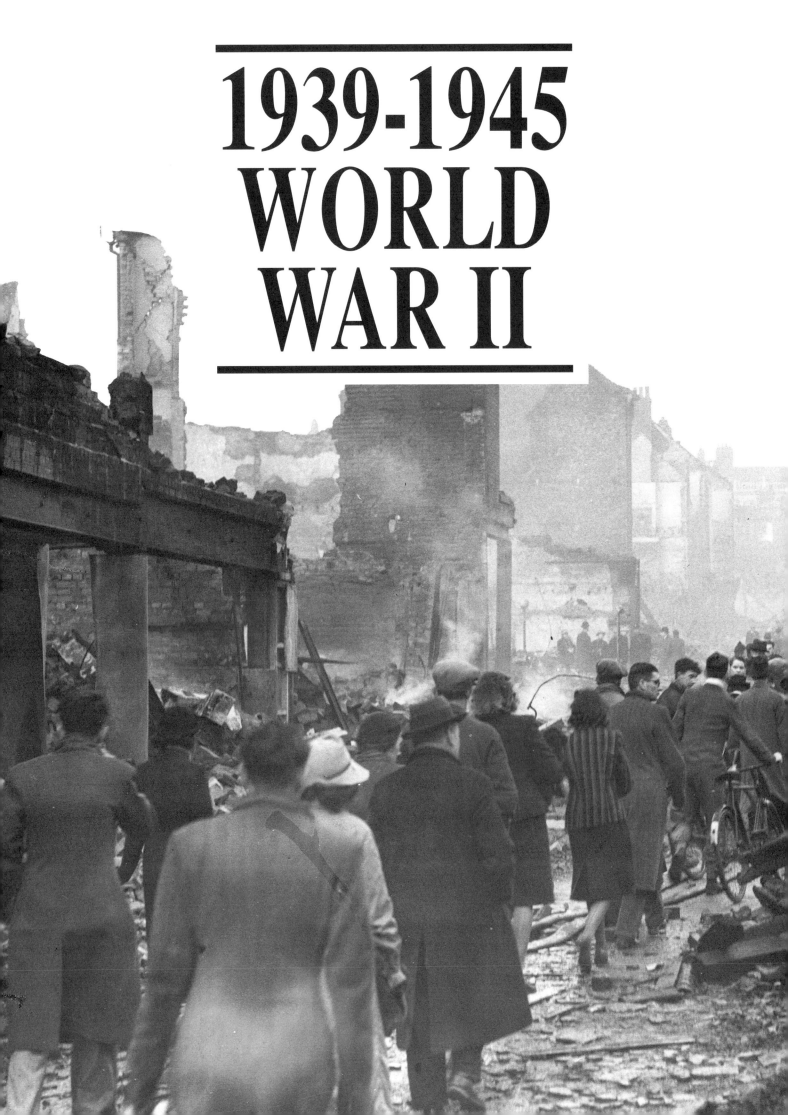

1939-1945
WORLD
WAR II

WHEN THE WEHRMACHT LAUNCHED ITS INVASION OF POLAND IN SEPTEMBER 1939, scarcely 20 years since the conclusion of what had been optimistically called 'the war to end all wars', the world was once again plunged into a bloody conflict. However, this time the conflict was to become a truly global one, since the efforts by the Allies to limit the ambitions of both Nazi Germany and imperial Japan ensured that the war spread far beyond Europe to Africa, the Middle East and the Far East. It entailed the mobilization of armies on a vaster scale than ever before, the introduction of fearful new weapons of destruction and the involvement of civilian populations, which had hitherto been largely spared the full horrors of war.

Although both German and Japanese armies gained spectacular early successes, the overwhelming superiority of the forces aligned against them ensured their ultimate defeat – but at a dreadful cost in human suffering. It has been estimated that 50 million people lost their lives in World War II (the true figure will never be known) and a majority of these were civilians – victims of genocide, aerial bombardment, mass starvation and, finally, atomic warfare.

FRANCO VICTORIOUS

GERMANS ENTER PRAGUE

Barcelona surrenders

Less than five weeks after it began, the Nationalist offensive against Catalonia resulted in the fall of Barcelona on January 26. The Republican government fled, first to Figueras, where Juan Negrín, prime minister, continued to defy Franco though reducing his 'irreducible' 13 points for peace to just three.

The rest of Catalonia was swiftly overrun, and refugees poured north into France. President Azaña resigned a month after the fall of Barcelona, and Franco's government was now officially recognized by Britain, France and the United States. Negrín's cabinet held out for a while in Madrid, where there was no fuel and practically no food, until overthrown by a 'council of defence', from which the Communists were excluded. There was fighting within Madrid between the Communists and Negrín's opponents, but there was little resistance to the Nationalist troops when they marched in on March 28. The end of the civil war, in which about one million people had died, was officially proclaimed by the Nationalist radio on the following day.

Top. Willing hands help carry an elderly Spanish refugee to safety.

Right. Spanish Nationalist soldiers on parade near the French frontier.

Czechoslovakia destroyed

On March 15 Hitler, in the wake of his soldiers, entered the ancient capital of Bohemia. The Nazi swastika was raised above Prague castle, and the Sudeten German leader, Konrad Henlein, was appointed head of the civil administration of a German protectorate.

Hitler had regarded the Munich agreement as a diplomatic setback and, although he had gained his main military objectives thereby, he did not cease efforts to destabilize the Czechoslovak government. In particular, he encouraged Slovak and Ruthenian separatism, and when the Prague government took action to suppress these movements, German pressure resulted in a Slovak declaration of independence (March 14) – read out by the Slovak leader, Josef Tiso, but drafted (in Slovak) by the Germans. After a barrage of propaganda similar to (and possibly directly copied from, in some cases) the outcry that preceded the Munich crisis, German troops marched into Czechoslovakia whose government, so Hitler informed the world, had disintegrated. The Czech president, Emil Hacha, after the customary bullying interview in Berlin at which Goering, head of the Luft-waffe, threatened to flatten Prague, central Europe's most beautiful city, ordered the Czech army to offer no resistance to the invasion. Slovakia was declared a German protectorate the following day, while Ruthenia was occupied by the Hungarians.

Internationally, the significance of the Nazi takeover of Czechoslovakia, Hitler's first conquest of a non-German-speaking territory, was to destroy the policy of appeasement. British public opinion turned violently anti-German. The result was Anglo-French guarantees to Poland and Romania, the two countries most threatened by Hitler's policy of expansion.

Czechs watch as German troops with artillery make their entry into Prague.

Lithuania loses its port

The town and port of Memel (Klaipèda) was surrendered to Germany on March 22 following a German ultimatum. Memel was Lithuania's only outlet to the sea, but by a convention of 1924 it enjoyed considerable local autonomy. It contained a large German minority (a majority in the town itself) and, encouraged by Berlin, had become a hotbed of Nazism. Nazis, agitating for union with the Reich, held a majority in the assembly. ▶ *page 189*

Ribbentrop signs the pact transferring Memel to Germany.

Japan tests strength of Russian bear

Amid the high political tension that gripped Europe, little attention was paid to the outbreak of heavy fighting between Japanese and Soviet forces on the border of Outer Mongolia at the end of May. In a battle lasting over a month the Japanese lost the equivalent of a whole division.

Despite its occupation of Manchuria and invasion of China, Japan regarded the Soviet Union as its main enemy. In 1938 it deliberately provoked a conflict on the Manchurian border but was checked by Soviet reinforcements under General Georgi Zhukov. The following year the Japanese essayed another trial of strength, sending a force of 30,000, together with tanks, artillery and aircraft, to Nomenkan. The Red Army, despite Stalin's purges, again performed well, and the Japanese eventually disengaged, partly because of shock and anger at news of the German pact with the Soviet Union. Germany was Japan's partner in the Anti-Comintern alliance and had been hitherto regarded as a firm ally against the Russians, although negotiations for a tripartite alliance of Japan, Germany and Italy against the western democracies earlier in the year had come to nothing.

Molotov signs the Nazi-Soviet agreement.

Italy seizes Albania

Anxious not to be outshone as a conqueror by his Nazi ally, Mussolini ordered the occupation of Albania in April. Backed by ships and aircraft, Italian troops invaded on April 7. The Albanians were totally unprepared and the only resistance came from isolated local units.

Albania was already practically a client state of Italy, and its annexation had been urged in the past by Italian nationalists. The invasion followed an ultimatum demanding a customs union and the stationing of Italian troops in Albania, which was rejected.

With the rapid military occupation and the flight of King Zog, Albania was reorganized as an Italian province. King Victor Emmanuel of Italy was declared king of Albania and Albania's natural resources, notably oil and

Albanian soldiers and peasants retreating from the Italians.

iron, were diverted to assist Italy's preparations for a greater war. The democratic nations warned Mussolini not to extend his territorial ambitions further and issued a guarantee to Greece similar to those given to Poland and Romania. ▶ *page 193*

Nazi-Soviet pact

The world was astonished by the announcement from Moscow on August 23 that Germany and the Soviet Union, whose governments represented opposite ends of the political spectrum, had signed a non-aggression pact. Amid general consternation, not the least embarrassed were the members of an Anglo-French delegation currently in Moscow in hope of negotiating a similar agreement with the Soviet Union themselves.

For Germany the immediate reason for the agreement, by which both sides undertook to refrain from any act of force against each other, whether singly or in conjunction with other powers, was to clear the way for an attack on Poland. For the Soviet Union, Stalin congratulated himself on having ended the threat of an anti-Soviet alliance by all the capitalist powers of Europe, which he seems to have regarded as a serious possibility, and on having made war between the fascist and the democratic states – with the Soviet Union on the sidelines – more likely. According to the memoirs of Nikita Khrushchev, Stalin remarked, 'Of course, it's all a game to see who can fool whom. I know what Hitler's up to. He thinks he's outsmarted me, but actually it's I who have tricked him.'

The price of Stalin's neutrality was contained in a secret protocol. It outlined German and Soviet spheres of interest in eastern Europe. The Baltic states and eastern Poland were recognized as lying within the Soviet sphere. ▶ *page 176*

The German army invades Poland

On September 1 German forces invaded Poland. The invasion was preceded by a grotesque incident in which a German concentration camp prisoner was killed, dressed in a Polish uniform, riddled with bullets and left at the frontier town of Gleiwitz (Gliwice) as evidence of a 'Polish attack' on German guards. The full German *Blitzkrieg* was then loosed on the Poles who, having stationed most of their troops near the frontier and relying on cavalry to repel tanks, were swiftly overwhelmed.

After the bloodless conquest of Czechoslovakia, Poland had moved to the top of Hitler's hit list. His quarrel with the Poles centred on the city of Danzig (Gdansk), where a majority of the population was German and, through intimidation and fraud, thoroughly Nazified. As always, Hitler was prepared to negotiate, but the Poles, secure in their guarantee from Britain and France, refused to do any deal with Hitler.

Polish foreign policy was inevitably based on maintaining a position of neutrality between two huge and mutually antagonistic neighbours, Nazi Germany and the Soviet Union. The German-Soviet Pact, secret clauses of which partitioned Poland between the two countries, rendered this policy unworkable.

Germany's non-aggression pact with the Soviet Union cleared the largest obstacle to the long-planned attack on Poland. Hitler believed that Britain and France, notwithstanding their guarantees, would offer no more opposition than they had over Czechoslovakia, and in any case would be in no position to prevent a rapid German conquest.

A Polish envoy discusses surrender terms with Germans.

German soldiers in Poland using various forms of transport.

1939 Britain and France declare war

On the morning of September 3 Britain and France delivered a joint ultimatum to Germany demanding a cessation of hostilities and immediate withdrawal of German forces from Poland. Fifteen minutes after the 11 a.m. deadline, no answer having been received from Berlin, the British prime minister, Neville Chamberlain, made his sombre announcement that the country was at war with Germany.

Hitler had miscalculated in assuming that Britain and France would not declare war, but he was correct in thinking that there was nothing they could do to prevent the conquest of Poland. A few French units crossed the frontier into the Saar, but did not engage in much actual fighting. The Royal Air Force dropped tons of propaganda leaflets on Germany but was told not to bomb the Ruhr as it was private property. Both countries embarked on frantic preparations for war, while the conquest of Poland proceeded unhindered.

Below left. Londoners running after an air raid warning.

Below. Proclamation of war at the Mansion House.

Stalin cashes in

On September 17 Soviet forces moved into eastern Poland. Moscow proclaimed that the occupation of what it called western Belorussia and western Ukraine was necessary because the Polish state had disintegrated. The Red Army swiftly occupied half the country, up to the line agreed in the German-Soviet pact, incurring under 1000 casualties.

The two allies hastened to improve their security. Hitler ordered that powerful defences should be constructed behind the new eastern borders of the Reich, while the Soviet Union compelled the three Baltic states, Estonia, Latvia and Lithuania, to sign 'mutual-assistance' pacts, which in plain language meant that the Russians could take them over whenever they liked.

A column of horse-drawn Soviet artillery crosses the Polish border.

Hitler decides to attack France

'Operation Yellow', the name given to an offensive against France and Britain, was the subject of a directive from Hitler to the German military chiefs on October 9. On the same day Hitler met the Swede, Birger Dahlerus, who was acting as an unofficial intermediary between Berlin and London, via Stockholm, on the subject of peace terms.

Hitler had no particular quarrel with Britain or France. However, since they had declared war on Germany, it would probably be necessary to fight them, and if so, the sooner the better. To his less-than-eager generals Hitler pointed out that, unlike 1914, this would be a one-front war, but the current neutrality of the Soviet Union could not be expected to last indefinitely. He wanted an attack launched through the Low Countries, thus circumventing France's famous Maginot Line, with the aim of seizing as large a chunk of northern France as possible, together with the Channel ports, preparatory to an air and sea attack on Britain.

Hitler's desire for an immediate attack on France was also influenced by the success of the *Blitzkrieg* against Poland. He wanted to keep the momentum going, although not even he expected the new German method of warfare to be as successful against France as it had been against the outclassed Poles.

Such was the disapproval of the army high command of Hitler's plans for an assault on France that there was talk of a military coup, though it came to nothing because of doubt whether German soldiers would obey an order to turn against the Führer. Bad weather forced postponement of Hitler's offensive and ultimately the plan was dropped because of fears that details had reached Paris and London. ▶ *page 185*

The *Royal Oak* goes down

Late on October 14, a German submarine, U-47, commanded by Günther Prien, approached the British naval base at Scapa Flow. That night she slipped through the defences and, the following morning, torpedoed the battleship *Royal Oak*, which sank almost immediately, taking over 800 sailors down with her.

The loss of the *Royal Oak* was a particularly severe shock to the British because the Scapa Flow base had been considered impregnable. It was not, however, the first naval disaster of the war. Apart from heavy losses in merchant shipping, the aircraft carrier *Courageous* had been sunk in the North Atlantic a month earlier. It was clear that the destructive powers of the U-boats would have a significant effect on Britain's war effort.

President Roosevelt gets a letter from Einstein

On October 11 the U.S. economist Alexander Sachs succeeded in obtaining an interview with the president. He presented him with a letter from his friend, Albert Einstein.

Einstein, the world-famous physicist who, as a Jew, had been forced to flee his native Germany, explained that scientists were on the verge of creating a hugely destructive weapon by means of atomic fission. Roosevelt noted that this news required action, though the development of the weapon was to take longer than he perhaps imagined. German scientists had informed Hitler of the possibility of such a weapon two weeks earlier.

The *Royal Oak* in Portsmouth in 1938. Its loss was a severe blow to British prestige.

Soviet machine-gunners training near Leningrad before the outbreak of war with Finland.

Finland invaded

On November 30 Soviet forces attacked Finland. Four armies, composed of 45 divisions, were involved in two main thrusts on either side of Lake Ladoga, whose shores were at that time shared by both countries.

In order to complete its defensive arrangements in the west, the Soviet Union needed control not only of the Baltic states but also of the Gulf of Finland and Finnish territory in the neighbourhood of Leningrad. When it failed to persuade the Finns to make the requisite territorial cessions, a full-scale invasion was launched.

Little serious resistance was expected, but the Finns were much better adapted to warfare in the extremely cold winter, whereas the Russians were both ill-equipped and unprepared. By the end of the year, with the Finns resisting heroically in hope of foreign assistance (not, however, forthcoming), the Soviet forces had been brought to a standstill. ▶ *page 184*

Battle of the River Plate

The first significant naval engagement of the war took place in December in the South Atlantic, when a British cruiser squadron encountered the German pocket battleship *Graf Spee*. Captain Langsdorff, his ship slightly damaged, took refuge in the estuary of the River Plate, Uruguay.

Although the active career of the *Graf Spee* was very short (about two months), she had done considerable damage, sinking nine ships including the Polish liner *Piłsudski*. Commodore Henry Harwood's cruiser squadron was hopelessly outgunned and had to break off, but it inflicted sufficient damage on the *Graf Spee* for Langsdorff to make for neutral waters. Intense British diplomatic efforts delayed him leaving until reinforcements were brought up. On December 17 Langsdorff, seeing no way of escape, scuttled his ship (according to his orders in such circumstances) and then shot himself.

The pocket battleship *Graf Spee* on fire and sinking outside Montevideo harbour.

STALIN'S SEARCH FOR SECURITY

THE THREAT to European peace represented by the Nazi accession to power in Germany was recognized in Moscow no less clearly than in other capitals. There was no change in policy and, despite Hitler's attacks on Communists, the Soviet government insisted that 'we have no wish other than to continue good relations'.

The Soviet government was in fact painfully aware of its international isolation, and sought to improve relations with the Western powers, in particular France. It was largely through French encouragement that the Soviet Union entered the League of Nations in 1935, and the two countries were associated in efforts to create an 'eastern Locarno', which would guarantee frontiers in eastern Europe as the Locarno treaties had done in the west. This never succeeded but did result in Soviet mutual assistance pacts with France (1935) and with Czechoslovakia, though action under the latter was conditioned by France acting first. Another aspect of the Soviet drive for security was the new policy of the Comintern, which endorsed the principle of the 'popular front', involving leftist parties other than Communists.

The failure to prevent Hitler's occupation of the Rhineland in 1936 led to a certain hardening in Soviet foreign policy. Foreign minister Litvinov, relatively pro-Western, remarked that it was not the Soviet Union that was most threatened by Nazism and that it was for other countries to decide what advantages could be gained from a Soviet alliance. The Spanish Civil War offered an opportunity for independent action. Its outcome was a defeat for Soviet policy, but by then Stalin had lost interest in Spain. The Munich agreement (from which the Soviet Union was excluded) confirmed the suspicion that the democracies were unreliable safeguards against Nazi aggression. Stalin began increasingly to suspect that their true aim was a war between Germany and the Soviet Union.

The British government distrusted the Soviet Union no less, but after the invasion of Czechoslovakia, with Poland or Romania apparently marked down as Hitler's next victim, the advantages of a Soviet alliance were increasingly obvious. Despite mutual dislike and suspicion, proposals for an Anglo-French-Soviet alliance were put forward. Representatives – 'low officials' as Molotov sneeringly called them – were sent to Moscow. German representatives were also in the Soviet capital – negotiating commercial arrangements. While the Anglo-French negotiations proceeded fitfully and suspiciously, the Germans dangled carrots before the Russians. At the beginning of August Joachim von Ribbentrop, the German foreign minister, let fall the remark that Poland might also be on the agenda.

As late as August 4 the Soviet Union might have been prepared to agree an Anglo-French treaty. But on that day Hitler decided to press for a Soviet alliance. When Molotov, who had replaced Litvinov, inquired whether Germany would be prepared to sign a non-aggression pact, he received a prompt and positive answer. The Anglo-French military talks, held up by the refusal of Poland to allow Soviet troops on its territory even if it were attacked, petered out. Ribbentrop made a flying visit to Moscow and the German-Soviet pact was signed – causing intense shock to western governments and no less to western Communists.

Above. Ribbentrop in Berlin with (left) the Romanian foreign minister.

Right. Viacheslav Molotov, Soviet commissar for foreign affairs from May 1939.

Far right. His predecessor, Maxim Litvinov, who advocated collective security against Nazi Germany.

BLITZKRIEG

THE TERM Blitzkrieg ('lightning war') was invented not by the Germans but by western journalists reporting the invasion of Poland. It was a very apt description of the new German tactics, designed to avoid the kind of expensive stalemate that had characterized the First World War. However, the method, like the name, was not a German invention. It had been worked out largely by British military theorists, and a young French army officer had in 1937 published similar ideas, which were largely neglected in his own country. His name was Charles de Gaulle.

The main purpose was to break through the enemy lines immediately and to destroy his communications. Attack was sudden and overwhelming, with as little advance warning as possible. The enemy air force was disabled as far as practicable before it could take to the air. Bombers then struck at communications and other large strategic targets, while dive-bombers attacked moving columns of troops wherever they could be found. On the ground, motorized infantry with light tanks and field guns advanced with great speed, avoiding cities, fortifications and other points likely to hold up the advance. In support came heavy tanks, in large formations, and behind them the ordinary infantry, to occupy the territory already bombed and penetrated and to deal with remaining centres of resistance.

In Poland, the SS regiments followed the infantry. Their job was officially classed as 'security'. In practice this meant obliterating any trace of resistance by means of terror and atrocity. Villages were burned. Groups of civilians, especially – but not only – Jews, were shot out of hand. A German staff officer, after a conversation with the army chief of staff, recorded Hitler's intention 'to destroy and exterminate the Polish nation'.

The German commander-in-chief, General von Brauchitsch, was told personally by Hitler, travelling by special train to witness the Polish defeat, to leave the SS alone. Nevertheless, their activities were offensive to the

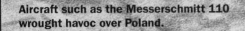

Aircraft such as the Messerschmitt 110 wrought havoc over Poland.

regular army. Field Marshal von Rundstedt ordered an SS unit out of the area of his command and put a stop to anti-Jewish measures. Admiral Canaris went to Hitler to complain of the brutality to civilians, but was dissuaded from making his protest by General Keitel. He returned to Germany shocked and disgusted. His state of mind was a not insignificant matter, since Canaris was head of German counter-intelligence. His performance of his duties in that post, which he retained until implicated in the bomb plot of 1944, was to reflect his lack of devotion to Hitler.

Admiral Wilhelm Canaris.

Field Marshal Keitel.

Field Marshal von Rundstedt.

NAVAL STRENGTH & STRATEGY 1939

Between the world wars Britain sought, in theory at least, to maintain a navy with twice the capacity of any two potential opponents. However, this was scarcely the case by 1939. Italy had declined to observe internationally agreed restrictions on warship construction in its ambition to dominate the Mediterranean. Germany, by the terms of the naval agreement with Britain of 1935, had the right to balance Britain in submarines, and in fact had potentially twice as many by 1939. The Versailles treaty had limited the permitted size of German battleships, a restriction that resulted in 'pocket battleships' like the Graf Spee, which could outgun any ship that they could not outrun. The Germans had also developed the magnetic mine, an indiscriminately powerful weapon until the British evolved an antidote. The German navy was about to launch the Tirpitz and Bismarck, the most powerful ships yet built, while the British battleships, though more numerous, were mostly antiquated. New battleships were under construction but would not be ready until 1941 or 1942.

The object of British naval strategy was: (1) to maintain the necessary flow of seaborne supplies to Britain; (2) to prevent an enemy attack on British coasts; and (3) to enable British forces to be transported overseas. Germany aimed primarily at preventing Britain receiving supplies, chiefly through submarine warfare, but also by the use of surface raiders and aircraft.

By the outbreak of war both sides had made certain preparations. The British fleet had been mobilized; it was based at Scapa Flow to contain the Germans in the North Sea, but another battle fleet was maintained at Malta as a check on the Italians. The convoy system, its effectiveness having been proved beyond doubt by experience in the First World War, was introduced at once, though in 1939 Britain was seriously short of escort ships, and the rapid building of mini-destroyers, called corvettes, began. By the beginning of September Germany was prepared for the forthcoming attack on British merchant ships, with the Graf Spee in the South Atlantic, and in addition a number of converted commerce raiders and U-boats in the vicinity of the main trade routes, with their supply ships nearby. The Atlantic battle was clearly of vital significance to both sides, and its ultimate result could not be foreseen, but by December the new first lord of the admiralty, Churchill, could report fair success in this and other naval endeavours: merchant ship casualties averaged only one in 750 sailings, and the British Expeditionary Force had been safely transported across the Channel.

A convoy of merchant ships in the North Sea.

A flying boat keeps watch over a convoy. Aircraft provided formidable protection against U-boat attacks.

The German pocket battleship *Deutschland* (later *Lützow*).

Minesweepers played a vital role in the war at sea.

The German heavy cruiser and convoy raider *Admiral Hipper*.

Altmark boarded

The German supply ship *Altmark* was boarded in Norwegian territorial waters on February 17 as she was making her way home. After a short fight with the German crew, sailors from the British destroyer *Cossack* (Captain Vian), released 300 British prisoners from her holds.

The *Altmark*'s prisoners had been captured by the *Graf Spee* during her brief career in the South Atlantic. The German captain had denied that he was carrying prisoners, and the Norwegians had found none during a superficial search. The 'cargo' of the *Altmark* was, however,

The supply ship *Altmark*, boarded in Norwegian waters.

known to British intelligence; hence the *Cossack*'s bold sortie. The action was against international law, but the British argued that Norway was also infringing the law by allowing prisoners of war to be transported through its waters.

The Germans attack Norway and Denmark

German forces swept over the Danish border on April 9. On the same day Norway was attacked. Denmark, in no position to resist, surrendered at once, and Copenhagen was occupied. Norway was less easily conquered.

The British and French had approved a plan to land forces in Norway early in February. Ger-

man intelligence was aware of this and Hitler planned his own invasion which, since the Anglo-French plan was postponed, took place first.

At stake in Scandinavia were Germany's iron-ore supplies from Sweden, which passed through the Norwegian port of Narvik, and valuable naval bases allowing the Germans swift access to the North Atlantic.

Anglo-French troops were hastily sent to Norway. By April 17 the British had 13,000 men ashore around Narvik and Trondheim, and there was fighting all along the coast. The Germans, however, had air superiority, and a British attack on Narvik itself was abandoned because of the inevitable civilian casualties. Ill-supported, the Allied forces were eventually compelled to withdraw.

The Norwegians, pinning their faith to neutrality, were taken by surprise by the German invasion. Their armed forces were very small in number, although, unlike the Danes, they derived some advantage in defence from the terrain. Once the Allied forces had withdrawn, they could no longer maintain the rearguard action, though unofficial resistance continued. The king and the government escaped to England in June, and the Germans forfeited any chance of widespread Norwegian acquiescence in the conquest by their support for the Norwegian fascist, Vidkun Quisling, whom they made puppet head of government.

Finland surrenders

An armistice was agreed between the Soviet Union and Finland on March 12, following the penetration of the Mannerheim Line by Russian forces, some of whom advanced over 30 miles of ice.

The Finns had put up stern resistance, which had prompted an optimistic revision of the probable length of the campaign among their friends. A British military expedition to Finland had been planned for March 20, but it was abandoned at the beginning of the month when the Finns advised that it would arrive too late. The Finnish prime minister was already in Moscow when the collapse of the Finnish defences ended any hope of further resistance. The armistice terms gave the Soviet Union what it wanted, including most of Karelia. The Finns lost nearly 30,000 men in the campaign, the Russians about twice as many.

Above. Motorized German army unit in a street in Copenhagen. Right. British soldiers disembarking in Namsos Fjord in Norway. Allied forces could offer little help to the beleaguered Norwegians.

Germans launch western offensive

On May 10 the war shifted gear as German forces swept into the Low Countries and the full force of the Nazi war machine was turned against its chief opponents, Britain and France. The main attack came in the west – inevitably since the Maginot Line protected France eastward from the Belgian border.

The original German strategy was similar to that of the Schlieffen Plan of 1914: a westward attack on a broad front, taking as much of northern France as possible and concentrating on the Channel ports. It did not envisage, at least not directly, knocking France out of the war. This plan was fundamentally altered early in 1940, partly as a result of documents from a crashed German plane falling into Allied hands, and partly because the new plan, whose chief architect was General von Manstein, appealed to Hitler. Manstein's plan called for the main thrust to be made through the Ardennes, where it would not be (and was not) expected because the country was considered impassable for tanks. Guderian, the brilliant panzer commander ('Fast Heinz' to his men), assured Manstein – correctly – that tanks could get through. ▶ *page 187*

Belgian artillerymen preparing their guns for action near the German border.

British soldiers in Bren gun carriers watch as Belgian refugees pass by.

Germans capture vital Belgian fort

A major target of the German assault on Belgium, the Eben Emael fort commanding the Albert Canal and its bridges – vital to ensure a smooth advance – fell within 24 hours of the start of the German offensive. Two of the three bridges were captured intact.

The capture of the fort, which was impregnable to ground assault, was an outstandingly skilful operation, the more remarkable for being the first attack of its kind in history – the 363 picked troops being transported by 41 gliders which arrived (all but two of them) silent and unsuspected. There were in fact very few casualties: 25 among the 1200 defenders and five among the attackers. Hitler personally decorated all the German participants with the Iron Cross.

The well-rehearsed attack on the Eben Emael fort stood in marked contrast to military tactics on the other side. In reaction to the German offensive, which was assumed to be the main thrust, French and British units moved forward into Belgium to link up with the Belgian army. Lack of planning, resulting from Belgium's hitherto neutral status, resulted in the French taking up positions where no defences had been prepared, and within two days the Allies' whole strategy was threatened by the German breakthrough farther south.

The Dutch surrender

Five days after the Germans simultaneously attacked the Low Countries and France, the Netherlands capitulated (May 14). The main object of the attack on the Netherlands was Rotterdam, which was subjected to the heaviest bombing raid yet experienced while negotiations were actually in progress.

Paratroops, an important element in German *Blitzkrieg*, spearheaded the attack on the Netherlands, and the main bridge in Rotterdam was taken by troops who landed on the water in seaplanes. Bombers attacked other communications centres and airfields. The air assault on Rotterdam, which virtually flattened the old city and killed about 1000 civilians, was probably a mistake. At least, local commanders attempted unsuccessfully to stop it, although Goering, chief of the Luftwaffe, was content to demonstrate the effect of such a bombardment. Rotterdam capitulated within hours, and the Dutch army surrendered next day.

German paratroops played an important part in the attack on the Netherlands.

The centre of Rotterdam after the devastating attack by the Luftwaffe.

The Germans break through

German armour under the command of General Rommel broke through the French lines without much difficulty on May 10–11. Of the ten existing German panzer divisions, no less than seven were committed to the Ardennes sector, where the defences were only lightly manned because an attack through the riven terrain of the Ardennes forest was unexpected.

Within four days the Germans had burst through into northern France and split the French forces in two. They advanced rapidly to the Somme. In this disastrous situation weaknesses appeared in the French command: one general suffered nervous collapse, a second shot himself, a third was dismissed. The commander-in-chief, Gamelin, had so positioned his forces that he had virtually no available reserves and he was soon replaced by Weygand (aged 72).

The immediate essential for the Allies was to repair the 50-mile-wide breach in their line which, as the German armour had run well ahead of its support, might have been feasible had not poor communications made a muddle of the operation. The Germans consolidated, but they were themselves astonished by the ease of their advance and Runstedt, the commander-in-chief, ordered a brief pause to regroup before continuing the northward momentum to 'bag' the Allied armies, including the British Expeditionary Force in Flanders and Artois. Without this pause the evacuation from Dunkirk would have been less successful. ▶ page 188

German soldiers with a troop carrier pass a burning farmhouse in France.

An artist's impression of the scene at Dunkirk.

The British turn defeat into victory

In a few days between May 27 and June 4 approximately 340,000 men, two-thirds of them British, were evacuated from the heavily besieged port of Dunkirk. The British had expected to rescue 100,000 at most. A further 190,000 men were evacuated from ports in Normandy and from Bordeaux. A vast and motley array of shipping took part in the operation, including small yachts and pleasure boats such as the *Brighton Belle*, a paddle steamer which failed to return, as well as French, Dutch and Belgian vessels.

Churchill had ordered ships to be collected in mid-May, when preparations were also being made in England against a German invasion. Three days later the British Expeditionary Force was cut off from its own supplies and depots as the Germans reached the Channel coast below Abbeville. Rommel was briefly halted by a British counter-attack at Arras, and at that point occurred the German halt: the enemy was in the bag, but the string was not drawn tight. There seemed to be no hurry. The number of troops trapped was underestimated by a factor of four, but in any case it did not seem possible that they could escape. Runstedt also wished to reserve the panzers to finish off the French.

On the same day British cryptologists cracked the cypher key being used for Luftwaffe communications, although the knowledge of German movements thus gained was now of little use. Hitler thought the war would be over in six weeks: France was clearly on the verge of defeat and he hoped then to conclude peace with Britain.

The British evacuation began on May 24, when about 1000 men were taken from Boulogne shortly before it was captured by the Germans. A German aerial attack was then launched on the Belgian ports, the heaviest assault being at Ostend, which the Germans assumed would be the chief evacuation point. The British order for 'Operation Dynamo' – evacuation from Dunkirk – to begin was issued on the evening of May 26.

The defeated troops at Dunkirk were exhausted, physically and mentally, and resentful of the relative scarcity of Royal Air Force support as they were dive-bombed by Stukas and pounded by artillery. Rain held up Luftwaffe operations on May 29 and 30, but fine weather on June 1 meant that daytime evacuation had to stop. The last British troops were brought off on June 2, the last French and other Allied troops two days later.

The Belgians, once the evacuation had begun, were forced to surrender. As the Belgian general Michiels wrote, 'We can no longer expect any support, or any other solution but total destruction.' Nevertheless, King Leopold's surrender, repudiated by the Belgian government which had take refuge in France, was regarded as precipitate. It certainly did not aid the British evacuation.

Exhausted members of the British Expeditionary Force receive a welcome drink on their return home after the evacuation from Dunkirk.

The Germans took about 40,000 prisoners, though they might have taken nearly ten times as many, and a vast quantity of equipment which Britain could ill afford to lose. Nevertheless, in British terms the operation could reasonably be interpreted as a victory for the Royal Navy and a defeat for the Luftwaffe, which lost more aircraft than the RAF. Incidents such as the massacre by an SS regiment of 100 men of the Royal Norfolks, who had surrendered when they ran out of ammunition, did not diminish the determination of the British to resist. (The SS officer responsible was hanged after the war.)

Italy declares war

As France stumbled toward defeat, on June 10 Italy declared war on Britain and France. Hitler remarked, 'They are in a hurry so that they can share in the spoils'.

The Fascist regimes of Italy and Germany had been drawn together by ideology. At first Mussolini was the 'senior partner'. By 1940, following Germany's lightning conquests, the balance had decisively changed. Mussolini had watched the German progress with mixed emotions. He had worked against the *Anschluss*, though ultimately accepting it as inevitable. He had aped Hitler's totalitarianism, making the state less efficient and his government less popular, and even copied Hitler's racial policies (the fact that the Italians were a 'non-Nordic' race and therefore, in Nazi eyes, inferior, was glossed over by all parties). In May 1939 he had signed the 'Pact of Steel', converting the understanding between the Axis powers into a formal alliance. He had invaded Albania largely to show that what Hitler could do (in Czechoslovakia) he could do in his own backyard. The failures in this campaign revealed that Italy was not ready for a major war. Mussolini told Hitler secretly that he would not be ready until 1942, which was about the time Hitler also contemplated a general war.

Events, however, moved faster. Mussolini had been disconcerted by the German-Soviet pact, of which he was not forewarned by Berlin, and by the ensuing invasion of Poland and outbreak of war. Italian military and naval chiefs advised neutrality, and the declaration of war was made by Mussolini without consulting his ministers. In the two weeks before the armistice, Italian troops advanced a short distance into the French Riviera, but Mussolini's hope of gaining Nice was frustrated as Hitler preferred to keep the French state intact.

Surrounded by his henchmen in full Fascist regalia, Mussolini delivers a speech. Seeing that France was on the point of collapse, he assumed that a complete German victory was inevitable and, anxious for a share of the booty, brought his fellow-countrymen into a war for which they were ill-prepared.

The Soviet Union occupies the Baltic republics

On June 17 Soviet forces occupied the Baltic republics of Lithuania, Latvia and Estonia. The act followed, in a matter of hours, an ultimatum to each country demanding a new government more amenable to the Soviet Union. After the occupation had taken place puppet governments were installed and in due course the three republics were incorporated into the Soviet Union. Vast numbers of people were deported to Siberia.

Hitler offers a dubious olive branch

In a speech on July 19 Hitler suggested that Britain might have peace if it wanted. The offer was phrased ungraciously, to say the least, and was not taken seriously by the British government.

Hitler's foreign policy during the 1930s had amounted to a claim for more German territory (*Lebensraum*, 'living space') in the east. The ease with which most of his aims had been achieved had made him overconfident, and the German attack on Poland had brought about a European war. With the fall of France, Germany had, for all practical purposes, won that war, and won it with devastating ease. What was to happen next? The only enemy still on its feet was Britain. Hitler had no particular wish to invade Britain, and the German military chiefs by and large opposed it. The Führer was more interested in attacking the Soviet Union, and advised his generals accordingly. However, while he had no special desire to conquer the British, he did need Britain neutralized. The country would therefore have to be conquered. For that to happen, however, it was necessary (as everyone recognized) for Germany to achieve air superiority.

France defeated

On June 5, the day after the Dunkirk evacuation ended, the Germans launched a major offensive southward against France. Though there were still some British (and Polish) troops fighting in France, the only substantial help the British could provide was in the air and it was not enough.

Many French units fought courageously but, apart from a brief check north of Paris, they were unable to hold up the German advance. In three days the Germans were across the Seine. By the middle of the month they were strolling around Paris admiring the sights (Paris had been declared an open city to avoid disastrous bombardment). The British sent more squadrons of aircraft to France than they could afford if they were to maintain the numbers thought necessary to defend Britain, but not as many as the French requested. They were losing Hurricanes at the rate of 25 a day and the chief of Fighter Command (Dowding) eventually threatened to resign if more aircraft were sent.

The French government retreated south, ahead of the invaders, visited several times by Churchill, desperate to keep France in the war. At the last moment Churchill even aired a romantic plan for political union of France and Britain. A day later Reynaud, who had all along been relatively bellicose, resigned, since a majority in his cabinet, like Weygand, favoured surrender. He was replaced by the aged Pétain, who sought an armistice. This was signed at Compiègne, in the railway carriage that had been the scene of the German sur-render in 1918. Hitler sat in Marshal Foch's chair.

Under the terms of the armistice, the Germans occupied roughly two-thirds of France, while an independent French state, with its capital at Vichy, remained in the southeast. The main purpose of keeping a French state in existence was to prevent the French overseas possessions continuing war against Germany.

Hitler in jovial mood before the signing of the French armistice.

Britain fires on French ships

In what Churchill described as a 'hateful action', British warships opened fire on the French fleet at Mers el-Kébir, near Oran, Algeria, on July 3, in order to prevent it falling into German hands. Two elderly battleships and the powerful new battle cruiser, ironically named *Dunquerque*, were sunk.

When the French government had gained Britain's consent to making a separate peace with Germany, it had been agreed that the French fleet should not be allowed to pass into German hands, but it continued to be stationed in ports abroad, a large part in Mers el-Kébir. The British boarded and took over French ships in British ports, and in Alexandria, without opposition, but because of some misunderstanding, plus wounded French pride, the fleet at Mers el-Kébir defied an ultimatum which offered several alternatives, including sailing the ships across the Atlantic for internment in U.S. ports. When

French warship on fire at Mers el-Kébir.

the ultimatum expired, the British opened fire. Over 1000 French sailors were killed. A number of the French vessels escaped to Toulon.

This ruthless British action, though resented by the French and leading to the Vichy government breaking off relations, had one advantageous result for Britain. It was convincing evidence – especially in U.S. government circles where the reports of the U.S. ambassador in London (Joseph Kennedy) had raised doubts – of Britain's unwavering determination to continue the war against Germany.

'The Day of the Eagle' dawns

On August 13, code-named by the Germans 'the Day of the Eagle', 1485 German aircraft attacked England, marking the beginning of an intensification of the assault on British air defences. The Luftwaffe lost 45 aircraft shot down, British Fighter Command 13 fighters. The crews of the German planes were, naturally, either killed or captured, but eight of the 13 British pilots were able to return to combat.

The raids of August 13 had been preceded by attacks, which had only limited success, on British radar installations on the south coast. These were the most advanced early-warning systems in the world and were vital in locating the approach of German aircraft, allowing the British fighter pilots to remain on the ground instead of constantly patrolling.

The air battle had been going on since before the fall of France, with attacks, in smaller numbers, mainly on coastal installations and shipping. By August 13, when the Battle of Britain began in earnest, the Germans had already lost about 200 aircraft.

The heavy bombing assaults continued daily for five days. Although the German casualties were nearly always higher, sometimes much higher (though never nearly as high as the optimistic estimates announced by the British authorities), British losses were at a level which could not be long sustained. The Germans were surprised by the efficiency of the British fighters, especially the Spitfire, and were forced to withdraw certain aircraft, notably the Stukas, which proved far too vulnerable. Meanwhile, British bombers retaliated, bombing German industrial areas and communications and Berlin itself, though the damage inflicted was much less than had been hopefully anticipated. ('Precision bombing' was not an accurate description: in an early British raid on the German island of Sylt, one British pilot had dropped his bombs on Bornholm, a different island, belonging to a different country, and in a different sea!)

After a brief pause the attack on British airfields, factories and fuel depots was resumed. However, on September 7, the day of an invasion 'scare' (one of many) in England, the primary targets were changed. Instead of airfields and the various air defence facilities, the Luftwaffe was directed against London, especially the docks. Some observers at the time, and most historians since, regard the change of tactics as a mistake. German air chiefs seem to have thought the battle was won (their estimates of enemy casualties were also wildly exaggerated). It was not won, although, but for the change in targets, it might have been.

A Heinkel bomber flies over London's dockland.

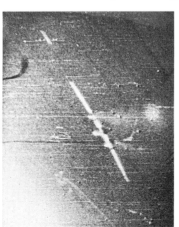

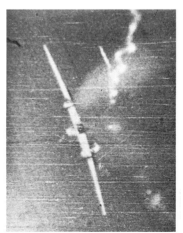
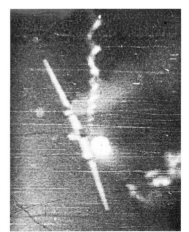

A German aircraft trying to escape bursts into flames as one of its engines receives a direct hit.

Japanese move into Indo-China

A Japanese army supply column moving through the streets of a town in Indo-China.

Japanese forces invaded northern parts of French Indo-China on September 22. The move was not unexpected, and followed a demand for bases in the region made two months earlier.

Japanese relations with the west had deteriorated steadily in recent years. The United States and Britain had attempted to bring assistance to the Chinese Nationalists, although supplies were small, and in this endeavour the 700-mile Burma Road, along which supplies could pass (the Japanese controlled the Chinese coast), had been constructed with great difficulty in 1937–9. The Japanese had made several attempts to stop this traffic, and in July 1940 the British agreed to close the road, for three months only, rather than risk war with Japan at such a critical moment. Meanwhile the United States, having renounced the U.S.-Japanese trade treaty of 1911, placed embargoes on exports to Japan of war and other materials.

Italians bring war to North Africa

On September 13 Italian forces from Libya crossed the border into Egypt. The previous month they had occupied British Somaliland and had bombed Gibraltar, marking the beginning of the campaigns in North Africa.

The collapse of France threatened British dominance of the Mediterranean at a time when the British were fully occupied defending their own island. The Italian navy was in some respects superior to the British fleet, notably in submarines, of which Italy had the largest number of any combatant. Nevertheless, the British were able to reinforce Egypt, sending warships through the Mediterranean without interference, at the height of the Battle of Britain, while Italian territorial advances were of minor importance. ▶ *page 194*

Indian troops, who played an important role in the desert war, on the march in Egypt.

Free French repulsed at Dakar

On September 23 the British, in co-operation with Free French forces, launched an offensive of their own. The objective was Dakar, in French West Africa, which was expected to renounce its allegiance to Vichy France without a fight.

This hope proved too sanguine. The authorities refused to acknowledge de Gaulle, who accompanied the expedition, and opened fire on the elderly British warships with the 17-inch guns of the battleship *Richelieu*. The operation was thereupon called off.

Italians invade Greece

On October 28 Italian forces invaded Greece from Albania. The attack was preceded by an unacceptable ultimatum; in fact the Italians had begun to cross the border before it was delivered.

The attack took place against the advice of the Italian chiefs of staff and to the annoyance of Hitler, for Germany was gaining control of the Balkans largely by diplomatic and economic pressure and did not wish to become embroiled in a Balkan war. Mussolini took care not to inform Berlin until it was too late for Hitler to stop him.

The Italian invasion soon went awry. It was carried out by only three divisions, on separate lines of advance. Within a week the Greeks had stopped the Italians in their tracks. Within three weeks they themselves had crossed the border into Albania as the Italians fell back.

Meanwhile, in fulfilment of Britain's guarantee to Greece, the Royal Navy struck at the Italian fleet. Torpedo bombers from the aircraft carrier *Illustrious* attacked the Italian fleet in the southern port of Taranto. One battleship was sunk and several other ships were put temporarily out of action. The Italians subsequently abandoned Taranto as a naval base, shifting all warships to the west coast. The British moved into Crete and Aegean bases, which brought the Romanian oilfields supplying Germany within range of their bombers.

The success of aerial torpedoes at Taranto was noted with interest by Japan's naval chief, Yamamoto, who was considering ways of 'taking out' the U.S. Pacific fleet. The same thought occurred to U.S. Navy secretary Frank Knox, who wrote that 'precautionary measures should be taken immediately to protect Pearl Harbor . . .'.

Italians captured by the Greeks in Albania.

Fire storm hits Coventry

Coventry cathedral in ruins after the air raid.

As part of the continuing German 'blitz' on England, a major assault was made on Coventry on November 14. Five hundred bombers were involved in the attack, which created a 'fire storm' in the city centre, killing 586 people and destroying about 60,000 buildings, including the cathedral.

The raid on Coventry, one of the most damaging of the war, was partly sparked off by a British raid on Munich on November 8, which ruined the festivities marking the anniversary of the Nazi putsch of 1923. The Coventry attack gave the Germans a new word, *koventrieren*, 'to annihilate'. It revealed the effectiveness of starting many fires instantaneously, so that fire-fighters were overwhelmed.

German air raids continued nightly, especially on London. During the month of November 4588 civilians were killed, and the British abandoned the principle, already frequently infringed inadvertently, of avoiding civilian targets. An RAF raid on Hamburg two days after Coventry left 233 German men, women and children dead.

Australian soldiers examining tanks abandoned by the Italians after an engagement in the Western Desert.

British counterattack in the Western Desert

With the advantage of first-rate intelligence on troop deployment and minefields, the British launched a counterattack on December 9 from Sidi Barani against the Italians. The assault was preceded by armoured-car patrols which confirmed certain gaps in Italian minefields.

General Wavell commanded two divisions in the attack, about half the troops being Indian with other units from Commonwealth, French and Polish formations. Though enjoying a numerical advantage of 2:1, the Italians were forced to retreat. The British suffered fewer than 100 casualties and all Egyptian territory was cleared in a week. ▶ page 199

St Paul's survives the flames

The Germans launched a particularly heavy raid with incendiary bombs on the City of London on December 29. The Guildhall was destroyed along with eight of Wren's churches and several halls of the livery companies. St Paul's cathedral, which at one time seemed to be engulfed by fire, was saved through the selfless endeavour of fire-fighters.

Left. Firemen direct a hose on to a still smouldering fire the morning after a German air raid on London.

Right. St Paul's Cathedral – miraculously it seemed at the time – survived the onslaught by the Luftwaffe on London, although many of the city's most famous buildings were destroyed. During the last six months of 1940 more than 23,000 civilians were killed in air raids on Britain.

Enigma

Alongside the great battles and campaigns of the Second World War, another, secret war was continually in progress, one in which the combatants sought to learn each other's plans, keep their own secret and mislead the enemy with false information. The usefulness of the activities of spies is a controversial subject – generally underrated by the military, perhaps exaggerated by others. Certainly there were some remarkable achievements in espionage and counter-espionage: the 'double-cross' system in Britain fed fictitious information to the Germans throughout the war from agents who were either nonexistent or had been 'turned round'. The Sorge ring in Tokyo, with intimate contacts in the German embassy, gave the Soviet Union advance notice both of Japan's intention not to attack in the east and of the German plan to invade in the west. There were hundreds of others.

Military intelligence was another matter. The source of the most productive intelligence in Britain, known as Ultra, was the top-secret government code and cipher school at Bletchley, and the most valuable information provided by Ultra came

Inspecting the Enigma decoding machine.

from an ability to crack the messages enciphered by the German cipher machine, Enigma. British intelligence had acquired knowledge of these machines at an early stage, indirectly through the Poles, and was thus able to receive messages between the German high command and the various commanders in the field. A great number of different ciphers were used, and it was comparatively rare for a cipher to be (1) completely understood and (2) (equally important), to be understood *in time* for the information derived from it to be useful.

The Enigma machine offered almost an infinity of possible solutions and, to a large degree, success in deciphering – at least until the experts at Bletchley perfected their system –

depended on small mistakes made by the operator. For some reason Luftwaffe operators tended to be less accurate than those of other services, and Ultra proved valuable in the Battle of Britain in providing information about targets and the extent and direction of attack. Ultra was also important in the battle of the Atlantic in 1943, after the Bletchley unit had at last solved the cipher used by the U-boats.

On the other side, the Germans also had successes. While Ultra saved many ships by allowing convoys to be re-routed to avoid the U-boat wolf packs, the Germans were reading British Admiralty messages on convoys, which until 1943 were sent in code, not cipher.

The true value of Ultra was not revealed until many years after the war, neither was the perhaps equally important U.S. penetration of Japanese ciphers ('Magic'). The full extent of the achievements of other participants (the Italian ciphers were notably secure) is still not known. It seems probable, for instance, that the Russians were, independently, no less successful than the British in solving the German Enigma.

HOME GUARD

WITH THE IMMINENT collapse of France, the British prepared for invasion. Churchill issued a warning in his 'This was their finest hour' speech on June 18, though it was known through intelligence that no major onslaught was likely before mid-July. Meanwhile, all Germans were hastily interned, though the majority of them were refugees from the Nazis. Those who were Nazis were sometimes found to be the most useful people to put in charge of the others. Some died on their way to internment in Canada. A few British Nazi sympathizers, like Sir Oswald Mosley, leader of the British fascists, were also interned. There were many instances of errors by over-conscientious security officials and many injustices, but in general, thanks to the relative ineffectiveness of Nazi propaganda in Britain and the leadership of Churchill (who seldom lost sight of the fact that the cause Britain was fighting for was liberty of the individual), the government's extensive authoritarian powers were exercised in a less oppressive manner than might have been expected.

Various means were adopted to confuse the potential invader, such as the removal of signposts and names of railway stations. Booksellers destroyed their stock of maps, though maps of Britain were not exactly unavailable in Germany. (The Germans had used British maps in the Norway campaign; but they were obsolete – the British did not have them – which created considerable difficulties when German signals were being interpreted by the British cryptanalysts.)

A home defence force was instituted, originally called the Local Defence Volunteers but soon renamed the Home Guard. Within a few weeks, over one million men had enrolled. Most of them were veterans of the First World War, for whom drilling and designing road blocks and home-made bombs came as a welcome antidote to restlessness. At first practically none had weapons – one Lancashire unit drilled with spears – and when they did get rifles (500,000 Lee Enfields 'surplus to requirements' arrived from the United States) they had no ammunition for them. The king, George VI, somewhat better equipped, practised revolver shooting in the gardens of Buckingham Palace (where, incidentally, he remained with the queen and their two young daughters throughout the war). As uniforms and equipment were provided the Home Guard took on a more military air, though its potential in case of an actual invasion remained doubtful. Later in the war the Home Guard was greatly reinforced, though by that time the danger of invasion had virtually disappeared.

Below. Workmen obliterating the name of a station to confuse German paratroops in the event of an invasion.

Opposite. Erecting barbed wire entanglements across a road in southern England.

Signposts removed to avoid helping enemy invaders.

Home Guard on parade at County Hall, London.

Germans and Austrians en route to internment camps.

Sir Oswald Mosley at a prewar rally.

THE *JERVIS BAY* FIGHTS BACK

The armed merchant cruiser *Jervis Bay*.

WITH GERMAN pressure on Atlantic shipping increasing, the pocket battleship Admiral Scheer (Captain Krancke) attacked a 37-ship convoy coming from Nova Scotia in mid-Atlantic on November 5. The convoy was escorted by the Jervis Bay, a former Australian passenger ship converted to armed merchant cruiser. Captain Edward Fogarty Fegen, an Irishman from Tipperary and a naval veteran of the First World War, ordered the convoy to make smoke and scatter as he steamed to engage the German raider.

In this David and Goliath contest, Captain Fegen did not have the advantage, so crucial to the original David, of a weapon that outranged the enemy's. His armament consisted merely of seven outdated 6-inch guns mounted on the deck of the 20-year-old liner, and his top speed was about 15 knots. The Scheer had six 11-inch guns as her main armament and the Jervis Bay had no chance whatever of escaping destruction. What she could do was delay the enemy, allowing the ships she escorted to make a break for safety.

The unequal contest lasted almost half an hour. Fegen's left arm was almost shot off at an early stage, but he remained in control of the battle. As a result the Scheer was able to catch and sink only five or six ships of the convoy. Of the crew of the Jervis Bay, 189 were killed, including Captain Fegen (posthumously awarded the Victoria Cross). The 65 survivors were later picked up by the Swedish Stureholm (Captain Sven Olander), which courageously returned to the scene.

Another ship, the 8000-ton oil tanker San Demetrio, was abandoned by her crew when largely disabled and on fire. One of her lifeboats, with Second Officer Hawkins in command, found her still burning the next day. He led the 13 men in the lifeboat back on board, notwithstanding the imminent threat of exploding fuel, and succeeded in putting out the fire. The scratch crew managed to raise steam and – eight days later – reached the Irish coast, where volunteers from a British destroyer came on board and helped her to limp into the Clyde. She berthed on November 19, 14 days after she was attacked.

The German pocket battleship *Admiral Scheer*.

1941

WAVELL CAPTURES TOBRUK

LEND-LEASE ACT

Tobruk captured

British artillery units firing into Tobruk.

Continuing the offensive begun the previous month, British and Australian forces captured Tobruk on January 22. The port then surrendered and 25,000 Italian prisoners were taken.

Wavell's offensive had begun as virtually a symbolic gesture, but it had turned into a victorious campaign. Though he had only about 30,000 men, they swept rapidly across Cyrenaica, covering about 500 miles in two months and shattering an Italian army more than five times the size. By the end of the first week in February, Benghazi, too, had fallen, but there the advance stopped. Chur-chill decided that the defence of Greece should have priority, and troops, aircraft and equipment were withdrawn from North Africa for that purpose. A few days later, Rommel arrived in Tripoli. The desert war was about to take on an entirely different aspect. ▶ *page 209*

Arsenal of democracy opens for business

The Lend-Lease act was passed by the U.S. Congress on March 11. President Roosevelt described it in homely terms as lending a hose to a neighbour whose house is on fire on the assumption that he will give it back when the fire is put out.

The act empowered the president to supply 'defence articles' (governmentese for 'weapons') to any country whose defence he deemed vital to U.S. security. In the immediate circumstances this meant Britain, and the effect was basically to place U.S. industry at the disposal of the British war effort with no question about payment.

Britain's total gold and dollar reserves had fallen from about $4.5 million at the start of the war to about $2 million at the end of 1940. Some war supplies had already been passed to Britain without further depletion of those fast-vanishing reserves, such as the exchange of 50 moth-balled U.S. destroyers for bases in the Caribbean. Lend-Lease made it possible for Britain, and later the Soviet Union and other countries, to acquire supplies from the United States with no financial strings attached.

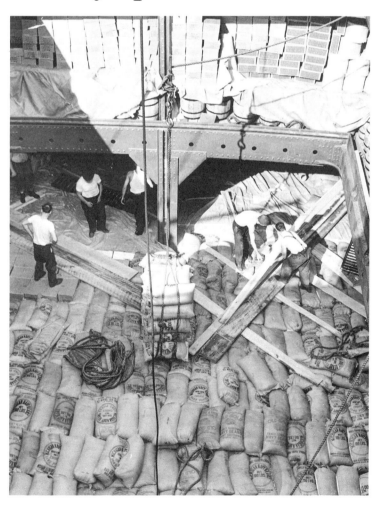

A British ship being loaded with American produce as part of lend-lease arrangements.

JANUARY
5 Wavell's forces take Bardia
10 Italians bomb Malta
10 Sicily-based German aircraft bomb British Mediterranean convoy
10 Greeks capture Klisura
11 Hitler issues directive for aid to the Italians
16 German air raid on Valletta harbour
19 Start of East African offensive against Italians
21 Riots and massacre in Romania
22 British and Australians take Tobruk
23 *Scharnhorst* and *Gneisenau* sail for the Atlantic
31 2000 die of hunger in January in Warsaw ghetto

FEBRUARY
6 Hitler calls for intensification of Atlantic battle
6 German troops sent to North Africa
6 Australians capture seven Italian generals at Benghazi
11 British war cabinet gives priority to defence of Greece
12 Rommel arrives in Tripoli
14 Yugoslavia declines to join Axis
17 Turkey compelled to sign non-aggression pact with Germany
28 Zhukov becomes Red Army chief of staff

MARCH
1 United States advises Soviet Union of impending German invasion
1 Bulgaria accedes to German occupation
4 Commando/Norwegian raid on Lofoten islands destroys factories and ships
4 Turkey refuses to join Axis
5 British troops transported to Greece
5 Richard Sorge advises Moscow of approximate date of German invasion
7 Allied forces invade Abyssinia (Ethiopia)
11 U.S. Lend-Lease act passed
13 17 members of Dutch Resistance executed
15 Rommel begins North Africa offensive
17 Britain introduces mobilization of women
25 Yugoslavia adheres to Axis
26 Yugoslav government ousted and German pact rejected
28 British naval victory off Cape Matapán

1941

Italian navy shattered

Good intelligence accounted for a British victory on March 28 in the largest naval battle of the war so far, when Admiral Cunningham's ships encountered the main Italian fleet south of Cape Matapán (Taínaron), at the southern extremity of the Greek mainland. At the cost of a couple of aircraft shot down, the British sank five Italian cruisers (leaving only three afloat) and three destroyers, although the flagship escaped. The Italian navy was emasculated as a fighting force, and the British task of moving troops across the Mediterranean to Greece was eased.

A British aircraft carrier, seen from the battleship *Warspite*, just before the battle of Cape Matapán which proved such a disaster for the Italian navy.

The Italians withdraw from Addis

Addis Ababa fell to mainly South African troops on April 6, following the withdrawal of the Italians. Emperor Haile Selassie was brought back from exile, and entered his capital on the fifth anniversary of the Italian conquest.

The previous summer the British had been forced out of British Somaliland, and for a time the Italians threatened Kenya and the Sudan. The offensive against them began in January, and involved African, Indian and French troops as well as some others. It was assisted by the ability of the British to read all Italian operational orders, and was notable for the exploits of the unconventional Gideon Force, consisting of Abyssinians and Sudanese troops under the command of the charismatic Colonel Orde Wingate.

With the capture of Addis the Italians had effectively lost East Africa, though some fighting continued in the north of Abyssinia and the final surrender was delayed until November.

Indian troops in Abyssinia manhandle armoured cars in mountainous country.

The Germans invade the Balkans

On April 6 a *Blitzkrieg* was launched again on small and relatively defenceless countries when the Germans simultaneously attacked Greece and Yugoslavia. A devastating bombing raid on Belgrade killed about 17,000 civilians. It was Palm Sunday and many people from outside the city had come to worship.

The bulk of the Yugoslav air force was also destroyed before it could take to the air. At the same time more German bombers hit the Greek port of Piraeus. Six ships were sunk, then a bomb hit the British merchant ship, *Northern Prince*, carrying explosives. In the explosion that followed a further ten ships were sunk and the port was devastated.

Hitler was not so foolish as to wage war when he could get what he wanted by less expensive means, and he had gained considerable success in the Balkans by diplomacy and blackmail. Hungary, Romania and Bulgaria had all been persuaded by various means to adhere to the Axis, and on March 25 the Yugoslav government had done likewise, the Regent Paul signing the relevant treaty in Vienna, to Hitler's satisfaction. However, it was not popular, and the government was overthrown in a revolt led by General Simovic, who wanted the country to remain neutral and cancelled the Axis pact. This was the immediate cause for Hitler's decision to invade the Balkans, even though it meant postponing Operation Barbarossa.

Three German armies now advanced across the borders. The first, from Austria and Hungary, made for Belgrade. The second and third advanced from Bulgaria, one into Yugoslavia and the other into Thrace, toward the Greek port of Salonika.

Belgrade fell within a week. A few days later, as the casualty figures mounted, the Yugoslav government surrendered. Hungary, Bulgaria and Italy all helped themselves to portions of the country, while Croat leaders seized the opportunity to create an independent (and fascist) state. Serbia was taken over by the Germans. It was, however, to prove a troublesome conquest, with guerrilla resistance organized on some scale.

Greece had a guarantee from Britain, and political considerations dictated that Britain, whose guarantees so far had not been worth much, should attempt to honour it. Nevertheless, the country was swiftly conquered, and it was soon obvious that another evacuation would be necessary. Muddles among the Allies resulted in most of the Greek forces being captured (a number of Greek officers, receiving the order to surrender, followed the example of their prime minister and committed suicide). The majority of the Allied forces – British, Australian and New Zealand, as well as some Greeks – were taken off to Crete, which had been occupied by Britain some months earlier.
▶ *page 202*

▶ *page 202*

Yugoslav soldiers lay down their arms after being captured by the Germans.

An unexpected visitor from Berlin

In one of the oddest incidents of the war, Rudolf Hess, Hitler's deputy and number two man in the Nazi party, arrived in Scotland on May 10. He had parachuted from his Messerschmitt, which he was flying alone, because he could not find a landing field, and he suffered a sprained ankle. He asked to see the Duke of Hamilton whom he had met before the war.

Hess's flight was apparently a solo initiative with the aim of issuing a last appeal to Britain to make common cause with Germany against the Soviet Union. It was clear, however, that he was mentally unbalanced.

Rudolf Hess.

British make sure of Iraq

On May 4 British troops invaded Iraq. One force was drawn from Palestine, the other consisted mainly of the Arab Legion under Brigadier Glubb (Glubb Pasha), from Transjordan. The purpose behind the invasion was to make sure of supplies of Iraqi oil and to forestall the Germans by overthrowing the pro-German regime of Rashid Ali.

Arab nationalists, especially those whose hopes of independence had been frustrated after the First World War, saw in the current conflict an opportunity to advance their cause. Britain's hasty adoption of a more pro-Arab policy in Palestine on the eve of the war was one sign of the advantages that might be drawn from the European conflict. Germany seemed to them a convenient lever with which to eject British and French imperialism from the Middle East.

Rashid Ali attempted to restrict British access to Basra and the Gulf, which was established by treaty, and looked for support from Berlin. He received some aircraft from Hitler and a suppor-

tive declaration, but Hitler's Middle East policy was vague and undecided (and complicated by Italian ambitions) and his declaration did not go as far as Rashid Ali would have liked.

The British forces encountered little serious opposition. Baghdad surrendered at the end of the month, Rashid Ali took refuge in Iran and a more co-operative regime took over in Baghdad.

Soldiers of the Arab Legion on guard on the Iraq-Transjordan frontier.

Attack from the skies

Following an aerial bombardment at dawn on May 20 German troops invaded Crete. They were transported there in about 500 aircraft and gliders. The Germans had total air cover, as the last British fighters on Crete had been withdrawn, to prevent further losses, to Egypt. Nevertheless, fighting was ferocious and casualties among General Student's airborne troops were very heavy.

Reliance on British superiority at sea had resulted in neglect of the defences of Crete. There was also a muddle over intelligence reports, which were good but not fully exploited (a matter that is still the source of argument). Besides the lack of air cover, the troops on the island were poorly equipped. The Greek troops, in particular, were said to have one rifle to six men and three rounds of ammunition each. Despite the ferocious resistance – experienced veterans said this was the fiercest fighting they had encountered – General Freyberg (a New Zealander, like many of the defenders) could not prevent the Germans gaining control of one of the main airfields. As a result

German paratroops taking part in mass landings on Crete.

the Germans were able to fly in reinforcements virtually unopposed. Attempts to bring in troops by sea were less successful: the convoys were severely dealt with by the British navy.

After a week of fighting the problem for the British was how to evacuate Crete. It was an operation fraught with danger. In the end, only about half the defenders got away, and the British ships, under constant air attack, suffered heavily. Three cruisers and six destroyers were sunk, and two battleships, three cruisers and an aircraft carrier damaged. Among

the casualties was the destroyer *Kelly* (Captain Lord Louis Mountbatten, whose nephew Philip also took part in the battle as an officer on the *Valiant*), which had performed heroically in the Norway campaign.

The capture of Crete was a remarkable victory in view of Britain's command of the sea. To an extent, however, it was due to British mistakes, and the Germans too suffered heavy losses – over one-third of the airborne troops and over 200 aircraft. They were not to attempt a similar type of operation again.

End of the *Bismarck*

In an engagement which occupied a large part of the British navy, the new, 45,000-ton German battleship *Bismarck* was sunk on May 27. Immobile and unable to fight, and surrounded by British warships, she was scuttled by order of her commander, Admiral Lutjens. Owing to a submarine scare in the area, very few of the crew were picked up by the British ships.

Accompanied by the formidable heavy cruiser *Prinz Eugen*, the *Bismarck* had sailed to attack British convoys in the North Atlantic on May 18. She was spotted taking on fuel in Bergen, and as she broke out through the Denmark Strait she was shadowed on radar by two British cruisers. Two large squadrons from Scapa Flow sailed hastily to guard the Atlantic convoys from this new and unexpected menace.

In the morning of May 24 the *Bismarck* was engaged by the first of these squadrons, which included the battle cruiser *Hood* and the battleship *Prince of Wales*. The first round proved to be a victory for the German leviathan: the *Hood* exploded, with the loss of all hands, and the *Prince of Wales* was damaged. However, the *Bismarck* had also been hit and a vital fuel line severed.

Later the same day another attack was carried out, by torpedo-carrying aircraft from the carrier *Victorious*, which, however, did no serious damage. At the same time another naval force had been dispatched from Gibraltar. It included the carrier *Ark Royal* and the battle cruiser *Renown*. The battleship *Rodney* was also coming from the northeast.

The following day, the two German warships separated, and the British lost track of the *Bismarck*, which was sailing for a French port to take on more fuel. She was not discovered again until the morning of May 26, when she was sighted by aerial patrols. Aircraft from the *Ark Royal* continued to track her, and in the evening she was again attacked with torpedoes. One hit her rudder, so that she could no longer steer.

In the night the torpedo attack was renewed by a destroyer, while the battleships *King George V* and *Rodney* closed in. Next morning they opened fire with their heavy guns, scoring hit after hit. The coup de grace was administered by torpedoes from the cruiser *Dorsetshire*.

The battleship *Bismarck*, the pride of the German navy, was sunk on its first mission.

The *Prince of Wales*.

Motorized German troops moving through scenes of devastation in the Soviet Union.

Vichy France loses another territory

On June 8 Free French and British forces invaded Syria. The immediate reason for the attack was the assistance rendered to Rashid Ali in Iraq, which was prompted by Admiral Darlan, currently foreign minister in the Vichy government.

After over a month's fighting the Vichy commander, General Dentz, was forced to surrender. His forces, though numerically superior, lacked most of the necessary equipment for modern warfare, and no help arrived from Germany. In the elation of victory, the Free French promised independence to both Syria and Lebanon.

The Germans invade the Soviet Union

The German-Soviet non-aggression pact of 1939 was abruptly terminated at dawn on June 22, when Germany launched 'Operation Barbarossa', its long-planned invasion of the Soviet Union and the largest single military operation ever attempted. In the first few hours, dozens of Russian cities and airfields were attacked by bombers while, before the bombs had stopped falling, German forces crossed the border on a 1000-mile front.

Stalin had known for a long time that a German attack was likely. His excellent agents in Tokyo, Switzerland and Germany itself had all informed him of it. Both the British and U.S. governments had warned him, on the basis of their intelligence. In any case, he could hardly have failed to observe the massive movements of German troops in the weeks before the invasion began.

Yet Stalin hoped, up to the last minute, that a German attack might be avoided. He made many efforts to appease Hitler in the months before the invasion. A few hours before it began, Stalin was arguing with General Timoshenko over whether a general alert should be issued. He was afraid that it might incite Hitler. As the German panzers stormed into Soviet territory, trains carrying Russian supplies were still dutifully making their way towards the Reich.

Such was the nature of the Stalinist government that whatever Stalin and his close associates might know was not communicated to the people. Nor was it communicated to local commanders. As a result, the German attack came as a total surprise to those most immediately affected.

On paper the Soviet Union was superior to Germany (and its allies) not only in manpower but also in aircraft, tanks and even artillery. The figures, however, were misleading. About 80 per cent of Soviet aircraft were obsolete types. Most of the tanks were too lightly armoured to be effective (the Russians produced, in the T.34, the best tank of the war, but it did not become operative in significant numbers until 1943).

In short, the Soviet Union was unprepared and ill-equipped to resist the German attack.

The Soviet line was at once breached at several points. A strategic error now became plain: a large part of the Soviet forces had been placed in forward positions, on territory such as eastern Poland and Bessarabia only recently acquired. Their communications and support were not yet properly organized. Many pieces of essential equipment were in short supply or unavailable.

The panzers sliced through Soviet territory, bypassing strong points and large cities and carving the country into chunks for the supporting troops to mop up later. Huge numbers of prisoners were taken, as the defence dissolved into something near chaos. On the second day of the battle, one Soviet bomber group was said to have lost 600 aircraft, and by the end of August aircraft losses were estimated at over 5000.

However, for all their sensational progress, advancing at 50 miles a day, the Germans had some cause for worry. In spite of the enormous destruction of aircraft, more kept arriving – from factories which had been moved beyond the Urals, out of range of the Luftwaffe. In spite of the overwhelming superiority of German tanks, the Russians continued to fight back, often suicidally.

The ferocity of the fighting took the Germans by surprise. The Russian forces, by any standards, were being resoundingly defeated. Yet they were still fighting. They were fighting, too, behind the German lines, where partisan bands were quickly formed – often from soldiers cut off from their units. The panzers continued to advance, basically in three directions – towards Leningrad, towards Moscow and towards the Ukraine. But they had advanced a very long way ahead of the main troops, on a total front which, by the nature of the land, was constantly widening. With unorganized bands roaming behind the lines, and groups of uncaptured troops in isolated pockets, there was a danger of a major breakout (there were one or two minor ones) in the German rear. The forces of the Reich began to look somewhat overstretched.

Advancing German soldiers pass a burning Russian tank.

The Germans take Brest Litovsk

On July 23 Brest Litovsk surrendered to the besieging Germans after a four-week bombardment carried out by aircraft and artillery. A new German mortar, nicknamed 'Karl', which fired a two-ton shell, was responsible for much of the destruction. Meanwhile, the German advance had proceeded far beyond the city.

It had already become clear that this was a campaign like no other. Although the Germans advanced inexorably and the Russians suffered terrible losses in men, tanks and equipment, their resistance was fiercer than the Germans had anticipated. They launched frequent counter-attacks, some of which were, at least temporarily, successful. The Russian soldiers, whose fighting spirit Hitler had supposed to be enfeebled by communism, fought with extreme tenacity. As one German general remarked, they seemed to have no fear of death. In the vast expanses of the Soviet Union the Germans were already encountering severe difficulties

posed by a scorched-earth policy and by partisan bands. Partisan warfare was to be an important, perhaps decisive, feature of the Russian campaign.

The campaign was unique in another way. It was marked by atrocities on a scale hitherto unknown, even in Poland. This was deliberate Nazi policy, though even some SS men expressed disgust and loathing (in private). Some of Hitler's allies were also guilty of massacring civilians, especially Jews.

In a Soviet guerrilla encampment. Partisans operated with great effect behind German lines.

1941

ATLANTIC CHARTER SIGNED

LENINGRAD UNDER SIEGE

GERMAN OFFENSIVE AGAINST MOSCOW

Churchill and Roosevelt sign Atlantic Charter

The British prime minister and the U.S. president met on board ship off Newfoundland on August 11. They agreed to aid the Soviet Union and issued a warning to Japan that any further encroachments would incur 'counter-measures'. They agreed too on a document, called the Atlantic Charter, issued a few days later, which expressed Anglo-U.S. determination to see freedom and democracy restored to those countries under Axis domination.

Churchill and Roosevelt with members of their entourage on board the U.S.S. *Augusta*.

Leningrad besieged

German soldiers besieging Leningrad find their movements hampered by appalling weather conditions.

On September 8 Leningrad was cut off and came under siege. The German line stretched south to Kiev, in the Ukraine, and Odessa, on the Black Sea, with a salient protruding beyond Dnepropetrovsk towards the Donetz basin. The Germans were less than 250 miles from Moscow, and the fall of the capital before winter set in in earnest appeared inevitable. The Russians had lost nearly half their ground forces and a huge quantity of equipment.

However, the front was 2000 miles long, too much even for the Luftwaffe to cover effectively, and the German forces were dangerously stretched. Moreover, the Germans could not be said to be in complete command of all the territory they had conquered.

They did not control, for instance, the 'partisan triangle' north-west of Vitebsk, and Hitler's order that commanders of areas behind the front should maintain order 'by employing suitably draconian methods' failed to crush resistance.

The shah of Iran abdicates

Following an Anglo-Soviet invasion of Iran, the shah was forced to abdicate on September 18. He went into exile, eventually to South Africa. His son, Muhammad Reza, succeeded him.

Before the war, the Germans had managed to achieve a dominant position in Iran, and after Syria and Iraq had been secured by the Allies, Iran became the centre of German political activity in the Middle East. With the advance of German troops in the Soviet Union, a military takeover was clearly a distinct possibility. To forestall it, the Soviet Union and Britain invaded Iran simultaneously in August, the Russians from the north, the British from the south. There was little serious resistance. Under the terms of the 1921 treaty, the Soviet Union had some justification for its invasion, though the only British justification was self-preservation.

Eventually an agreement was made between the three parties which established Russian and British occupation for the duration of the war.

A British soldier stands guard near a sunken ship at the Abadan oil refinery.

The Panzers drive towards Moscow

On October 2 the Germans launched an offensive in the direction of Moscow. Guderian's armour was switched from the Ukraine, where Kiev had finally fallen (and the Russians had lost four armies), for this final thrust of the year. Moscow was in a state bordering panic, with millions leaving the city. Stalin, however, remained.

The weather turned against the Germans. Heavy rain made the battlefields into swamps, and when the frost came at last it came with a vengeance. Severe blizzards grounded the Luftwaffe. The German troops had inadequate clothing. Their supplies could not reach them and their guns would not fire. There were thousands of cases of frostbite and dysentery, and some suicides. Early in December the attempt to reach Moscow – then only 20 miles away – was abandoned.

Leningrad also survived – just. Invitations, already printed, to a party in the city which Hitler would attend had to be pulped. Thousands of Leningrad's citizens died each day, and desperate expedients for survival were adopted. That the siege was to last another two years would have seemed incredible.

DECEMBER

10 *Prince of Wales* and *Repulse* sunk
11 Germany and Italy declare war on the United States
12 Germans fall back on Moscow front
19 Italian midget submarines cripple two battleships at Alexandria
19 Hitler takes over from Brauchitsch as German commander-in-chief
22 Churchill arrives in Washington
23 Japanese take Wake Island
24 British recapture Benghazi
25 Japanese capture Hong Kong

Russian soldiers firing under the protection of a tank during the winter counter-offensive.

A disabled enemy tank seen from a Russian tank during an advance against German positions.

Japan smashes the U.S. Pacific fleet

A gigantic explosion aboard the U.S.S. *Arizona*, one of three battleships sunk at Pearl Harbor, witnessed from the nearby Ford Island.

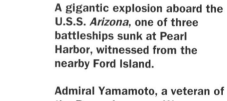

Admiral Yamamoto, a veteran of the Russo-Japanese War, masterminded the attack on Pearl Harbor.

Early on Sunday morning, December 7, the Japanese attacked the U.S. naval base at Pearl Harbor in Hawaii. Although the attack had necessitated moving a large fleet from Japan through the northern Pacific to a position 220 miles from Hawaii, it achieved total surprise. The Japanese declaration of war, which was supposed to be made 30 minutes before the attack, was held up by slow communications and actually arrived after the attack had begun.

The main assault came from over 350 carrier-based aircraft, many of them carrying torpedoes similar to those used in the British attack on the Italians at Taranto. In two hours 19 warships, many of which were lined up less than 1000 yards apart, were sunk or badly damaged; they included eight battleships (four sunk), out of a total of ten in the Pacific fleet. About 200 aircraft were destroyed on the ground, and nearly 2000 people, nearly all naval personnel, were killed. The great U.S. base was a smoking ruin.

The Japanese lost about 30 aircraft and 60 men. They also lost five midget submarines, inserted through the harbour gates from larger submarines but totally unsuccessful in their mission – a significant failure, since it led the Japanese to place a low priority on submarine warfare.

The catastrophe of Pearl Harbor, which resulted partly from skilful planning by the Japanese naval genius, Admiral Yamamoto, and partly from indisput-

able negligence as regards U.S. defence, might, nevertheless, have been worse. The Japanese failed to destroy the huge U.S. oil reserves on Oahu island. Even more important, the four large aircraft carriers which were normally with the Pacific fleet were all, coincidentally, off station (one was tracked by a Japanese submarine in the Pacific but its pursuer was sunk first). The destruction of the carriers, seen as vital by Yamamoto, the apostle of naval air war, had been a primary aim of the attack. Their survival slightly tarnished his triumph.

War between the United States and Japan had seemed inevitable long before Pearl Harbor. Relations, deteriorating fast since the Japanese invasion of China, reached a nadir when the United States placed an embargo on exports which cut Japan off from its only oil supply. Additionally, Japan saw Britain and the United States as Western imperialists frustrating its own empire-building, or what it described as the

'Greater East Asia Co-Prosperity Sphere', which already included most of Indo-China.

In many respects Japanese policy was vague and undecided – a result of the governmental set-up in which the armed services functioned more or less independently. The government had lost its way: it could not conceive any policy that would lead it out of its current predicament, except an ultimately suicidal resort to war. The Japanese were, however, sincere in their Asian crusade. They expected to be welcomed in the

countries they occupied, as leaders of the Asian 'New Order'. The United States was an obstacle to that 'New Order' and therefore became the target for attack. The United States, in spite of its excellent intelligence (having broken the Japanese diplomatic cipher it could read every message between Tokyo and the Japanese embassy in Washington), anticipated that the Japanese attack, when it came, would be launched against an Asian target, probably Malaya or the Philippines. ▶ *page 210*

Total war

In the wake of Pearl Harbor, what had so far been primarily a European conflict became truly a world war, encompassing every continent except South America and nearly every country. Within a few days in December Britain, having declared war on Finland, Hungary and Romania (all engaged in the attack on the Soviet Union) primarily to appease Stalin, also declared war on Japan. Germany and Italy declared war on the United States. Even China, which had hitherto stubbornly maintained that its conflict with Japan was an 'incident', finally declared war (on Germany, as well as Japan).

The entry of the United States against the Axis apparently worried Hitler very little. He seems to have thought that the United States, as a democracy, was morally rotten, and not to have realized that, even if his failure to defeat the Soviet Union was not fatal to Germany, war against the United States most certainly was.

A small boat rescues a seaman from the doomed battleship *West Virginia*.

The Afrika Korps take a step back

The first German campaign in North Africa came to an end on December 18 when, after a confused passage of fighting, Rommel decided to withdraw.

His offensive, begun in March, had carried him across Cyrenaica and into Egypt, though he failed to capture Tobruk, where the Australian (later British and New Zealand) garrison held out against heavy odds. Suez, if not the Persian Gulf, beckoned, but just as Wavell's plans had been frustrated by the withdrawal of British forces for Greece, the Afrika Korps now had to play second fiddle to the German attack in the Balkans, which Hitler regarded as an essential prerequisite to Operation Barbarossa – the long-awaited onslaught on the Soviet Union. Rommel remained on the Egyptian frontier, suffering growing difficulties with his trans-Mediterranean supply lines. A British counter-attack under Auchinleck (who had replaced Wavell) in November had no very clear result but, rather than risk encirclement (the British forces being superior in numbers), Rommel slipped back, in good order, to Tripolitania. Tobruk was at last relieved, though on the British side there was recrimination over Rommel's successful withdrawal with his panzers intact.

▶ *page 218*

South African troops advancing through the desert under a smokescreen.

Field Marshal Rommel with his aides studies a map during the desert campaign.

Members of the Australian
Imperial Forces taking part in
defence exercises in Malaya.

The Japanese open Malaya's back door

On the same day as the assault on
the Philippines and the bombardment of Pearl Harbor, the attack
on Malaya also began. Following
the capture of Bangkok, Japanese troops began landing on the
northern neck of the Malay
peninsula (part of Thailand).

At the tip of that peninsula lay
the naval base of Singapore,
fondly believed to be impregnable
because of its powerful fortifications on the seaward side and 200
miles of impenetrable rubber jungle on the landward side.

Fortress defence is, obviously,
static, but the defenders of Singapore were provided with mobility by the despatch, despite
demands elsewhere, of two powerful warships, the *Prince of
Wales* and the *Repulse*. On their
way to attack a naval force
making landings in northern

Malaya they were spotted from
the air and attacked by torpedo-
carrying aircraft. Both ships were
sunk, a devastating illustration of
the vulnerability of battleships to
air attack. The defenders of
Singapore were compelled to sit
tight and wait. ▶ *page 212*

Rising sun over Hong Kong

The British colony of Hong Kong
surrendered to the Japanese on
December 25. It had held out for
nearly two weeks, longer than
might have been expected in view
of its extreme strategic vulnerability and the absence of any hope of
relief.

As part of the efforts of the
Japanese to weaken resistance,
pamphlets were dropped which
aimed to divide Scots from English in the British garrison. Why
should the Scots, the Japanese
propagandists wrote, die in an
English quarrel? Several Chinese
leaders, including a one-legged
admiral, managed to escape to
the hinterland and reached the
Kuomintang forces.

For three months after Pearl
Harbor the Japanese enjoyed a
string of triumphs. The crippling
of the Pacific fleet prevented the
United States from bringing relief
to its Pacific bases. Isolated outposts like Guam and Wake Island
fell swiftly, though not without

spirited resistance. The Gilbert
Islands were invaded and, by
the end of the year, the Philippines were under attack. General

MacArthur withdrew his forces,
about ten per cent of them American, to fortified bases such as
Corregidor and Bataan.

**A view over one of the coastal
gun emplacements in Hong
Kong which were intended to
help ward off a seaborne
assault.**

PACIFIC PROSPECTS

GOVERNMENT, like war, is not an exact science. The Japanese, though seen by the Americans – understandably enough – as a hideously devious, scheming nation, had in fact blundered helplessly into a war which they had no real chance of winning. The omens were clear to intelligent people like Admiral Yamamoto, who pointed out more than once that starting a war was easier than finishing it. 'This war will give us much trouble . . .' he wrote in a private letter. 'The fact that we have had a small success at Pearl Harbor is nothing. The fact that we have succeeded so easily has pleased people. Personally, I do not think it is a good thing to whip up propaganda to encourage the nation. People should think things over and realize how serious the situation is.'

Yamamoto saw that Japan's only realistic chance was to take advantage of the surprise victory achieved at Pearl Harbor by throwing everything into a short campaign (a prime necessity being to neutralize the carriers that had escaped at Pearl Harbor) in the hope that the United States would be prepared to make peace. The situation was much the same in Europe. In six months the Germans had achieved considerable success against the Russians. But they had not defeated them. If they could not defeat them in six months, they could not defeat them at all and Germany's only option (whether recognized or not) was to force its opponents into a negotiated peace.

The democratic powers had been very reluctant to go to war. In the end they had been forced into it. Their reluctance was seen by their opponents as a sign of weakness. However, once engaged in war, the democratic powers proved fiercer than their opponents. They became utterly determined to win crushingly and conclusively. The governments of Germany and Japan were in a position to seek a negotiated peace if they so desired. The governments of the United States and Britain were, arguably, not in that position. Such was the hatred and determination of their citizens – encouraged by their own propaganda – that no other end was possible except the unconditional surrender of their enemies.

Hitler did not see this, nor did Tojo, nor even did people like Yamamoto. The Japanese, however, could see the ominous writing on the wall. Unless the United States could be persuaded to make peace fairly soon, its industrial muscle, indirectly the cause of Japan's attack in the first place, would bring about its defeat. A comparison of U.S. and Japanese production of the chief weapons of the Pacific war – ships and aircraft – during 1941–3 could, alone, leave no doubt of the outcome.

U.S. AND JAPANESE PRODUCTION 1941-43			
	Battleships	Aircraft Carriers	Aircraft
United States	7	95	153,000
Japan	0	16	30,500

THE PARTISANS

PARTISAN WARFARE of some kind existed in nearly all the occupied countries but proved particularly important in the Soviet Union, where it was less of a novelty owing to the experience of the civil wars after 1917. Guerrilla warfare had an ideological appeal for Communists, and there was less distinction between regular and irregular warfare in the Soviet Union, heightened by the fact that the Red Army was fighting on its own territory often in direct contact with partisan bands.

Stalin's call for guerrilla resistance on July 3 had a tremendous effect, especially in encouraging other Communist partisans, such as Tito in Yugoslavia, who had been hitherto sitting uncomfortably on the fence as a result of the German-Soviet non-aggression pact. Perhaps of greater significance in raising resistance in the Soviet Union (where there were many groups prepared to welcome the Germans as liberators – partisan warfare could work both ways), was the insensitive German policy towards the conquered. Savage repression did not encourage co-operation.

Being so long, the German front was porous. It could be penetrated almost at will, and behind it lay large bands of leaderless men and abandoned equipment.

The Central Committee of the Communist party took the lead in organizing partisan activity, issuing instructions and setting up training centres. Many of these were staffed by NKVD (secret police) men, a liability since it led to confusion at higher command levels. Partisan groups, generally about 100 strong though very variable, were often based on local communities such as village or workplace but existed largely 'underground'.

The main purpose of the partisans was to harass the Germans by sabotage; less was said about the assassination of collaborators. Partisans often covered the retreat of the army, going underground as the area was overrun by the advancing Germans. Their numbers, and their effectiveness, are hard to calculate. There were said to be 10,000 actively engaged behind the German lines during the battle for Moscow, but it was not the partisans who were responsible for the Germans calling off the assault. Even the difficulties with communications were due mainly to other causes, such as the weather. However, as the tide began to turn, and the Red Army began to make successful counterattacks, partisan activity was greatly encouraged and expanded accordingly. So did German massacres in reprisal.

The savagery of the Great Patriotic War and the remarkable heroism displayed by countless thousands of ordinary people are symbolized by the partisan heroine Zoya Kosmodemianskaya, who was hanged by the Germans after torture in December 1941. She was 18 years old. Her body was found, still hanging, by a reporter from Pravda, and thus her story became widely known. There were thousands, partisans or not, like her.

Singapore surrenders

The great base on the island of Singapore fell to the Japanese on February 15. The British had been retreating steadily through Malaya for the previous two months, and were to some extent demoralized. As Singapore fell, so did the prestige of the British Empire in the Far East, if not throughout the world.

The Japanese conquered Malaya in 54 days with casualties of under 5000. The British lost 25,000, mainly prisoners, and a large quantity of equipment. The straits dividing Singapore from the mainland, about a mile wide, were crossed on the night of February 8, some of the troops apparently swimming across. The defence, which had been thoroughly inadequate in preparation (and had not been improved by some bitterness between British and Australians, which reached

as high as government level), proved no better in execution. Arguments have raged ever since over why certain things were done or, more particularly, not done.

By the next day, General Yamashita had about 30,000 men on the island, with another two divisions on the mainland close by. The defenders were far more numerous, but many were poorly trained and had already been mentally defeated. Leadership was imperfect and there was virtually no defence against Japan-

ese air attacks. The big guns of the fortress, all pointing out to sea, were useless, and Churchill's call to fight to the bitter end was not calculated to inspire the defence.

Within a week of the landings, the defenders were forced back into the city itself. With food supplies running out and the water supply in immediate jeopardy, the British army commander of Singapore, General Percival, raised the white flag. The defenders, including a British force recently disembarked which had not fired a shot, were marched off to dreadful imprisonment, and the mainly Chinese inhabitants of Singapore were subjected to a Japanese regime only slightly less brutal.

Japanese landings in Dutch East Indies

The victorious progress of the Japanese in the islands of the southwest Pacific continued on January 6 with landings in the Dutch East Indies. Dutch Borneo, with its valuable oil resources, fell within 24 hours, while paratroopers took the city and air base of Manado in the Celebes. This gave them the necessary launching pad for an attack southwards.

The Dutch had a large army in the Indies, but there was doubt about the willingness of the native troops to fight for their European masters against the Japanese, whose propaganda leaflets, dropped beforehand, proclaimed them as liberators. Some of the most serious fighting took place in the Java Sea, where the Dutch lost five cruisers at the end of February. The capital, Batavia (Djakarta) fell a week later, followed by the Dutch surrender, though all resistance did not finally cease until the end of April. The Japanese took about 100,000 prisoners, a large proportion of whom later died in captivity.

Above. British officers in Singapore on their way to discuss surrender terms.

Right. British soldiers taken prisoner in Singapore eye their captors with apprehension.

The British evacuate Rangoon

With the inexorable Japanese advance through Burma, General Alexander ordered the evacuation of Rangoon which fell on March 10. The Japanese had taken Pegu, only 40 miles from the Burmese capital, two days earlier, and the Pegu-Rangoon road remained closed.

The Japanese rapidly overran southern Burma with two divisions, proving that the jungle country of the border region was not impenetrable to tanks, as had been thought, and easily pushing back the thin British defence, which was also deficient in air cover. The civil administration, which had acquired a reputation for incompetence, rapidly disintegrated. After Singapore fell, another two divisions became available to the Japanese, who advanced steadily northwards. An offer of help from Chiang Kai-shek was accepted, in spite of fears that the Chinese had ulterior motives relating to Burmese territory, but the Chinese were swiftly driven out along with the British.

The Japanese made more careful preparation for their Burma campaign than for other conquests. They had considerable

An artist's view of Japanese cycle troops in Burma.

support inside the country and, although this did not amount to much in military terms, it made Burma, hitherto a relatively placid and pleasant region of the British Empire, particularly unpopular with the British soldiers, who were sometimes betrayed by local people.

The Japanese also had a remarkable agent inside Burma before the war, Colonel Suzuki, a brilliant and unorthodox soldier akin to Lawrence of Arabia, not least in his genuine support, what-

ever Tokyo intended, for Burmese independence.

With the fall of Mandalay, the British were driven out of Burma by the end of April. The majority of the troops managed to struggle back to India, though relinquishing most of their equipment. There remained one small area in the north unconquered by the Japanese, where the British were more popular (few of them had been there). It was held by irregular troops drawn chiefly from the Chin. ▶ *page 244*

MacArthur vows to return

On March 12 General MacArthur, commanding the army in the Philippines, obeyed (none too promptly) the order of his superior, the U.S. president, to get out of the doomed islands and retire to Australia in order to reorganize resistance to the Japanese conquest from there. He slipped through the Japanese blockade in a motor torpedo boat, passing within hailing distance of a Japanese battleship, on to Mindanao, whence he flew to Darwin. There he told waiting reporters, 'I shall return!'

The attack on the Philippines had begun on the same day as that on Pearl Harbor, with the destruction of most of the warplanes at Clark air base while the pilots were having lunch. MacArthur, in the middle of a ten-year assignment to train the Filipino army, realized that he could not resist the ensuing Japanese invasion, which captured Manila on January 2. He accordingly withdrew his forces to Corregidor, an island fortress in Manila Bay, and

Bataan, the peninsula opposite. Bataan, heavily forested, contained well-concealed supply depots, hospitals and even factories. MacArthur's troops, about ten per cent American, were outnumbered by about three to one.

The defensive plan worked well. The Japanese, who had expected to overrun the Philippines very quickly, found themselves held up. But MacArthur's plan was based on a siege that would last, at the very most, six months. He expected relief well before then from the U.S. navy. What he found difficult to grasp was the fact that, since Pearl Harbor, the navy was unable to bring relief. He was cut off and no help was forthcoming.

Despite reinforcements, the Japanese attack was held up (its commander showed none of the flair of General Yamashita in Malaya). Nevertheless, the ultimate outcome was in no doubt, especially after the inspirational leadership of MacArthur was removed, although, under Gen-

eral Wainwright, the Filipinos continued to resist for some time, and Corregidor did not surrender until early May.

General MacArthur, Allied commander in the southwest Pacific.

JANUARY
1 First declaration of 26-member 'United Nations'
2 Japanese take Manila
6 Japanese landings in Dutch East Indies
15 Most South American countries agree to break off relations with Germany
15 First U.S. troops arrive in Great Britain
18 Red Army parachutes troops behind German lines
20 Eichmann appointed to oversee 'Final Solution'
23 Japanese invade New Guinea and Solomons
29 Rommel takes Benghazi in new offensive
29 Anglo-Soviet treaty with Iran
31 Japanese besiege Singapore

46 ships sunk by U-boats off U.S. east coast in January

FEBRUARY
1 U.S. naval attacks on Japanese in Marshall Islands
8 German munitions chief Fritz Todt killed in plane crash
8 Japanese troops land on Singapore island
14 Japanese invade Sumatra
15 Singapore surrenders
16 More U-boats exploit 'Happy Time' off U.S. east coast
19 Japanese bomb Darwin
19 Roosevelt signs order permitting internment of all Japanese Americans
23 Harris takes over British Bomber Command
27 British raid destroys radar station at Bruneval
27 Heavy Allied losses in Java Sea battle

MARCH
7 Archbishop of Zagreb protests at arrest of Croatian Jews
8 British begin intensive bombing of German industrial areas
7 Java surrenders to Japanese
12 MacArthur leaves the Philippines
22 Cripps mission to India promises independence but fails to stop nationalist opposition
22 First coded bulletin broadcast from London to French resistance
25 British convoy from Alexandria reaches Malta
26 First Jewish prisoners sent to Auschwitz
28 RAF begins terror bombing campaign at Lübeck

Allied merchant shipping losses in March total 273

1942

APRIL–JUNE

BATTLE OF THE
CORAL SEA

BATTLE OF
MIDWAY

Battle of the carriers

On May 3 the first naval air battle of the war was fought in the Coral Sea. It lasted three days, and the main combatants never saw each other, since the battle resolved itself into a search and destroy operation by aircraft from the distant rival carriers.

The U.S. carriers *Lexington* and *Yorktown* were accompanied by an Australian cruiser squadron, a British battleship and various other craft. The Japanese had two carriers which had been diverted from Nagumo's fleet returning from the Indian Ocean to join a squadron accompanying troops intended for New Guinea, consisting of a light carrier, six cruisers and other craft, including transports.

Tactically the battle was a draw. The Japanese light carrier was sunk and the two heavy carriers were put out of action for several months. The *Lexington* was sunk and the *Yorktown* seriously damaged. Aircraft losses were heavy on both sides, with the Japanese losing three-quarters of their attack bombers. The battle revealed that the Japanese pilots generally were less competent than the hand-picked men who had attacked Pearl Harbor, and in the longer term the battle was a victory for the United States, more easily able to replace its losses. The battle also forced the Japanese to call off their assault on Port Moresby (New Guinea) which they had hoped to make a base for threatening Australia.

Raid on Ceylon

A Japanese attack on Ceylon (Sri Lanka) on April 1 was relatively unsuccessful. The plan was the brainchild of Yamamoto and the attacking force was led by Admiral Nagumo, who had been in command at Pearl Harbor. His fleet consisted of five aircraft carriers, three battleships, six cruisers and 20-odd destroyers.

The British authorities were alerted to the Japanese approach and well prepared. The Japanese aircraft found no targets in Colombo harbour, nor at the naval base at Trincomalee, though they later located an aircraft carrier and sank it. The British naval forces in Ceylon, though large, were no match for Nagumo's fleet and concentrated on keeping out of trouble. Two cruisers were lost.

The carrier *Lexington* sinking. The U.S. and Japanese fleets were evenly matched at the Coral Sea.

The Allies invade Madagascar

On May 4 the British embarked on Operation Ironclad – the invasion of Madagascar. In an effort to prevent the Japanese from gaining bases in the Indian Ocean, the British landed at Diégo-Suarez (Antseranana) with orders to take over the Vichy French colony. Although the landing was successful, the French troops resisted, and it was not until late in September, following the arrival of reinforcements, that the campaign could be successfully concluded.

The British battleship *Resolution* taking part in the landings at Madagascar.

Yamamoto chances his arm at Midway

Following the drawn battle of the Coral Sea, the Japanese and U.S. fleets clashed again off the sun-drenched coral island of Midway on June 4. This time the Americans, who had learned valuable lessons in the Coral Sea, were the clear victors.

Midway was an obvious strategic target – a possible bomber base for the United States against Japan (carrier-borne bombers had already raided Tokyo, the planes flying on to land in China). If captured, it could serve similarly for a Japanese attack on the U.S. west coast. But Yamamoto's chief motive for advocating its conquest was his hope that the Americans would defend it, offering an opportunity for the decisive victory over the U.S. carriers that he believed was an essential and urgent preliminary to a negotiated peace.

A vast Japanese fleet assembled: eight aircraft carriers, 11 battleships, 22 cruisers, 65 destroyers and 21 submarines. The main force, including four large carriers, made for Midway, with the battleships (Yamamoto himself oddly choosing to remain with them) 300 miles behind, and a third section making a feint towards the Aleutian Islands. Although the whole operation had been put together with the utmost speed, elaborate ceremonies accompanied the departure of the ships.

The Americans could read the Japanese naval cipher and knew that Midway was the main target: the feint to the Aleutians did not deceive them. This was just as well, since they could collect only three carriers, including the hastily patched-up *Yorktown*, eight cruisers and 15 destroyers.

The Japanese, who had no radar, were surprised by a U.S. air attack on the morning of June 4. Three carriers, including Nagumo's flagship, were crippled. Savage fighting continued, with the U.S. pilots proving their superiority, although the Japanese Zeke fighter (successor to the Zero) was perhaps the best plane. So confusing was the battle that it was some time before its effects became evident. The Japanese had lost all four carriers, plus a cruiser and over 330 aircraft. U.S. losses were the gallant *Yorktown*, one destroyer and 150 aircraft.

Midway decisively ended the long string of Japanese successes. Enormous efforts were made to prevent the defeat becoming public knowledge in Japan itself, but henceforth Japan was on the defensive – precisely the situation which Yamamoto had recognized as fatal. ▶ *page 222*

A Japanese cruiser at Midway sinking after being heavily bombed.

The carrier *Yorktown* on fire at Midway after an attack by Japanese planes.

Disaster strikes at Arctic convoy

German success in the secret war

In June a Dutch agent of the British, named Lauwers, parachuted into the Netherlands and was captured by the Germans. They took over his radio transmitter and dictated his messages to London. The deception was not detected, and as a result the Germans in the next few weeks captured about 50 agents.

Some aspects of the 'secret war' remain unknown. Present knowledge suggests that the Allies had considerably more success than the Germans. Operation North Pole, as the Germans named their Dutch double-cross, was an example of the contrary, and probably the worst defeat for the British SOE in the whole war.

London was largely to blame. Not only was Lauwers's 'fist' not recognized, he even managed to transmit the word 'caught' without arousing the suspicion of the Germans – or the British!

The German double-cross was not discovered until one of the captured agents escaped and got back to Britain. The Germans concluded this episode by broadcasting, *en clair*, to the head of the Dutch section in London, whom they addressed by name: '. . . you are trying to make business in the Netherlands without our assistance. We think this rather unfair in view of our long and successful co-operation as your sole agents. But never mind, whenever you come to visit our continent you may be assured that you will be received with the same care and result as all those you sent us before. So long.'

On the first day of July a large convoy of 36 ships, including 22 U.S. and eight British vessels, was spotted by German reconnaissance in the Arctic Ocean as it made its way from Iceland with precious war materials for the beleaguered Russians. Its escorts consisted of six destroyers and a number of other small armed ships.

Although the Russians had performed marvels in moving factory production to the east, beyond the Urals, where it was relatively safe from attack, the Soviet Union was desperately short of war material, and in response to Stalin's requests Churchill promised regular convoys to Archangel. This meant a hazardous voyage through up to 2000 miles of Arctic waters, much of it within range of the Luftwaffe, not to mention powerful warships like the *Tirpitz*, poised in Norway.

Admiralty policy was that if such a powerful surface force appeared, the escorts (in very short supply) should withdraw and the convoy should scatter. Admiralty intelligence indicated on July 4 that the *Tirpitz*, together with the pocket battleship *Admiral Scheer* and heavy cruiser *Admiral Hipper*, had put to sea (they had, but they soon returned, playing no part in the ensuing events). The naval escort accordingly withdrew, leaving the merchant ships to find their own way individually to Archangel. The result was a slaughter. Only 11 ships reached the Russian port, the others being sunk by U-boats and torpedo-bombers. Material losses included over 400 tanks, 3000 trucks and other vehicles, and 200 aircraft.

The convoys continued, after a spell in which ships sailed individually (with losses of over 50 per cent). A total of about 100 ships was lost on the Arctic route, with nearly 3000 men, mainly merchant seamen.

A ship in Convoy PQ-17 sinking after being hit by a U-boat torpedo.

German advance on the Caucasus

The dust cloud in the sky, thickened by smoke from burning villages and guns, could be seen 40 miles away as the Germans launched their spring offensive in Russia in May, codenamed Operation Blue. Manstein rapidly completed the conquest of the Crimea (except for Sevastopol), while, farther north, a Russian counter-attack at Kharkov resulted only in one of those German pincer movements that cut off a Russian army and reaped thousands of prisoners.

Hitler's main plan for the 1942 offensive was a drive through the Caucasus to capture the Russian oil fields, equally vital to both the Germans and the Russians. To protect the flank of this assault against new forces from the east, it was necessary to take Stalingrad, a city of both strategic and psychological importance. Unknown to Hitler, the Russians made great efforts to turn it into an impregnable fortress.

The advance over the grassy steppe beyond the River Don went well at first. Oil wells were sighted at Maikop which fell on August 9. However, the main oil fields lay beyond the Caucasus, and as the Germans entered more mountainous country, the advance slowed. Meanwhile, the 6th Army (General von Paulus), unsupported by tanks, advanced on Stalingrad. So far the Russians, though outfought, had managed to beat off the attack on their two greatest cities, Leningrad and Moscow. Stalingrad was equally important. ▶ *page 218*

Heavy casualties at Dieppe

The British launched a cross-Channel raid on the port of Dieppe on August 19. About 7000 troops were involved, the great majority Canadians.

Like the earlier raid on St Nazaire in March, the Dieppe raid was intended primarily as a test for a future invasion of France. The results were not promising. Although some damage was done and about 50 German aircraft were destroyed, nearly half the total force failed to return – about 1000 killed and 2000 captured. Several Victoria Crosses were awarded, one to a Canadian chaplain, Captain John Foote.

The raid did nothing to encourage the British to establish a second front in Europe, for which Stalin was pressing hard.

Canadian prisoners, under German guard, rest by the roadside after being captured at Dieppe.

Blindfolded Germans, taken prisoner at Dieppe, are brought back to England.

1942

AUGUST–SEPTEMBER

GERMANS REACH
STALINGRAD

MALTA RECEIVES
GEORGE CROSS

An aerial view of the ruins of Stalingrad, the scene of some of the most ferocious fighting of World War II.

Germans in Stalingrad

On August 23 the Germans reached the Volga north of Stalingrad. German bombing virtually destroyed the wooden buildings of the city which flanked the central strip, containing large modern factories lining the Volga for about 20 miles. The battle for the city, where Zhukov, after his successful organization of the defence of Leningrad, was now in overall command (General Chuikov commanded the forces inside the city), was about to begin.

By 23 September the main factory complex was surrounded, and the German artillery was within range of the quays on the river, across which the Russians evacuated wounded and brought in reinforcements. Ferocious street fighting, hand-to-hand conflict of the most savage kind, now ensued. Stalingrad became a maelstrom, a hell of noise in which an individual shot could not be heard amid the constant clamour of guns – a fog of fury in which smoke and dust reduced visibility to a few yards.

Exhaustion and deprivation gradually sapped men's strength. Hitler, who had become obsessed with the battle for Stalingrad, refused to countenance a withdrawal. Von Paulus, in desperation, launched yet another attack early in November. The 4th Panzer Army, brought up in support, reached the Volga south of the city, which was then completely surrounded. But that was as far to the east as the Germans were to go, not only in this battle, but in the whole Russian campaign. ▶ *page 223*

Rommel renews the attack

On August 30 Rommel launched the offensive which, he hoped, would take him all the way to Cairo. Thanks to the cracking of the Enigma ciphers, the British were well prepared. Besides revealing Rommel's plans, this intelligence had enabled the British to sink several ships carrying fuel to the Afrika Korps, and Rommel's advance was soon checked, near El Alamein, by British and Commonwealth troops commanded by General Bernard Montgomery. ▶ *page 220*

Rommel in conference with his officers. During his August offensive he faced a worthy opponent in General Bernard Montgomery.

George Cross for Malta

On September 13 the island of Malta, suffering massive bombardment, was awarded the George Cross by King George VI. The award, for bravery, was normally given to individuals. The inhabitants and garrison of Malta, though appreciative, would have preferred a few squadrons of Spitfires.

Malta had been under siege for several months. The Germans badly wanted to take this valuable base, but ruled out a Crete-type airborne invasion and elected to put the major effort into conquering Egypt. While Rommel was in the ascendant, they could attack Malta and the Mediterranean convoys from North Africa and from Crete, which they did with devastating effect.

Desperate efforts had been made to supply Malta, but few ships had got through. The island itself was attacked by air several times a day: the harbour of Valletta was out of action for long periods and the fighters that the British did manage to bring to the island were as often as not destroyed before they could get into the air. The people became accustomed to living like troglodytes, emerging only at night. The air attacks diminished somewhat to enable aircraft to be diverted to the reinforcement of Rommel's summer offensive, but the blockade remained almost impenetrable. A few ships got through, but more were sunk, including the carrier *Eagle* with a squadron of Spitfires on board. The U.S. tanker *Ohio*, twice torpedoed, made it to Malta lashed between two destroyers to prevent her capsizing. Relief for Malta came only with the victory of the Allied forces in North Africa, beginning with El Alamein.

1942

SEPTEMBER
22 Hitler dismisses chief of staff Halder
23 U.S.-Australian forces attack Japanese in New Guinea
23 British forces take Antananarivo (Madagascar)
23 General Groves appointed to head Manhattan (atomic bomb) Project
23 Zeitzler becomes Hitler's chief of staff
26 Gold from dead Jews' teeth is assigned to the SS

OCTOBER
3 V2 rocket successfully tested at Peenemünde
8 Arrests and executions in Norway amid mounting resistance
14 Renewed German offensive at Stalingrad
23 General Mark Clark lands secretly at Algiers
23 British victory at El Alamein
26 Unsuccessful attack on *Tirpitz* with 'manned torpedoes'
29 Germans attack again at Stalingrad
31 German air raid on Canterbury

NOVEMBER
1 Strikes in Vichy France against recruitment for labour in Germany
3 Yugoslav partisans capture Bihać (Bosnia)
8 Allied landings in French North Africa
8 Hundreds of German aircraft transferred from Russia to Tunisia
9 Darlan orders cessation of resistance to Allies in Algiers
11 Axis forces occupy southern France
11 Russian defences split in two at Stalingrad
11 Japanese defeated in naval battle at Guadalcanal
13 8th Army recaptures Tobruk
19 Soviet counter-offensive at Stalingrad
20 Convoy reaches Malta from Egypt undamaged
20 8th Army recaptures Benghazi
22 Germans encircled at Stalingrad
27 Admiral Jean de Laborde orders French fleet at Toulon to be scuttled

Italian aircraft shedding their deadly load over Grand Harbour, Valletta, Malta. The island had the unenviable reputation of being one of the most bombed targets in World War II but, against appalling odds, repelled every assault by the Axis powers.

Advancing through a dense smokescreen, which effectively hides their movements from the enemy, Australian soldiers prepare to mount an attack on a German strong point.

Desert victory for Britain

On October 23 the war in the desert, which had swung back and forth across Libya, moved decisively in favour of the British. Montgomery's forces, including many Commonwealth troops, registered a resounding victory in the (second) battle of El Alamein, which lasted five days and ended with the Axis forces in full retreat from Egypt.

Montgomery had superiority in practically every sphere. He had over 1000 tanks, including many of the reliable new U.S. Shermans, against less than 500. He also had more men, more aircraft and more artillery, as well as better intelligence and fuel supplies. Another advantage was that Rommel (recently promoted to field marshal) was temporarily absent from North Africa, though he was hastily recalled when the battle began.

Montgomery's tactics were also unexpected. The battle began with a heavy artillery barrage. The infantry then advanced, opening a path for the tanks. However, Montgomery's greatest contribution to success was probably not tactical. He had built up the morale of the 8th Army – depressed since the fall of Tobruk – and commanded an unusual degree of esteem from his men. Moreover, he was no respecter of politicians, and refused to launch his attack until he was ready (at one point, under pres-

sure to do so, he threatened to resign). Not least, he enjoyed the full support of his superior, General Alexander.

The result of the battle, given the unequal strengths of the opposing forces and the determination of Montgomery to take no risks, was never in doubt. In the end Rommel extricated most of his men with his well-known skill and imagination. Nevertheless, nearly 30,000 German and Italian prisoners were taken.

Part of the massive British artillery barrage which preceded the second battle of El Alamein. German resistance was fierce and, despite Montgomery's overwhelming superiority in manpower and equipment, the enemy's defences were not finally breached until November 4.

Allied 'Torch' lights up North Africa

Following the British victory at Alamein, Operation Torch – the Anglo-U.S. invasion of French North Africa, took place on November 8. The operation, commanded by General Eisenhower, deployed nearly 700 ships, almost half of them warships, and 100,000 men. The troops disembarked simultaneously at Algiers, Oran and Casablanca, and met only minor resistance.

Operation Torch had not been regarded with great enthusiasm by many service chiefs, even the British, whose operation it was. Stalin, demanding a second front in Europe, regarded North Africa as an insignificant sideshow, but Churchill, backed by Roosevelt, was eager to clear the Mediterranean. It was largely a political operation, involving the tricky question of French authority. The Americans underestimated de Gaulle and were hoping to use General Giraud, who had recently escaped from a German fortress-prison at the age of 63, to supplant him. A further complication was the presence, coincidentally, of Admiral Darlan in Algiers. Fortunately, Darlan ordered the Vichy troops in Algiers not to resist. Soon afterwards he was assassinated, and eventually Giraud, having agreed to co-operate with the Gaullists, faded from the scene, leaving de Gaulle triumphant but extremely irritated with the Allies. The situation remained extremely complicated, since three competing authorities occupied the region – the French, the Allied military command and the sultan of Morocco.

With French North Africa now in Allied hands, and Rommel retreating westward before Montgomery's cautious advance, the Axis forces were in danger of an imminent squeeze. Early in the following year, they held only Tunisia. However, Axis forces there, under General von Arnim, had been hastily reinforced, and they were to prove far from easy to dislodge. ▶ *page 230*

Right. German soldiers on the move in Tunisia.

Below. American troops marching through Algiers.

1942

U.S. FORCES INVADE GUADALCANAL

GERMAN 6TH ARMY TRAPPED

Germans occupy southern France but French fleet eludes them

In reaction to the Allied invasion of French North Africa, the Germans moved in to occupy Vichy France on November 11.

A major reason for the occupation of the whole of France was the desire to secure the main French fleet, lying idle in Toulon since the fall of France. This failed when the French sailors scuttled their ships in the port. Thus, in the end, Darlan's promise of 1940, when the French surrender was imminent, that the navy should not be allowed to fall into Germany's possession, was fulfilled.

French naval vessels at anchor at Toulon. The whole fleet was scuttled to prevent its being seized by the German army.

Heavy Japanese losses at Guadalcanal

On November 11 the latest and most destructive sea battle took place off the disputed island of Guadalcanal, in the Solomons. The Japanese attempted to land 10,000 men in order to overwhelm the U.S. forces occupying the island, but lost 7 out of 11 troop transports, as well as two battleships and a heavy cruiser.

After air reconnaissance had revealed a skeleton Japanese force on Guadalcanal, the Americans had invaded in strength.

What was generally expected to be a short contest turned into a long and bloody campaign, which lasted six months – the first of a series of intensely savage battles, perhaps the fiercest battles of this or any war, which were to be repeated at many other places in the Pacific. The Japanese fought with – often literally – suicidal determination. Admiral Nimitz's well-staffed war machine, spearheaded by the marines, was equally remorseless.

American marines on patrol in Guadalcanal investigate a suspicious noise. Here, as elsewhere during the long campaign in the Pacific, they were opposed by an enemy who fought with grim determination against overwhelming odds and often preferred suicide to surrender.

Russian counter-attack at Stalingrad

On November 19 Zhukov launched the counter-stroke at Stalingrad which he had planned with Stalin. The manoeuvre, one which the Germans themselves had several times employed against the Russians, involved a pincer movement around the city, which easily broke through the thin, outlying defences manned by German 'satellite' troops (Romanians, Hungarians and Italians). Within three days the arms of the pincers met on the Don. The 4th Panzer Army was forced to retreat, and von Paulus's 6th Army in Stalingrad was surrounded. ▶ *page 229*

A German soldier emerging from a dugout.

A Russian antitank unit moving up to Stalingrad.

Operation Double-Cross

The exploits of perhaps the most successful double agent in Britain were not made public until 1972. Even then his real name was kept secret. It was Juan Pujol García.

A Spaniard who was antipathetic to fascism, 'Garbo' (García's codename) was turned down when he applied for work as a British agent in Italy or Germany early in 1941. Nothing daunted, he set up as a freelance. He applied to the German embassy in Madrid, and persuaded them that he could get himself sent to England by the Spanish government, and would there become a spy for them. With forged Spanish documents and the Germans' blessing, he went no farther than Lisbon, where he spent the next six months composing letters about the situation in Britain, using guidebooks and other rather inadequate sources, supplemented by brilliant imagination. These he sent to the Germans, explaining that they came from England by courier to Lisbon. He showed astonishing skill; for example, learning from an old railway timetable that a certain line was a busy one, he invented elaborate defence works for it.

Some of his made-up reports were, in fact, very close to reality. The Germans appreciated all this, and Garbo was able to make use of the specific questions they asked him in order to invent likely but untrue information. For example, when his German contacts asked if armoured units had been seen moving south to the north of London, he shortly afterwards reported a sighting of just such units farther south. He was somewhat handicapped by his almost total ignorance of Britain. He had trouble submitting his expenses because he was unsure how many British pennies there were in a pound and, since he knew only two common British names, he adopted the all-inclusive nom de guerre of 'Mr Smith-Jones'.

The British, to whom he reapplied, eventually took him on early in 1942 (how he had survived so long in Lisbon without giving himself away is something of a miracle). He went to England and was taken on by the secret service. Soon he controlled an imaginary team of subagents, including a Dutch airline steward, a U.S. soldier, a Welsh nationalist and a typist in the cabinet office. Occasionally, it proved necessary to get rid of one of these dummy agents. For example, when Operation Torch was being organized, a difficulty arose over the presence of one of Garbo's agents in Liverpool, where he would presumably be bound to notice the preparations in the port. Garbo therefore reported that the man was sick, travelled (supposedly) to Liverpool himself, and subsequently advised the man's death. A phoney obituary notice was published in a Liverpool newspaper and the Germans expressed sympathy with the sorrowing widow.

Garbo was one of a whole network of double agents, some of them former German spies forced to 'turn round' or face a firing squad, who supplied the Germans with information compiled exclusively by British intelligence.

WAR FOR TWO OCEANS

THE OUTCOME of the Second World War rested largely on the contest for supremacy in the Atlantic and the Pacific. The nature of the two ocean wars was, however, entirely different.

The Battle of the Atlantic (so named by Churchill) was fundamentally between the German U-boats and the convoys carrying vital supplies to Britain. The role of surface raiders and (until comparatively late) aircraft was secondary.

Admiral Karl Doenitz, the German U-boat commander, had only 27 long-range, ocean-going U-boats at the beginning of the war. He did not acquire the 300 he reckoned he needed until July 1942, at which time the tide was turning in the Allies' favour. Nevertheless, the tonnage sunk by the U-boats far exceeded replacement capacity until the vast U.S. and Canadian shipbuilding programmes got going.

Many other factors entered the equation, not least the intelligence war which at different times favoured one side or the other, but up to mid-1942 Doenitz could be said to have been winning. In 1941 200 U-boats were built; less than 50 had been lost since September 1939. Better weaponry, longer-range aircraft, more escorts, etc. nevertheless turned the tide against the U-boats in 1942. Though they made record kills in May (off the North American coast) and again in November (in the North Atlantic), Allied shipping replacement was by this time exceeding losses, while U-boat losses rose to equal replacements. By May 1943 the U-boat fleet was shrinking and the Battle of the Atlantic was virtually won.

In the Pacific, the battle was simply for command of the sea which, as both sides recognized, depended on naval air power. At the start the odds favoured the Japanese. Their carriers outnumbered the Americans' by ten to three, though four were light carriers. Their aircraft were more numerous and arguably superior – their fighters certainly were. However, in the extremely hazardous art of flying an aeroplane from a carrier (and finding it again), the U.S. pilots ultimately proved more skilful. The Japanese were more experienced, and extremely confident, but in some respects this was a drawback. Careless signalling proved a boon to U.S. naval intelligence. (The Americans learned that Midway was the target of the assembling Japanese fleet by a particularly clever trick.) Midway – one of the three ultimately decisive battles fought in 1942 (the others being El Alamein and Stalingrad) – was the turning point. The Japanese defeat left the balance equal in terms of ships and aircraft, but with the important difference that the rate of construction was far higher in the United States than in Japan.

Preparing for action on board an aircraft carrier.

A U-boat being depth-charged in the Atlantic.

View of U.S. battleships from a carrier.

The Japanese battleship *Ise* carried 14-in guns.

FRENCH RESISTANCE

THE 41-year-old Jean Moulin remained at his post as prefect of Chartres (the youngest such official in the country), when France surrendered, but quickly found himself at odds with the Germans. His refusal to sign a document blaming French troops for atrocities carried out by the Germans resulted in arrest and torture, and an attempt at suicide. On recovering, he went south and made contact with many resistance groups, on whose behalf he travelled to London late in 1941 for discussions with de Gaulle. He might, perhaps, have made a challenge for de Gaulle's position, but chose to remain a loyal subordinate. Early in 1942 he was parachuted back into France, and during the next year and a half welded the main resistance groups into a single Gaullist organization – a truly remarkable feat.

In 1943 Moulin and other Gaullist leaders were betrayed, arrested and tortured by the Gestapo, and killed. The same fate befell many resistance workers, some now famous, some virtually unknown.

Despite the general supervision – sometimes resented – of the British SOE, the resistance comprised a great number of different groups and individuals with a great number of different purposes, ranging from guerrilla warfare to forgery of documents.

Of the almost unlimited instances of useful work done by the resistance, one example concerned the Peugeot factory in Montbéliard, an episode described by the SOE agent (later a well-known educationalist) Harry Ree, who organized it. The decision having been taken in London to put the Peugeot works out of action, it was bombed by the RAF. Much damage was done to the town and to nearby Besançon, and many innocent French people were killed or wounded, but the factory itself suffered little. Contact was then made by the resistance with a foreman inside the works who was already organizing a little subtle sabotage on his own account. The authorities in London were asked to keep the bombers away and leave the job to the locals, and for the rest of the war production at the factory was almost permanently disrupted by a succession of minor incidents so arranged that the Germans, though suspicious, were never able to pin the charge of sabotage on the workmen. On one occasion an explosive device, destined for the plant's transformers, accidentally fell from a workman's pocket. A German guard kindly drew the man's attention to the fact that he had dropped something.

In view of the relative failure of precision bombing (virtually abandoned by 'Bomber' Harris in favour of saturation), the incident demonstrated how skilful resistance workers could sometimes achieve more – and at vastly less cost – than regular military forces.

Opposite. Seen through the window, a post office telephonist who used the telephone network to convey information about German troop movements to the maquis.

The redoubtable Jean Moulin.

Members of the French resistance with an American army officer.

German soldiers standing over the bodies of French maquis.

1943

CASABLANCA CONFERENCE

GERMAN SURRENDER AT STALINGRAD

Churchill and Roosevelt at Casablanca with their military and naval advisers, including General Marshall (far right, seated) and Lord Louis Mountbatten (behind Roosevelt).

Roosevelt and Churchill discuss strategy

Early in the new year, on January 14, Churchill and Roosevelt met in Casablanca to discuss the future of the war. While most decisions were naturally secret, they publicly confirmed the war aim of 'unconditional surrender'.

They agreed, reluctantly but inevitably in the light of the advice of the military chiefs of staff, to postpone the invasion of occupied Europe until the early summer of 1944 – a decision deplored by Stalin. Meanwhile, the

bombing of Germany was to be increased, not only to disrupt industrial production but also to destroy morale. An Allied landing in Sicily was fixed for July, though Churchill pressed for an earlier date. ▶ *page 234*

Australian troops moving towards Sanananda, the last centre of Japanese resistance in Papua (eastern New Guinea).

Australians take Sanananda

With the capture of Sanananda by the Australian 18th infantry brigade on January 16, following by a few days the U.S. capture of Buna, Japanese resistance in eastern New Guinea was now vir-

tually at an end.

Plans for securing the region as a useful base for operations farther north had been laid by MacArthur's command in 1942. The Japanese had forestalled

them by invading the north and advancing overland on Port Moresby. Resisted by the Australians, they nevertheless reached to within about 30 miles of the port, but with supplies proving a major

problem, they got no farther, retreating to defensive positions around Buna and Gona (Garara), where they were attacked by U.S. and Australian forces at the end of 1942. ▶ *page 231*

German disaster at Stalingrad

On January 31 the headquarters of General von Paulus in Stalingrad was overrun and he finally surrendered. He would have done so long before but for Hitler's insistence on holding out. Hitler had that very morning raised him to the rank of field marshal, with the reminder that no German field marshal had ever surrendered. Paulus, declining the invitation to suicide, became the first.

The remains of the German 6th Army amounted to about 110,000 men, many of whom were wounded. A roughly equal number had been killed in the previous month. The survivors were marched off to prison camp. Many never arrived, and few ever returned.

Hitler was badly rattled by the first really serious military defeat his forces had suffered, and the German radio played ponderous music for three days. In Moscow the mood was different, and all the bells of the Kremlin were joyfully ringing. Meanwhile, Chuikov, the victorious Russian commander, began preparations to move his troops to the west.

Field Marshal von Paulus.

German soldiers at Stalingrad are checked off by Russian officers as they surrender.

Red Army soldiers on the attack running along a railway track in a Stalingrad suburb.

229

Rommel threatens Tunisian breakout

COUNTER-OFFENSIVE IN TUNISIA

RED ARMY AT KHARKOV

BATTLE OF BISMARCK SEA

On February 14 the Germans in southern Tunisia staged a counter-offensive. Following attacks on French colonial troops ill-equipped to resist tanks and on newly arrived U.S. troops holding the mountain passes, Rommel's tanks advanced on the Kasserine Pass.

Rommel had hoped to break through into Algeria, but he was stopped by a combination of Allied defence and the difficult country – narrow, rocky valleys not being ideal territory for tanks. He thereupon fell back to the Mareth Line, which was about to be attacked by Montgomery.

Early in March, Rommel was withdrawn from Africa to organize the defence of Greece, but General von Arnim was left to fight to the last in Tunisia in spite of dwindling air support and erratic supplies. ▶ *page 232*

An American M-3 tank moving up to defend the Kasserine Pass in Tunisia.

The Chindits behind the lines

A somewhat unusual expedition was launched by the British from India on February 14. The troops consisted of 3000 Britons and Gurkhas of 77th Indian Brigade, the 'Chindits', and it was devised and commanded by the unorthodox and controversial Brigadier Orde Wingate.

Wingate was convinced that the dense, largely trackless and disease-ridden jungles of Burma lent themselves to guerrilla warfare, though he had some difficulty persuading more conventional military minds. From Imphal his troops penetrated about 500 miles deep into Japanese-occupied Burma, blowing up several bridges and a railway. Three columns crossed the Irrawaddy, but were halted by the impossibility of supplying them by air at any greater distance. They ambushed a Japanese force and killed 100 while losing only one man themselves. Casualties overall were high, however.

Wingate was later to mount a similar operation on a larger scale, but was himself killed at the outset. The effectiveness of such operations received some proof when the Japanese organized a similar raid themselves.

Orde Wingate (centre) in discussion with his men at an outpost on the Burma-Assam border.

Battle for Kharkov

The Russian advance against the Germans, which had started even before the surrender at Stalingrad, brought Vatutin's forces to Kharkov in February. A ferocious street-to-street battle ensued before the Germans were forced to withdraw on February 16.

The steady advance of the Red Army led to a certain euphoria. Though the situation was radically different from that of a year earlier, the army was still inexperienced and in some respects ill-organized, while the Germans were far from finished as a fighting force. Manstein, one of Hitler's best generals, commanding Army Group South, now set in motion a counter-offensive against the over-extended Russians. The spearhead of the advance, under General Popov, was cut off by converging Panzer armies. Hitler sent in reinforcements from the west, and the Germans set about recapturing Kharkov. The city was reclaimed by the Germans only a month after the Red Army had taken it. The goal of the Russian offensive, to reach the Dnieper, had become clearly impracticable.

Troop transports sunk in the Bismarck Sea

Beginning on March 2 a three-day naval battle raged in the Bismarck Sea, north of New Guinea. It scotched an attempt by the Japanese to bring reinforcements to New Guinea from their base at Rabaul, northern New Britain.

This was the first major action in the southwest Pacific since the defeat of the Japanese in eastern New Guinea in January. U.S. and Australian aircraft did most of the damage, sinking the majority of the transports in the convoy as well as four destroyers, while U.S. torpedo boats conducted mopping-up operations. The Japanese also lost about 100 aircraft.

A Japanese merchant ship hit by a bomb.

Subhas Chandra Bose travels to Tokyo

On April 26 in the Indian Ocean a passenger was transferred from a German to a Japanese submarine. This was Subhas Chandra Bose, the Indian nationalist, who after a residence in Germany was on his way to Japan preparatory, he hoped, to entering Delhi with a conquering Japanese army.

Other Indians had already helped the Japanese to form an Indian National Army recruited from prisoners of war. It was used, however, chiefly for intelligence gathering and sabotage. Subhas Bose transformed it into a revolutionary movement, whose motto, *Jai Hind!* ('India for ever!'), became a form of greeting among his supporters. The British in India, where Wavell was to be appointed viceroy in October, generally ignored him, and his support in India itself was apparently slight. Gandhi regarded him as a 'misguided patriot', and Nehru was thoroughly hostile to the notion of Indian 'liberation' by means of Japanese forces. By the time the Indian National Army was actually used in battle by the Japanese, they were already on the retreat. Bose himself was mortally wounded soon after the end of the war when the plane taking him back to Japan crashed in Taiwan. He became, after death, something of a legendary hero.

Subhas Chandra Bose.

The end of the Axis empire in Africa

The remnants of the German and Italian forces in Tunisia surrendered on May 12. They had no more territory left to defend. The Allies took 275,000 prisoners, including General von Arnim.

Hitler had foreseen the inevitable defeat two months earlier, yet had refused to evacuate the troops. At the beginning of May von Arnim was reduced to 76 tanks, whose crews were fashioning makeshift alcoholic fuel from wine. The last Luftwaffe bases were evacuated as the Axis forces were confined to a small region around Tunis and Bizerta. Both cities fell on May 7 and resistance petered out soon afterwards. All Axis forces were thus cleared from North Africa. Mussolini had suffered a disastrous defeat, his dreams of empire turned to dust. For the Germans, the defeat was less serious, since the North African campaign, in spite of occasional hopes of advancing to Suez, had never been more than a valuable distraction, undertaken in support of the Italians.

German and Italian prisoners in Tunisia escorted by American, British and French soldiers.

Dead man deceives the Germans

A curious but effective British subterfuge was enacted on April 30. The dead body of a naval officer was washed up on the Spanish coast at Huelva, apparently the casualty of a plane crash on a flight from Britain to North Africa. He carried documents relating to an 'Operation Husky'.

This was a plant and the body had in fact been deposited from a British submarine. 'Operation Husky' was the genuine codename for the planned invasion of Sicily, but the fake documents gave the impression that the landings would be, not in Sicily, but at two places in Greece, and further implied that the current air attacks on Sicilian bases were merely a feint.

The British learned of the success of the trick when, a few days later, messages were intercepted from Berlin to the German commanders in Greece ordering steps to be taken to defend against an invasion at the places named. The German high command, it was said, had learned of the coming attack on Greece from an 'absolutely reliable' source.

Heavily laden American assault craft approach a beachhead at Holtz Bay on Attu. The island was recaptured after nearly three weeks of fierce fighting.

Japanese driven from the Aleutians

A U.S. infantry division landed at different points on the island of Attu in the Aleutian chain on May 11, and after the usual savage fighting which the regaining of territory from the Japanese always demanded, aggravated by appalling weather, the defending garrison of about 2000 was wiped out, the last troops dying in a suicide attack. The Japanese thereupon evacuated nearby Kiska.

By driving the Japanese from the Aleutians, which they had invaded as a subsidiary operation to that which ended at Midway, the United States secured its northern flank in the Pacific and deprived the Japanese of bases from which they were able to bomb Alaska. Conversely, U.S. bombers were now able to attack the northern Kuriles.

Dams busted

In the ever-growing aerial assault on Germany, the Royal Air Force carried out a notable raid on May 17. The targets were three major dams, Möhne, Eder and Sorpe, in the Ruhr industrial region.

The British scientist Barnes Wallis had developed a special type of bomb to destroy these inaccessible and heavily defended targets. Dropped on the reservoir behind the dam, the bomb, which was circular, was designed to bounce along the surface until it reached the dam. It had to be dropped at very low – and precise – level. Eighteen Wellington bombers made the attack, led by Wing Commander Guy Gibson (subsequently awarded the Victoria Cross), and two of the dams were successfully breached. Over 1000 people were killed and much damage was caused, though the results were less destructive to German industry than had been hoped, and fewer than half the aircrews returned safely.

Water pours through the Möhne dam – a spectacular achievement by the RAF.

A wounded American soldier receives blood plasma.

Axis homeland invaded

The Allies' invasion of Sicily, agreed at the Casablanca conference earlier in the year, took place early on July 10. Two task forces, the British 8th Army under Montgomery and the U.S. 7th Army plus others under General Patton, landed on the southeast of the island.

Sicily had been chosen as the objective because its capture would help clear the Mediterranean. It left the Allies with a long landward advance up the Italian peninsula, however, which as events were to prove was an extremely arduous undertaking.

The danger of landing on open beaches with no regular port immediately available created initial difficulties with supplies, and the new amphibious vehicle, the 'Duck' truck, proved its usefulness. Within two days, nearly 100,000 men, 7000 vehicles and some 300 tanks had been brought ashore. Initial resistance was light, and the Allies were able to capture the airfields in a few hours, enabling aircraft to be brought in from North Africa.

The American forces captured Palermo and advanced east along the coast, using amphibious operations to help overcome the coastal defences. The British approach up the east coast was shorter but more difficult, and entailed overcoming the main German forces. By mid-August both armies had reached Messina, completing the conquest of the island. The Germans, however, were able to withdraw the bulk of their troops and equipment over the straits.

Among the beneficiaries of the conquest of Sicily were the Mafia, who had been suppressed under Mussolini. Their numbers augmented by American colleagues who had come over with the army, they quickly restored their rule in Sicily, Allied military government or no.

General Eisenhower visits Canadian soldiers in Sicily.

Mussolini dismissed

Following the invasion of Sicily, with about one million Italian troops fighting Hitler's war in other theatres, the fate of Mussolini was sealed, and he was dismissed on July 23 by King Victor Emmanuel. Marshal Badoglio took over as prime minister.

Most Italians were heartily sick of a war they were ill-equipped to fight, and even Mussolini had become aware of the hopeless situation into which he had allowed his country to be drawn. The Sicilian invasion demolished his prestige, even among Fascists,

and made it possible to remove him. He was arrested and taken to an island, later to a mountain resort, while Badoglio entered into secret discussions with the Allies about an armistice. To prevent a German takeover, he wanted an Allied invasion of

Italy reaching as far north as possible, preferably Rome. The Allies, a little misled by the ease of their conquest of Sicily, were seduced by the prospect of taking Naples, which was within flying distance of their Sicilian bases.

Italy surrenders

The document agreeing Italy's surrender was signed on September 3 and announced five days later. Badoglio would have preferred to delay the announcement longer in order to augment his plans to circumvent a German takeover. In the event the Germans moved fast, occupying Rome and its adjacent airfields within 24 hours. The Italian government fled to Brindisi.

On the day the armistice was agreed Montgomery landed in Calabria, while another mainly British force landed at Taranto. Neither encountered any serious opposition, as the Germans had not yet decided how much of Italy they could reasonably defend.

Among the unpleasant results of Italy's surrender were the killing of some unarmed Italian soldiers by their German captors, the despatch of many more to prison camps and a heightened campaign against Italian Jews, who had been relatively little molested under Mussolini's regime. The Allies acquired some, though not many, Italian aircraft, and while most of the fleet at Taranto succeeded in slipping away to Malta, the battleship *Roma* was spotted by the Germans and sunk. ▶ *page 236*

A night barrage by Allied artillery before the landings in Italy.

Troops embarking on landing craft at Catania before the assault on Italy.

1943

**BATTLE
FOR NAPLES**

**ALLIED ADVANCE
HALTED**

**TEHRAN
CONFERENCE**

Fight for Naples

On September 9, the day after the announcement of the Italian surrender, a large Allied invasion force commanded by General Mark Clark landed at Salerno, south of Naples. The local German commander, in the process of taking over from the Italians, put up fierce resistance and at one point General Clark was forced to contemplate evacuation.

The need for that was avoided by determined fighting, disruption of the defence by parachute troops and heavy air attacks. As Montgomery's 8th Army advanced from the south, the Germans withdrew northwards, ultimately to a defensive line on the River Volturno. Meanwhile, news of the Allied landings had sparked off a revolt in Naples itself. Three days of fierce fighting and savage reprisals followed before the Allied forces reached Naples at the end of the month.

Meanwhile, at the height of the Salerno battle, the Germans mounted a daring operation, led by an SS officer, Otto Skorzeny, to rescue Mussolini. A small aircraft spirited the deposed dictator away to Germany and thence to northern Italy where he was established as head of a token and entirely powerless government.

Partisans marching through the streets of an Italian town.

General Mark Clark attends a church service in Naples.

Allied soldiers attend bomb victims in a Naples street.

Italy changes sides

On October 13 Badoglio's Italian government, which had been Germany's ally just five weeks earlier, declared war on Germany. Since the government had little authority in the current confused state of Italy and two-thirds of the country was under German occupation, this had no very decisive results. Some Italian units were recruited to fight alongside the Allies, but they received small encouragement from Allied commanders, most of whom had a (mistakenly) low opinion of Italian fighting qualities. A substantial number in German-occupied territory took to the hills and waged guerrilla warfare against the Germans, incidentally demonstrating that Italian soldiers were as brave and as capable as any others when they felt they had something worth fighting for.

Stalemate in Italy

In November the Allied force advancing slowly northward in Italy was brought to a halt at the Gustav Line. This defensive position, which the Germans had prepared since the Allied landings, stretched across the peninsula between Naples and Rome.

The Allies had met fierce and growing resistance as they advanced from Naples, and the destruction of facilities by the retreating Germans caused further delays to their movements. The rivers proved difficult to cross, and although the British and Americans had open ports on both coasts, including Naples itself, the need to ship in food for the civilian population of southern Italy as well as the soldiers caused hold-ups. More troops did arrive, including U.S.-equipped French forces and Polish units. By December, when there was a major changeover in command (Eisenhower and Montgomery returning to Britain to plan Operation Overlord), winter weather had imposed a deadlock on the campaign. ▶ *page 245*

Battle for Chang-te

A vigorous, fluctuating battle for Chang-te (Changde) in Hunan, centre of China's 'rice bowl', began on November 2. The Japanese threw over 100,000 men into the attack on the city, which changed hands several times in a few days but ended up still held by the Chinese.

The Sino-Japanese war had become merged with the world conflict after Pearl Harbor. Chinese forces had taken part in the Burma campaign under the U.S. general Stilwell. Though soon forced to withdraw, they had continued the fight and performed valuable work, such as the rescue of an Allied force trapped on the Irrawaddy in April 1942.

China's main problem, however, remained poor communications. U.S. aircraft, successors of the volunteer 'Flying Tigers' of General Chennault in 1941, played an increasingly important part. U.S. air power also largely dictated Japanese strategy, which was directed at the destruction of air bases and at driving a communications corridor through eastern Asia to compensate for their desperate shortage of merchant shipping as well as for the onslaughts of U.S. aircraft. Chinese ground forces were compelled to fight a war of defence and attrition while they built up their armies and awaited an Allied counter-offensive.

A Chinese machine-gunner in action during the fierce battle for the control of Chang-te.

'Big Three' meet at Tehran

On November 26 the leaders of the main opponents of Germany met in Tehran. It was the first time Stalin had been outside the Soviet Union since the 1917 Revolution.

Roosevelt, Churchill and Stalin celebrate Churchill's birthday at a dinner party in Tehran.

The main purpose of the meeting was to discuss plans for Operation Overlord, the invasion of western Europe promised for spring or early summer of 1944 (though under certain conditions, relating to the current strength of German troops in France). On his side, Stalin promised that the Soviet Union would declare war on Japan as soon as Germany was defeated. A few days earlier, Roosevelt and Churchill had met Chiang Kai-shek in Egypt, where they had agreed that Japan must be forced to relinquish all its conquests, including Manchuria. One subject not discussed with Stalin or Chiang Kai-shek, however, was the progress being made on developing an atomic bomb.

Lieutenant Kennedy sends a coconut

In the war of the islands in the southwest Pacific a lively, daring and dangerous role was performed by the U.S. PT boats or, as the British called them, motor torpedo boats.

In August 1943 a squadron of these fast-moving hunter-scavengers left their base at Rendova Island in the Solomons to attack four Japanese destroyers carrying supplies to the garrison on Kolombangara. They were unsuccessful, and on August 8 PT-109 was rammed by one of the destroyers. She exploded and broke apart, apparently, with the loss of all hands.

Eleven men (most of the crew) had in fact survived, including the commander, Lt John F. Kennedy. After clinging for several hours to floating wreckage, they reached a small coral atoll three miles away. Later, Kennedy swam out to sea in the hope of flagging down a passing PT boat and, caught by a strong current, only just managed to get back. Undaunted, two days later the whole party swam to a larger, inhabited island, Nauru (as they thought: in fact it was Cross Island). They persuaded two islanders there to take a message south, hoping to locate one of the Australian coast-watchers who were scattered throughout the region. For lack of other material, Kennedy scratched his S.O.S. message on a coconut.

This stratagem worked. The coconut was delivered to Lt Arthur Evans on Gomu, an unoccupied island. Evans, who was keeping watch on Japanese-held Wana Wana nearby, sent a canoe, paddled by another islander, Benjamin Kevu, to bring the stranded men to Gomu. Meanwhile he radioed the U.S. base at Rendova, to which other islanders were also travelling, with a report of the incident. Within a week of the destruction of PT-109, Kennedy and his crew were picked up by another PT boat.

The Russian general Vatutin at Kursk.

Russians examine a shattered German tank.

A dejected German soldier after the battle.

Russian soldiers at Kursk preparing to beat back an attack by enemy armour.

THE BATTLE OF THE TITANS: KURSK 1943

THE RAINS of spring inhibited campaigning in Russia, but both sides used the interval to build up for the inevitable battle that would come in the summer. The Germans, for whom attack was essential, selected an obvious target: the Kursk salient, a westward bulge in their line with the city of Kursk at the centre. The Russians hastened to defend the salient with an enormous system of earthwork defences. Both sides massed their armour for what was to be the decisive military engagement of the European war.

Hitler had a lot on his mind – defeat in North Africa, the need to shore up Italy, confusion over the target of the next Allied Mediterranean offensive, above all perhaps the growing pressure on German morale exerted by Allied bombing of German cities. For once he allowed his generals almost a free hand in preparing for the battle.

The Red Army had recovered rapidly from the exhaustion of the post-Stalingrad campaign. The factories were now working at full blast: tanks were being produced at twice the German rate, along with artillery and aircraft. Deficiencies, such as motor transport, were made up by lend-lease. By the time of the battle of Kursk the Russians had nearly 200,000 U.S. trucks. Moreover, the quality of the Russian equipment was well up to the German standard, in some respects more advanced.

The Germans attacked at dawn, the 9th Army (General Model) to the north of the salient, the 4th Panzer Army (General Hoth) to the south. They aimed to meet, cutting off the salient and bagging the 60 Russian divisions (Generals Rokossovsky and Vatutin) within. Both made progress, though the hastily dug defences slowed them down. Model's Panzer divisions advanced 30 miles towards the high ground of Olkhovatka, from which they could look down on Kursk. Hastily summoned Russian reinforcements, however, deprived them of this view. In the south, too, Hoth pierced the Russian defences, but was forced to draw on his reserves to maintain progress. Russian armoured reserves were brought in from other sections of the front, and there ensued the greatest tank battle in history, with 900 involved on each side. Casualties were heavy. Some German Panzer divisions lost three-quarters of their tanks.

By nightfall, with thundery rain hissing off hot metal, the German offensive had clearly failed. Worse, the losses were so heavy that German production was scarcely able to replace them and was certainly unable to build up a greater force for a new offensive. By contrast, the Russians still had reserves in hand and were rapidly increasing them (by 1944 they were producing over 2000 tanks a month, whereas the Germans, despite the best efforts of Speer and Guderian, could manage only about 350).

Although, in the immediate aftermath, the Russians did not make the best use of their victory at Kursk, the inevitable result was German retreat. Kharkov was retaken, for the last time, in August, and in September, with the autumn rains threatening, the Germans were forced back to the Dnieper. Whether they could hold that position during the winter campaign seemed extremely doubtful.

Russian soldiers advancing under the protection of their tanks. The failure of the Kursk offensive made German defeat in Russia inevitable.

TITO AND THE YUGOSLAV PARTISANS

THE MOUNTAINOUS terrain, paucity of roads and tradition of resistance to the ruling power made Yugoslavia, like Greece, an excellent country for guerrilla warfare. Both countries similarly failed to unify national resistance and hostility among rival groups was as fierce as hostility against the occupiers.

In Yugoslavia, where the speed of conquest left many soldiers, still armed, at large, resistance was first organized by Colonel Mihailovich, whose Serbian Chetniks, however, were equally opposed to the Croat fascist ustase, while Mihailovich hated communism as much as fascism. Moreover, the Chetniks' activities were inhibited by the fear of reprisals against the civilian population. In the end, therefore, it was the Communist partisans led by Tito (Josip Broz) who, less concerned over reprisals and less riven by ethnic conflicts, appeared as the more effective force against the Germans and thus gained the most support from the British.

The first British liaison officers entered Yugoslavia in the autumn of

A partisan supply column moving through a village.

Men and women partisans at an assembly point.

240

1941. They were attached to Mihailovich and found the task of co-ordinating the operations of the rival groups difficult to the point of impossibility. Conflicts between Serb and Croat, Christian and Muslim, Communist and Monarchist generated growing violence. It has been estimated that 600,000 people in Yugoslavia killed between 1941 and 1945 were slain by fellow Slavs, perhaps half of them Serbs killed by the genocidal ustase.

The British did not make direct contact with Tito until March 1943. Six months later, Brigadier Fitroy Maclean arrived, to be followed by stepped-up British supplies, which could then be flown in from southern Italy. Some material also came from the Russians, though, as Tito complained, aid from fellow Communists was much less than he received from the capitalist British.

Maclean was the personal emissary of Churchill (who placed a high priority on helping the Balkan resistance), and he encountered hostility in the feud-ridden intelligence world in Cairo (responsible for Balkan operations). Maclean was later to write that, on the plane taking him to Yugoslavia, he took care 'not to accept the first parachute I was offered'.

Early in 1944 British aid to the Chetniks was ended and all resources were diverted to Tito. Defending this policy in Parliament, Churchill asserted that the partisans were holding down 14 German divisions in Yugoslavia while the Chetniks were doing little or no fighting against the Germans.

Funeral of German soldiers killed by Yugoslav partisans.

Tito (right) in conversation with his chief of staff.

Yugoslav women partisans training in Italy.

BEACHHEAD AT
ANZIO

JAPANESE IN
RETREAT

A bridgehead gained

The Allied offensive in southern Italy was resumed in the second half of January. While new attacks were launched against the Gustav Line, an Allied force sailed from Naples to land in the rear of the German defences at Anzio on January 22. Complete surprise was achieved. Within 24 hours nearly 40,000 troops landed with only a dozen casualties and a bridgehead nearly ten miles deep was created.

The ease of the landings gave a false impression. Having secured the bridgehead, the commanding officer, General Lucas, hesitated to advance into the hills since he had, as yet, no armour, while the German commander in Italy, Kesselring, reacted with his usual speed and decisiveness. A series of heavy counter-attacks effectively sealed the bridgehead, and the Allied forces were left clinging to

their precarious foothold in very difficult conditions for over four months.

The attack in the south made little progress. The U.S. 5th Army was held on the Rapido river, while the British and French made scarcely more progress. The whole advance came up against the formidable defences at Cassino, which lay across the main northward route to Rome.

In the area of Cassino the Allies encountered that furious resistance which characterized the German troops throughout the long months in which their ultimate defeat became ever more certain. Bitter fighting raged for two months. The Allies made attack after attack and the destruction wrought by aerial and artillery bombardment was such that bulldozers had to be brought in to clear away the debris for tanks and vehicles to pass. After the last of these attacks in mid-March, with the famous monastery of Monte Cassino in ruins, the Allied commanders called off the battle. ▶ page 245

The Russians cross the Polish border

On January 4 General Vatutin's armies in the Ukraine crossed the old (prewar) frontier of Poland. With the Germans strung out along such a wide front, there was little to stop the Russian advance except their own supply problems.

Manstein did produce another surprise manoeuvre which halted Vatutin in his tracks, but it involved withdrawing units from other sections of the front, and the Russians made further advances in the north and the south, where part of Vatutin's forces linked up with Koniev's, on their left, to 'bag' ten German divisions (sorely depleted in strength) on the Dnieper. ▶ page 244

British tanks and Bren gun carriers being disembarked at the Anzio beachhead.

Russian soldiers in house-to-house fighting.

Leningrad relieved

The long and terrible siege of Leningrad came to an end on January 27. An attack on the Leningrad front forced a German withdrawal from the Moscow-Leningrad railway. The siege had lasted nearly 900 days, though the casualties had been worst in the first winter, and some supplies had subsequently been brought in across Lake Ladoga.

Though much harassed by partisans, the Germans withdrew in comparatively good order to a more easily defensible position.

Russian ski troops moving through a Leningrad suburb.

One result, however, was to isolate the Finns, who had been involved in hostilities against the Soviet Union since 1941. They now began approaches to the Russians regarding an armistice.

War of the islands

The slow and painful U.S. advance continued in the southwest Pacific, with the Marshall Islands secured before the end of February. Particularly fierce fighting occurred on Kwajalein atoll, taken on February 6.

The next objective was the Marianas, especially Saipan and Guam, where the Japanese were strongly entrenched. Long-range air attacks were launched, and the Japanese base on the Truk Islands was neutralized by a series of heavy bombardments. In June Saipan was bombarded from the sea and a landing made four days later. Japanese resistance, as always, was fierce. The Japanese committed much of their declining naval strength to knocking out the beachhead, but suffered severe losses in both ships and aircraft. Guam came next, with U.S. forces landing in July. Everywhere the Japanese fought fanatically – and refused to give up, so that mopping-up operations often continued long after the main battle was over.

Meanwhile, in New Guinea Australian and U.S. forces were steadily driving the Japanese out. Seizure of the Admiralty Islands in February and the subsequent isolation of Rabaul made the seas safe, and in April landings were made around Hollandia (Jayapura) on New Guinea. Wade Island fell the following month, followed by Biak Island, and by the end of July New Guinea was virtually cleared of Japanese.

The Pacific war was largely a U.S. affair, with command shared between Admiral Nimitz in the central Pacific and General MacArthur in the southwest. Inter-service rivalry, the vague division of the two commands, and the contrasting personalities of the two commanders created difficulties but did not stop the U.S. advance. ▶ *page 244*

Japanese dead on the beach at Saipan, killed in a suicidal counterattack.

A U.S. Navy aircraft flies over a badly damaged Japanese destroyer.

Red Army marches west

The Russians renewed their advance on March 4 with a three-pronged attack. It was led by Zhukov, who had taken over from the dying Vatutin, and struck towards eastern Galicia. To the south (north of the Black Sea) Malinovski advanced more slowly, while between them Koniev launched a dynamic thrust across the River Bug.

Koniev's advance was so rapid that it carried him on to the Dniester, where he was able to make use of German pontoon bridges, still in place. By the end of the month he was on the Romanian border. Meanwhile, Zhukov had come level with him with an impetus that for a moment promised to carry him through the Carpathians on to the Hungarian plain.

In response to this threat the Germans hastily occupied Hungary. Communication problems, plus the exhaustion of the Russian troops after their sustained advance, combined to call a halt, though part of Koniev's forces, turning south along the Dniester, reached the Black Sea coast, isolating Odessa which, threatened from east and west, was captured by the Russians in early April.

U.S. marines roll drums of gasoline ashore on Emirau Island.

Stroke and counter-stroke in Burma

In March the Japanese in Burma began their 'march to Delhi'. Crossing the border into India, on March 30 they attacked the town of Imphal, but failed to take it.

The siege of Imphal, which lasted two months, involved some of the fiercest combat of the war, comparable only to the similar hand-to-hand struggles in the Pacific islands. Some of the most vicious fighting took place in attempts to defend or capture quite insignificant objectives.

The Anglo-Indian troops displayed much better morale than those who had trailed defeated out of Burma or been mopped up in Malaya in 1942 (the Japanese had then formed a low opinion of the fighting qualities of the British and considered the Indian troops more formidable foes). However, the most important factor in deciding the outcome was airborne supply. The Royal Air Force, considerably reinforced since 1942, was able to keep the defenders of Imphal constantly supplied with food and ammunition. The Japanese, on the contrary, ran short of equipment and medical supplies, and were unable to seize food stocks. The result was a disastrous defeat, in which they lost most of their 85,000 men.

Meanwhile, airborne troops had landed in northern Burma with the object of capturing Myitkyina, while a second, diversionary attack was made farther west, towards Akyab (Sittwe). With General Stilwell's troops advancing from the north, the stage was set for the clearance of the Japanese forces from Burma. ▶ page 259

British soldiers move along a jungle path during the battle for Imphal.

Rabaul neutralized

Emirau Island in the Bismarck Archipelago was occupied by U.S. marines on March 20 without opposition. Work began at once to build an airfield.

The significance of this acquisition was that it completed the ring of U.S. bases around the great Japanese base of Rabaul. The reconquest of the Solomons and New Guinea which made this possible had been extremely costly. The Japanese constantly fought to the death. The few prisoners taken were usually wounded and thus unable to kill themselves and avoid the dishonour of capture (some Japanese were prevented from surrendering by their officers, nevertheless). Although U.S. and Australian casualties were far less than the Japanese (often less than ten per cent), a direct assault on Rabaul would have been very costly. It was more economical to cut it off, leaving about 100,000 troops isolated as the war moved north and west. ▶ page 250

The Russians clear the Crimea

On April 8 the Red Army began the reconquest of the Crimean peninsula, which Hitler had insisted on holding long after its loss had become inevitable. While the Soviet forces already established on the Kerch peninsula struck westward, General Tobukhin invaded from the north. The Crimea was swiftly overrun, although Sevastopol held out for a month.

Alexander breaks through in Italy

Monte Cassino finally fell on May 18, overrun by Polish units after a skilful flanking manoeuvre by French forces. The whole Gustav Line was swiftly overrun and the U.S. troops bottled up at Anzio broke out to link up with the advancing 5th Army.

Allied bombing of their communications made German withdrawal difficult and costly and, although the German forces provided stubborn resistance south of Rome, there was now little to stop the Allies overrunning central Italy. Rome was liberated on June 4, General Clark fulfilling his ambition to get there first, and the advance continued to another, hastily constructed German line of defence, the Gothic Line, in Tuscany.

Florence was captured in August and the Gothic Line penetrated in several places, but Allied strength had been depleted by the withdrawal of troops for the campaign in southern France and by declining U.S. interest in Italy. Though some troops were replaced (among the replacements was a Brazilian division), the Germans held out until winter halted operations. ▶ *page 261*

The shattered remains of the town of Monte Cassino after the battle.

The centre of the historic town of Caen after an Allied bombing raid.

D-Day: Allies invade Normandy

In the largest, most complex invasion ever launched, Operation Overlord, Allied forces landed in Normandy on June 6. Following airborne troops who had gone in earlier to protect the flanks, the main assault began at 6.30 a.m. on the beaches between the Cherbourg (Cotentin) peninsula and Le Havre. Five divisions – two U.S. two British and one Canadian – landed on the beaches codenamed Utah, Omaha, Gold, Juno and Sword.

A crowded Normandy beach on D-Day.

There was little initial resistance from aircraft or guns, owing to the efficient preliminary bombardment. As it was, the Germans had only about 200 fighters immediately available, while the Allies deployed a total of about 12,000 aircraft, nearly half of them fighters, and including the strategic bomber forces withdrawn temporarily from their daily assault on Germany.

Although there were four German divisions in defence, only one of them, the 352nd Division, was of top quality. This happened to be stationed immediately behind Omaha beach, where the U.S. troops, who also lost a lot of their amphibious Sherman tanks during the chaos of disembarking, suffered very heavy casualties on the beach. Nevertheless, even at Omaha a beachhead was established, and by the end of D-Day the invading forces were on the verge of creating a united front several miles inland.

The following weeks witnessed very heavy fighting, and the Allied forces made much slower progress than had been anticipated in the meticulous planning of the operation. An immediate British objective was the town of Caen, which Montgomery, the operational commander, had hoped to take on D-day itself. Three separate attacks failed, and eventually the effort had to be called off. West of Caen, the 12th SS Panzer Division, made up of recruits from the Hitler Youth, arrived on June 7 and inflicted heavy losses on the Canadians. But it failed to break through to the sea, and Allied reinforcements, under almost total air cover, were being shipped in rapidly. Montgomery launched another attack on Caen on July 7 in which the old city was largely

Commandos disembarking from landing craft.

flattened by 2500 tons of bombs. It finally fell a few days later.

In the Cherbourg peninsula the U.S. troops made steady progress, but were hampered by the ancient hedgerows, perfect tank barriers (one detail the Overlord planners had overlooked). However, Cherbourg fell on June 26.

In early July the Germans,

pulling in reserves, seemed to have established a united defensive line to contain the invasion. Fearful casualties were incurred by the Americans in the battle for Saint-Lô, but German losses were even worse, and six weeks after D-Day, General Bradley's 1st Army was on the point of breaking through. ▶ *page 248*

The Russians drive to the Vistula

In accordance with Stalin's promise to Churchill at Tehran, the Russians launched a major summer offensive on June 22, north of the Pripet marshes. The German commanders, who had wanted to make a strategic withdrawal, were ordered by Hitler to stand firm.

Following preliminary, probing attacks by infantry, the main assault was launched a day later on an 800-mile front. Zhukov's forces consisted of 166 divisions with 2700 tanks and 1300 mobile guns. The German Army Group Centre had just 37 divisions. Within a week, two of the three German armies had been encircled and virtually destroyed – Hitler did eventually allow a retreat, but it was too late. A huge gap yawned on the eastern front, and the remaining German army was trapped after rapid movement by Rotmistrov's tanks east of Minsk. It suffered about 40 per cent casualties in breaking out.

While thousands of prisoners were marched back to Moscow, the Red Army's advance continued. Early in August the Russians were on the River Vistula, south of Warsaw. In the Polish capital itself fighting had already begun.
▶ *page 256*

Hitler blasted but unbowed

While the battle for Normandy was raging, on July 20 Hitler was in conference in a wooden building at his headquarters in Rastenburg (Ketrzyn). As he leant over the table, studying the map, the room was shaken by an explosion. When the smoke cleared, four officers were dead among the ruins of the hut. Hitler himself, clasping his arm, had a few cuts and bruises.

Shortly before the explosion, the briefcase containing the bomb had been idly pushed away from Hitler's feet by an aide. That, and the intervening table, saved him.

The deadly briefcase was planted by Colonel von Stauffenberg. He was a safe distance away when the bomb went off and, seeing the building blown up, he assumed that Hitler was dead. The conspiracy of which Stauffenberg was the principal architect was thus exposed. Beginning with Stauffenberg himself, about 5000 people were executed within the next few months, many hanged with piano wire from a meat hook. One of the conspirators was Rommel, recovering from a wound suffered in Normandy, who was offered the choice of suicide. Declared to have died of wounds, he was given an elaborate state funeral.

This was not the first attempt to kill or neutralize Hitler by army officers, and it is amazing that men who displayed such ability on the battlefield proved so inept at assassination. The majority of German generals were not Nazis. Even those who were most in sympathy with Nazi ideology, notably the younger ones, were exasperated with a leader who was apparently bent on leading them to total destruction.

One of the conspirators on trial for his life.

Hitler's headquarters after the explosion.

A second invasion of France

On August 15 the Allies invaded the south of France. Heavy aerial bombardment of communications and strong support from U.S. and British warships as well as from the French resistance assisted the invasion – by mainly U.S. and French troops. A British-U.S. airborne force, preceding the invasion, landed west of St Raphael to secure a vital pass.

The invasion of the south of France had originally been planned to take place at the same time as Overlord, but was postponed because of a shortage of landing craft. Its aims were to draw German forces, which otherwise might threaten the flank of the Normandy invasion, southward, and also to secure more port capacity.

Resistance was relatively light. Toulon and Marseilles were soon

captured and within a month the troops had linked up with Patton's army to join the advance towards the German frontier.

American troops on a coastal road in southern France marching past a steel and concrete wall built by the Germans along the beach.

Falaise pocket closed

After desperate German attempts to hold open the gap between Falaise and Argentan in Normandy, the advancing Allied forces closed the pocket on August 21. Although some German troops managed to get through, about 250,000 were killed or captured, together with most of their equipment.

In late July, while the British and Canadians pressed forward from Caen, the newly constituted 3rd Army of General Patton, the last exponent of *Blitzkrieg*, advanced rapidly, ignoring the ports of Brittany in his rear and reaching Argentan by August 13. As the danger of envelopment in the Falaise 'pocket' appeared, Kluge (who had replaced Rundstedt, dismissed for advising Hitler to make peace), launched a major armoured attack with the aim of cutting off Patton from the rear. The biggest tank battle of the campaign – in terms of mobile tanks, perhaps of the war, with ten divisions on each side – took place, covering about 800 square miles and lasting two weeks. The victory opened the way for rapid Allied advances into France.

Tanks and personnel carriers of the Free French 2nd Armoured Division passing through the Arc de Triomphe during the liberation of Paris.

French forces enter their capital

A French armoured unit entered Paris early on August 24. For Parisians the eagerly awaited day had arrived. A few German pockets still held out, and some of the shooting was not directed at the remaining German intransigents. There were old scores, not all

connected with the war or the resistance, to be paid off.

The Parisians themselves had rebelled a week earlier, when the Paris police had joined members of the resistance, who came out openly against the Germans in vengeful street fighting. This

revolt accelerated the Allied advance, and the French 2nd Armoured Division was swiftly despatched to the capital. De Gaulle himself, who had already secured the presidential palace at Rambouillet for himself, was not far behind.

British airborne force in disaster at Arnhem

On September 17, one of the most brilliantly planned operations of the war came badly unstuck at Arnhem. The British 1st Airborne Division, dropped at Arnhem to secure the bridge over the Rhine, was defeated before supporting ground forces could arrive. Casualties, killed and captured, were enormous.

From mid-July onwards the Allied advance from Normandy was rapid. The British and Canadians entered Belgium, capturing Antwerp early in September (though not the Schelde, where a fierce battle had to be fought by the British to take Walcheren Island in November). The U.S. 1st Army liberated much of northern France, while the 3rd Army swept east, taking Reims and Verdun and reaching the Moselle in the first week of September. The 7th Army was level with them after its rapid advance up the Rhône valley.

Thus by early September the Allies had formed a front stretching unbroken roughly along the Dutch and French frontiers to Switzerland (although there were areas where the Germans still held out – on the Loire and the Atlantic and Channel ports which Eisenhower, remembering the destruction at Cherbourg, preferred to bypass). As they fell back to the Siegfried Line, the Germans fought the more determinedly. At the same time, the Allies were running ahead of their supplies. One of the Mulberries (artificial concrete harbours towed across the Channel to Normandy) was still in operation, transport aircraft flew to and fro, trucks formed a constant procession and fuel came from England via PLUTO (Pipe Line Under The Ocean). Even so, Antwerp was badly needed.

The Arnhem landing was part of Operation Market-Garden, an attempt to turn the German line and establish a bridgehead on the Rhine. In addition to the British drop on Arnhem, U.S. airborne troops descended in thousands of gliders to secure the crossings over the Meuse and the canal linking it with the Schelde. The latter objectives were safely achieved, and the link with supporting ground forces was made.

The failure at Arnhem itself was the cause of bitter recriminations.

To frustrate the Allies' effort to open Antwerp, Hitler diverted his V-1s and V-2s, which had caused many civilian casualties and some panic in England, against the Belgian city. Nevertheless, the Schelde was cleared and the estuary swept clear of mines by mid-November.

British airborne troops in action at Arnhem.

Awaiting a German assault, British paratroops armed with antitank weapons keep watch.

Japanese defeat at Leyte Gulf

OCTOBER–DECEMBER

**BATTLE OF
LEYTE GULF**

**CIVIL WAR IN
GREECE**

**SLOVAKS RISE
IN REVOLT**

Germans leave Greece but conflict continues

British airborne troops landed in Greece early in October, occupying Athens on the 13th. Little fighting was necessary since, with the Allies in northern Italy and the Russians in Romania and Bulgaria, Hitler conceded that his troops should leave Greece.

Partisan activity in Greece had been widespread and vigorous. As in Yugoslavia, however, resistance was divided between nationalist and Communist organizations. Churchill was to complain that ELAS, the pro-Communist liberation army, used British-supplied arms to fight its compatriots, especially EDES, the democratic republican force under the command of General Zervas. EAM, the political arm of ELAS, set up its own provisional government in the mountains, disregarding the king and the government-in-exile.

After the withdrawal of the Germans and the return of the royal government, civil war broke out in Athens, provoking intervention by British forces and a flying visit from Churchill. A Communist takeover was prevented, though Greece's domestic conflict was far from over.

General MacArthur's long-expected attack on the Philippines began on October 20. The Japanese, who had proclaimed that the battle for those islands would decide the war, prepared a rigorous defence, while placing their main hope in a naval victory.

The Japanese navy had lost the carrier war but was still strong in capital ships, including the two most powerful warships in the world, the super-battleship *Yamato* and her sister vessel *Musashi*. MacArthur's invasion force had very powerful naval protection, but as it approached Leyte Gulf, in the central Philippines, it was venturing beyond the point where air superiority could be relied on, being out of range of land-based planes. The Japanese aimed to decoy the U.S. warships away from the troop convoy, then send in their most powerful battleships to destroy the transports.

The decoy plan worked, in that it drew off Admiral Halsey's fleet, including aircraft carriers. In the event neither of these forces took part in the battles, since Halsey never made contact with the Japanese decoy fleet.

Meanwhile, two stronger Japanese fleets, including five modern battleships, made for the transports. One fleet was skilfully ambushed and almost totally destroyed by the U.S. warships left behind to cover the troops. They included old and shabby battle-ships which had been reconstructed from the wrecks of Pearl Harbor. The other fleet pierced the U.S. defences but, because of failures in intelligence and communications, never got to grips with the transports, and eventually left with heavy losses.

The battles of Leyte Gulf, the largest in naval history, lasted three days. Six U.S. warships were lost, including the carrier *Princeton*, sunk by a lucky hit with a single bomb. The Japanese lost 36 warships, and their navy was, in effect, finished. Though hard fighting lay ahead, the loss of the Philippines was assured.

A feature of the battles of Leyte Gulf was the first appearance of *kamikaze* ('divine wind') suicide pilots, who deliberately crashed their aircraft, loaded with explosives, on to U.S. ships. The carrier *St Lo* was one victim. By the end of the war 34 U.S. ships were lost to such attacks, in which 5000 *kamikaze* pilots died.

General MacArthur strides ashore at Leyte Island.

Churchill makes third Moscow visit

Churchill flew to Moscow for talks with Stalin on October 9. The conflict over the Warsaw rising, when Churchill had been ready to use Soviet bases to supply the Poles in spite of Stalin's refusal (gambling that the Russians would not actively resist), was a foretaste of future trouble, and it was important to settle some postwar territorial questions in advance, particularly in the Balkans. Churchill told Stalin that he regarded Romania as within the Soviet sphere of interest, but that Britain should have priority in Greece. Yugoslavia should be subject equally to Soviet and Western influence.

Churchill in Moscow with (right) Molotov.

D-Day Deception

For the planners of Operation Overlord, it was vitally important to maintain secrecy until the last possible moment, in order to prevent the Germans from massing their forces at the point of invasion. For the Germans it was equally important to find out where the invasion would take place.

Given that the point chosen had to be within fighter range and had to have beaches suitable for landing, there were really only two likely candidates, the Pas de Calais and Normandy. Calais had certain obvious advantages: the crossing was shorter and it was nearer Germany. Elaborate efforts were made to persuade the Germans that this was the objective of the main invasion force. A wholly fictitious army group was invented in southeast England, opposite the Pas de Calais. General Patton was its commander and he made some high-profile appearances in Kent and Sussex. Many signals were made to and from this nonexistent force, and the bombing was actually more concentrated in the Pas de Calais area than it was in Normandy. Messages issuing from Garbo's circle and from other double agents were designed to heighten the impression that the Pas de Calais was the target.

The creation of a mythical invasion force for the Pas de Calais was not the only Allied effort at deception. German suspicion that an attempt would be made to liberate Norway was encouraged by manipulating the Oslo stock exchange and by false reports of troop concentrations in northeast England. Even after the invasion had taken place, Hitler was still unsure whether it was the main thrust, or whether another might not be coming in the Pas de Calais area. It was not until more than six weeks after D-Day that he allowed the defensive forces stationed there to move to Normandy.

An incidental advantage for the Allies was a disagreement about strategy between Rommel, in charge of the defence of France, and his superior, Rundstedt. Rommel's plan (correctly forecast by his former opponent, Montgomery) was to station the panzer divisions close to the coast, where they could strike quickly and prevent the invaders from establishing a bridgehead. Rundstedt, more conventionally, wanted to keep the armour in a central reserve, from which it could be despatched to the right place when that became known. (Unlike Rommel, Rundstedt had never had to fight a battle without air cover.) A compromise was eventually reached and, as a result, Rommel had only one panzer division close enough to the beaches to carry out a speedy counterattack.

The vast Overlord armada occupied all the numerous good harbours on the south coast of England (some units even sailed from East Anglia and South Wales), but German intelligence was poor. The shortage of fuel restricted aerial reconnaissance to an absolute minimum, and the first warning that the Germans had of the arrival of the invasion fleet was the roar of its approach.

The Slovaks rise too soon

In October, as Soviet and Czech troops were combating fierce German resistance in the Carpathians, the Slovaks rose in revolt. Like the Poles in Warsaw, they expected to be soon joined by the Russians but, like them, they were disappointed.

Slovakia had been in a state of ferment throughout 1944, and the partisan army that rose against the German occupiers numbered about 65,000. Before the end of the month, however, the rising had been defeated, thousands of Slovaks had been slaughtered and many villages burned to the ground. The Russians were later to protest that they had received insufficient warning of the Slovak rebellion.

The end of Admiral Horthy

Such was the strategic importance of Hungary to the Germans that, when it was threatened by the advancing Russians, the Germans decided to take over, and on October 15 the regent, Horthy, was removed. This was accomplished in another startling coup by Otto Skorzeny, the SS officer who had rescued Mussolini. He captured the citadel of Budapest with just four tanks. A puppet fascist government was installed in Budapest, but by the end of the year the Red Army was at the gates.

Admiral Horthy (left), who was deposed when he attempted to negotiate with the Russians.

THE WARSAW RISING

W ITH THE RUSSIAN guns audible from the city, the Polish Home Army, which at its height numbered about 40,000 men and had organized a very active and sometimes brilliant resistance in German-occupied Poland, gave the signal for a general uprising in Warsaw at the end of July. At most the Warsaw leaders reckoned to hold out for two weeks, but they did not expect to wait so long.

The Home Army had been formed as early as 1939. Its leaders were generally nationalist and conservative, but it had the support of most of the people, excluding some on the far right – and the Communists. It was loyal to the Polish government-in-exile, headed until his death in an air crash by General Sikorski. This government was recognized by the Soviet Union until the discovery of the Katyn massacre, when Stalin, in indignation at the (correct) assertion that the killings had been carried out by Russians, broke off relations.

The Warsaw rising, one of the most heroic and most ghastly battles of the war, was the cause of bitter controversy at the time and has remained so. It may be that the Home Army command made a serious mistake in starting a revolt inside the city. On the other hand, it is hard to see how they could have remained passive on the apparent eve of liberation. The extent of Stalin's duplicity may be uncertain, but there is little doubt that his failure to give sufficient assistance in time was deliberate, even if the immobility of Rokossovsky's army on the edge of the city can be explained by honest military reasons, i.e. a forceful German counterattack.

The Home Army was also too sanguine, not only in assuming that the Russians would arrive sooner, but in its apparent expectation of aid from the United States and Britain (though Churchill did his best). To have dropped the Polish Parachute Brigade into Warsaw, as requested, would have required over 250 Liberator aircraft – an impossibility two months after the Normandy landings.

The Poles fought to the bitter end. A 12-year-old boy destroyed a Tiger tank with a home-made petrol bomb, but such expedients as stringing a line of (empty) bottles across a street to inhibit advancing tanks were of little avail against an occupying force which deployed artillery units that included a 600 mm battery. Old Warsaw was almost completely destroyed, and the Poles were eventually forced into the sewers. Hand-to-hand fighting took place in pitch darkness with the combatants up to their waists in the slime of decaying excrement.

In the end Stalin relented sufficiently to allow Allied planes to use his airfields, and the Russians eventually dropped weapons and supplies themselves – though without parachutes so that most of the weapons were broken. Most of the supplies fell into German hands.

After four desperate weeks General Bor-Komorowski, the leader of the insurrection, sought surrender terms. The Germans promised that the fighters of the Home Army would be treated as regular soldiers. That promise at least was (on the whole) kept.

Opposite. Germans fire rocket shells against Polish positions.

German soldiers lift a Pole out of the sewers.

Poles are blindfolded before discussion of surrender terms.

A German patrol in the ravaged streets of Warsaw.

BATTLE OF THE 'BULGE'

IN AN EXTRAORDINARY repeat of 1940, in December the Germans launched an offensive in the Ardennes which took the Allies by surprise and broke through weak U.S. defences. Like the French in 1940, the Allies had assumed the front in the Ardennes region to be safe from serious attack.

Despite all evidence to the contrary, Hitler still believed, or said he believed, that a powerful counter-offensive could knock the Allies out. The panzers in the Ardennes were less than 100 miles from Antwerp, and if the port could be regained the Allies' war effort, already slowed by communications difficulties, could be disrupted.

Another view of the planned offensive was held by General Dietrich, one of the two army commanders. All Hitler wanted him to do, he remarked was to 'cross a river, capture Brussels, and . . . take Antwerp. And all this in the worst time of the year through the Ardennes, when the snow is waist deep and there isn't room to deploy four tanks abreast let alone armoured divisions. When it doesn't get light until eight and it's dark again at four, and with reformed divisions made up chiefly of kids and sick old men. And at Christmas.' Among other drawbacks, there was insufficient fuel; success depended on capturing supplies from the Americans.

However, the attack took the Allied command by surprise. The U.S. defenders, some of them fresh from their homeland, were overrun. Eisenhower, taking a more serious view of the offensive than either of his subordinates, Bradley and Patton (who was battling his way into the Saar), moved in two armoured divisions to guard the flanks of the German breakout. The U.S. 101st Airborne Division hastened by road to protect Bastogne, a vital objective in the German advance, and held it in spite of being ill-equipped to deal with tanks. However, they were soon surrounded. Called upon to surrender, the U.S. commander, General McAuliffe, issued his famous rejoinder, 'Nuts!'

Elsewhere, the German impetus was dying as hasty Allied reinforcements moved in and clearer weather permitted the full deployment of Allied air power and the dropping of supplies to Bastogne. Counterattacks by Montgomery against the northern line of the German 'bulge' compelled the panzers to withdraw and by the third week of January the Allied front line stood where it was before the German offensive began. The U.S. forces nevertheless lost about 35,000 men (half of them prisoners) while a large number of atrocities had been committed by the graduates of the Hitler Youth, mainly against Belgian civilians but also, in a notorious case at Malmédy, 72 captive U.S. soldiers.

American vehicles pass a knocked out German tank.

A solitary German escorting American prisoners.

American infantrymen advancing through a wood in the Bastogne region.

Marshal Zhukov, the leading Soviet military commander.

Eisenhower's forces reach the Rhine

Having repaired the Ardennes 'bulge', and with German divisions being drawn off for the eastern front, in late January Eisenhower resumed the Allied drive in the west. There were three main lines of attack, the British and Canadians in the north and the U.S. armies in the south, towards the Ruhr and the Saar.

The Red Army advances on Germany

The Red Army renewed its offensive in Poland on the Vistula on January 12. The Germans had drawn off several armoured divisions for the (unsuccessful) relief of Budapest, yet Hitler refused to countenance withdrawal from the Vistula. The Russians, having had five months to make good their supplies and communications, were prepared to make a major advance.

The three Russian spearheads – commanded respectively by Koniev, Zhukov and Rokossovsky – broke through the inferior German forces, isolating Warsaw, which fell within the week. Koniev then advanced on Silesia, while Rokossovsky reached the southern frontier of East Prussia. German reinforcements arrived from Czechoslovakia, but too little and too late.

Before the end of the month Rokossovsky reached the Baltic, cutting off considerable German forces, while Koniev cut through to the Oder. Zhukov, bypassing Poznan, reached the German frontier and on the 31st his vanguard was on the lower Oder only 40 miles from Berlin. At this stage, the Russians were held up, both because they had run ahead of their support and because the narrowing front favoured the defence.

After some bitter fighting the Canadians reached the lower Rhine near Wesel by mid-February. The U.S. 1st Army, delayed when the Germans opened the dams on the Rur, took Düren towards the end of February, while the 9th Army, after clearing München-Gladbach, reached the Rhine north of Düsseldorf a few days later, forcing the Germans to the south of them to withdraw across the river. The 1st Army, with the 9th on its left, took Cologne, while at Remagen, farther south, the Americans had a great stroke of luck. The Germans had omitted to destroy the Remagen railway bridge, the only one still standing on the Rhine. A platoon of men seized it and held out until reinforced. Charges on the bridge failed to explode and General Bradley lost no time in moving across to establish a bridgehead on the east bank.

Meanwhile, in another offensive backed by especially powerful air support, the U.S. 3rd and 7th Armies crossed the Moselle and attacked the Saar region. Mainz fell on March 22 and the same night General Patton 'sneaked a division across' the Rhine. No substantial German forces remained active west of the river, and the way lay open for an advance on Berlin. ▶ *page 262*

Russian tanks passing through a town in German Silesia.

Tanks crossing a pontoon bridge spanning the Rhine.

An American tank receives a direct hit in a street near Cologne cathedral.

Burma Road reopened

On January 27 Chinese forces succeeded in reopening the Burma Road. Direct overland contact was thus opened up again between Allied bases in India and the region of Chungking, the Chinese capital.

Chiang Kai-shek's army was, in theory, the largest in the world. In practice, it was less formidable, and almost entirely dependent on the Americans for weapons and supplies, which British aircraft airlifted over the vast mountains that divide China from India.

The war in China was heavily influenced by the war in the Pacific. The Japanese pinned down the Communist army in the northwest and effectively called the tune in the south. The advance of Nimitz's forces in the Pacific threatened Japanese control of the South China Sea, essential to the viability of its new empire, and this had provoked the Japanese offensives in South China in 1944 which, at one time, seemed to threaten Chungking. At the end of the year, however, the tide

had turned in favour of Chiang Kai-shek's forces, largely U.S.-trained, although no longer commanded by General 'Vinegar Joe' Stilwell.

The Japanese remained powerful in southern China, but as their strength was sapped in the Pacific they also became more vulnerable in China. Chinese counter-offensives at the end of April regained Nanning and Liuchow – soon lost again but recaptured in June. By that time the Japanese were staring defeat in the face.

General Stilwell (centre) in northern Burma with members of his personal bodyguard.

JANUARY
9 U.S. landings on Luzon
12 Red Army renews advance in Poland
14 Bastogne relieved
17 Soviet and Polish troops take Warsaw
18 Thousands die on 'death marches' as Germans move prisoners eastwards
18 Budapest surrenders
23 Ardennes 'bulge' straightened out
26 East Prussia cut off
27 Soviet forces overrun Auschwitz
27 Burma Road reopened
29 Red Army crosses Polish-German border
30 Berlin police fire on food rioters
30 6000 refugees die when Soviet submarine sinks German transport from East Prussia

FEBRUARY
4 Yalta conference
3 MacArthur's forces in Manila
12 Amnesty granted to Greek Communists
13 Dresden destroyed
19 U.S. invasion of Iwo Jima
20 Churchill and Roosevelt meet in Cairo
21 Turkey declares war on Germany
23 100,000 Filipinos slaughtered by Japanese in Manila
24 Egyptian prime minister assassinated after declaring war on Axis
27 U.S. forces recapture Corregidor

MARCH
2 U.S. forces reach the Rhine
3 Finland declares war on Germany
3 Fall of Manila
5 Meiktila captured in Burma campaign
6 Killings and deportations of Poles by Russians reported in detail
6 Cologne occupied
7 Rhine bridge captured at Remagen
9 84,000 civilians killed in Tokyo firestorm
11 Vietnam declares independence
11 Huge air raid destroys Krupp works in Essen
19 Japanese evacuate Mandalay
21 Precision raid destroys Gestapo records in Copenhagen but kills 86 children
21 Guderian dismissed for advising an armistice
22 Kesselring replaces Rundstedt in command of defence of Germany

Big Three meet at Yalta

The Big Three, Churchill, Roosevelt and Stalin met for the last time at Yalta in the Crimea on February 4.

The outstanding problem was Poland. Stalin gave assurances that democratic methods would be allowed to determine Poland's government, assurances which he did not honour. It was also agreed that citizens of the Soviet Union captured fighting for Germany should be sent home. Southern Sakhalin and the Kurile islands were to be sent home to the Soviet Union after the war, and Germany was to pay reparations for damage done in the course of its occupation.

Churchill, Stalin and Roosevelt together for the last time.

Dresden destroyed

On February 13–14 Allied air forces bombed the city of Dresden, one of the showpieces of Europe. The target was the railway marshalling yards, with the aim of slowing down the movement of German reinforcements to the eastern front. The result was one of the greatest single pieces of destruction of the war.

The attack began with a raid by 150 British bombers, followed by a second wave numbering 500. The attack was resumed next morning by 450 U.S. bombers, but by that time there was little of Dresden left. A firestorm set off in the first two raids had consumed 11 square miles of the city, destroying everything within the area. It was not possible to count the bodies, because many of them had been completely burned up. Total civilian casualties were probably about 60,000.

Bodies lie piled in the streets of Dresden following the massive air raid by British and American bombers. Casualties were appalling in a city already crowded with refugees fleeing from the advancing Russians.

The Stars and Stripes on Iwo Jima

U.S. marines landed on Iwo Jima on February 19. The island was small and barren, but offered potential as a base from which bombers could comfortably operate over Japan. The U.S. flag was raised on the highest point three days later, but the fighting for the island had barely begun.

The fighting was particularly savage, partly owing to the terrain and the technical problems it presented to an assault. In the battle, which lasted a month, the defenders were wiped out almost to a man, and U.S. casualties totalled about a third of the invading force. At this time the average span for an infantryman before becoming a casualty was three weeks. ▶ *page 260*

American soldiers crawl cautiously ashore on Iwo Jima.

Japanese defeated in Burma

On March 19 the Anglo-Indian force of Slim's 14th Army took Mandalay. The offensive had been delayed by the Japanese attack on Imphal. Its defeat allowed Slim to resume his plans.

While fighting fiercely against Stilwell's U.S.-Chinese troops and the Chindits in the northeast, the Japanese became less concerned with Burma after the Imphal defeat owing to the steady reduction of their power in the Pacific. Slim's advance was rapid.

Operation Dracula, the assault on Rangoon, began on May 1 with an aerial bombardment. Two days later an aircraft flying over the city spotted a message laid out in the prison camp: 'Japs gone. Exdigitate.'

British soldiers in Rangoon on the lookout for Japanese suicide squads.

MARCH
22 Arab League formed in Cairo
25 Allied forces cross the Rhine
25 Underground Nazi group assassinates Allied-installed mayor of Aachen
25 Heavy air attacks continue on Japanese cities
27 Non-communist Polish negotiators arrested by Russians
28 Swedish diplomat Raoul Wallenberg arrested by Russians in Poland
29 Russians enter Austria

APRIL
1 U.S. marines invade Okinawa
3 Churchill warns of possible Soviet dominance of Europe after the war
4 Eisenhower views 4000 corpses at Ohrdruf camp
7 Japanese battleship *Yamato* sunk off Okinawa
8 Canaris, Pastor Bonhoeffer and others executed in Germany
11 Soviet Union and Yugoslavia sign friendship treaty
11 U.S. troops enter Buchenwald
12 Death of Roosevelt and succession of Truman
13 Russians capture Vienna
17 British discover 35,000 corpses at Belsen
18 Churchill diverts Montgomery to Lübeck to preserve Denmark from Soviet occupation
18 U.S. war reporter Ernie Pyle killed off Okinawa
20 U.S. forces take Nuremberg
21 French forces occupy Stuttgart
25 U.S. and Soviet troops meet on the Elbe
25 Provisional government set up in Austria
25 46 states attend inaugural meeting of UN in San Francisco
28 Mussolini shot by Italian partisans
29 500 guards at Dachau massacred by U.S. troops and inmates
29 German forces in Italy surrender
29 Hitler writes last testament blaming 'international Jewry' for the war
30 Red Army takes Berlin
30 Hitler commits suicide
30 Dönitz succeeds Hitler as German head of state
30 Truman declines Churchill's plea for U.S. advance to Prague and Trieste

MAY
3 British occupy Rangoon
3 German officers from the east attempt to surrender to British
7 Final unconditional surrender of Germany agreed
7 Rising in Prague

U.S. marines invade Okinawa

The Japanese island of Okinawa was invaded on April Fool's day. An extremely heavy bombardment had preceded the landing, in the hope that the heavy casualties suffered during the invasion of Iwo Jima might be avoided. In the event the landing was virtually unopposed.

Manila recaptured

After a month's siege, marked by bitter street fighting which left the city as ruinous as Warsaw, Manila was secured by the Americans on March 3. At the same time, MacArthur's troops, assisted by Filipino guerrilla units, were clearing the Japanese from the strongholds of Corregidor and Bataan.

Advance airborne units had invaded Luzon, the island on which Manila is situated, before Leyte was fully secured and the main invasion began in January. Simultaneously with this operation, the southern islands of the Philippines were being reclaimed. The capture of Palawan and rapid construction of airfields on that island aided the movement of the U.S. 3rd Fleet into the South China Sea to attack the Japanese on the coast of China and Indo-China.

As in Okinawa, the Japanese on Luzon, with no hope of actual victory, concentrated on static but tenacious defence. The U.S. forces received considerable aid from Filipino units, which were soon organized within the reconstituted Philippines army. Resistance was particularly fierce in Manila and in the region of the Clark air base, but once the central plains and the Manila Bay area were secured, the campaign became largely a mopping-up operation. The mountainous areas of the northwest were the most difficult, and resistance had not been entirely overcome there when the war ended.

A Japanese *kamikaze* bomber dives into the sea.

The Japanese had also changed their strategy. They aimed to let the marines on to the island, destroy the ships with suicide attacks (planes, boats and mines), then wear down the U.S. forces on land as they were confronted by a series of strong defences. Thus the fiercest battle of the Pacific war began fairly quietly.

In the meanwhile the battleship *Yamato* sailed from Japan; she had enough fuel for a one-way trip only. She and her escorts were sunk by air attacks before they could do any damage, but the U.S. ships suffered heavily from *kamikaze* attacks, which also took out many of the destroyers operating the distant radar screen to give warning of incoming attacks. British aircraft carriers, equipped with armoured flight decks, proved less vulnerable to the *kamikaze* pilots.

On land the Japanese defended with their customary tenacity, and all resistance was not finally overcome until June. The casualties of the battle were horrendous. Over 100,000 Japanese died, the senior officers all committing suicide, and probably a similar number of Okinawan civilians. (Many took refuge in caves where, since the marines could not tell whether the inhabitants were Japanese soldiers or, as in one case, student nurses, they were blasted or burned.) About 7000 U.S. soldiers died.

A wrecked bridge sprawls across the river in the shattered centre of Manila.

An American marine charges towards a Japanese machine-gun emplacement on Okinawa.

The Germans crumble in Italy

On April 9 the 15th army group, now commanded by General Mark Clark, opened its offensive in the Po valley. Advances in the preceding winter had been small owing partly to the removal of troops for the invasion of France.

Having crossed the river, the U.S. 5th Army and British 8th Army advanced rapidly northwards, gradually enclosing the main German forces. Italian partisans rendered valuable assistance. Milan was taken before the end of April and part of the U.S. forces continued moving west-ward to link up with the French, while the 8th Army advanced toward Trieste and made contact with the Yugoslav partisans. The Germans surrendered on April 29, the formal ceremony taking place a day or two later at Alexander's headquarters.

Enthusiastic crowds greet American troops as they move through the streets of Milan.

MAY

8 Soviet troops enter Prague
8 VE Day celebrated
15 Last Germans in Yugoslavia surrender
26 Japanese forces evacuate Nanning
30 In 'Sétif massacre' hundreds of Algerians and 88 French killed in nationalist rising and reprisals
31 Ceasefire in Syria after clashes between French and Syrians

JUNE

5 Allied control commission created to administer postwar Germany
10 Australian troops invade North Borneo
11 Sudeten Germans forced out of Czechoslovakia
13 Australians take Brunei
18 Japanese resistance on Mindanao weakened by starvation
20 Emperor Hirohito urges peace negotiations
21 Members of Polish government-in-exile imprisoned by Russians
22 Okinawa captured
24 British bombers destroy bridges over the River Kwai
26 UN charter signed by 50 states
29 Czech-Soviet treaty assigns eastern Ruthenia to Soviet Union

JULY

6 U.S. chiefs of staff plan evacuation of 400 top German scientists
16 Admiral Halsey steps up raids on Tokyo
17 'Big Three' conference at Potsdam
25 Japanese resistance on Mindanao ends
26 Labour Party victory in British election; Churchill ceases to be prime minister
26 Japan rejects Potsdam declaration calling for unconditional surrender
29 Many of 883 casualties lost to sharks after USS *Indianapolis* is torpedoed

AUGUST

4 Last Japanese resistance in Burma extinguished
6 Atomic bomb falls on Hiroshima
8 London agreement on creating war crimes tribunal
8 Soviet Union declares war on Japan
9 Second A-bomb destroys Nagasaki
14 Japanese soldiers attack imperial palace protesting at surrender proclamation

 Germany overrun

After crossing the Rhine, the U.S. armies cut off the Ruhr in April and advanced towards the Elbe. About 300,000 German troops, including 30 generals, were surrounded in the Ruhr 'pocket', while Montgomery's forces swept across the north German plain and the Canadians advanced through the Netherlands.

Meanwhile, the Russians, after being held up on the Oder, finally broke through and within a week they were in the suburbs of Berlin. The city was encircled by April 25. Soviet and U.S. forces joined hands on the Elbe, but fierce street fighting took place in Berlin itself.

As authority at the centre had disappeared, there was no neat and tidy end to the war, the Germans surrendering piecemeal. All those who could endeavoured to surrender to the Americans or the British, rather than the Russians, and of all the sufferings of helpless civilians during the Second World War, few were worse than those endured by the people of eastern Germany as the war drew towards an end.

HITLER COMMITS SUICIDE

VICTORY IN EUROPE

British soldiers disembark rapidly from landing craft, rifles at the ready, after crossing the Elbe.

The end of two dictators

The day preceding the German surrender in Italy, partisans intercepted a party of Fascists trying to make their escape to Switzerland. Hiding underneath a pile of coats was Mussolini. The whole party, including Mussolini's mistress, Clara Petacci, were summarily shot on April 28. Their bodies were taken to Milan and hung up on public display, upside down.

On April 30 in Berlin, as a Russian soldier raised the hammer and sickle on the Reichstag building a matter of yards away from the Führer's bunker (*see* the illustration opposite), Hitler asked his remaining associates, who included Goebbels and Bormann, to leave him. As they waited outside, they heard a shot. Hitler had put a bullet through his mouth. He was dead. His mistress, Eva Braun, who had hastened from the relative safety of Munich to join him, was also dead. She had taken poison.

Mussolini at his last interview – with a Hungarian reporter.

A haggard-looking Hitler a few days before his suicide.

VE day

The Russian-speaking General Krebs opened surrender negotiations with the Russians in Berlin on May 1. Long discussions ensued (Krebs talked to Chuikov, who telephoned Zhukov, who telephoned Stalin), but the Russians refused to accept anything less than unconditional surrender simultaneously to the Soviet Union, the United States and Britain. They resumed bombarding the tiny area of Berlin that was still unconquered. Next morning the commander of German forces in Berlin surrendered, and the Russian guns stopped firing.

Other places still held out, but gradually the Germans surrendered everywhere – in Italy (May 2), in Scandinavia and north Germany (May 3) – though isolated pockets held out several days longer. On May 7 General Jodl, the German chief of staff, with the authority of Karl Doenitz, Hitler's designated successor, went to Eisenhower's headquarters in Reims and signed a general, unconditional surrender.

Europe was free. But it was awash with the dead, the dying and the displaced. Nevertheless, everyone who was physically able to do so celebrated VE (Victory in Europe) Day on May 8.

A triumphant Russian soldier raises the Soviet flag over the Reichstag amid the smouldering ruins of Berlin.

Londoners in a euphoric mood (with the exception of one small child) celebrate VE-Day. For Britain it had been a long, hard war which left the country spiritually exhausted and economically nearly bankrupt.

Hiroshima destroyed

Shortly after 8 a.m. on August 6 a specially adapted B-29 bomber named the 'Enola Gay', completing a five-and-a-half hour flight from Tinian Island in the Marianas, dropped an atomic bomb on the Japanese city of Hiroshima. After a blinding flash, a huge mushroom cloud arose to obscure the stricken city. One of the bomber's crew remarked, 'What a relief, it worked.'

Instant casualties amounted to about 80,000 killed and about half as many injured. Two-thirds of the city was destroyed, including 52 out of 55 hospitals and medical centres. During the next two weeks another 12,000 people died, and radiation, the full effects of which were unforeseen even by scientists on the Manhattan Project, continued to kill people for the next two generations. The memorial in Hiroshima lists 138,890 victims. (Approximately double that number were killed during the carpet bombing of Japanese cities with conventional explosives and incendiaries between March and June.)

The U.S. military and political chiefs had decided to use their new super-weapon to bring the war to a speedy end and thus save lives – U.S. lives, naturally, though it could be argued that it would save Japanese lives too. The battle for Okinawa had shown that an invasion of the Japanese mainland (planned for November), seen as an Okinawa-type operation on a far larger scale, would result in more casualties than the United States had suffered so far in all theatres since the war began. Strategic bombing had not proved the answer, and the Japanese had shown no sign of willingness to surrender. The Soviet campaign against the Japanese was not thought likely to affect the situation other than marginally, and some far-thinking experts, such as the chief of staff, General Marshall, deplored it as likely to lead to undesirable Soviet gains in the Far East. ▶ page 266

Opposite. Utter desolation prevails at Hiroshima six months after the dropping of the first atomic bomb.

Japanese surrender demanded at Potsdam

The 'Big Three', meeting at Potsdam on July 17, issued a joint declaration calling on Japan to surrender, while implying that unconditional surrender would not mean the deposition of the emperor – a major Japanese objection. It warned that the alternative was the 'utter devastation of the Japanese homeland'.

There were changes among the Big Three. Stalin was at the Potsdam conference but, Roosevelt having died in April, President Harry S Truman represented the United States. The British representative at the start was Churchill but at the end Clement Attlee, Britain's first postwar general election having been won decisively by Attlee's Labour Party.

The Potsdam Declaration did not specifically mention the atomic bomb, which had been successfully tested in New Mexico a week earlier. Truman told Stalin that the United States possessed a super-weapon of incomparable destructive power. Stalin in fact knew more than Truman realized, since there was a Soviet spy, Klaus Fuchs, in the Manhattan Project team.

Churchill, the new American president, Truman, and Stalin, in joyful mood at Potsdam.

Russians invade Manchuria

On August 8, two days after the A-bomb was dropped on Hiroshima, the Soviet Union, having renounced its non-aggression pact with Japan, attacked the Japanese in Manchuria. This fulfilled the promise made by Stalin at the Tehran conference.

The attack was made by three Soviet army groups. The Japanese Kwantung army was numerous, of good reputation, but largely unmechanized – in marked contrast with the Soviet divisions. Initial Japanese defence was fierce, but once the Soviet tanks had broken through into open country, the defensive forces were rapidly outmanoeuvred and surrounded. Those who managed to escape fell back across the Yalu River, and the Red Army moved into North Korea. By the third week in August Japanese resistance was at an end. Korea was subsequently divided at the 38th parallel into Soviet and U.S. zones.

Major war criminals to be tried

British, French, Soviet and U.S. officials in London signed an agreement on August 8 which provided for the establishment of a military tribunal to try the leaders of the Axis as war criminals. At the first session – held in October in Berlin, although subsequent sessions were held at Nuremberg – 24 Nazi leaders were indicted. Half of them eventually received death sentences, carried out in October 1946.

A UN War Crimes Commission, charged with investigating, arresting and punishing all those guilty of criminal acts, had been set up nearly two years earlier, 17 nations adding their signatures to the agreement. Earlier still, the intention to carry out retribution for Nazi atrocities had been listed among Allied war aims, and the Big Three had agreed that those guilty of atrocities in occupied countries should, at the conclusion of the war, be sent back to those countries for trial.

A view of Nagasaki showing the appalling destruction caused by the bomb.

Second bomb forces Japanese surrender

After the appalling destruction of Hiroshima, the United States again called upon Japan to surrender. No response was made, and accordingly the second U.S. A-bomb (they had only two) was dropped on Nagasaki on August 9. About 25,000 people were killed.

On August 15 the Emperor Hirohito made a broadcast to the Japanese army (the first public speech by a Japanese emperor) in which, in the characteristically indirect Japanese manner, he told his soldiers to 'accept peace'. This was interpreted by most Japanese, apart from a few extremists, as an acceptance of the Potsdam Declaration terms for surrender. MacArthur arrived in Yokohama on August 28 and five days later the formal surrender was signed on board the battleship *Missouri* in Tokyo Bay.

Vietminh seizes power

Ten days after the bombing of Nagasaki in August the Japanese withdrew from Indo-China. In Hanoi power was seized on August 19 by the Vietminh, the Vietnamese nationalist organization formed in China during the war under the Communist leadership of Ho Chi-Minh.

The Japanese authorities had finally overthrown the Vichy French administration, with considerable slaughter, in March. Under their declared policy of 'Asia for the Asians', they had installed a puppet Vietnamese government. At the Potsdam conference it was agreed that, after Japan's defeat, North Vietnam should be occupied by the Chinese and South Vietnam by the British. When the Vietminh took over, they set up committees throughout Vietnam and declared it to be independent. The French, who had taken over from the British, were left to reach agreement, with the Vietminh.

A Formosa oil refinery attacked by American bombers.

Allied forces land in the East Indies

On September 29 Anglo-Indian and Dutch troops landed in the East Indies. The country, a Dutch colony before the Japanese conquest, had declared its independence after the collapse of Japan six weeks earlier.

The Japanese occupation of the islands had started promisingly, with widespread acceptance among the local peoples of the Japanese claim of 'Asia for the Asians'. The reality of Japanese rule had provoked much hostility, but it nevertheless allowed rapid development of nationalist sentiment, if only because the Japanese, short of manpower, were compelled to let the East Indians govern themselves. However, the declaration of independence was not accepted by the Dutch, who claimed that the new republic of Indonesia was merely a Japanese manufacture, and a long struggle began.

Chinese take over Formosa

On October 25 the island of Formosa (Taiwan) was taken over by Chiang Kai-shek's government. This reflected an agreement made at Cairo in 1943.

Taiwan, whose inhabitants were predominantly Chinese (with a large aboriginal minority), had been Japanese-controlled since 1895, when it was surrendered to Japan by China in a treaty ending the Sino-Japanese war. Under Japanese rule Taiwan made rapid progress, becoming an important producer of rice and sugar. During the Pacific war it had served as 'Japan's largest aircraft carrier'.

THE CAREER OF GENERAL VLASOV

THE TRAGEDIES of war are numerous and terrible, so terrible that perhaps no person can really comprehend them. The utter hideousness of Nazi ideas and actions, the appalling fate of the European Jews – these are almost beyond rational understanding. There, however, the issues are clear cut. But even in the Second World War, the issues were not so clear for everyone. In parts of the Soviet Union the invading Germans were welcomed with open arms.

The career of General Vlasov is an object lesson in divided loyalties. He is of interest particularly because he was such a distinguished figure. His appearance, intelligence and personal charm were appropriate for the Coriolanus-like tragic hero he became.

He had a very distinguished military record and was one of the heroes of the defence of Moscow. Stalin apparently considered appointing him to command at Stalingrad. Not surprisingly, having seen so many of his fellow-officers destroyed by Stalin's paranoia, Vlasov disliked Stalin and the Stalinist system. He also had some disillusioning experiences in the field as a result, he felt, of Moscow's disloyalty. In 1942 he was captured by the Germans and, convinced that nothing could be worse than Stalinism, he changed sides. He was appointed to command a Russian 'army,' more propaganda than firepower, with the Germans. He was given no chance to fight until 1944, when the Germans were in full retreat. He then commanded two divisions, one of which was moved up to the Russian front (where it was almost destroyed). The other, under Vlasov himself, went to Prague. There, having seen enough of the Nazis to realize they were just as bad as the Stalinists, he turned against the Germans and joined the Czechs.

At that stage it looked as though U.S. forces would liberate Prague. As it became evident that the city would be relieved, as a result of political decisions, by the Red Army alone, Vlasov attempted to escape to the west. He was captured and, with a number of his officers, hanged by the Russians. Several thousand of his men who did avoid capture by their compatriots were later turned over by the Americans (another political decision) to the Russians.

Vlasov was certainly a traitor by any standard. He saw himself, however, as a potential saviour of his people, and hoped for another revolution which would get rid of Stalinism. He wanted nothing to do with the British or the Americans because they were Stalin's allies. His great mistake was to think the Germans could achieve his aim, and perhaps his chief fault was in taking too long to change sides the second time. In different circumstances, however, he might have ended up as a national hero.

The cost of the Second World War

No one knows exactly how many people died as a direct result of the Second World War. Fifty million, a good round number, is probably as nearly accurate as is possible. The figures below are therefore unreliable, though probably close to the truth in nearly all cases.

The country that suffered the most casualties was the Soviet Union. As a proportion of total population, however, Polish casualties were higher, while Romania lost the highest proportion of its – admittedly small – army (about 50 per cent), largely as a result of Stalingrad.

Germany also suffered heavily, especially if the terrible misery among German refugees from the east is taken into account.

Despite the savagery of the Pacific war against the Japanese and what came to be the predominance of U.S. forces in western Europe, the United States, which endured no significant attack on its own territory, suffered least among the major combatants. Britain and its Commonwealth and imperial partners also suffered lightly by comparison with others. French losses, in view of France's early removal from the combat, were relatively heavy.

A mourner at the grave of a British soldier in Normandy.

HUMAN CASUALTIES

	Military deaths	As % of armed forces	Civilian deaths
Soviet Union	7,000,000[1]	35	7,700,000
Poland	320,000	32	6,000,000
Germany	3,300,000	36	1,000,000
Japan	1,300,000	23	933,000
Great Britain[2]	265,000	6	70,000
Italy	280,000	6	93,000
France	200,000	4	173,000
United States	292,000	2	5,000

[1] A large proportion of Soviet soldiers died in captivity

[2] Not including Commonwealth and Imperial: Australia 23,000, Canada 37,000, India 24,000, New Zealand 10,000, South Africa 6000.

Among occupied countries, Yugoslavia suffered worst, with 1.4 million civilian dead. The Netherlands lost 200,000, nearly all civilians, Greece 170,000.

THE CAMPS

T HE FIRST concentration camp was opened in Germany, at Dachau, within weeks of Hitler's coming to power. Several more were built in the next five years, especially after 1938, when the expansion of the Reich produced more victims.

Essentially, a concentration camp is a prison. The inhabitants of prisons, however, are normally people who have been convicted of a crime by a court. The inhabitants of the concentration camps were not criminals and had not appeared in any court. They were there because they opposed the Hitler regime or simply because the Nazis disliked them. They had not been sentenced to a term of detention: they were there for life, which, owing to the conditions in the camps, usually meant not very long.

When the war began, the camps changed their character and at the same time were vastly expanded along with the German conquests. Most were labour camps, sometimes attached to specific factories, where the inmates were forced to work for Germany in conditions that killed them off in months if not weeks. Others were death camps. The first, largest, and most efficient of these was Auschwitz, where the gas Cyclon B was first introduced (it killed within ten minutes). Gas came to be preferred to shooting, as it was simpler and did not require the firing squads to be kept permanently drunk and frequently relieved of duty.

Women SS guards at Belsen concentration camp.

Polish Jews en route to Auschwitz.

Auschwitz also pioneered the furnaces designed to overcome the considerable difficulty of disposing of so many corpses. Auschwitz could handle 12,000 bodies a day – a murder factory without parallel.

All the death camps were in Poland. This created logistical problems later, as people destined for destruction sometimes had to be brought great distances and, with the adoption of the 'Final Solution', in very large and growing numbers.

When the concentration camps were overrun by the advancing Allied and Soviet armies in 1945, the horrors they contained were a revelation to the soldiers. Unsurprisingly, there were many cases of instinctive reprisals – at one camp 500 guards were machine-gunned. But while the full extent of Hitler's programme had not until then been comprehended, the perpetration of atrocities by the Nazis was well-known before the war began. Overwhelming evidence of massacres on an unheard-of scale emerged soon after the conquest of Poland, and Hitler's decision to adopt the 'Final Solution' was known officially in 1942.

On the whole, governments and institutions such as the churches had, in general, been ineffective in opposing Nazi persecution and unhelpful towards its victims. The British refused to let more Jews into Palestine; the Americans refused to accept German Jewish refugees without birth certificates – which could be obtained only by application to German officials. The British and their allies in 1939, the Americans two years later, had not gone to war against the Nazis to help the Jews, or the Slavs, or the Gypsies, etc., they had gone to war against Germany to prevent German hegemony in Europe.

The indescribable horrors witnessed by the liberating forces.

Women prisoners use the boots of the dead as fuel.

1946-1965
INDEPENDENCE
AND IDEOLOGY

WITH THE ENDING OF WORLD WAR II THE RELATIONSHIP BETWEEN THE UNITED STATES AND THE Soviet Union rapidly deteriorated. Stalin's gradual absorption of the countries of eastern Europe fuelled American suspicions of Russian expansionism, precipitating the nuclear arms race. Henceforth world politics were to be conducted under the threat of atomic war.

Momentous events were taking place in other parts of the globe. India and Pakistan became independent in 1947, but the birth of the new nations was accompanied by appalling communal violence. The state of Israel, created the following year, was to prove a source of future conflict in the Middle East and in 1949 Communist China emerged victorious only after a long civil war.

Peace seemed as elusive as ever in the 1950s, which began with the outbreak of war in Korea. It was also the decade of Suez and the Hungarian uprising, and of French involvement in colonial wars, first in Vietnam and then in Algeria, where the conflict threatened to engulf mainland France. Elsewhere in Africa, from Morocco to Mozambique, colonial rule was undermined by a variety of nationalist movements. In the early 1960s black nationalism found an echo in the growing strength of the civil rights movement in America. Towards the end of 1962 the United States and the Soviet Union came as close as they had ever been to nuclear war.

1946

Independence for Trieste

An agreement signed by Italy and the World War II Allies on February 10 made the city of Trieste and the surrounding region a 'Free Territory'. It was to be neutral, independent and unarmed, and divided into two zones, one under Anglo-U.S. administration, the other Yugoslav.

After the collapse of the Austro-Hungarian Empire, the cosmopolitan port city of Trieste had been given to Italy in the peace treaty after World War I. In 1943 it was occupied by the Germans. In the last week of the war Tito's

British and U.S. military police in Trieste.

Yugoslavs marched in and claimed it as their own. The compromise of February 1946 soon proved unworkable. After various proposals had been rejected, it was finally divided more or less equally between Yugoslavia and Italy in 1954.

Civil war in China resumes

On May 5 fighting broke out between Nationalist and Communist forces on the Yangtse River. It marked the renewal of the civil war in China which had been interrupted by the Japanese invasion and ensuing world war.

The co-operation between Nationalists and Communists during the war had always been half-hearted, partly because their forces were a long way apart, making combined operations difficult. After the Japanese surrender, both sides attempted to gain as much vacated Chinese territory as they could. Nationalist troops, aided by U.S. air and sea transport, took over most of the eastern cities and railways, while Mao Tse-tung's Communists occupied much of the hinterland in the north and Manchuria. Prolonged attempts were made

by U.S. representatives, in particular General George C. Marshall, to arrange a compromise, and early in 1946 the prospects looked hopeful. A cease-fire was arranged and talks were held to establish a coalition government. In February, the rival leaders agreed to Marshall's plan to merge their armies.

However, after the renewal of fighting in the spring, Mao's formal declaration of war on the Nationalists in August confirmed that the fight would continue until one or other side had gained control of China. ▶ *page 283*

General Marshall (left) on his return from China.

Irgun terrorists blow up King David hotel

One wing of the main hotel in Jerusalem was destroyed by an explosion on July 22. The hotel was being used as British military headquarters, but the explosion killed over 50 Arabs and Jews as well as 17 British personnel.

The bomb had been planted by

the terrorist organization led by Menachem Begin, the Irgun Zvai Leumi, in reprisal for tough British security measures. It was the most notorious incident in the increasingly bitter conflict between Jews and the British (the occupying power). ▶ *page 277*

Removing a casualty from the King David hotel.

Thousands die in Hindu-Muslim riots

Following the call for a 'Direct Action Day' by the Muslim League, serious fighting broke out between Hindus and Muslims in Calcutta on August 16. The violence spread to other regions, and estimates of the total killed in three days' conflict ranged up to 7000.

The British Labour government was eager to concede independence to India as soon as practicable. In March, to the accompaniment of violent anti-British demonstrations and a mutiny in the Indian navy, a government mission arrived in India to discuss its constitutional future. It proposed to set up a provisional government (to be led by Jawaharlal Nehru), but the Muslim League, led by Mohammed Ali Jinnah, demanded a completely independent Muslim state. This was rejected, resulting in the increase of Muslim opposition to the Congress party, and the outbreak of violence in August. When the constituent assembly did meet, in December, it was boycotted by the Muslim League. ▶ *page 276*

A dead Hindu surrounded by Muslim assailants.

1946

Conflict in Greece over the monarchy

A referendum held in Greece on September 1 produced a vote heavily in favour of the restoration of the monarchy. The Communists, who had abstained from the vote, went underground.

Following the British suppression of the Communist revolt in Athens at the end of 1945, peace was agreed and the Communists now abandoned their resistance. There were violent clashes after the announcement of the referendum result, as well as frequent incidents on the borders with Greece's Communist-controlled neighbours.

Big bangs at Bikini

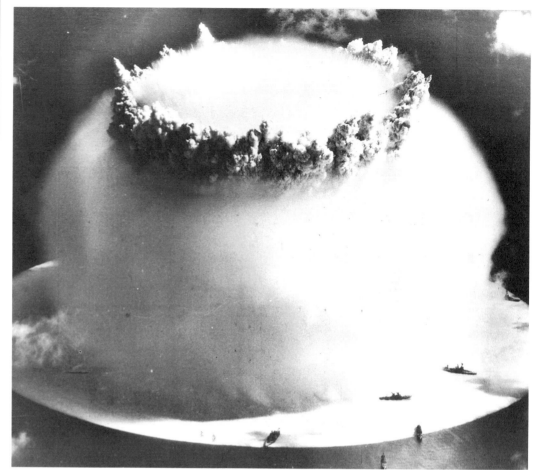

The awesome spectacle of an atomic bomb explosion above Bikini atoll.

On July 1 the United States began a series of nuclear weapons tests off Bikini atoll in the Marshall Islands. The first explosion occurred 500 ft above the water, and the blast sank the aircraft carrier *Independence*.

Subsequent explosions, which provoked protests in the United States, took place underwater.

In the same month the United States proposed at the newly founded UN Atomic Energy Commission an international authority to which it would surrender its atomic knowledge in exchange for a pledge by other nations not to develop nuclear energy for warlike purposes. This was rejected by the Soviet Union. ▶ *page 316*

The French bombard Haiphong

On November 23 the French attempted to stop the flow of arms into northern Vietnam. Shots were exchanged in Haiphong, and the French navy bombarded part of the city.

French troops had landed at Haiphong and occupied Hanoi in March, but had reached a settlement with the Vietminh, the Communist-dominated nationalist movement, in which the Democratic Republic of Vietnam, under the leadership of Ho Chi Minh, was recognized as an autonomous state within French Indo-China. Subsequent negotiations in France, however, failed to reach agreement on major issues, and it became clear that the Vietminh was preparing to renew the conflict. Four weeks after the incident in Haiphong, the Vietminh made a surprise attack on the French, but were beaten off and took to the forest. One of the longest and bitterest struggles of the postwar period had begun. ▶ *page 284*

The French prime minister, Georges Bidault, receives Ho Chi Minh during the latter's visit to Paris in July 1946.

1947

United States backs Greek government in civil war

JANUARY–MARCH

CIVIL WAR IN GREECE

TRUMAN DOCTRINE PROCLAIMED

On February 21, the British government announced the withdrawal of its troops from Greece. Its role there was taken over by the United States, which pumped in large amounts of aid as well as military 'advisers'.

Full-scale guerrilla warfare was renewed early in 1947 by the Communists, who had never given up their bases in the mountains and now received support, indirectly at least, from the Soviet Union, through the Communist-controlled countries on the border. In the course of the year they succeeded in taking over considerable areas and proclaimed a Communist provisional government in the north.

Soldiers of the Greek regular army, equipped with British weapons, manning an outpost in Macedonia.

'Truman Doctrine' promulgated

In a speech to the U.S. Congress on March 12, President Truman declared that the United States should 'support free peoples who are resisting attempted subjugation by armed minorities or by outside pressures'.

The 'Truman Doctrine', as it was called in reference to the Monroe Doctrine of an earlier president declaring the western hemisphere off-limits to European powers, put an end to any chance of the United States resuming its isolationist stance of the 1920s and 1930s. The immediate proposal was for funds for the governments of Greece and Turkey to combat communism (British troops were on the point of leaving Greece). The Soviet Union was not mentioned, though there was no doubt what 'outside pressures' referred to.

President Truman speaking before a battery of microphones.

1946

JULY
1 U.S. A-bomb test in Marshall Islands
4 Philippines gain independence
17 Mihailovich executed in Yugoslavia
22 Irgun terrorists blow up King David hotel in Jerusalem

AUGUST
16 Thousands die in Hindu-Muslim riots in India
19 Mao Tse-tung declares war on Nationalists in China
24 Nehru appointed head of provisional Indian government

OCTOBER
16 Ten leading Nazis executed at Nuremberg
16 UN General Assembly opens in New York

NOVEMBER
17 Jewish terrorists step up bombing campaign
23 French bombard Haiphong

DECEMBER
9 Indian constituent assembly meets
28 French impose martial law in Indo-China

1947

JANUARY
19 Truman condemns Polish elections as contrary to Yalta agreement
21 South African prime minister General Smuts refuses UN trusteeship for South-West Africa
31 British civilians evacuated from Palestine

FEBRUARY
10 Peace treaties signed with Italy, Finland and Balkan states
20 Mountbatten appointed viceroy of India
21 Britain informs the United States of intended troop withdrawal from Greece

MARCH
4 Anglo-French treaty of alliance
5 Reign of terror in the Punjab following Sikh leader's denunciation of the Muslim League
12 Truman Doctrine proclaims world defence against Communism
14 Philippines grant U.S. naval and military bases
19 Chinese Nationalist offensive captures Communist capital of Yenang
22 Mountbatten arrives in India amid communal violence

Burmese cabinet massacred

Prime minister Aung San.

On July 19, armed men burst into a cabinet meeting in Rangoon and killed the prime minister, Aung San, and six ministers.

Aung San's Anti-Fascist People's Freedom League, which had supported General Slim in the liberation of Burma from the Japanese, had widespread support in Burma, though not among some of the hill people, including the Karens, nor among the Communists. Having secured victory in popular elections, it proposed a Union of Burma, which was accepted by the British. The massacre of the cabinet had little effect on these political developments: U Nu took over and negotiations with the British continued, resulting in a treaty in October providing for Burmese independence in January 1948.

British repel *Exodus* refugees

The *Exodus*, carrying 5000 European Jewish refugees, arrived at Haifa on July 18. A battle took place as British troops acted to prevent them landing, in which three people died.

This was the worst incident in the campaign to bring unlicensed Jewish refugees into Palestine in the face of British restrictions (it subsequently became the subject of a highly inaccurate legend).

Most of the refugees were carried back to France, where they had been picked up, but the French refused to admit them and they eventually returned to – of all places – Germany.

Rape of Kashmir

On October 22, thousands of Muslim tribesmen invaded Kashmir, intent on rape, looting and murder of the Hindus. They were responding to the massacres in the Punjab and to the attacks on Muslims in Kashmir by Hindu and Sikh refugees. Their weapons, including light artillery, were apparently supplied by Pakistan, while some of them were led by Pakistani officers said to be 'on leave'.

Jammu and Kashmir was a princely state, ruled by a Hindu maharajah and largely administered by Hindus, though the majority of its population (except in Jammu) was Muslim. After August 15 the maharajah was faced with the choice of attaching his beautiful and strategically significant land to either India or Pakistan. Independence was impractical because of Kashmir's geographical situation, entirely dependent on supplies from outside. Pakistan was the obvious choice, on religious, economic as well as geographical grounds, but there were also strong reasons for joining India. Nehru was particularly keen for this, since he hated the idea of political division on purely religious grounds (and perhaps because his ancestors came from Kashmir). The decision was delayed, and fighting broke out in Kashmir itself, mainly between Muslim rebels and the maharajah's Hindu troops.

The invaders of October 22, who swept across the country killing and burning as they went, prompted the maharajah to cede Kashmir to India, with a request for immediate help. Indian troops were flown in and, after a struggle, they repelled the invaders. The immediate reaction of Jinnah and the Pakistan government was to send in Pakistani troops, but open war between India and Pakistan was avoided after delaying action by the Pakistani army commander who, like the commander of the Indian troops, was British.

The question of the border in Kashmir was left unresolved – a festering sore which was to erupt again in the future. ▶ *page 283*

A rioting mob invades a shopping centre – a familiar scene in India in 1947.

UN votes for Palestine partition

A plan for the partition of Palestine was approved by the UN General Assembly on November 29. It provided for a separate Jewish state and made Jerusalem a neutral zone under international control.

The plan, which, surprisingly enough, was supported by the Soviet Union, caused celebration among Zionists and disgust among Arabs. The British, disillusioned by the activities of underground Jewish terrorist groups, were determined to get out of Palestine (and out of a conflict to which they had no solution) as soon as possible. They announced their intention of withdrawing their forces by August (later brought forward to May) 1948. They also refused to admit a UN supervising force until their own troops had completely withdrawn. ▶ *page 280*

In Jerusalem an Orthodox Jew is searched by a British soldier before entering a compound where suspects are screened.

Soviet grip tightens on satellites

King Michael of Romania was forced to abdicate on December 30, with Communists, some Moscow-trained, gaining increasing power in the government. The incident was a symptom of the tightening control imposed by the Soviet Union on those countries of eastern Europe within its zone of influence.

U.S. pressure for free, democratic elections in countries such as Bulgaria, Poland, Hungary and Czechoslovakia was seen by Moscow as merely a part of the assumed capitalist plan to encircle the Soviet Union. The elections were not free, and democratic leaders like Maniu in Romania were not only forced out of office but tried on trumped-up treason charges. Maniu died in prison in 1952. ▶ *page 281*

King Michael of Romania, with Princess Anne of Bourbon-Palma, during a visit to England in November 1947 for the wedding of the then Princess Elizabeth. His forced abdication came a few weeks later.

THE END OF THE RAJ

AT 8.30 IN THE MORNING of August 15 celebrations began in Delhi and Karachi. While 31 guns boomed a salute, the flags of the newly independent nations of India and Pakistan were proudly raised. Lord Mountbatten, who was chiefly responsible for the speedy accomplishment of Indian independence, changed roles – from the last viceroy of British India to the first governor-general of the Dominion of India. The first governor-general of Pakistan was Mohammed Ali Jinnah. He was the first non-white to hold such a post (though not because of British progressiveness; he had simply insisted on it).

The partition of the country into two independent states, one of which was itself divided geographically into two widely separated territories (East and West Pakistan), had proved to be the only solution to the conflicting ambitions of the parties involved. Unfortunately, there was no easy way of doing it. In particular, it meant dividing Bengal and the Punjab between the two new nations. It was in those provinces that serious trouble could be expected, and even while the guns were firing in celebration in the capitals, they were sounding in earnest elsewhere.

Bengal was thought to be the most explosive. It was feared that in Calcutta, as the Hindus gained control, there would be a slaughter of Muslims in revenge for the killings of the previous year. Gandhi moved into a Calcutta slum and his presence undoubtedly saved thousands of lives.

He also spent some time in the Punjab, where his influence among the Sikhs was, however, more limited. They had been more or less openly preparing for war with the Muslims ever since the partition plans became known (the final details had not, even on the day of independence, been published). The troops who had been sent to the Punjab to control the violence found the task too much for them, while public services had come to a stop as the people that ran them moved from one part of the country to another.

After August 15 the stream of refugees became a torrent. Some convoys stretched unbroken for 50 miles. Stragglers were cut off by armed bandits. The monsoon broke and cholera invaded the refugee camps. Violence spread to Calcutta. Gandhi, aged 77, threatened to fast until death and, amazingly, this action was sufficient to stop the slaughter.

Delhi, the Indian capital, was flooded with refugees, whose stories of their sufferings provoked revenge attacks against Muslims. One day, after a massacre at the railway station, blood streamed down the platforms. British and Gurkha troops eventually succeeded in restoring order. The press grew hysterical, and relations between the two new states approached total rupture.

Casualty figures are hard to determine. Over 500,000 people died in the Punjab alone. More than 20 times that number were made homeless.

Main picture. Muslims waiting to leave New Delhi for the journey to Pakistan.

Below left. Crowded trains carrying Sikh refugees from Pakistan arriving at Amritsar, India.

Opposite, above right. A victim of communal rioting in New Delhi.

Opposite, below right. Gandhi, shortly after abandoning his fast undertaken in an effort to stem the violence in Calcutta.

1948

JANUARY–MAY

**APARTHEID
IN SOUTH AFRICA**

**ARAB-ISRAELI
WAR**

**COUP IN
CZECHOSLOVAKIA**

Costa Rican rebels take capital

The forces of the Costa Rican National Liberation party, led by Colonel José Figueres, entered San José on April 24. Civil war had broken out several weeks ear-lier following a move by the in-cumbent president, Teodoro Pic-ado, to annul the election results.

Later in the year there was an armed incursion from Nicaragua in support of the former presi-dent Calderón Guardía. The insurgents took the town of La Cruz but by Christmas had been driven out.

President José Figueres with his wife arriving on a visit to Hamburg.

Revolt in Indonesia

South Molucca proclaimed its independence from Sukarno's Indonesian state on April 26. The Moluccan revolt was symptom-atic of the widespread antipathy among Indonesian peoples to the dominance of Java and the poli-cies of Sukarno. Sporadic out-breaks of unrest occurred in several parts during the next ten years, as the creation of an Indo-nesian nation from so many different lands and peoples proved problematic. ▶ *page 314*

President Sukarno of Indonesia during a tour.

South Africa embraces *apartheid*

Elections in South Africa on May 26 resulted in a victory for the National Party, the official doc-trine of which was *apartheid*, or 'separation' of the races. The new government embarked upon leg-islation to enforce this principle and set up a huge bureaucracy to cope with the considerable admi-nistrative problems.

Under the Government of South Africa act of 1909 the so-called 'Cape Coloured' (mixed race), as well as a few property-owning blacks, had the right to vote, but in fact racial separation in South Africa was institutional-ized from the time of its colonial beginnings. The system of *apar-theid* was to lead to growing opposition, increasing violence and eventually to an internat-ional boycott of South Africa, as well as inflicting cruel and often ludicrous restrictions on the maj-ority of the population. ▶ *page 308*

Arab attempt to crush Israel

On May 14, a few hours before the official end of the British mandate in Palestine, the republic of Israel was proclaimed by David Ben Gurion, veteran leader of the Jews in Palestine. The armies of the Arab League – Lebanon, Syria, Jordan and Egypt – immediately attacked.

The war between Arabs and Jews within Palestine had, in effect, been going on for some time, and Arab refugees had been fleeing Jewish-held territory, especially after a massacre of Arab villagers by Jewish terror-ists at Deir Yassin on April 9.

The Israelis, with an army of about 30,000, were vastly out-numbered, but they were very well led and they were committed. They had also acquired consider-able experience of war. The Arab forces, on the other hand, were in general very badly led (the Jor-danian Arab Legion was an exception) and less committed. They were also ill co-ordinated and relatively inexperienced.

Nevertheless, an Israeli victory looked highly unlikely, and at the beginning of the war some places were lost (though nearly all subse-quently regained). The conflict lasted over six months, with inter-mittent truces arranged by the UN. Israeli casualities were about 6000; Arab casualties were much higher, though the exact numbers were uncertain. In addition, Israel expanded its boundaries far beyond those of the partition plan. It consisted of a solid swathe of territory west of the Jordan (except for the region later known as the West Bank) from southern Lebanon to the Red Sea.

The legacies of the conflict were heightened Arab-Jewish hostility (the Arabs rejected Israel's right to exist, never mind its consider-able accessions by conquest), and up to one million homeless Pales-tinian Arabs, occupying desolate refugee camps in the Lebanon.

Armoured forces of the Arab Legion preparing to move against Israel.

Communists take over Czechoslovakia

In the elections held in Czechoslovakia at the end of May, the vast majority of electors voted for the so-called National Front. No other party was standing.

The new constitution, establishing a 'people's democracy' (i.e. total Communist party control), was rejected by President Beneš, who resigned. He died a few months later, the new Communist president, Gottwald, having meanwhile ratified the constitution. The foreign minister, Masaryk, son of the founder of Czechoslovakia, also died, after falling from a window – a traditional fate for political opponents in Prague.

The takeover in Czechoslovakia was merely the most blatant example of the Soviet Union's use of intimidation to seize control in the countries on its borders in eastern Europe. By the end of 1948, democratic parties and virtually all non-Communist political leaders had been in one way or another eliminated. Communists monpolized power not only at national level but also in towns and villages, factories and businesses. No opposition was allowed and the dominance of the party soon extended to every aspect of society.

Prime minister Gottwald addresses a mass rally of Communist supporters in Prague.

Jungle war

A state of emergency was declared in the British colony of Malaya on June 18. It followed a series of murders of managers of European rubber plantations and attacks on government posts and police.

The Communist insurgents in Malaya aimed to destabilize the country through guerrilla warfare, mainly by disrupting the economy. The guerrillas, the Min Yuen, were almost wholly Chinese, and the British adopted a policy of gathering the Chinese workers of the mines and plantations into new villages which, though they caused social upheaval, offered many advantages

Police question a Malay villager about Communist bandits.

and ultimately proved successful in depriving the guerrillas of popular support. The British also developed good guerrilla tactics themselves. Aided by Dayak

trackers, they combed the country, district by district. Though the state of emergency continued for many years, the Min Yuen were eventually driven out.

Berlin cut off

On June 24 a blockade was imposed on West Berlin, which lay within the Soviet zone of occupied Germany. Within a few weeks, all traffic by road, rail or water was cut off.

The blockade, the first serious conflict of the 'Cold War', was not totally unexpected, as the Soviet authorities had begun to impede the traffic by prolonged customs checks several months earlier. The relations between East and West were already poor, and the Soviet authorities strongly objected to moves towards the restoration of self-government in West Germany and to the introduction of the new Deutschmark in West Berlin.

The Allies responded by organizing a massive airlift, which continued for over a year. U.S. and British aircraft flew about 1.6 million tons of food and other supplies into West Berlin during that time, and carried out a sizeable proportion of the city's exports. Nevertheless, the people of Berlin suffered considerable hardship, especially through shortage of fuel during the winter.

Attempts at the UN to get the blockade lifted were unsuccess-

ful, but an embargo on some trade with countries of the Soviet bloc had more effect, and after just under a year the Soviet authorities lifted the blockade unilat-

erally. They continued to impose tight control on communications with the city from the west, and there were sporadic interruptions for several years.

An RAF transport aircraft, one of many bringing vital food supplies to the beleaguered city of Berlin, makes a night landing at Gatow airport.

Nationalist disaster in Manchuria

The Nationalist Chinese suffered a major defeat at the hands of the Communists on October 30. The capture of Mukden (Shenyang) completed the Communist takeover of Manchuria: over 300,000 Nationalist troops surrendered.

As the Soviet forces retreated from Manchuria after Japan's surrender, they bequeathed weapons and supplies to the Communists and in places deliberately delayed their withdrawal so that the Communists could take over

from the Japanese.

Apart from the costly defeat in Manchuria, the Nationalist cause looked, increasingly, a losing one. U.S. aid ($2 billion in 1945–8) did not compensate sufficiently for the collapsing morale of Chiang

Kai-shek's regime. A second military disaster occurred in northern China towards the end of the year, when around 500,000 men were lost, the majority through desertion, in the region of the Huai river basin.

1949

KASHMIR CEASE-FIRE

CHINESE COMMUNISTS VICTORIOUS

Truce in Kashmir

On January 1 fighting between Indian and Pakistani forces in Kashmir finally came to an end. The truce was arranged by the UN, which was also charged with organizing a referendum in the disputed province.

In military terms the Kashmiri conflict was hardly a war – more an affair of occasional skirmishes. There were no pitched battles and very few direct confrontations between substantial units. It left most of Kashmir in Indian hands, and failed to resolve what was to prove a long-running dispute.

The *Amethyst* reaches Hong Kong

There was a warm welcome for the British frigate *Amethyst* when she reached Hong Kong on June 30. She had been trapped up the Yangtse river when the Chinese Communist forces advanced on Shanghai.

The *Amethyst* had been damaged by artillery fire and 40 members of her crew, including the captain, were killed. As food and fuel ran low, she escaped during the night, making a dash down river and breaking through a boom that barred her progress.

The *Amethyst* arrives in Hong Kong for a refit after its epic journey along the Yangtse.

The People's Liberation Army takes Shanghai

After a month's siege, Shanghai fell suddenly and without much resistance to the Chinese Communist forces on May 26. Many people had already fled the city, including the still-substantial European population.

Although the Nationalist leaders, weakened by corruption and factional disputes, had spoken of making a stand in Shanghai, their forces were crumbling. They withdrew to Canton. There was fierce fighting to the east as Nationalist troops endeavoured to keep a corridor open for escape, but by October Canton itself had fallen.

Communist victory in China

In December Chiang Kai-shek acknowledged the defeat of his forces in mainland China by resigning the presidency of the Nationalist government. On December 8 the regime moved to the large island of Taiwan and was re-established in Taipei. The 'People's Republic' of China had already been proclaimed in Peking, and Mao Tse-tung installed as chairman.

Although people of different persuasions were included in the new government, what looked like a coalition was in fact completely dominated by the Communist party, which had five or six million adherents throughout the country. ▶ *page 296*

1950

WAR IN KOREA

CHINESE INVADE TIBET

Divisions harden in Vietnam

On February 7 the Western powers formally recognized the French-supported regime of Bao Dai in Vietnam. The move followed the Soviet Union's recognition of Ho Chi Minh's government a week earlier.

Bao Dai's regime failed to gain the hoped-for popular support, and French authority was now increasingly confined to the towns, with movement between them possible only in armed convoys. Following Vietminh victories, by the end of the year the French were compelled to abandon the region adjoining the Chinese border. ▶ *page 295*

The emperor Bao Dai.

North Korea invades the South

On June 25 North Korean troops crossed the 38th parallel and invaded South Korea in support of their government's claim to sovereignty over all Korea. The invasion had been preceded by a number of border incidents during the two previous years.

Notwithstanding agreements during World War II that Korea should become free and independent, in 1945 the country was divided along the 38th parallel, temporarily by intention but permanently as a result of failure to agree on a united government. A Communist regime backed by the Soviet Union existed in the north, and a (more or less) democratic government under President Syngman Rhee was established in the south. Both claimed to be the rightful government for the whole country.

On the basis of the Truman Doctrine, and more particularly the security of Japan, the United States was unwilling to countenance a Communist takeover in South Korea. At the time of the invasion the Soviet Union was boycotting the UN Security Council over the refusal to substitute the Chinese Communist government for the Nationalist government holding China's UN seat, and accordingly the UN passed a resolution condemning the North Korean invasion and approving direct aid to the south. The war in Korea was therefore waged by the North Koreans, supported by the Soviet Union (later by China), against the United Nations. Although the United States provided the great mass of the UN force, Britain, France, Australia and other governments also sent troops.

Within two months, the North Korean forces had occupied almost the whole of South Korea, including the capital, Seoul. U.S. troops at that stage were insufficient to prevent the conquest.

U.S. soldiers accompanied by tanks moving up to the front in South Korea.

U.S. landings at Inchon

U.S. troops climbing down into their assault craft during the landings at Inchon.

On September 16 U.S. troops from Japan landed at Inchon, on the west coast of Korea, not far from Seoul. In spite of the short time available for planning, the invasion was a remarkable feat, confirming General MacArthur's already high reputation.

MacArthur's forces quickly liberated Seoul and the rest of South Korea. Upon reaching the 38th parallel, the *de facto* boundary between north and south, he ordered an invasion of the north and rapidly advanced towards the Chinese frontier. After issuing several warnings, the Chinese, anticipating an invasion of China (as MacArthur had advocated), attacked.

The combined Chinese and North Korean forces, in a devastating counterattack, recaptured Seoul and all but drove the UN forces into the sea. MacArthur managed to establish a defensive line in the south which held, while President Truman proclaimed a state of international emergency.
▶ *page 286*

Chinese invade Tibet

Chinese troops invaded the eastern borders of Tibet on October 21. There was little resistance, and protests from India were dismissed by the Chinese as interference in China's internal affairs.

Under an agreement formalized six months later the Chinese promised autonomy to Tibet, with the position of the Dalai Lama unimpaired. The Chinese were to set up military headquarters at strategic points in Tibet, absorb the Tibetan army and conduct Tibet's foreign policy. On this basis, the Dalai Lama, who had fled the country in December, returned to Lhasa, while India implicitly recognized Chinese sovereignty in Tibet.
▶ *page 306*

The Dalai Lama.

Egypt attacks British influence

A speech by the Egyptian king, Farouk, in November, echoing the greater militancy of the recently elected Wafdist government, raised the temperature of the dispute with Britain. He demanded the removal of British troops from the Suez Canal zone and the cession of the Sudan to Egypt.

The long-running Anglo-Egyptian dispute had died down in the period of the Arab-Israeli conflict, when the British had appeared mainly intent on preventing Israeli conquest of Egyptian territory, and a new agreement had given Egypt a larger share in the profits and administration of the Suez Canal Company. However, moves towards making the Sudan independent aroused fierce indignation in view of Egypt's claim to that country.
▶ *page 287*

JANUARY
6 Britain recognizes Communist regime in China
10 Soviet UN envoy walks out in protest at Nationalists' retention of China seat
25 U.S. government official Alger Hiss sentenced to five years for perjury
31 Soviet Union recognizes Ho Chi Minh government in Vietnam

FEBRUARY
7 Western nations recognize Bao Dai regime in Vietnam
9 U.S. Senator McCarthy begins crusade against communism
14 Sino-Soviet treaty of alliance

APRIL
8 India and Pakistan sign agreement to protect minorities
24 Jordan annexes Palestine territory of West Bank

JUNE
25 North Korean forces invade South Korea
26 President Truman pledges military aid for South Korea
27 UN votes for direct assistance to South Korea
28 Seoul falls to North Koreans
28 General MacArthur arrives in Korea

JULY
1 U.S. troops land in Korea
26 Britain and France agree to send troops to Korea
31 King Leopold of the Belgians abdicates

AUGUST
7 U.S. forces launch Korean offensive at Chinju
29 British troops arrive in Korea

SEPTEMBER
16 U.S. amphibious landings at Inchon

OCTOBER
1 UN troops reach 38th parallel
10 Vietminh defeat French at Kaobang
15 Truman confers with MacArthur on Wake Island
21 Chinese troops enter Tibet
26 UN forces take North Korean capital of Pyongyang

NOVEMBER
16 Egypt demands British evacuation of Suez Canal Zone
26 Chinese launch invasion in support of North Korea

DECEMBER
5 UN troops evacuate Pyongyang
16 President Truman declares national emergency after Korean defeats
19 Eisenhower appointed NATO supreme commander
19 Dalai Lama flees Tibet
24 Chinese troops invade South Korea

Retirement of an old soldier

To the surprise of everyone, General Douglas MacArthur, commander of the UN troops in Korea, was summarily dismissed on April 11. Conflicting views between the nominal commander-in-chief, i.e. the president, and MacArthur had been known to exist, but their conference on Wake Island the previous October was assumed to have clarified the situation. MacArthur, however, continued to make statements infringing on the prerogatives of politicians.

With the Chinese invasion, the Korean conflict had become, as MacArthur put it, 'a new war', and he urged the bombing of Communist bases in Manchuria, a blockade of the Chinese coast and the involvement of Chinese Nationalist troops in the UN force. Whatever generals might say, however, politicians were determined to avoid widening the conflict in this way, which threatened to lead to a third world war.

Truman later characteristically commented, 'I fired him because he wouldn't respect the authority of the president. I didn't fire him because he was a dumb son-of-a-bitch, although he was, but that's not against the law for generals.'

MacArthur, who was to be succeeded as UN commander by General Matthew Ridgway, made a memorable farewell speech to the U.S. Congress on his return, when he remarked that old soldiers never die, they merely fade away.

General MacArthur during a visit to Korea.

Iran nationalizes oil

On May 3, five days after Mohammed Mossadegh became prime minister, the Iranian parliament passed a bill to nationalize the oil industry. Immediate protests were made by the Anglo-Iranian Oil Company, which controlled the industry in the southern part of the country, and by the British government.

The AIOC had signed an agreement with the Iranian government in 1949 increasing the royalty rate. In February, with the campaign for nationalization of the industry growing more intense, the AIOC offered a fifty-fifty agreement, while the prime minister, Ali Razmara, was informed by expert studies that nationalization was impracticable. This decision caused frantic resentment and Ali Razmara was assassinated a few days after presenting his conclusion to parliament.

Mossadegh's enforcement of the nationalization act and his general recalcitrance, which was such that he was suspected, in the West at least, of being mentally unbalanced, inflamed the dispute with Britain, leading eventually to the complete close-down of AIOC's operations and a break in diplomatic relations. ▶ *page 291*

Prime minister Mossadegh en route to New York.

Truce talks in Korea

On July 10 representatives of both sides in the Korean war met at Kaesong to discuss the possibilities of seeking a truce. Meetings took place in an atmosphere of mutal hostility and suspicion, complicated by the fact that Kaesong had been in no man's land when fixed as a meeting place but had meanwhile been captured by the Communists.

Difficulties over establishing neutral territory were characteristic of the painful progress of the negotiations and caused several recesses, one lasting over two months. Another major problem concerned prisoners of war. When the Communists at last agreed to exchange lists, the UN list of missing men proved to be about ten times longer than the Communist list. The matter of appointing a supervisory commission from neutral countries caused lengthy argument, the Communist nomination of the Soviet Union being refused by the UN command.

The question of where the truce line should lie also provoked disagreement, the Communists arguing that the 38th parallel was the obvious point, the UN preferring a line that made more strategic sense.

The fighting in the first half of the year had ended up roughly even. A UN offensive regained Seoul in March and advanced across the 38th parallel, only to be forced south by a series of Communist offensives in the spring, culminating in a savage battle for Seoul, which restored the position of January. Early in June the UN advanced again, against fierce resistance. Fighting continued while the truce talks were in progress, but generally on a smaller scale, a characteristic being the use of small task forces and patrols. By November, when the Communists accepted the UN preference for a demarcation line roughly coinciding with the front, the fighting had stabilized a short way north of the 38th parallel. ▶ *page 288*

U.S. and North Korean liaison officers discussing the demarcation line.

Egypt renounces 1936 treaty

The Anglo-Egyptian dispute worsened on October 8 as Egypt renounced its 20-year treaty of 1936 with Britain and renewed its claim to the Sudan.

The government of Nahas Pasha, appointed in January, at first seemed inclined to seek more amicable relations with Britain, but domestic problems and pressure from extremist groups (responsible for killing two prime ministers and the Cairo chief of police in the previous two years) combined to make the quarrel with Britain a welcome distraction.

Britain rejected the unilateral cancellation of the treaty and the proclamation of King Farouk as king of the Sudan, being supported in this by France and the United States. British troops in the Canal Zone were reinforced, as increasingly frequent clashes took place, sometimes involving the Egyptian police. ▶ *page 288*

King Farouk (centre) dining with the Duke of Edinburgh and Ernest Bevin.

1952

JANUARY–DECEMBER

**EGYPTIAN
MILITARY COUP**

**MAU MAU
REVOLT**

Military coup in Egypt

On the night of July 22 a group of Egyptian army officers led by Colonel Gamal Abdul Nasser seized control of Cairo. Within hours they controlled most of the country. The king abdicated, and a new government was set up under General Mohammed Neguib, a hero of the Israeli war.

The Egyptian coup, a turning point in the history of the Middle East, was rooted in many causes, not least the disgust of younger army officers at the poor performance against Israel in 1948. Farouk, the immensely fat 'playboy king', was an antiquated figure in the 1950s and his friends, if not he himself, were openly corrupt. Palace and parliament were mutually hostile. More immediately, the king and the government lost prestige as a result of the British seizure of the Ismailia police headquarters, in which nearly 50 Arabs died. This was followed by riots in Cairo which the embittered police did little or nothing to check. The ease with which the military takeover was accomplished – with virtually no bloodshed – was evidence of the power vacuum into which Colonel Nasser and his colleagues stepped. ▶ *page 298*

General Mohammed Neguib.

Revolution in Bolivia

Victor Paz Estenssoro.

A revolution in Bolivia overthrew the military government on April 11. It was popular in character, a leading role being taken by labour unions and tin miners.

The revolution opened the way for the return to office of the MNR (National Revolutionary Movement) leader, Victor Paz Estenssoro. He had been legally elected president in 1951, though in exile at the time. The current incumbent had annulled the election and had turned power over to the army, under General Hugo Ballivián.

Paz Estenssoro's presidency was swiftly recognized by the United States, and he undertook the economic reforms, such as nationalization of the mines and redistribution of land, which the revolution demanded. He served his full presidential term – the first Bolivian president to do so since the 1920s.

Operation Stranglehold

On August 18 an extensive bombing campaign began in Korea. The object was to destroy Communist supplies and communications, and railways were a special target. Because of the stabilization of the ground fighting, more aircraft were available for operations. At the same time, Communist air action, as well as artillery fire, increased. About 60 MiG-15s (the standard Soviet jet fighter) were destroyed in the month of September alone.

The air attack switched mainly to night-time raids in October, the targets being storage areas and marshalling yards. Nearly all North Korean airfields were rendered unusable, while a total naval blockade denied Communist forces the use of the sea.

Towards the end of the year ground action increased, requiring more air support. Sometimes the front lines were barely 50 yards apart, with stubborn, hand-to-hand fighting for vantage points that changed hands many times. Close air support and more accurate artillery fire compensated for the UN inferiority in numbers. ▶ *page 291*

U.S. artillery 'Long Toms' firing in support of infantry in Korea.

Emergency in Kenya

As British troops were flown in from Suez, a state of emergency was declared by the British governor of Kenya on October 20. The Mau Mau, hitherto considered a small, essentially criminal force of obscure tribal origin, was moving towards an open campaign against the colonial regime.

The Mau Mau movement grew among one of Kenya's most numerous people, the Kikuyu. It revived the traditional custom of oath-taking and violence and set out to terrorize local inhabitants, especially European planters, in order to rid the Kenya Highlands, traditionally Kikuyu territory, of whites. Victims included Kikuyu and other African opponents as well as Europeans. The suspected leader of the Mau Mau, Jomo Kenyatta, was arrested when the state of emergency was declared, and hundreds of other Kikuyu were rounded up in the next two months. ▶ *page 290*

Following a night raid organized by the army and the police a Mau Mau suspect is taken into custody for interrogation. The state of emergency was the beginning of more than four years of military operations against rebel Kikuyu tribesmen.

Pérez Jiménez wins election but not votes in Venezuela

In Venezuela a period of disorderly government by a largely military junta came to an end on December 2 when Marcos Pérez Jiménez was declared president, notwithstanding that in the election he was a clear loser. He proceeded to establish a rigorous dictatorship which was to last for eight years.

1953

UPRISING IN BERLIN

CEASE-FIRE IN KOREA

COUP IN IRAN

Kenyatta jailed

In a courtroom lit by oil lamps because of a power failure, Jomo Kenyatta and several other Kikuyu were sentenced on April 8 to seven years' hard labour for organizing the Mau Mau. Some legal experts considered the verdict surprising in view of the flimsy nature of the evidence.

Mau Mau terrorism had caused considerable panic among the large and influential white community, who earlier in the year had staged a demonstration in Nairobi calling for tougher measures against the terrorists. Kenyatta, essentially a nationalist leader who always insisted that he was not anti-white, did not serve his full sentence, being released in 1961 (after the Mau Mau revolt had been suppressed) in plenty of time to become independent Kenya's first president.

Jomo Kenyatta outside the courtroom during an adjournment of his trial.

Revolt in East Berlin

On June 16 a largely working-class rising erupted in the Soviet zone of Berlin. Demonstrators waved the old German national flag and shouted 'Ivan go home!' at Soviet troops.

Discontent in East Berlin was aggravated by conditions of near famine, which had vastly increased the numbers seeking refuge in West Berlin. A tactless call to increase productivity provoked a spontaneous strike soon joined by thousands. After two days of demonstrations, which spread to other cities, the Soviet authorities sent in tanks to restore order. A number of people were killed and hundreds injured.

Russian tanks moving through hostile crowds in East Berlin. They were brought into the city, together with infantry reinforcements, to put an end to the disturbances after violent street battles between strikers and demonstrators on the one hand and Soviet sector police on the other.

Peace comes to Korea

After some of the longest negotiations for a ceasefire on record, a truce was finally signed at Panmunjon in Korea on July 26.

Of several long-running disagreements, the most stubborn was the repatriation of prisoners. The UN and President Syngman Rhee of South Korea were unwilling to repatriate North Korean prisoners who did not want to go. In the end the Communists tacitly accepted this principle, and a truce was agreed along the line of battle with a neutral buffer zone intervening. Five nations – Poland and Czechoslovakia nominated by the Communists, Sweden and Switzerland by the UN and India as a 'neutral' – were to police the ceasefire.

Although the truce remained just a truce (negotiations for a more formal armistice got nowhere), and various infringements took place later (the neutral peacekeepers were ineffective), the Korean war was over. Approximately one million people had been killed.

U.S. and North Korean army officers signing the truce at Panmunjom.

Mossadegh falls from power

The struggle for power in Iran came to a decisive climax on August 20. In a popular, pro-royalist revolt backed by the army, Mossadegh was ousted and thrown into prison.

Opposition to Mossadegh's government, whose nationalization of the oil industry had failed to bring economic benefits, centred on General Fazlollah Zahedi, a former minister. The Mossadegh government was accused of co-operating with the Communist-dominated Tudeh party and the Soviet Union (traditionally, with Britain, the great power most involved – and most resented – in Iran). An attempted coup d'état, in which Zahedi was appointed prime minister and an attempt was made to arrest Mossadegh, misfired. The shah was forced to flee the country and Zahedi to go into hiding, and there were open demonstrations by the Tudeh in favour of a republic. Four days later came the second coup, launched in the shah's absence, which was successful. Zahedi assumed office, the shah returned from his short exile, steps were taken to restore relations with Britain and reach an agreement with the Anglo-Iranian Oil Company, and Mossadegh was given a prison sentence for treason.

General Fazhollah Zahedi, who became prime minister of Iran after the coup which brought the downfall of Mossadegh.

1954

EMERGENCY IN CYPRUS

ALGERIAN REBELLION

Carrying out counter-terrorist measures, British soldiers in Cyprus carefully examine the contents of a car.

Enosis provokes Cyprus emergency

Terrorist attacks against the British administration in Cyprus began on April 1. They were the work of EOKA, an organization led by a Greek ex-army officer, Georgios Grivas, which sought *enosis* ('union') with Greece.

Though containing a substantial Turkish minority, Cyprus was historically a Greek island. It held no real strategic interest, yet the British government was determined to hold on to it. Colonel Grivas proved highly elusive, and most Greek Cypriots were sympathetic to his objective, if not his methods. ▶ *page 298*

Bananas behind Guatemalan revolution

Ten years of democratic government and moderate social reform came to an end in Guatemala on June 18. An invasion by a small force of dissidents and mercenaries led by Colonel Castillo Armas and planned by the CIA (U.S. Central Intelligence Agency) brought down the government of President Guzmán.

The chief motivating force behind this episode was the United Fruit Company, anxious about its investments in Guatemala. The Company engaged the CIA (whose director later became a director of United Fruit) and a coup was planned. It was stopped by the Truman government, but under the Eisenhower administration the situation was more promising, and the Arbenz government, which had Communist support, provided its opponents with good propaganda by purchasing arms from Communist Czechoslovakia. The coup was virtually unopposed: only one person died. Castillo Armas became a dictator, backed by substantial U.S. aid.

The 1954 Guatemala coup was significant not only for Guatemala but for relations generally between Latin America and the United States, which were permanently soured.

Colonel Castillo Armas (left), the Guatemalan rebel leader.

Nationalist revolt breaks out in Algeria

In what was a particularly troubled year for the old imperial powers, rebellion broke out in Algeria on October 31. Sporadic minor acts of anti-French violence had occurred earlier, but this was a long-planned revolt by nationalists who took the name Front de Libération Nationale (FLN). Several people were killed in attacks on police stations and guard posts.

The 'Sétif massacre' of 1945 had delivered a salutary shock both to the French and to Algerian Muslims. The response was a statute making Algeria a group of French departments (provinces) with certain acknowledged distinguishing features, and creating an assembly in which Algerians could play some part. Liberal reforms were promised, but the European majority in the assembly was in practice invincible, and few reforms were enacted.

The manifesto of the FLN called for an independent sovereign state, in which all residents of Algeria would have equal rights. At the outset, many Algerian political leaders kept their distance, but as violence grew, hostility between the two communities became more intense and compromise less possible. ▶ *page 299*

A patrol of French soldiers searching suspects during operations in Algeria.

McCarthy brought down

On December 2 Senator Joe McCarthy's astonishing four-year witch-hunt for Communists within the ranks of the U.S. government was finally extinguished. By a majority of 67 to 22 the Senate condemned him for abusing his colleagues. The term censure was not used, but that was what it was.

Joe McCarthy's extraordinary career, in which, with the aid of counsel Roy Cohn, he had insidiously exploited the public hysteria against Communism in the years after World War II, came to grief after he turned his attention to the U.S. army. For some six weeks the daily discussions of the Senate Permanent Investigations subcommittee on the Army-McCarthy hearings were shown on television. They produced an unlikely hero in the elderly Boston attorney Joseph Welch, whose decency, courage and wit made McCarthy look like a scheming and unprincipled bully.

Senator Joseph McCarthy.

French aircraft waiting to attack Vietminh positions.

A helicopter above French trenches at Dien Bien Phu.

Cease-fire talks between French and Vietminh delegates.

DIEN BIEN PHU

*I*N THE PROLONGED *decline of European imperialism which was a major theme of the generation after 1945, one of the most epic and decisive events was the French defeat at Dien Bien Phu. The French forces in Vietnam had only recently captured this base, and it became apparent early in 1954 that General Giap, the military commander of the Vietminh, was determined to recapture it. The base was well fortified and was defended by crack French troops. Its chief vulnerability lay in lack of access. It was solely dependent on supply or reinforcement by air. While the Vietminh could offer little threat to French aircraft, the loss of the airfield meant that Dien Bien Phu was entirely cut off and could be supplied only by parachute. There was certainly no means of evacuation.*

The siege lasted 55 days. The French lost the airfield and though they did receive supplies, and 3000 more paratroopers, from the air, the Communist forces, who were well supplied with artillery, proved too strong. On May 7, shortly after the commander, General de Castries, had ordered his own men to fire on his command post when the Vietminh broke through the last defences, the base was overrun. Nearly 20,000 French troops were killed or captured, and the French endeavour to hold on to Indo-China was clearly at an end.

An international conference was already in session at Geneva, and a ceasefire was negotiated there in July. It was signed by France (whose new prime minister, Pierre Mendès-France, was eager to end costly colonial engagements), Britain, Communist China, the Soviet Union and the United States, as well as the representatives of the four states of Indo-China. It provided for a more or less arbitrary division of Vietnam between North and South. Internationally supervised elections were to take place to decide the terms on which Vietnam was to be reunited. The Vietminh were to withdraw from the other, independent states of Cambodia and Laos.

Whereas, under Communist rule, North Vietnam became a strongly unified state, political authority in South Vietnam was far less secure. Bao Dai, the head of state, had little popular appeal (he was soon to be deposed), and the government was disputed between various religious and military groups, with frequent changes of prime minister. However, the U.S. government, currently influenced by the 'domino theory' of states successively falling to aggressive Communism, promised aid to Bao Dai, though without specifying its precise nature. Ho Chi Minh, who had disappeared into the background during the seven-year Indo-China war, re-emerged in Hanoi to become president of North Vietnam.

Opposite. Ho Chi Minh while on a visit to New Delhi.

Left. A soldier crouches deep in a trench at Dien Bien Phu. Although the French were supplied from the air, their position was hopeless.

**WARSAW PACT
SIGNED**

**COUP IN
ARGENTINA**

Chinese Nationalists and Communists maintain the tension

On January 28, shortly after several Communist gunboats venturing near Taiwan had been sunk by the Nationalists, and a few shells had been fired at the Nationalist-controlled island of Quemoy, the U.S. government took steps to defend Taiwan.

The United States still regarded the Nationalists as the rightful government of China and, unlike its Western partners, refused to recognize Mao's regime. The Communists never made a real effort to conquer Taiwan, though there were to be more serious assaults on the islands of Quemoy and Matsu.

An elderly refugee is helped ashore by a sailor after his arrival at the port of Keelung in Taiwan. The sporadic fighting between Chinese Communists and Nationalists during the 1950s led to the evacuation of people from outlying islands to the safety of Taiwan.

Middle Eastern powers sign Baghdad Pact

On February 24 Turkey and Iraq signed the British-sponsored Baghdad Pact. Pakistan and Iran also added their signatures before the end of the year.

The purpose of the Baghdad Pact was security against Soviet expansionism. All the signatories (except Great Britain) had common borders with the Soviet Union and were apprehensive of the spread of Communism. Although Iraq was to withdraw in 1958, the pact was enlarged in 1959 into the Central Treaty Organization (CENTO), with the United States as an associate member, and it became part of the fabric of defensive treaty organizations designed to resist the expansion of the Soviet Union.

Delegates at a meeting of the economic committee of the Baghdad Pact. The Pact was intended to provide security against Soviet expansionism and the United States promised economic aid to the signatories.

Communist riposte to NATO

The Warsaw Pact, a defensive alliance between the Soviet Union and seven Communist countries in Europe, came into existence on May 14. It was essentially a reaction against the acquisition of sovereignty by the Federal Republic of (West) Germany, which was followed by the rebuilding of a German army and the inclusion of the country in the anti-Soviet NATO alliance.

Later the same month, another small step was taken to increase Soviet security when Bulganin and Khrushchev, the new leaders of the Soviet Union since the forced resignation of Malenkov, re-established relations with Tito during a visit to Yugoslavia.

Warsaw Pact delegates at a wreath-laying ceremony.

Perón overthrown

After growing opposition, in which the army had to be called out to suppress demonstrators, President Perón of Argentina was overthrown on September 19. His personal popularity had perhaps waned since the death of his charismatic wife, Evita, though the main reasons for his fall were economic failures – inflation, unemployment and poor industrial performance. Perón was forced into exile.

Peronismo was the dominant feature of Argentine politics for 30 years after World War II. Perón achieved power in 1945 through the support of the army (ordinary soldiers rather than the officer corps) and of organized labour, and these were the sections of the population which benefited most from his policies. His popular, nationalistic, and moderately socialist regime, like European fascist regimes, made effective use of mass rallies and the communications media, though Perón was not a fascist in the sense that Mussolini and Hitler were. His enormous popular appeal gradually faded as his government failed to overcome the outstanding economic problems of Argentina, and he was never very popular with the professional middle classes, who broadly supported the coup.

A crowd of Perón's supporters in front of the Parliament in Buenos Aires.

The commissioner for Cyprus, Lord Radcliffe.

Makarios banished

The British administration in Cyprus, under the governor, Field Marshal Harding, took a drastic step towards neutralizing EOKA activity on March 9 when Archbishop Makarios, the leader of the Greek Cypriot community on the island, was exiled to the Seychelles. With him went his colleague, the bishop of Kyrenia.

If the British really believed this would lead to a reduction in violence, they were seriously misled. During the next year, terrorist activity was at its peak, though the number of casualties was relatively small. The British forces which, including police, amounted to some 40,000 (not enough to capture General Grivas, however), suffered about 200 killed in the period up to March 1957, but the great majority died in accidents, such as forest fires. Deaths among Greek civilians, mainly EOKA men, were about the same.

The position was complicated by the rising opposition of the Turkish community, supported by the Turkish government, to *enosis*. A pogrom was carried out against Greeks in Istanbul in 1955, and a conference between the foreign ministers of the three countries involved failed to reach agreement on Cyprus. An atmosphere of mistrust and suspicion prevailed, as Lord Radcliffe, a commissioner appointed by the British government, produced a plan for a new constitution for Cyprus in December 1956.
▶ *page 307*

Nasser seizes the canal

President Nasser (right) with his foreign minister, Mahmoud Fawzy, and the Australian prime minister, Robert Menzies (left).

To an enthusiastic crowd, the Egyptian president, Colonel Nasser, announced on July 26 that Egypt was taking over the Suez Canal. Britain and France reacted angrily. The British prime minister, Anthony Eden, perhaps forgetting that Britain no longer ruled India, spoke of 'Nasser's thumb on our windpipe'.

The last British troops had left the Suez Canal Zone a few weeks earlier, according to an agreement with Egypt through which the British had hoped to gain influence in the Arab world. In that agreement, the Egyptian government guaranteed free passage through the Canal. It acknowledged its control by the Suez Canal Company and Britain's right to reoccupy the zone in case of war. However, the immediate cause of Nasser's precipitate action was the refusal of Britain and the United States to finance construction of the Aswan Dam, a refusal motivated by Nasser's relationship with the Soviet Union and the recent purchase of arms from Communist Czechoslovakia. Nasser proposed to use the revenue from the nationalized canal to finance the dam.

The British had come to regard Nasser as the chief obstacle to the maintenance of their influence in the Arab world. With Nasser refusing to reconsider the matter of sovereignty (though he did propose an international board to operate the canal), discussions took place against a background of growing crisis. ▶ *page 302*

Revolt in Hungary

The first successful revolt against Communist totalitarianism took place in Hungary on October 23. Following earlier clashes, the government surrendered to a massive popular demonstration in favour of the 'liberal' Imre Nagy, who was thereupon restored as prime minister. As Soviet forces withdrew, Nagy, under strong popular pressure, agreed to introduce a multi-party system, leave the Warsaw Pact and make Hungary a neutral state on the model of Austria.

Hungarian premier Imry Nagy.

Nagy had been a relatively moderate and popular leader until he was overthrown in 1955 by another former prime minister, the Moscow-trained Stalinist, Matyas Rákosi. A number of Nagy's associates remained in place, however, and there was considerable social and political tension within the party. Rákosi's unpopularity grew, while news of Khrushchev's denunciation of Stalin at the Moscow party congress and, still more significant, the return to power of the moderate Gomułka in Poland, encouraged opponents of the regime. In July 1956 Rákosi, out of favour in Khrushchev's Moscow, lost his position, and demands for the rehabilitation of Nagy grew. The mass protest of October 23, during which there were clashes with Soviet forces, was not the first demonstration against the influence of the Stalinists in the Hungarian government, but it was the largest and proved decisive. Nagy returned to power the following day. ▶ *page 301*

Algerian leaders seized

Ahmed Ben Bella and several other Algerian nationalist (FLN) leaders were arrested in Algiers on October 22. They had been travelling between the newly independent states of Morocco and Tunisia when their plane, chartered by the Moroccan government, was diverted to Algiers.

The conflict in Algeria became increasingly bitter and intractable in 1956, and was marked by atrocities on both sides. The new Socialist French premier, Guy Mollet, visited the country in February and was confronted with furious European demonstrators who feared a 'sell-out'. Mollet's declared policy was to enforce a ceasefire and then to hold elections, to be followed by direct negotiations with the Algerian representatives. Extra troops had to be flown in, and an attempt was made to isolate Muslim villagers from FLN influence by resettlement. A further complication was the discovery of extensive oilfields in southern Algeria, which resulted in that country's two southern provinces being administered directly from Paris. ▶ *page 304*

Ben Bella handcuffed and under escort after his arrest in Algiers.

299

Hungarian revolutionaries with a member of the hated secret
police, many of whom were summarily executed.

HUNGARY CRUSHED

O N THE LAST DAY of October Soviet forces were withdrawn from Budapest. The newly restored prime minister, Imre Nagy, having informed Moscow of his intention to take Hungary out of the Warsaw Pact and adopt a neutral international stance between East and West, began negotiations with Soviet officials concerning the evacuation of all Soviet troops from the country. Four days later, shortly before dawn, the Soviet forces came back. They returned in strength, with over 1000 tanks, backed by artillery and aircraft: it was a full-scale invasion.

The Soviet forces met fierce resistance from Hungarian army units and from workers and civilians. The streets of Budapest witnessed the grim spectacle of ordinary people fighting tanks with petrol bombs. It was a heroic but unavailing struggle. Key points, including the Ministry of Defence and the parliament building, were taken within a few hours. Hungarian radio was silenced in the midst of an appeal for international help, but dramatic news of the fighting in the streets came from a Hungarian reporter who divided his efforts between a teleprinter and a rifle, which he fired from the office window.

By lunch-time Moscow radio was announcing the end of the Hungarian 'counter-revolution' – the customary term to describe democratic opposition to Soviet control. A new government was formed under János Kádár, at heart an anti-Stalinist but a man who believed in keeping in tune with the times. There was no immediate news of Imre Nagy. He had been arrested while under a safe conduct; he was later tried in secret and executed. Buried in an unmarked grave, his body was to be disinterred and given a more fitting resting place after the success of the next 'counter-revolution' in 1989.

The suppression of the Hungarian rising was not the first example of the brutal destruction of political opposition in eastern Europe – similar events on a smaller scale had taken place in Poland only a few weeks earlier – but it was the most flagrant example so far, and permanently soured the impression of greater liberality that Khrushchev had seemed to promise. In retrospect, it was perhaps the first milestone on the road that led to the destruction of the Communist system in Europe over a generation later, for it caused a 'crisis of conscience' among sincere Marxist-Leninists throughout Europe. Many veterans of the party in western Europe and North America were disillusioned, as the determination of the Soviet leaders to maintain power in the satellite countries with total disregard for the wishes of their peoples could no longer be ignored.

János Kádár, who headed the new pro-Soviet government.

A young woman freedom fighter.

Main picture. Soviet tanks rumbling through the streets of Budapest. The Hungarian people enjoyed only a brief taste of freedom before the reimposition of Communist rule.

Israeli soldiers in consultation before the attack on the Sinai peninsula.

Anglo-French army in Suez

On October 29 Israeli forces crossed the Egyptian border. The following day Britain and France issued an ultimatum demanding that both Israeli and Egyptian forces withdraw ten miles from the Suez Canal and requesting Egyptian consent for temporary occupation of the canal zone by Anglo-French forces. The Egyptian government rejected the ultimatum, and on October 31 the European allies launched an attack, beginning with the bombing of Egyptian airfields by aircraft from Cyprus.

Although the British and French governments denied it, many critics of their policy accused them of collusion with Israel (this was later proved to be true). The military operations themselves were a success. The Israelis rapidly took the Gaza Strip, occupied key strategic points in the Sinai peninsula and defeated the Egyptian forces east of the canal. British and French forces landed in the northern canal zone on November 5, capturing Port Said and Port Fuad. Meanwhile the United Nations called for the withdrawal of all foreign troops from Egyptian territory and voted for a UN force to supervise the evacuation. Britain, followed by France and later Israel, agreed to end its occupation as soon as a UN force was available to take over.

The precipitate withdrawal by the three countries was the result of a miscalculation about U.S. policy which, muddled by the excitement of a presidential election, was currently subject to shifts. The British had been anti-cipating tacit approval in Washington, but ran into unexpectedly strong opposition. A sharp drain in gold reserves proved decisive in convincing the British government that it had embarked on an unwise adventure.

The results of the Suez episode included a dramatic rise in Nasser's prestige throughout the Arab world and bitter divisions in Britain, where Eden (in poor health anyway) was compelled to resign, his attempt to increase British influence in the Arab world having had precisely the opposite effect.

An Egyptian in Port Said surveys the devastation caused by British bombing raids. A tank stands in the background. The Anglo-French attack on Egypt was militarily a successful operation, but politically it proved to be disastrous and led to a further decline in British influence in the Middle East.

1957

CRISIS IN JORDAN

FEDERAL TROOPS AT LITTLE ROCK

Nikita Khrushchev at a ceremony with Marshal Zhukov (left), whom he dismissed later in the year. Bulganin (right), the Soviet premier, was removed from office in 1958.

Hussein defies opponents

An attempted army coup against the rule of the 20-year-old King Hussein was foiled on April 14. It followed a political crisis in which the prime minister had been dismissed after stating his intention to form a republic in close co-operation with Egypt and Syria. The king took a considerable risk by driving in person to the rebel headquarters and successfully defying the dissident officers.

Tension within the Arab world had increased since Nasser's accession to power in Egypt. Jordan had incurred resentment among other Arab states for its incorporation of central Palestine within its borders in 1950, and the government was suspected of being 'soft' towards the West. Hussein attempted to defuse criticism in 1956 by dismissing Glubb Pasha, the virtual founder of the Jordanian army, and by abrogating his treaty with Britain.

Khrushchev disperses opponents

An eventful session of the Soviet Communist party central committee ended on July 4 with a victory for Khrushchev over his opponents. His occasionally idiosyncratic rule was fiercely criticized, especially by the Kremlin 'old guard'.

The decisive factor seems to have been the support of the army for Khrushchev, although that did not prevent Marshal Zhukov, defence minister and hero of the Great Patriotic War, being himself purged later in the year. Meanwhile, the old guard were banished. Molotov, foreign minister under Stalin, became ambassador to Outer Mongolia, while Malenkov (who had been party leader before Khrushchev superseded him) was given the job of managing a power station in Kazakhstan. ▶ *page 319*

Stand-off at Little Rock

The governor of Arkansas, Orval Faubus, sent national guardsmen to the all-white central high school in Little Rock on September 3. Their purpose was to prevent nine black children from entering the school. His action defied the ruling of a federal district court, which ordered the children to be admitted.

Faubus, recently elected, had the reputation of being a liberal, but not (it appeared) on the subject of race. His defiance of federal law was condemned by President Eisenhower, and FBI agents in Little Rock applied for an injunction to compel admittance of the schoolchildren. The president ordered 10,000 Arkansas national guardsmen into federal service and sent in 1000 paratroopers. The federal troops dispersed the hostile white crowds and, after nearly a month of confrontation, the children entered the school. ▶ *page 312*

1956

AUGUST
1 Britain, France and the United States hold talks on Suez
4 British paratroopers sent to Cyprus

SEPTEMBER
29 Anglo-French talks on Suez
29 Luis Somoza takes over in Nicaragua

OCTOBER
23 Uprising against Soviet and Stalinist control in Hungary
29 Israeli forces cross the Egyptian frontier
30 Anglo-French ultimatum to Egypt and Israel
31 Anglo-French forces attack Egypt in Canal Zone

NOVEMBER
5 Hungarian revolt crushed by Soviet forces
7 UN calls for Anglo-French withdrawal from Suez
8 Hostilities in Egypt halted
9 UN calls for Soviet withdrawal from Hungary
21 First UN peacekeeping troops arrive in Suez

DECEMBER
1 Castro relaunches Cuban revolt with 80 men
22 Last Anglo-French troops leave Suez

1957

MARCH
1 Israel agrees to withdraw from Gaza Strip and Sinai
25 Treaty of Rome creates six-member E.E.C.

APRIL
4 State of emergency in Cyprus relaxed as Makarios is released
14 King Hussein defeats attempted army coup in Jordan

JULY
22 Rising against the sultan of Oman

AUGUST
11 Omani rebel base captured by British troops
30 Malaya gains independence

SEPTEMBER
3 U.S. federal court orders desegregation of Little Rock schools
4 Segregation upheld in Little Rock by Arkansas governor

OCTOBER
4 Soviet Union launches first artificial Earth satellite

DECEMBER
19 NATO governments agree to U.S. nuclear bases in Europe
26 Afro-Asian Solidarity conference opens in Cairo

303

1958

JANUARY–DECEMBER

DE GAULLE
COMES
TO POWER

COUP IN IRAQ

MARINES IN
LEBANON

De Gaulle returns

On May 31, as the Algerian conflict brought France to the edge of civil war, the country's greatest national hero, General Charles de Gaulle, returned to power as prime minister. In view of the frequent failures of government in recent years, de Gaulle took office on the understanding that he should rule by decree for six months, and during that time a new constitution should be drafted.

The defeat of France in Indo-China, followed by Nasser's victory over Suez, fuelled the Algerian crisis. Muslim Algerians became more militant in their desire for independence, and the French army became more determined not to suffer another defeat. Independence had already been granted to Tunisia and Morocco, but Algeria was a different case. It had been French for over a century, it was administratively part of France, and it contained a large minority of European descent, many of whom had been established in the country for generations. In May, with the Paris government in yet another crisis, rioting *colons* (Europeans) occupied government offices in Algiers and encouraged a military revolt, in which the French officers in Algeria were supported by many colleagues in France. De Gaulle seemed to be the only man who could end the revolt.

Those who called for his return, however, were mainly on the political right, including the army officers themselves and the *colons*. They anticipated a victorious end to the savage Algerian war which had divided French society more sharply than Suez had divided the British.

For some time they had no cause to regret their decision. In September the new constitution, which bestowed vastly expanded executive powers on the president, was approved by referendum. In December, de Gaulle was elected president. The constitution included the creation of a French community to include the remaining French colonies in Africa, which turned out to be a considerable success. Algeria, however, was not part of this arrangement and the war continued. ▶ *page 308*

Murder in Baghdad

King Faisal (left) and his uncle.

General Salan greets de Gaulle in Algiers.

The Iraqi government was overthrown in an army coup on July 14. The revolt was led by Brigadier Abd el-Karim Kassem, who with other officers had been plotting such a move for years.

The coup took place at the height of a Middle Eastern crisis, with supporters of Nasser-style Arab nationalism planning to seize power in Jordan, Syria and the Lebanon, as well as Iraq. The young King Faisal was well aware of the unreliability of the army, which was therefore not issued with ammunition. However, an exception was made for forces being sent to the Jordan frontier to support the royal regime of the even younger King Hussein in the event of an anticipated revolt. These troops were under the command of officers loyal to Kassem, and were diverted to Baghdad.

The palace was besieged and, after a few hours, surrendered. King Faisal, his uncle the crown prince, and about 20 other people, including the king's sister and other members of his family, were summarily shot. The prime minister, Nuri es-Said, was caught next day while trying to escape. He was lynched and his body, along with those of the crown prince and numerous royal officials, was dragged through the streets.

Kassem subsequently became president of the newly proclaimed republic. Suspicious of Nasser and the Ba'ath party, he proved incompetent as well as brutal. He narrowly escaped assassination in 1959 at the hands of an officer named Saddam Hussein, and his rule marked the beginning of a bloody and bitter era in Iraq's history. ▶ *page 316*

Marines land in the Lebanon

On July 16, two days after the Iraqi coup, U.S. marines landed in the Lebanon in response to an appeal from President Chamoun. Civil war had broken out over the news of Chamoun's intention to run for a second term as president. At the same time British paratroopers landed in Jordan, at King Hussein's request, to bolster the regime there against radical pan-Arabists inspired by Nasser.

Though furiously condemned by the Soviet Union, these incursions by the Western powers were relatively low-keyed and short-lived. Sunbathers greeted the marines on the beach. What fight-ing there was stopped for lunch. The U.S. forces were out of the Lebanon by mid-October and the last British troops left Jordan a few weeks later. As a compromise Chamoun was removed from power in Beirut, but Hussein hung on to his throne in Amman.

Later developments in the Lebanon were to be more savage. The basic problem was that the Lebanon was not any kind of national state (the Syrians, not without justice, regarded it as rightfully part of Syria). The people of Lebanon were either Maronites (Christians), Druse, or Shi'ite; those were the affiliations that commanded their loyalty (with the additional complication that divisions existed within them, for example among the three main clans of the Maron-ites). The Shi'ites, together with the Palestinian refugees, were the poorest and, increasingly, the most numerous. They were large-ly excluded from power and from the wealth that had accumulated in Beirut, a great financial and business centre and the West's gateway to the Arab world. They sympathized with radical pan-Arabism, while the dominant groups, particularly the Maron-ites, looked to the West.

U.S. marines making warlike preparations after their landing in Lebanon.

Constitutional collapse in Pakistan

On October 7, after a succession of crises within both East and West Pakistan and a continuing lack of stability at the centre which had characterized Pakistan since independence in 1947, President Iskander Mirza declared martial law. The governments, both provincial and central, were dismissed and all political parties were abolished. The supreme army commander, Mohammed Ayub Khan, took over the admin-istration and later in the month he replaced Mirza as president, expelling him from the country.

Mohammed Ayub Khan, the new president of Pakistan.

**CUBAN
REVOLUTION**

**EMERGENCY IN
LAOS**

**GENOCIDE IN
RWANDA**

Fidel Castro emphasizes a point during his inaugural speech after being sworn in as Cuba's youngest ever head of government.

Castro victorious

The New Year opened with the flight of the corrupt dictator, Fulgencio Batista, from Cuba on January 1. Castro proclaimed the victory of the revolution, which was widely welcomed, even in the United States. He named a new president and prime minister.

Within a few weeks Castro himself became prime minister and signed a crucial trade agreement with the Soviet Union. In April he made a week-long trip to North America and reassured Congressional leaders in Washington that his regime was not Communist. However, further misgivings were aroused by his agrarian reform, in which large estates were confiscated, some of the land being handed over to landless peasants, some being reorganized as state farms. President Urrutia Lleo was forced to resign in July and the Argentinian, Ernesto 'Che' Guevara, was made head of the National Bank.

▶ *page 311*

Dalai Lama dodges the Chinese

Tibetan women in Lhasa in a mass protest against the Chinese presence.

In March the Chinese invited the Dalai Lama, the spiritual and political leader of Tibet, to visit Chinese headquarters in Lhasa – without his usual bodyguard. This was seen as a device to capture him (he had recently declined an invitation to Peking), and he slipped away to India on horseback on March 17.

Resistance to the Chinese occupation, encouraged by the movement of Chinese settlers into the country, had continued since 1950, gaining strength after 1955. In one battle, Kampa guerrillas in the east had annihilated a large Chinese garrison.

Vast numbers of Tibetans surrounded the Dalai Lama's palace as the Chinese attempted to capture him, and after his escape the frustrated Chinese turned on the crowds, killing many hundreds. Resistance broke out all over Tibet, which the Chinese crushed with widespread slaughter. According to Tibetan estimates, 65,000 Tibetans were killed, while an equal number fled to India and Nepal.

The Chinese, who had hitherto not interfered greatly with Tibetan institutions, proceeded to crush Tibetan society, closing down the monasteries and imposing Chinese law, language and customs, and a Communist government.

Civil conflict in Laos

On September 4 a state of emergency was declared in Laos. The government had been moving towards the right and, as the Communist Pathet Lao increased its armed opposition, the situation degenerated into civil war, with the two sides supported by the rival superpowers.

The Geneva convention of 1954 provided for the 'neutralization' of Laos, but its provisions were open to various interpretations, and conflict had broken out almost immediately between the government and the Pathet Lao. After the elections of 1955, from which the Communists were barred, there was a prolonged constitutional crisis and Prince Souvanna Phouma, who eventually became prime minister, was unable to come to terms with the Pathet Lao. Under the state of emergency, control of most of Laos passed to a rightist military leader, General Phoumi Nosavan, leading to civil war in which the forces of the right were opposed by the neutralists as well as the Pathet Lao.

Prince Souvanna Phouma.

Rwanda massacres

Soldiers in Rwanda, the scene of bloody and recurrent tribal warfare.

In November extensive killings were reported from the Belgian territory of Ruanda-Burundi, soon to become the independent republics of Rwanda and Burundi. The Tutsi, an aristocratic people of unusual height, had for generations been dominant in the territory, though outnumbered by subservient peoples, of whom the Hutu were most numerous. The Tutsi were in this case the main victims: casualties were estimated at 20,000, and their dominance was largely broken. Genocidal outbreaks of this kind occurred at intervals during the next few years. Some 200,000 Hutu are said to have died in revenge attacks by the Tutsi in 1972.

Lumumba arrested

On November 1, the nationalist leader Patrice Lumumba, was arrested in the Belgian Congo. He was accused of instigating anti-white riots in Stanleyville in which a number of people died after police opened fire. The Congo was scheduled to become independent in 1960, but already there was conflict between those, like Lumumba, who favoured a centralized state and those who wanted a federation. ▶ *page 311*

Patrice Lumumba in conference at London Airport.

Makarios presides over Cyprus

On December 14 Archbishop Makarios, who had returned to an ecstatic welcome in Cyprus a few weeks earlier, was elected president. In a situation which somewhat resembled that of Palestine a decade earlier, the British had lost patience with the ongoing Cyprus conflict and a settlement was arranged at an international conference in Zur- ich by which Cyprus was to become independent in 1960.

Though the Turkish Cypriots numbered less than 20 per cent of the population, the British showed considerable tolerance of their feelings. Thus union with Greece was ruled out, although partition of the island into separate Greek and Turkish states (the preferred Turkish solution) was also discounted. Later agreements provided for a Greek president and Turkish vice-president, with an assembly and civil service divided between Greeks and Turks in a ratio of 70 to 30. Britain was to retain two military bases, the independence and integrity of the future republic being guaranteed by Britain, Greece and Turkey. ▶ *page 318*

1960

JANUARY–JUNE

INSURRECTION IN ALGERIA

SLAUGHTER AT SHARPEVILLE

European revolt in Algeria

On January 23 an insurrection among Europeans in Algeria broke out in protest against de Gaulle's policies. It was sparked off by his recall and subsequent dismissal of the popular General Massu, who had expressed criticisms of de Gaulle's Algerian policy. For a moment it seemed as though the army in Algeria might refuse to act against the rebels, but the revolt fizzled out. De Gaulle took emergency powers and visited Algeria himself in March and later in December, when he again insisted that self-determination would decide Algeria's future. ▶ *page 312*

Soldiers on patrol in Oran during the European revolt.

Massacre at Sharpeville

On March 21 a demonstration was organized by the Pan-African Congress (a more militant offshoot of the ANC), in protest against the South African pass laws, at Sharpeville, an African township 40 miles south of Johannesburg. The crowd became unruly and some stones were thrown at the police. A police officer lost his head and opened fire. In the next few minutes 69 people were shot dead and many more wounded.

Although the Sharpeville massacre – the worst but by no means the first such incident – was caused primarily by panic and poor discipline, it seemed to world opinion more like a declaration of war on the part of the ruling whites in South Africa against the blacks. The reported remarks of the police commander, that if people did not behave they would have to 'learn their lesson the hard way', reinforced this opinion.

In the immediate aftermath of Sharpeville, it looked as though South Africa was disintegrating. Divisions within the white community, particularly between British and Afrikaners, deepened, and fear of the future, exacerbated by events in the Congo, caused heavy emigration of whites. Capital migrated elsewhere with equal speed, and the government was forced to impose tough exchange controls. In a referendum held in October South African whites voted in favour of their country becoming a republic, which it did in the following year, when South Africa also left the Commonwealth. As a token reprimand to the practitioners of *apartheid*, Chief Albert Luthuli, leader of the ANC, was awarded the 1960 Nobel Peace Prize.

Ultimately, the South African economy was saved by the world demand for its minerals, especially gold; and by the 1970s, with the price of gold rocketing upward, it was growing faster than any other country's, except Japan's. The fundamental problems of South African society, however, remained unsolved.

The grim scene after the Sharpeville killings, which led to worldwide protest.

Chief Albert Luthuli (centre), the Nobel Prize winner, in conversation with farmers.

Communist giants fall out

In what was a bad year generally for international relations, a sharp division between the world's two Communist giants, the Soviet Union and Mao Tse-tung's China, was publicly acknowledged on June 22. Khrushchev denounced Mao as a Stalinist; the Chinese regarded him as a dangerous revisionist. Signs of the break had first been evident at an international conference of Communist nations held in Moscow in February, when the Chinese failed to attend. Soviet technicians and advisers were withdrawn from China, and the quarrel grew steadily more acrimonious, with both Moscow and Peking vying for leadership of the Communist world.

Nikita Khrushchev with Mao Tse-tung at Peking airport during a visit to China.

FLIGHT OF THE U-2

AT THE END of April Francis Gary Powers, a U.S. pilot stationed at Incirli in Turkey, took off on a routine flight on which, after stopping at Peshawar in Pakistan, he would fly to Bodø in Norway, a distance of nearly 4000 miles. The route would take him over the Soviet Union. His aircraft, a U-2, was basically a powered glider with wings so long and flimsy they literally flapped. It could not carry much of a load, but it was equipped with highly sophisticated photographic equipment. Powers was on a spying mission.

Of course, the Russians would know he was there. But they would not be able to do anything about it. As the CIA had explained, they possessed no weapon capable of reaching the great altitude at which the U-2 flew. These aircraft had been making overflights of Soviet territory for four years with complete impunity. Powers was able to watch without a tremor of trepidation the condensation trail of an impotent Soviet fighter, flying a parallel course miles below him.

Four hours into the flight, somewhere over Sverdlovsk, 'there was a dull thump, the aircraft jerked forward, and a tremendous orange flash lit up the cockpit and sky. Time had caught up with us.'

More prosaically, what had caught up with Powers's U-2 was a Soviet SAM missile. The CIA's information on Soviet air-defence systems was a little out of date.

Powers managed to eject and parachuted down safely. He was put on trial in Moscow as a spy. The Soviet government had been presented with a remarkable propaganda gift, and made the most of it. The United States' initial reaction was to deny espionage. The plane had flown off course, and its cameras were merely for photographing clouds. Since absolutely no one believed this, the pretence was dropped, but President Eisenhower still refused to make the apology demanded by Khrushchev, justifying the U-2 flights as necessary peace-keeping operations.

The incident took place only three weeks before a scheduled summit meeting of the 'Big Four' (United States, Soviet Union, Britain and France) in Paris. Though the meeting did go ahead as arranged, and lasted for three days, no reasoned discussion took place. Khrushchev, something of a specialist at righteous indignation, bellowed recriminations. Eisenhower looked pained but stubborn, and Prime Minister Macmillan hopped over the British Embassy wall after announcing that he was off to a pub. In an atmosphere approaching farce, East-West relations reached a nadir. In Moscow Gary Powers was sentenced to ten years but released after two in exchange for the Soviet spy known as Colonel Abel.

Below. Francis Gary Powers (left) taking part in a senatorial hearing in Washington. He was completely exonerated for his part in the U-2 affair.

Inset. Khrushchev in Paris during the summit conference.

Patrice Lumumba at Léopoldville being given rough treatment after his arrest by Colonel Joseph Mobutu's soldiers. He was captured while trying to reach Stanleyville.

1960

AUGUST
7 Castro nationalizes all U.S. property in Cuba
9 Souvanna Phouma heads new neutralist government in Laos
16 Cyprus becomes independent
19 U-2 pilot Powers convicted of spying in Moscow
29 Jordanian prime minister Hazza Majali and others assassinated in bomb attack
31 East Germans close West Berlin border to check rising flow of refugees

SEPTEMBER
14 Mobutu takes over in the Congo
23 Khrushchev demands dismissal of Hammarskjöld and removal of UN from United States

OCTOBER
25 Clashes between Vietcong guerrillas and South Vietnam forces

NOVEMBER
11 Attempted military coup in South Vietnam
21 Fighting breaks out between UN and Congolese troops in Léopoldville

DECEMBER
2 Lumumba captured near Stanleyville
13 De Gaulle insists on Algerian self-determination in Algiers speech
16 Failed coup against Emperor Haile Selassie in Ethiopia
31 North Vietnamese incursions prompt Laos appeal to UN

The Belgian Congo disintegrates

The former Belgian Congo became an independent republic on June 30. In the last weeks Belgian authority had collapsed and it remained to be seen whether the new government could impose order. The independence ceremony itself developed into a fiasco when the king of Belgium, having made a conciliatory if somewhat patriarchal speech, had to listen to a diatribe from the new prime minister, Patrice Lumumba, on Belgian iniquities.

The personnel of the new government were divided roughly between those in favour of a strong, centralized state, pre-eminently Lumumba, and those who preferred a looser, federal system. This group included the president, Joseph Kasavubu. Disorders began almost immediately, with tribal fighting in Kasai and a mutiny in the Congolese army, whose officers were still Belgian. Lumumba thereupon dismissed the Belgian officers and appointed a Congolese NCO to be commander-in-chief. Belgian forces remained to guard areas of European residency, but after Lumumba had appealed to the United Nations in July, they were gradually replaced by UN troops.

Meanwhile, the provinces of Kasai and Katanga seceded. The latter, under the leadership of Moïse Tshombe, was especially significant, since it contained much of the Congo's mineral wealth. Its declaration of independence was not acknowledged by Belgium or by other countries.

In September President Kasavubu dismissed Lumumba and appointed another prime minister. Lumumba refused to acknowledge the president's right to dismiss him, and for a short time there were two governments, with some individuals holding office in both. This anomalous situation was dissolved when Colonel Joseph Mobutu dismissed both prime ministers and the president and installed yet another government made up mainly of students. He later came to a working arrangement with Kasavubu, still generally recognized internationally as head of state, while turning against the Soviet Union, which supported Lumumba. In December Mobutu's forces arrested Lumumba. He was sent to Katanga for greater security, and was murdered there early in 1961, 'while trying to escape'.

The conflicts in the Congo were to have an important international dimension and contributed to a sharpening of the cold war. Khrushchev denounced the role of the United Nations, called for the resignation of its secretary-general, Dag Hammarskjöld, who played an active part in the Congo crisis, and demanded that UN headquarters be removed from U.S. soil. ▶ *page 313*

President Joseph Kasavubu.

Castro takes over the banks

Foreign banks in Cuba were nationalized on October 14. Most industrial enterprises, including the interests of such U.S. giants as United Fruit, had been taken over earlier in the year, as Cuban-U.S. relationships sharply deteriorated. The CIA was already engaged in plots to get rid of Castro, and the United States finally broke off relations officially in January 1961. ▶ *page 312*

1961

**BAY OF PIGS
FIASCO**

**FRENCH GENERALS
IN REVOLT**

**BERLIN WALL
BUILT**

Castro triumphant in Bay of Pigs

On April 17 a motley collection of about 1500 troops, mostly half-trained Cubans, invaded Cuba, after an initial attack by U.S. bombers. They landed at Cochinos Bay (Bay of Pigs), but the anticipated rising inside Cuba against Castro failed to materialize and the invaders were defeated within three days.

The Bay of Pigs fiasco got the new administration of President John F. Kennedy off to a poor start. He had been informed of CIA plans for the invasion by 'Brigade 2506' after he won the presidential election the previous November, and approved it in spite of strong doubts. Apart from planning and training, and the initial – ineffective – bombardment of Cuban airfields, the United States offered no further assistance to the Cuban rebels, with inevitable results. The majority of the invading force was captured. Most were allowed to return to the United States towards the end of the year.

U.S. denial of responsibility for the Bay of Pigs invasion was not taken seriously, and the United States suffered a severe diplomatic setback internationally, while the Castro regime was greatly strengthened. At a summit meeting in June between Khrushchev and Kennedy in Vienna, friendly relations were superficially maintained, but little progress was made towards improving relations and Khrushchev apparently formed the impression that the new Kennedy government lacked steel and was vulnerable through Cuba. ▶ *page 315*

Freedom riders spark riots in Alabama

Violence broke out in Montgomery, Alabama, and other places in the southern United States in May. Segregationists retaliated against 'freedom riders', both black and white, who on May 4 set out to test desegregation on interstate buses. In Montgomery martial law was declared, the National Guard was mobilized and federal marshals were sent in. Elsewhere, the riders were beaten up and a bus was burned, while at Jackson, Mississippi, the riders were arrested. ▶ *page 316*

The Austrian president with Kennedy and Khrushchev at a reception in their honour.

Revolt of the generals

After little more than a year since the last outbreak, a revolt of Europeans took place in Algiers on April 21. The leaders this time were four generals, of whom the most prominent was Raoul Salan.

Troops took over the main governmental and military institutions in Algiers and a radio broadcast announced that the province was now controlled by the army. Weapons were distributed to the OAS (Organisation de l'Armée Secrète). In France de Gaulle assumed powers which made him in effect a dictator. Tanks and troops were drawn up outside the Elysée Palace as an airborne invasion of Paris from Algiers seemed possible.

De Gaulle's incisive action, including a passionate televised public appeal during which he wore his old army uniform, together with the popular demonstrations in his favour in France (and less support than the generals had expected in Algeria itself), resulted in the revolt subsiding in two or three days.

Meanwhile, negotiations concerning Algerian independence took place in secret between an FLN delegate, Belkacem Krim, foreign minister in the provisional republican government, and the French minister for Algerian affairs. ▶ *page 314*

Tanks massed before the Elysée Palace in Paris.

The wall goes up

East German workers erecting the Berlin wall.

On August 13 the East German authorities closed the border between East and West Berlin. Barbed wire was used at first, then a concrete wall was built, initially only five feet high but soon to grow taller. Transport between the two sectors was stopped and 50,000 East Germans who worked in West Berlin were turned back.

There had been many warning signs that a clamp-down on the trickle of refugees from the East was imminent, and in the weeks immediately before the border was closed the trickle had become a flood. At its peak, over 1000 people were taking flight daily. The refugees included at least one border guard, who leapt over the barbed wire in helmet and uniform, carrying his rifle.

The Western powers complained that the wall infringed the postwar agreements on the occupation of Germany, but neither their protests nor the angry demonstrations by Germans on both sides of the wall had any effect.

UN chief among Congo casualties

Dag Hammarskjöld arriving in New York.

The secretary-general of the UN, Dag Hammarskjöld, was killed in an air crash on September 18. The aircraft was about to land in Northern Rhodesia, where Hammarskjöld was to meet Moïse Tshombe, the leader of the secessionist province of Katanga. Although the reason for the crash was unclear, it was apparently an accident.

The UN forces became yet more deeply involved in the continuing Congo crisis when the decision was taken to combat directly the secession of Katanga (a decision which was ultimately to cost the brilliant but unorthodox Irish UN official, Conor Cruise O'Brien, his job). On the whole the West – and in particular the white-governed countries to the south – tended to support Katanga, and the excesses of the Congolese troops, including the massacre of some Belgian nuns, did not help the cause of the central government headed by Kasavubu (Mobutu had withdrawn from the political scene temporarily, having decided, with some foresight, that he would be best employed building up the army). Tshombe agreed to end the secession in the summer, but later changed his mind and took refuge in Northern Rhodesia, where Hammarskjöld was to hold discussions with him. Towards the end of the year, he again agreed to co-operate with the central government, now under the Kasavubu appointee, Cyrille Adoula, though this agreement also proved abortive. Meanwhile, violence continued in the Congo in conditions of near-chaos.

End of the UAR

The precipitate union of Egypt and Syria, as the United Arab Republic, came to an end on September 28. A military coup was staged by Syrian officers discontented with their Egyptian superiors. The new Syrian government promptly declared the dissolution of the UAR.

Algeria independent

On July 3 President de Gaulle signed the agreement recognizing the independence of Algeria. It followed a ceasefire agreed at Evian-les-Bains in March and referenda in which both the French and the Algerians voted overwhelmingly for Algeria's independence, with future socio-economic co-operation with France.

The OAS continued violent resistance up to the end, though their brutal tactics alienated many potential supporters. De Gaulle himself survived several assassination attempts, including one in which his car was riddled with bullets. The OAS leader, General Salan, was captured in April and, despite an OAS order to stay, the *colons* began to leave Algeria for France in great numbers after the peace agreement. A few days after Algerian independence was recognized OAS terrorists set fire to oil wells in the south of the country, but this was their last major act of defiance, and a week later their campaign was called off.

The bitter struggle for independence, which had brought France to the verge of civil war, had lasted for nearly eight years. Casualties among Algerian nationalists were estimated at over 100,000, French casualties at 15,000, including about 4000 Muslim Algerians fighting with the French army.

Triumphant Muslims in the streets of Algiers celebrating their country's independence.

Ben Bella takes over in Algeria

The Algerian republican government, headed by Prime Minister Ben Yusuf Ben Khedda, arrived in Algiers at the beginning of July, but the deputy premier, Ahmed Ben Bella, was absent. He was closely linked to Egypt and the Soviet Union and critical of 'neo-colonialist' aspects of the independence agreement.

Ben Bella formed an FLN politburo at Tlemcen in order to 'continue the Algerian revolution along socialist lines'. In September Colonel Houari Boumédienne led Algerian forces, which had been assembled in Tunisia and Morocco, to Algiers in support of Ben Bella. In the elections for a constituent assembly which were held later that month the names of Ben Khedda and most of his close supporters did not appear. When the assembly was convened, Ben Bella was elected prime minister with Boumédienne as minister of defence.

Dutch marines rounding up Indonesian paratroops captured in West Irian. Placed under U.N. administration, the territory was eventually transferred to Indonesia in 1963.

Dutch finally cede West Irian

The expansionist ambitions of Indonesia under President Sukarno achieved another success on July 31 when the Dutch ceded West New Guinea (West Irian). The United Nations, acting as intermediary, was to supervise the territory for a brief period.

The wishes of the inhabitants, many of them living in Stone Age conditions, were not much considered. In 1960 Sukarno had sent 'volunteers' into the country, which the Dutch planned to make independent in due course. By 1962, with fighting intensifying, the Dutch had had enough.

Subsequently settlers from Java were moved in. This was resented locally and sporadic guerrilla resistance to Indonesian rule – virtually impossible to quell given the nature of the New Guinea terrain – continued.

Nuclear war looms over Cuba

For a few days in October the world appeared to hover on the brink of nuclear war. U.S. President Kennedy anounced on October 22 that the Soviet Union had bases for nuclear missiles in Cuba. The missiles, he said, were capable of reaching most of the major cities in the Americas. He made it clear that their presence was unacceptable to the U.S. government.

The news came as a shock to most people, but suspicions of what was afoot in Cuba had existed in the U.S. government since the summer, and aerial reconnaissance on October 16 now provided indisputable photographic evidence. Kennedy considered an invasion of Cuba but feared it would provoke a Soviet takeover of West Berlin. He confronted the Soviet foreign minister, Andrei Gromyko, on October 18, but was told that only defensive armaments were involved.

Kennedy demanded the withdrawal of the weapons and instituted a naval blockade of Cuba. Khrushchev's first reactions were bellicose, and work on the missile sites was speeded up, but the Soviet ships approaching Cuba with more missiles turned back. On October 26 he offered to withdraw the missiles from Cuba if the United States would do the same with its missiles in Turkey and undertake not to invade Cuba. The U.S. response was that the work on the sites in Cuba must stop before any negotiations could be entertained. Two days later Khrushchev caved in, consenting to removal of the missiles and dismantling of the sites under UN supervision. Privately, the U.S. government agreed to the Soviet demand for removal of Turkish-based missiles.

Castro, infuriated at his exclusion from negotiations, refused to allow UN observers into Cuba, but U.S. reconnaissance confirmed the fulfilment of the Soviet pledge in November and the U.S. blockade was lifted. Kennedy, whose tactics won widespread approval in the non-Communist world, had greatly enhanced his international prestige, while the Soviet Union, and particularly Khrushchev, had suffered a clear defeat.

Deck of a Soviet ship showing missile transporters.

Clash of the Asian giants

The image of Nehru's India as a great Third World force for peace and moderation suffered a blow on October 11 when war broke out with China. The dispute took place in a remote and inhospitable area, the mountainous border region between India and Tibet.

The official frontier was known as the McMahon Line, after the British cartographer who had drawn it. However, the British had never actually penetrated as far as the hypothetical border, and in places there was doubt about where it ran; moreover, the Chinese had never accepted it. Trouble arose as a result of China's need for access to Tibet, which led them to build a road from Sinkiang to western Tibet through the virtually uninhabited country of the Aksai Chin. Part of it ran through territory claimed by India. When the dispute arose China offered to negotiate, but Nehru, who had demonstrated that he could be as bellicose as any other leader of a new state by seizing Goa the previous year, refused to concede an inch and Indian forces were moved to the border.

Clashes occurred in 1962 and at one point the Indians themselves penetrated beyond the McMahon Line. In October 1963 a decision was taken in Delhi to expel the Chinese from all those sections claimed by India. The Indian troops were easily defeated and the Chinese advanced until they threatened the plains of Assam. There, however, they stopped, announcing a unilateral ceasefire, and withdrew to their former positions. They sent back captured weapons, nicely cleaned, to the Indians.

The border question remained unresolved. India had received an unpleasant shock, possibly contributing to Nehru's stroke two months later (from which he never recovered). India strengthened its alliance with the Soviet Union and devoted a larger portion of its budget to rebuilding its armed forces.

Kassem (left) seen in 1958 with Colonel Aref who was later responsible for his assassination.

Kassem overthrown in Iraq

On February 8 a well-organized army plot was put into effect to overthrow the government of Abd al-Karim Kassem. He had held power since the anti-monarchist coup of 1958.

The leaders of the coup were Colonel Arif, who had co-operated with Kassem in 1958 (and was subsequently sentenced to death but reprieved), and Colonel Hasan al-Bakr, a leading Ba'ath-ist. Kassem was shot with his aides in a television studio. However, divisions existed within the new regime. Arif, who became president, was a Nasserite. Al-Bakr, who became prime minister, was, as a Ba'athist, favourable to Syria. Once Kassem's supporters, the mainly Shi'ite Communists, had been crushed (to the accompaniment of great slaughter), Arif initiated another coup in November, dismissing the Ba'athist government and banning the Ba'ath party. Subsequently Arif himself turned more towards Syria, and against the Iraqi Nasserites, before being killed in a helicopter crash in 1966.

A further complication in the political warfare that passed for government in Iraq was the rebellion of the Kurds in the north of the country, which, since Kassem had reneged on his promise for an autonomous Kurdistan, was to continue sporadically throughout the 1960s.

Nuclear tests banned

A treaty welcomed throughout the world was signed in Moscow on August 5. Though it did not end the cold war, it banned nuclear tests, the dangers of which, once underrated, were now more apparent. The treaty was signed by the Soviet Union, the United States and Britain, whose prime minister (Macmillan) regarded it as his supreme achievement. It was later signed by most other countries – though not by the world's fourth nuclear power, France, nor by China.

Cold war hot line

On August 30 a special telephone link was set up between Washington and Moscow. In the wake of the Cuban missile crisis a reliable method of quick and direct communication between the heads of government of the superpowers seemed desirable. Instant contact between the White House and the Kremlin became possible.

The dream of Martin Luther King

Martin Luther King addresses an enthusiastic crowd during the massive March on Washington in support of civil rights. The following year he was awarded the Nobel Peace Prize.

A huge demonstration by nearly 250,000 people in support of civil rights, was held in Washington on August 28. The massive crowd was addressed by Martin Luther King, who said, 'I have a dream ... that one day this nation will rise up and live out the true meaning of its creed: "We hold these truths to be self-evident, that all men are created equal".'

The civil rights movement in the United States, which aimed to secure equality for blacks, rose to a crescendo in 1963. A particular centre of strife was Alabama, whose governor, George Wallace, emerged as the leader of racist reaction. He attempted to block integration in education, but was foiled by National Guardsmen under federal orders. Meetings between the Alabama governor and the U.S. attorney-general, Robert Kennedy, ended in impasse. Martin Luther King was briefly jailed in Birmingham, Alabama, in April. Medgar Evans, an official of the National Association for the Advancement of Colored People, was shot dead in Jackson, Mississippi, two weeks before the Washington rally. A bomb planted in a Birmingham church in September exploded during a service, killing four black schoolchildren. James Meredith, the first black to attend the University of Mississippi, received his diploma and President Kennedy sent a civil rights bill to Congress. ▶ *page 320*

Ngo Dinh Diem ousted

On November 2, the South Vietnam government headed by Ngo Dinh Diem was overthrown. Diem and his brother, the chief of security Ngo Dinh Nhu, were killed.

A decisive factor leading to the coup was the withdrawal of U.S. support from Ngo Dinh Diem, which was the result of the extreme unpopularity of his government. The country had been administered under martial law since April, and protests against the government had included the suicide by fire of several Buddhist monks. Even the pope had expressed concern. Duong Van Minh took over the government, but he in turn was ousted by General Nguyen Khanh two months later.

The South Vietnamese president, Ngo Dinh Diem.

Kennedy assassinated

The whole world was shocked by the assassination of the young and progressive U.S. president, John F. Kennedy, on November 22. He was shot as he was driving through Dallas, Texas, in a motorcade with his wife and the state governor. Mrs Kennedy was unhurt, Governor Connally was wounded. Kennedy died in hospital less than 30 minutes after being shot.

The police arrested Lee Harvey Oswald, a misfit who had defected to the Soviet Union in 1959 but returned to the United States in 1962. Two days later, while in police custody, Oswald was fatally shot by a Dallas night-club proprietor, Jack Ruby. The new president, Lyndon Johnson, set up a commission under the chief justice, Earl Warren, to investigate the assassination.

The Warren Commission, which issued its report ten months later, criticized security and law-enforcement agencies but concluded that the assassination was the work of Oswald alone. Such was the shock of the deed, however, that theories of a conspiracy of some sort were already legion. Such a devastating deed required a sensational explanation: the insignificant Oswald failed to satisfy the emotional need. Theories, both plausible and implausible, have flourished ever since.

Kennedy's assassin, Lee Harvey Oswald, is fatally wounded by Jack Ruby.

1964 Engagement in the Gulf of Tonkin

On August 2 U.S. warships in the Gulf of Tonkin were attacked by the North Vietnamese. It was not the first such clash though it was the most serious so far. A few days later the U.S. Congress passed the so-called Gulf of Tonkin Resolution, empowering the president to wage open naval warfare against North Vietnam. It was a decisive step in the escalation of the Vietnam War, bringing the United States into direct conflict with the North.

The goal of the United States in South Vietnam was to prevent its takeover by the Communists. At the same time it did not wish to commit its troops to another land war in Asia. As the first aim became more pressing the second policy was gradually superseded. President Kennedy had committed more men and materials to South Vietnam, but no combat troops. However, during 1963–4 the attacks of the Vietcong were becoming increasingly effective. Their success was bolstered by the unsatisfactory nature of the regime in Saigon. Diem, whose repressive and incompetent rule had provoked widespread and passionate opposition, especially from Buddhists and students, had finally been ousted in 1963, but he was followed by a rapid succession of military men no more successful in achieving national support.

By 1964 the U.S. personnel in South Vietnam could no longer be described as mere 'advisers'. As they took a larger role the recent advances of the Vietcong were reversed. That, however, had the effect of drawing in support for the Vietcong from North Vietnam. By scarcely perceptible stages, the war became one between the United States and North Vietnam, the latter being armed and supplied by the Soviet Union. At the end of the year there were 23,000 U.S. personnel in South Vietnam. Within three years the number rose to over half a million. ▶ *page 332*

President Johnson talking with the South Vietnamese foreign minister, Phan Huy Quat.

UN troops sent to Cyprus

As forecast by Archibishop Makarios, the constitutional arrangement under which Cyprus became independent in 1959 had broken down by August, when UN troops were sent in to divide the warring Greek and Turkish communities. Turkish planes flew menacingly over the island, while a Turkish naval invasion was averted by low-profile activities of the U.S. 6th Fleet in the Mediterranean.

The UN force, comprising Canadian, Irish and Scandinavian troops besides the British units already present, gradually succeeded in damping down the conflict, although occasional outbreaks continued and were often followed by further reprisals directed against the unfortunate Greek community in Istanbul. The United Nations and the United States also endeavoured to seek a political solution to the Cyprus problem, but without success, all schemes being rejected either by the Turks, the Greeks or the Greek Cypriots.

Turkish Cypriot women and children are evacuated to safety after their village had come under fire.

'Confrontation' in the Pacific

Indonesian infiltrators, arrested on Singapore Island, are taken away for interrogation.

Indonesian units landed in central Malaysia on September 3 but were repulsed. The incident was a characteristic of the Indonesian policy of 'confrontation' with Malaysia.

Sukarno's Indonesia harboured extensive territorial ambitions in the region. The impulse for 'confrontation' had been provided by the creation in 1963 of the Malaysian federation, which included North Borneo (Sabah) and Sarawak. It was to have included Brunei also, but the sultan of Brunei withdrew at the last moment. Indonesia, which objected to the federation on general grounds, regarding it as a manufactured, Western-orientated counterweight to itself, interpreted Brunei's withdrawal as a sign of unpopularity and instability in the new state, and Sukarno calculated that it might be broken up by small-scale attacks and large-scale propaganda. The confrontation continued for two years but without achieving its desired result.

Khrushchev takes up gardening

Leonid Brezhnev (right) and Alexei Kosygin (left) in Red Square, Moscow.

The Soviet leader Nikita Khrushchev was unceremoniously ousted in a Kremlin coup on October 15. The plot, hatched while he was out of Moscow on holiday, took him by surprise, and he found himself isolated.

Khrushchev was replaced as party leader by Leonid Brezhnev and as prime minister by Alexei Kosygin. Apart from certain failures in foreign policy, especially the breach with Communist China, Khrushchev's weakness in the eyes of the Politburo was in allowing too much freedom and dissent within the Soviet Union. No one, probably, wanted to restore Stalinist terror, but many wanted a return to Stalinist discipline and conformity. Khrushchev, the least unattractive leader the Soviet Union had until Gorbachev, was later to say that the only thing he regretted doing while in power was banning Boris Pasternak's *Dr Zhivago*.

War over the Rann of Kutch

The devastation caused by Pakistani guerrillas in Kashmir.

U.S. marines in Dominican Republic

At the request of the government of the Dominican Republic on April 27 U.S. marines landed in Santo Domingo to help suppress rebellion. They were subsequently replaced by an American-led force made up of several members of the OAS (Organization of American States).

The political situation in the Dominican Republic had been unstable since the assassination of the dictator Trujillo in 1961. Political exiles had returned home, full of plans and ambitions, and Cuban influence was also present. In December 1962, in the first free elections for over 30 years, Juan Bosch was elected president, but he was overthrown in a military coup the following September. The military installed a three-man junta, and a new constitution with free elections was promised. These did not transpire, and a popular insurrection broke out in April. Order was swiftly restored but the political situation remained deadlocked. Eventually a compromise government was established according to a plan approved by the OAS.

On September 6 Indian forces launched an invasion of Pakistan, moving towards Lahore. The army had been much improved in training and morale since the conflict with China, and a Pakistani force was defeated before a UN-sponsored truce was accepted by both sides two weeks later.

The second Indo-Pakistani war originated earlier in the year, in a dispute over the Rann of Kutch, where serious clashes occurred before a ceasefire was arranged through British mediation. Subsequently, Pakistani guerrillas infiltrated Kashmir, with the aim of provoking a general rising against India. In August Indian forces re-established the position, before carrying the war into Pakistani territory.

The Soviet Union acted as intermediary in securing a more concrete ceasefire, which was signed by President Ayub Khan and the Indian prime minister, Lal Bahadur Shastri, at Tashkent in January 1966.

Explosion in Watts

A rioter in Watts is forcibly restrained by heavily armed police.

The single most violent outbreak of racial tension in the United States occurred on August 11, which, in California, happened to be even hotter than usual. A large part of the black ghetto of Watts, in Los Angeles, was burned.

Trouble arose after a black man was arrested for drunken driving, and rioting was soon out of the control of the police and the fire department. A curfew was ignored as snipers shot at policemen from rooftops, looters ransacked stores and hundreds of fires were started. The National Guard eventually restored order, though Watts continued to simmer.

In view of the scale of the violence, deaths were relatively few – less than 30. They included several children. About 700 people were injured, including 100 police and firemen. Damage was estimated at up to $200 million.

The PKI miscalculates

On September 30 the PKI, or Indonesian Communist party, attempted a coup. Allegedly, it was provoked by a false report of the death of Sukarno, whose health had been poor for some time. Six Indonesian generals were murdered in a peculiarly savage manner (the small daughter of one, who escaped, was also killed), but General Suharto was not on the hit list and his prompt action defeated the coup.

A struggle for power between the Indonesian army and the pro-Chinese PKI had always appeared to be likely. Sukarno had prospered partly by balancing the two, though he had become increasingly dependent on the Communists in recent years. Following the failure of the coup, a frightful massacre of Chinese – Communist or not – ensued. The total number who died may have been over 500,000. Meanwhile, Sukarno was edged out of power and Suharto became president of an authoritarian regime.

Direct rule in Aden

The British high commissioner in Aden abandoned the constitution and imposed direct rule on the colony on September 23. The move evoked protests in Aden and outside, particularly in Egypt where Nasser supported the campaign of Adeni nationalists to drive out the British.

Aden was a British colony attached, by a complicated constitutional arrangement, to the Federation of South Arabia, an association of sheikhdoms. Hitherto the British had been anxious to hold on to Aden because of its strategic importance. Nationalist strikes and acts of terrorism, backed by Egypt, had been increasing for several years and were complicated by incursions from Yemen, where a civil war, involving Egypt and Saudi Arabia on opposite sides, was continuing after a republican revolution in 1963.

Rhodesia opts for UDI

On November 11 Ian Smith, the prime minister of Rhodesia, made his long-threatened unilateral declaration of independence. The British high commissioner thereupon dismissed the government, but was ignored. The British government protested and imposed sanctions, while black African states demanded, vainly, the removal of the Smith regime by force.

As Southern Rhodesia, the country had been part of the Central African Federation which, never liked by black Africans, had broken up in 1963. The two other members, Northern Rhodesia and Nyasaland, then proceeded, steadily if not altogether smoothly, towards independence (as Zambia and Malawi) in 1964. Southern Rhodesia, now simply Rhodesia, also wanted independence, which the British government was unwilling to grant because, although the country had been self-governing for many years, power belonged totally to the whites. In contrast to the situation in Zambia and Malawi, whites formed a substantial minority of the Rhodesian population, and UDI was a device to maintain white control.

Despite sanctions, which were approved by the United Nations, for some time the Rhodesian economy hardly suffered. Not only was South Africa positively disposed, but sanctions were widely evaded – not least by British companies. However, guerrilla activities inside Rhodesia increased, despite splits among black leaders, while South Africa became less supportive and developments in Angola and Mozambique turned to Smith's disadvantage. The numerous attempts by various parties to arrange a compromise settlement failed, but by the 1970s, with the guerrillas becoming steadily more successful, it was made increasingly clear, even to white Rhodesians, that they could not win. ▶ *page 359*

Ian Smith at a press conference after talks with the British government had failed.

AFRICAN CONFLICTS

W ARS, sometimes relatively small-scale, were endemic in Africa in the early 1960s as the colonial powers pulled out. Many of these wars could be ascribed very largely to the colonial legacy. The Congo was the worst example: an almost total absence of a solid political base and the fragility of administrative structures resulted in seven years of disorder and civil war, further aggravated by the use of European mercenaries.

The boundaries of colonies had been drawn in the chancelleries of Europe, often in ignorance of the situation on the ground, and as a result had often cut across national and tribal lines as well as grouping different peoples, sometimes traditionally hostile, in one political unit. Thus, many of the conflicts in black Africa arose from national or tribal antagonisms, or over disputed frontier regions.

A third cause of conflict, and one of the most bitter although the one most easily capable of short-term solution, arose in countries where a large number of Europeans had settled. Someone who is born in a country thinks rightfully of that country as his own. White South Africans, for instance, are indisputably African, no less than Xhosa or Zulu. However, a right to citizenship is not the same as a right to benefit from a government which discriminates against the majority of the population. No such right, it is now universally admitted, exists. The conflict in Algeria almost tore France apart. The unilateral declaration of independence by Rhodesia also resulted in a long guerrilla war. Portugal's attempt to hang on to its colonies created a tradition of violence in Angola and Mozambique which made peace all the more difficult to achieve when the Portuguese revolution brought eventual withdrawal.

Somalia's efforts to regain what it considered its lost territories resulted in sporadic fighting with Kenya (1963–67), and a conflict, most intense in 1964, with Ethiopia over the Ogaden. Civil war broke out in

Portuguese soldiers begin an offensive operation in Angola.

Removing road blocks placed by Angolan rebels.

Above. An Angolan village destroyed by rebels.

Right. Guerrilla fighters in Mozambique undergoing training.

Chad in the mid-1960s, eventually attracted an avaricious Libya, and remained unresolved until the 1990s. Namibia's war of independence lasted almost as long (1966–89); Angola's, with the civil war that followed the Portuguese exit, even longer. A particularly savage civil war beset the federation of Nigeria (1967–70), while tribal hatreds provoked sporadic massacres and bouts of civil war in Rwanda and Burundi.

There were many other areas of unrest, and in most if not all of them, local conflicts were exacerbated by the influence, interference or support of other, more powerful countries with axes of their own to grind. Some of them were nearby – for example, South Africa and Egypt; some of them were former colonial powers; others, like the Soviet Union, the United States and, to a much smaller degree China, were engaged in a struggle for world domination.

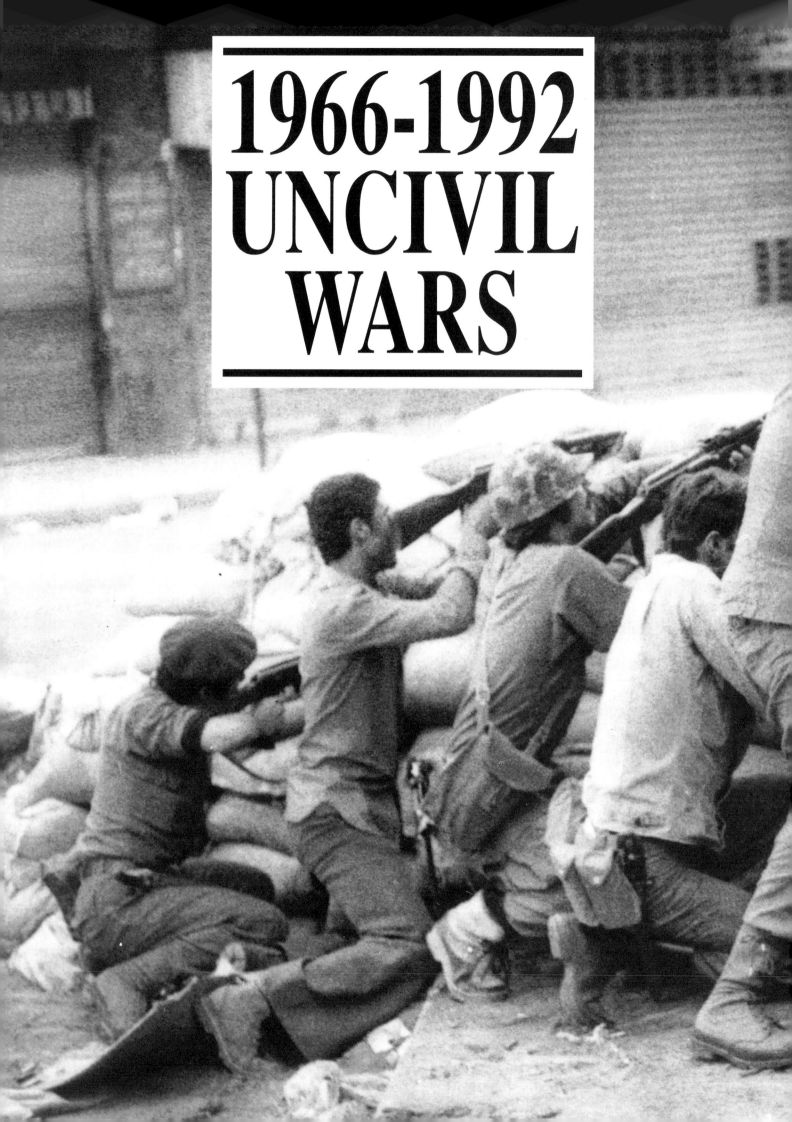

1966-1992 UNCIVIL WARS

THE HIGH HOPES THAT HAD ACCOMPANIED THE CREATION OF AN INDEPENDENT AFRICA were doomed to disappointment. By the late 1960s many of the new states were riven by internal dissensions and democracy had given way to dictatorship. In the Middle East Israel emerged victorious from a war with the Arab states, and in Prague liberalism flowered briefly .

The most frightening phenomenon of the 1970s was undoubtedly the growth of international terrorism. A series of spectacular hijackings, the murder of Israeli athletes at Munich, the bombing campaign by the Bader-Meinhof gang in West Germany and by the IRA in Northern Ireland and mainland Britain brought terror into the streets. Nevertheless, it was also the decade in which the United States withdrew from Vietnam and Egypt made peace with Israel.

At the beginning of the 1980s the triumph of Islamic fundamentalism in an Iran involved in a bloody conflict with Iraq introduced a new element into world politics. Britain defeated an Argentinian army in the Falklands, Lebanon descended into anarchy and Russia became embroiled in Afghanistan. Although by the end of the decade the collapse of communism in eastern Europe had transformed the global scene, the Gulf War and the growth of ethnic violence in Azerbaijan, in Armenia and in Yugoslavia ensured that the 1990s would not usher in a new era of peace.

1966

JANUARY–DECEMBER

COUP IN NIGERIA

NKRUMAH OUSTED

RIOTS IN U.S. CITIES

CULTURAL REVOLUTION

The cracks appear in Nigerian unity

On January 15 a military coup took place in Nigeria. Its leaders were junior officers of the Ibo, who were discontented with the government and resented the dominance of the northern region. The federal and northern prime ministers, Sir Abubakar Balewa and the Sardauna of Sokoto, were assassinated with many others. Senior officers then stepped in and General Johnson Ironsi, an Ibo, was proclaimed head of state.

Nigeria was the largest black African country, but it was made up of very different groups and cultures with little concept of national unity. The north, predominantly Hausa and Muslim, was the largest region, with more than half the total population; the eastern (Ibo) and western (Yoruba) regions had more obvious economic assets. At independence in 1960 Balewa, a northerner, had become federal prime minister. The eastern leader, Nnamdi Azikiwe, became president in 1963.

Early co-operation between east and north did not last, partly because of northern fears of Ibo domination. There were also divisions in the western region, which resulted in the creation of a fourth, mid-western region in 1963. The new western leader, Chief Akintola (who would be another victim of the 1966 coup), sought closer co-operation with the north, partly at Ibo expense. Outbreaks of violence occurred in several parts during 1965.

Ironsi's job was to prevent the federation breaking up. Many northerners feared that this would be done by abolishing the federal constitution, and in July a second coup took place. Ironsi was killed and replaced by Yakubu Gowon, a northerner though a Christian. Agreement was reached on a new constitution, but massacres of Ibo in the north and the flight of survivors to their homeland left the eastern region discontented and disillusioned.
▶ *page 328*

Nkrumah overthrown

The charismatic Ghanaian president, Kwame Nkrumah, was overthrown on February 24 while on a visit to China. The brilliant leader, who in 1957 had become the first prime minister of an independent black African country, had deteriorated into a demagogue whose primary concern was to keep his own power and privileges. He had dissipated Ghana's wealth (considerable at independence) and allowed corruption to gain a grip on administration which successive, mainly very short-lived governments were unable to root out.

President Kwame Nkrumah.

Sir Abubakar Balewa in London for a conference of Commonwealth prime ministers.

Black riots in northern U.S. cities

Looters removing goods from a store in Cleveland, Ohio, while police stand by.

In another bad year for race relations in the United States, serious riots broke out in several northern cities on July 31. Black, Puerto Rican and white gangs fought in New York; 4000 national guardsmen were drafted in to quell violence in Chicago; and there were several deaths and many injuries in similar outbreaks in Cleveland, Ohio. Meanwhile, the struggle for equality was continuing in the South, where James Meredith, the man who broke the colour bar at the University of Mississippi, was shot (not fatally) during a civil rights march in that state in June.

Red Guards versus revisionists

Young wall poster artists use their talents to advance the Cultural Revolution.

The extraordinary episode in China known as the Cultural Revolution moved into top gear in mid-August. Masses of young people were mobilized as Red Guards to attack 'revisionism' as the aging Mao Tse-tung strove to reinvigorate the revolutionary process which, he feared, had gone flabby.

The motive for the Cultural Revolution was to be sought in failures of social and economic policy. An example was education, where all entries to institutes of higher education had to be postponed for one year. From these unemployed young people – perhaps as many as 20 million in all – the Red Guards were recruited. In the course of this ideological crusade, officials at every level of Communist society were purged. Many unfortunate people were subjected to mental and physical abuse. As counter-revolutionary tendencies could be ascribed to practically anyone, no one was safe. Property was destroyed on a large scale, resulting in serious breakdowns in communications, transport and industrial production.

JANUARY
15 Military coup in Nigeria
17 Unexploded H-bomb falls into Atlantic after U.S. aircraft collide
31 U.S. bombing of North Vietnam renewed

FEBRUARY
7 President Johnson holds talks with South Vietnam leaders
22 Five ministers arrested as Obote consolidates power in Uganda
24 Nkrumah ousted in Ghana coup

MARCH
10 De Gaulle withdraws French troops from NATO
11 Suharto takes over executive powers in Indonesia
12 Communist party banned in Indonesia

MAY
15 Anti-war demonstrators surround the White House in Washington

JUNE
1 Purges underway in China
28 Nonviolent military coup in Argentina
29 Kurds accept settlement with Iraqi government
29 U.S. bombers attack Hanoi

JULY
1 NATO HQ moved to Brussels as French withdraw forces
14 Israeli aircraft attack Syrian targets after border raids
29 Ironsi killed in Nigerian coup
31 Blacks riot in U.S. cities

AUGUST
11 Indonesia calls off 'confrontation' with Malaysia
18 Cultural Revolution accelerates after Peking rally

SEPTEMBER
5 Black rioting in Atlanta, Georgia
6 South African prime minister, Hendrik Verwoerd, assassinated
29 20 Argentinians 'invade' Falkland Islands in hijacked plane

OCTOBER
2 Many deaths reported among Ibo in northern Nigeria
5 Franco regime tightens Spanish blockade of Gibraltar

NOVEMBER
1 Vietcong attack Saigon with rockets
19 Mobilization ordered in Jordan after Israeli attacks

DECEMBER
22 Ian Smith declares Rhodesia a republic

1967

JANUARY–DECEMBER

MILITARY COUP IN GREECE

BIAFRA IN REVOLT

SIX-DAY WAR

BRITISH LEAVE ADEN

King Constantine (centre) with members of the new ruling junta in Greece.

Greek colonels take over

Democracy came to a sudden end in Greece on April 21. A coup was carried out by army officers of middle rank in anticipation of a general election. The coup was justified as necessary to avoid an alleged Communist threat, and was at first supported by traditional conservatives.

The struggle between Communists and anti-Communists had gradually subsided during the 1960s. From 1963 a centrist government under George Papandreou had carried out social reforms which aroused some antagonism among those who equated all vaguely socialist policies with communism. Particular hostility was shown towards the prime minister's son, Andreas, who was supposedly involved in secret leftist intrigues.

The crisis which created the opportunity for the coup arose from a quarrel between the prime minister and the king, the young and headstrong Constantine. Their dispute concerned control of the army, a powerful force in Greece since it had been built up by the United States in opposition to communism. The intrigues of the king and some of Papandreou's colleagues brought down the government and led to disorders. In this atmosphere, and with the prospect of the forces of reform winning the election, the colonels acted.

The military junta which took over Greece ruled with a mixture of barbarity – employing torture as a deliberate instrument of policy – and stupidity. However, in December it survived an ill-planned attempt at a counter-coup by King Constantine, who then fled the country.

Biafra secedes

On May 31 Colonel Odumegwu Ojukwu declared that the eastern region of Nigeria was seceding from the federation as the independent republic of Biafra. The Biafran declaration was rejected by the Nigerian government, and civil war began.

Ojukwu had been made governor of the eastern region at the time of the first Nigerian coup. After the second coup and the massacres and persecution of Ibo in the north, he came to the conclusion that the Ibo would be safe only in their own republic.

The war proved to be long and bitter. Dreadful suffering occurred in Biafra, with famine and disease among the overcrowded, besieged population.

The much stronger federal army was supplied with arms by Britain (though fiercely opposed by many Biafran supporters) and by the Soviet Union. Biafra was supplied by France. The Organization of African Unity attempted mediation, but several African countries recognized Biafra's independence.

With the Biafrans resisting manfully, the war lasted two and a half years before the internal situation forced the breakaway republic's surrender. The federal government promised no reprisals and reconciliation, promises which were largely kept.

Biafran children suffering from malnutrition.

War breaks out in Middle East

A remarkable war broke out in the Middle East on June 5. One of the shortest on record, it formed an episode in one of the most persistent conflicts – between Arabs and Israelis. In six days the Israelis inflicted an overwhelming defeat on their numerically superior enemies and captured a vast amount of territory.

The new Ba'athist government of Syria had stepped up bombardment of Israel in the spring and, with Jordan and Lebanon, planned to divert the Jordan river to deprive Israel of two-thirds of its water. In April, the Syrian air force clashed with Israeli planes bombing the artillery positions on the Golan Heights. Fearing a much stronger Israeli reaction, Syria appealed to Egypt, which launched a big political offensive against Israel and closed the Straits of Tiran, the entrance to the Gulf of Aqaba, which was tantamount to an act of war. In May President Nasser demanded withdrawal of UN troops from Sinai and moved in his own. He proclaimed that the time had come to destroy Israel. A joint military command was announced with Iraq and Jordan, in which King Hussein was forced

Triumphant Israeli soldiers in Jordanian Jerusalem.

to accommodate Nasser under pressure of Arab popular feeling. The tourists left Israel as the journalists moved in.

War began early on June 5. In six days it was over. The Arab forces were decimated. The Israelis were on the Suez Canal, the Golan Heights, the West Bank and in Old Jerusalem.

The Six-Day War was followed not by peace but by a fierce war of attrition, with the Israelis raiding Egypt from fortifications on the Suez Canal and the Egyptians calling on the Soviet Union to provide assistance, including SAM missiles. A ceasefire was arranged shortly before Nasser's death in 1970. ▶ *page 343*

The British pull out of Aden

On November 29, after large-scale risings in Aden, British forces were withdrawn from Aden and South Yemen. A month earlier Egyptian forces had left North Yemen. The two Yemeni republics now entered upon a troubled era of coups, assassinations and civil wars.

The region of the Yemen had been largely isolated from the outside world until the 1960s, with the exception of the port and region of Aden, a British colony since the early 19th century. The traditional Yemeni rulers were the highly conservative imams of Saana (San'a), who combined absolutism with assassination.

Rising Arab nationalism had presented the British in Aden with increasing problems after the Suez crisis of 1956. Nasser's influence was also at work in North Yemen, where plots were incubated against the imam. The Egyptians were behind the coup in Saana in 1962 and sent in troops to support their puppet regime. Violent opposition was

launched by the tribes, who were supported by the Saudis and the British. The position of the Egyptians in the Yemen and of the British in the Aden protectorate grew equally untenable. Nasser withdrew after his shattering defeat by Israel. The British pulled out a month later.

British soldiers round up civilians in Aden following the violent demonstrations which greeted the arrival of a UN mission. The rising tide of Arab nationalism led to an increasing number of acts of terrorism, making the colony virtually ungovernable.

THE SIX-DAY WAR

IN THE ATMOSPHERE of crisis which preceded the outbreak of the Six-Day War, the Israelis formed a government of national unity in which the chief of staff, the charismatic, one-eyed general, Moshe Dayan, became responsible for the nation's defence. The striking Israeli success is ascribed largely to his skilful strategy.

On June 2, a Friday, it appeared that the threat of imminent war was receding, as Israel showed signs of reversing its warlike preparations, even demobilizing part of the armed forces (which included practically the entire fit, adult, male population – making constant mobilization problematic). What ought to have been evident in Cairo and elsewhere was that the current situation made an attack by Israel virtually inevitable: the alternative was to endure gradual suffocation.

On the morning of June 5, the Israeli air force attacked Egyptian airfields. The planes flew low over the Mediterranean, evading Egyptian radar, and approached from the west, the opposite direction, and at a

slightly later time than expected. The Egyptian pilots were at breakfast, and practically the entire air force was destroyed on the ground in a matter of minutes. The Syrian and Jordanian air forces then attacked and were also overwhelmed. Altogether the Arab air forces lost about 450 aircraft while the Israelis lost 26.

With complete control of the air, the Israelis then wiped out the Egyptian forces in the Sinai. Entire columns 20 miles long were destroyed by disabling the leading vehicles first, then attacking the remainder, which were lined up like ducks in a shooting gallery across the desert.

Israel had promised not to attack Jordan unless provoked. However, the Jordanian army was under the command of an Egyptian general, and King Hussein did not dare to countermand his orders. Some damage was caused by shelling in Tel Aviv and West Jerusalem, but within three days the Israelis had taken the whole of the West Bank and

An Egyptian soldier surrenders to Israelis.

Israeli defence minister Moshe Dayan at a press conference.

Right. Egyptian aircraft destroyed on the ground.

Below. Egyptian vehicles after an Israeli air attack.

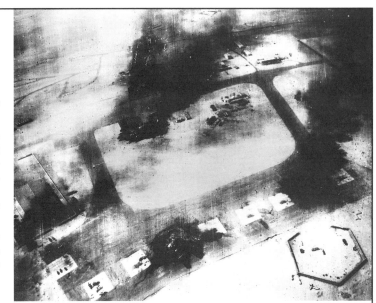

had captured Old Jerusalem.

Syria, though it had been chiefly responsible for starting the war, had played little part in it beyond cross-border shelling. The Israelis took the opportunity of ending this persistent aggravation by storming the Golan Heights. Damascus was at their mercy when the ceasefire was arranged on June 10. Egypt had admitted defeat two days earlier, Nasser subsequently offering his resignation as president, though it was rejected by the Egyptian assembly.

Arab casualties in the war were over 20,000, Israel's about 700. Israel had gained huge new territories but its defensive position was improved, as its new frontiers were shorter and easier to defend. At first the Israelis regarded their territorial acquisitions as bargaining counters, to be handed back in exchange for Arab recognition and peace. As time went on, however, and such aims went largely unrealized, the new territories, or some of them, came to be regarded as permanent Israeli possessions.

Israeli soldiers at a captured Egyptian air base.

An Egyptian general taken prisoner by Israelis.

Prague spring

Dramatic changes took place at government level in Czechoslovakia on January 5. The Stalinist party chief, Novotný, was voted out by the party central committee and Alexander Dubček, a Slovak with a reputation for liberalism, replaced him. Two months later Novotný was removed from the presidency in favour of another liberal, General Jan Svoboda. The Prague Spring began.

Mindlessly obedient to Moscow, the Novotný government had become politically bankrupt. Jokes about the stupidity of Novotný himself were invented daily over glasses of *pils*. The Czechs, especially the professional and intellectual classes, were now completely disillusioned with the Communist party, and Dubček thus had to overcome initial inertia before his policy of 'socialism with a human face' was embraced by the people.

The new Dubček government ended censorship and removed civil disabilities from non-party members. It instituted liberal economic reforms which swept away the stifling doctrines of the Stalinist system. In May elections cleared out the old guard altogether.

Dubček proclaimed loyalty to Moscow which, having lost faith in Novotný, had no serious objection to the economic reforms. But the Brezhnev regime was increasingly concerned with the liberalization of society that went with them. From May onwards, doubts began to be expressed by Czechoslovakia's neighbouring satellites, while in Czechoslovakia itself Dubček came under pressure from reformers to take his 'Action Programme' even further. Soviet premier Kosygin visited Prague, seeking compromise; but soon after him came another Soviet visitor, the chief of Soviet military intelligence. Dubček assured the Soviets that Czechoslovakia was not going to become another Yugoslavia, or another Romania, but Moscow remained worried. In June Warsaw Pact manoeuvres were held in Czechoslovakia. This was a long-term plan – but when the manoeuvres were over the Soviet tanks were in no hurry to leave.

A South Vietnamese soldier in action in Saigon.

Communists launch Tet offensive

The U.S. command and South Vietnam were taken by surprise during the Tet festival on January 31 when the Communist forces launched a major offensive. About 100,000 troops were involved, and every major city and base in South Vietnam was attacked simultaneously.

Saigon, the South Vietnamese capital, nearly fell to the Vietcong, while Hue, the second city, was taken and held until regained by U.S. and South Vietnamese forces in March.

General Giap's offensive was ultimately unsuccessful, but it was a spectacular stroke which demonstrated that the United State's opponents in Vietnam were militarily far more formidable than had generally been assumed, although incapable of winning a war of set battles. It had a number of indirect results. The U.S. commander-in-chief, General Westmoreland, was replaced; opposition to the war in the United States increased; another bombing pause was followed by a U.S. offer to withdraw; and discussions opened between the United States and North Vietnam in Paris in May.

The Paris talks, later joined by the South Vietnamese and the Vietcong, led nowhere; the North Vietnamese realized now that they could maintain guerrilla operations despite the heavy U.S. bombing, and they were aware that the U.S. government was anxious to withdraw. Richard Nixon campaigned for the U.S. presidency on a platform which included ending the Vietnam war. Time was therefore on the side of General Giap. ▶ *page 342*

North Koreans capture U.S. spy ship

North Korean forces boarded the USS *Pueblo* on January 23. One crew member was killed, but there was no serious resistance as the ship was virtually unarmed (and, surprisingly, unescorted). The Koreans claimed the ship was within their territorial waters, though this was denied by the United States. The object of the attack was clearly to gain possession of a ship full of advanced intelligence-gathering equipment. The North Koreans refused to return the vessel, though the crew were ransomed in December.

Massacre at My Lai

On March 16 at least 100 people – over 300 according to some accounts – in the Vietnamese village of My Lai were massacred by a U.S. army unit. The dead included women and children.

The My Lai massacre was the most notorious incident in a brutal war. The junior officer in command of the unit was later court-martialled and sentenced to life imprisonment (the sentence was subsequently reduced), although his commanding officer was not charged.

Atrocities were frequent in Vietnam, but the coverage of the war by the media, particularly television, made its horrors more immediate and shocking to ordinary people, and contributed to its rising unpopularity. By 1968 it was causing serious internal divisions in the United States, and President Johnson's fear of losing the presidential election because of the Vietnam war persuaded him not to stand for another term.

Lt Calley, implicated in the My Lai massacre.

French students in revolt

On May 2 French students confronted the police in a pitched battle on the streets of Paris. The outbreaks continued for several days, and the students were joined by workers, who declared a general strike, and by other revolutionary elements. Extensive damage was caused in Paris and France was brought almost to a standstill.

The near-revolution in France was the most dramatic episode in the movement of protest among students generally in the 1960s, which was almost a world-wide phenomenon. Outbreaks had occurred earlier in Germany, where an assassination attempt against Rudi Dutschke, a leading student radical, had provoked violent attacks on right-wing newspaper offices, and in Italy.

The main grievance of the Italian students concerned conditions in the universities, which formed the core of revolt generally. Other causes were also involved, including a particularly acute 'generation gap' – the older generation being conditioned by World War II and its aftermath, the younger by the liberal atmosphere of the 'Sixties' (already apparent in the mid-1950s), which embraced the hippy movement and 'pop' culture. There was widespread dissatisfaction with entrenched bureaucratic power and the emphasis on materialism, which seemed to stunt spiritual and artistic development. The Vietnam war and the Soviet suppression of the Prague Spring provided international issues on which youthful protest could unite.

The revolution failed because students alone did not form a sufficiently powerful force to overthrow society and, ultimately, they had no allies. Peace returned to France when the workers, soothed with higher wages, forsook the students. A significant legacy of the student revolt was terrorist activity by small groups of political extremists, especially in West Germany, Italy and France.

Soviet tanks enter Prague

On August 21 Soviet tanks and troops, which had been stationed on the border for some time, moved into Czechoslovakia. The Czechoslovak army did not resist (as Dubček had promised), and although the citizens, mainly young, of Prague formed flimsy barricades and removed street signs and even house numbers, the Soviet force was irresistible.

There were a few outbreaks of fighting; otherwise the Czechs put up only passive resistance, and milled around the tanks explaining to the often bewildered soldiers that they were not engaged in an act of liberation, as they had been told, and that they were not in Germany, as some supposed.

Having taken over, the Soviet authorities moved rather slowly to demolish the Prague Spring, being aware not only of the hostility in the West but also of con-

Czech students demonstrating against Soviet tanks in Prague.

siderable dismay within the Warsaw Pact countries (which supported the action and provided some units). The 'Brezhnev doctrine' affirmed the limits of sovereignty in the countries of the Warsaw Pact, which was an unwelcome restatement of their subservience to Soviet policy. In Prague the reformers were gradually edged out of power, and a regime similar to the one Dubček had tried to reform was reinstalled.

1969

**UNREST
IN ULSTER**

**SINO-SOVIET
CLASH**

British troops sent to Northern Ireland

After a spate of violent civil rights demonstrations in Belfast and Londonderry and several political murders, British troops were sent to keep order in Northern Ireland on August 14. They were requested by the Northern Ireland government and were welcomed by the Roman Catholic minority in the province.

The civil rights movement in Northern Ireland, encouraged by the example of the United States, was provoked by the dominance of the Protestant majority and the exploitation of the Catholics. Its objectives were generally approved by the British government in London, while the need for reforms was recognized by the Unionist Northern Ireland government. But the Unionist government was coming under increasing pressure from right-wing extremists such as the Rev. Ian Paisley, who regarded any surrender to Catholic opinion as a move towards integration with the hated Republic of Ireland.

The forces of law and order were almost entirely Protestant. Particularly objectionable to Catholics were the B-Specials, a supplementary police force widely suspected of conniving with, and perhaps taking part in, acts of violence against Catholics. British troops were initially seen by Catholics as a far preferable alternative. The British government subsequently insisted on the suppression of the B-Specials and the disarming of the Royal Ulster Constabulary, while pressing the Northern Ireland government for reforms. This helped to alienate Unionists and, since Britain now became the chief force for law and order, it eventually provoked conflict with the Catholics and encouraged the rise of the terrorist IRA (at first, particularly the breakaway group known as the Provisionals). ▶ *page 338*

An injured policeman is attended by his colleagues.

Chinese attack Soviet forces on the border

Chinese forces occupied a small, uninhabited island in the Ussuri river on March 2. The river forms part of the easternmost frontier between China and the Soviet Union. In a clash with Soviet troops, probably unaware of the Chinese move, about 30 Soviet soldiers were killed.

This dispute, which spread to other parts of the frontier (China recorded over 500 Soviet 'infringements'), was of mainly symbolic importance. It was rooted in China's claim to a larger part of the eastern Soviet Union which it had relinquished in the 'unequal treaties', signed under pressure with Russia and other European powers by the Manchu government. It became active in 1960 after the falling-out of the two Communist giants, and encouraged the diplomatic 'revolution' which drew China closer to the United States in the 1970s.

Police coming under attack in the predominantly Roman Catholic Bogside area of Londonderry. The British army was subsequently brought in to shield the Roman Catholic minority from the violence of the Protestant majority, but came into conflict with that section of the population it had set out to protect.

1970

JANUARY–DECEMBER

U.S. STUDENTS SHOT DEAD

JORDAN-PALESTINIAN CONFLICT

Death on the campus

The worst incident in the student unrest that had become familiar in Western universities in the preceding decade occurred in Ohio on May 4. The location was Kent State University, hitherto not known for student militancy. The occasion was a demonstration against the Vietnam War, and specifically its extension into Cambodia, which degenerated into riot. National Guardsmen, who were called to the campus by the state governor after Molotov cocktails were thrown at police, opened fire on the students. Two young men and two young women were shot dead.

The disaster resulted from poor discipline. The guardsmen, many of them no older than their 19-year-old victims, were tired and nervous. Tear gas had failed to disperse the students, who replied with makeshift missiles. Hearing what they thought was a gunshot, the guardsmen opened fire at a range of less than 30 yards. Those killed were said not to have been involved in the rioting: one was a member of the Reserve Officer Training Corps.

Anti-war protests reached a new pitch with the invasion of Cambodia at the end of April. Hundreds of colleges and universities were partly or totally closed down by student strikes.

Black September for Palestinians

In early September fighting broke out between the Jordanian army and the Palestinians in Jordan. The Palestinians, who outnumbered the Jordanian population and were turning the north of the country into an armed camp, suffered heavy casualties before a ceasefire was agreed in Cairo.

King Hussein's government had become increasingly anxious about the presence of the Palestinians, who were largely outside its control and whose activities invited Israeli attacks. Though the army proved more than capable of containing the Palestinians, the Arab world was shocked by Jordan's action, and Syrian tanks crossed the border in support of the Palestinians. They were swiftly repulsed (largely because internal rivalry in Syria resulted in the absence of air cover), but at the truce agreed in Cairo on September 27 (the day before Nasser died of a heart attack), Hussein was, in effect, compelled to recognize Yasser Arafat, head of the PLO, as equivalent to a head of state. Nevertheless, the Palestinians were ultimately forced to surrender their power bases in Jordan. The centre of PLO activities shifted to the Lebanon. ▶ *page 340*

Jordanian artillery firing on Palestinian positions in Amman.

Obote ousted in Uganda

The president of Uganda, Milton Obote, was relieved of his office on January 25 while he was attending the Commonwealth conference in Singapore. The leader of the coup was Colonel Idi Amin, who subsequently declared himself president.

Uganda, even more than most new African states, was riven by internal divisions – racial, tribal, religious and political. Obote had antagonized many people while, in the seven years of Uganda's independence, raising himself from constitutional prime minister to dictatorial president. Following an attempted assassination in 1969, he had tried to curb the power of Amin and the army, on which he had become dangerously dependent.

Amin was a very large, apparently genial man who had been commissioned by the British in the East African Rifles after showing considerable ability as an NCO. His seizure of power was regarded with some complacency by those whom Obote had antagonized. Earlier conceptions of his character, however, proved incorrect, as he proceeded to institute a reign of terror in which hundreds of thousands of Ugandans died and the country's economy was completely ruined.
▶ *page 338*

Milton Obote, the deposed president of Uganda.

Pakistan breaks apart

Pakistan's president, Yahya Khan, declared a state of emergency in East Pakistan on March 25. Sheikh Mujibur Rahman and other leaders of the Awami League were arrested, and Pakistani troops began a brutal suppression of the Bengalis.

Political parties had been re-established in Pakistan under Yahya Khan, who took over from Ayub Khan in 1969, but the elections, held in December, emphasized the rift between the two sections of the country. In West Pakistan the victors were Zulfikar Ali Bhutto and his Pakistan People's party. In the East, 160 out of 162 seats were won by the Awami League led by Mujibur Rahman. The policy of the Awami League was complete internal autonomy, with the federal government retaining power only in foreign affairs and defence. This was rejected by Yahya Khan and by Bhutto, whose negotiations with Mujibur got nowhere (the Awami League was actually the largest party in the federal parliament). The government then turned to force to resolve the deadlock. Estimated numbers killed between March and December range up to 3 million, although the actual number was perhaps one-tenth of that. Besides those slaughtered, every other form of savagery was perpetrated, and refugees poured into India in millions, compelling closure of the border.

Among the refugees were the remaining leaders of the Awami League, who declared the complete independence of East Pakistan, as Bangladesh, in April in response to the army's attack. They received full support from the Indian government, which assisted in training and arming the guerrilla army, the Mukti Bahini, officered by Bengali deserters from the Pakistan army.

Rickshaw passengers and their drivers at Saidpur in East Pakistan brutally murdered by soldiers from West Pakistan during savage but ultimately futile attempts to prevent secession.

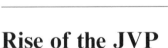

Rise of the JVP

The JVP (People's Liberation Front) in Ceylon (Sri Lanka), a revolutionary Sinhalese organization, began a revolt against the government on April 5. The crisis lasted for several weeks before the movement was crushed by government forces. The government put total casualties at 2000, its opponents quoted a much greater figure. Many of the victims were not supporters of the JVP. The state of emergency declared by Mrs Bandaranaike's government would remain in force until 1977, when the JVP was legalized. ▶ *page 353*

China joins the United Nations

On October 25 Communist China became a member of the United Nations. Its membership had hitherto been barred by the United States, which had invariably used its Security Council veto to block China's admission.

The UN also voted to expel Nationalist China (Taiwan) at the same time as its rival was admitted (since both claimed to be the legal government of all China), a development that the United States had hoped to avoid. The ending of the U.S. exclusion of China was symptomatic of the policy of detente pursued by President Nixon and his secretary of state Dr Henry Kissinger, and made possible by the winding-down of the Vietnam war. It coincided with a Chinese reappraisal of world affairs in which more amiable relations with the United States were seen to be desirable, partly because of the Sino-Soviet split. Other tokens of improving Sino-U.S. relations were the ending of the U.S. trade embargo and the visit of a U.S. table tennis team to China later in the year, practically the first contact of that kind between the two countries for over 20 years.

Detente, though faltering, was a policy universally applied, and the United States was anxious not to hazard its relations with the Soviet Union, improving generally since the Cuba crisis, through its rapprochement with China.

Pakistan attacks India

Yahya Khan's air force launched a surprise attack on Indian airfields on December 3. The aim was to destroy the Indian air force on the ground, but it failed almost completely. Pakistani actually lost more aircraft than India.

The guerrilla war in Bangladesh (East Pakistan) had grown steadily more intense since April. In November the Mukti Bahini launched a new offensive with the active aid of India, whose troops crossed the border in Bengal. War became inevitable, and the Pakistani air strike was an attempt to establish an initial advantage. India's response was to grant formal recognition to the rebel government of Bangladesh and to invade in full force. The Pakistani troops in East Bengal were totally defeated within two weeks, while Indian forces also overran the Rann of Kutch in West Pakistan. Mrs Gandhi then declared a ceasefire.

Yahya Khan's government fell, and Zulfikar Bhutto took over as president of a truncated Pakistan. Mujibur Rahman was released to become prime minister of the new state of Bangladesh.

Indian soldiers moving back to the border after their victory against Pakistan.

1972 Bloody Sunday in Londonderry

As the security situation in Northern Ireland worsened, relations between the British army and the Catholic population reached a nadir, and on January 30 British troops opened fire on rioting Catholics in Londonderry. Thirteen people were killed. South of the border, the British embassy in Dublin was burned down in protest by a furious crowd.

The advent of British troops in 1969 had reinvigorated the IRA, as the troops looked increasingly like an army of occupation. Barricaded 'no-go' areas were set up in Catholic urban districts. The soldiers became the target of IRA attacks, while acts of terrorism by both Catholics and Protestants increased.

The British imposed direct rule from London in March, terminating the authority of the Northern Ireland government. Towards the end of the year a brief truce was called by the IRA and secret meetings were held with a British minister, though nothing was achieved. In 1969 14 people had died in political violence in Northern Ireland: in 1972 the figure rose to 475. ▶ page 344

An angry mob storming the British embassy in Dublin.

The funeral procession of the victims of 'Bloody Sunday'.

Slaughter in Burundi

The conflict between the ruling Tutsi minority and the Hutu majority in the central African republic of Burundi came to a head again on April 29. Several thousand people were killed in a Hutu guerrilla attack. Nevertheless, the Tutsi-dominated government retained control.

With some help from Zaïre (the former Belgian Congo), the army suppressed the rebels and in the process killed a vast number of Hutu (estimates ranged up to 200,000). Many more fled across the border to Rwanda and Tanzania. In May Hutu guerrillas launched another attack, from bases in Rwanda and Tanzania. In driving them back, Burundi forces entered Tanzania and killed several people. Peace was eventually restored during the following year.

Uganda Asians driven out

On August 9 the Ugandan dictator Idi Amin announced that Asian residents were to leave the country. Initially the order was restricted to those who still held British citizenship, though ultimately almost the entire Asian population (mainly Indian in origin) was forced to leave.

Many people were robbed of all they possessed before leaving. Their shops and businesses were looted by Amin's soldiers, or taken over by people unable to administer them. The results were disastrous for the Ugandan economy. The refugees, together with other Asians expelled (in less savage fashion) from Kenya, were admitted to Britain.

Amin repels invaders

Idi Amin in an expansive mood at the microphone.

On September 17 a small guerrilla force numbering only a few hundred invaded the country from Tanzania in support of the deposed president Obote. They were swiftly expelled by the army, which was being supplied by Gaddafi's regime in Libya.

The Ugandan air force then raided two towns in Tanzania in reprisal. Full-scale war was avoided by the mediation of the OAU (Organization for African Unity) and peace was restored early in October. ▶ *page 357*

War for the cod

One of the least bloody 'wars' of the 20th century began on September 12 when an Icelandic gunboat fired warning shots over two British fishing vessels.

The conflict originated in Iceland's unilateral decision to extend its fishing limits to 50 miles, contrary to international agreement. The British refused to co-operate and provided naval protection for their trawlers. A compromise was reached in 1973, but Iceland then extended the limit to 200 miles. Though Britain was legally in the right, Iceland was struggling for economic survival, and the British eventually gave in. The only real losers in the four-year Cod War were British fishermen.

Revolution in Madagascar

On October 11 the president of Madagascar (the Malagasy Republic) was forced to resign by military pressure, after extensive rioting. Although President Tsiranana, who had held office since independence in 1958, had recently been re-elected, a referendum – of suspect validity – held after the coup approved it. Madagascar entered upon a long period of exploitative government, with virtual anarchy prevailing in much of the countryside.

Philibert Tsiranana, the ousted Malagasy leader.

1972

JANUARY
12 Mujibur Rahman becomes Bangladeshi prime minister
13 Colonel Acheampong leads military coup in Ghana
30 British troops kill 13 in Londonderry

FEBRUARY
2 British embassy in Dublin burnt down
21 U.S. President Nixon visits China
22 IRA bomb kills seven civilians at Aldershot barracks
25 West Germany pays Arab hijackers $3 million for release of hostages

MARCH
12 United States establishes diplomatic relations with China
30 British government imposes direct rule in Northern Ireland
30 North Vietnamese troops invade South Vietnam

MAY
10 U.S. air force raids North Vietnam cities
10 Hutu rebels invade Burundi from Rwanda and Tanzania
26 SALT I treaty signed in Moscow
30 Japanese terrorists kill 27 in attack at Tel Aviv airport

JUNE
2 German terrorist Andreas Baader arrested
16 German terrorist Ulrike Meinhof arrested
17 Five men caught bugging Democratic party offices in Washington's Watergate building

JULY
3 Peace agreed between India and Pakistan at Simla
25 French nuclear test in South Pacific

AUGUST
9 Idi Amin orders 60,000 Asians out of Uganda
11 Last U.S. combat troops in Vietnam withdraw

SEPTEMBER
2 22 die in terrorist attack on Montreal nightclub
5 11 Israeli athletes killed in Munich
8 Israelis bomb guerrilla bases in Lebanon and Syria
17 Uganda invaded by exiles from Tanzania

OCTOBER
5 OAU mediates peace between Uganda and Tanzania

NOVEMBER
7 Nixon re-elected U.S. president
21 SALT II talks begin in Geneva

339

Andreas Baader, leader of the Baader-Meinhof group.

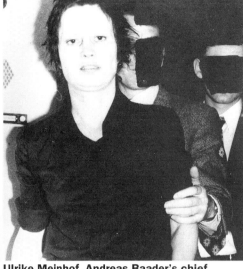

Ulrike Meinhof, Andreas Baader's chief accomplice, pictured after her arrest.

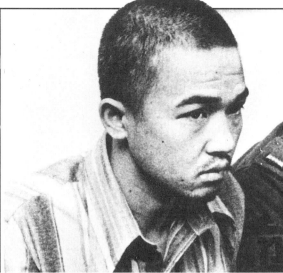

Kozo Okamoto, the Japanese Red Army terrorist implicated in the Lod airport massacre.

The wreckage of a British airliner after it had been blown up at a Jordan airfield.

A terrorist (right) in conversation with officials in Munich.

Women and children arriving in Amman, Jordan, after their release from one of the aircraft hijacked by members of the Popular Front for the Liberation of Palestine.

TERRORISM

Leila Khaled (second left), who attempted to hijack an Israeli airliner, pictured at a training camp.

The scene at Lydda Airport, Israel, after the bodies of the Munich massacre victims had been flown home.

Terrorism, the use of the bomb and the gun by relatively small underground groups in pursuit of broadly political aims, is often seen as the characteristic form of violent conflict in the late 20th-Century world. Practically every country in the world outside the communist bloc experienced some form of terrorism in the 1970s and 1980s. Some, such as Uganda, have experienced 'state terrorism', a more terrible phenomenon. Many more have experienced terror tactics in the process of civil war and revolution. Terrorist groups themselves often justified their actions by pointing out that governments were guilty of worse atrocities (an argument that leads to total anarchy).

In spite of their frequent espousal of left-wing doctrines, most terrorist groups were not primarily motivated by political ideology but by nationalism, often combined with religious fanaticism. The Palestinian groups that waged international terrorism in pursuit of local aims fell into this group, as did the IRA in Northern Ireland. Although these groups achieved little or nothing beyond creating individual misery, they proved ineradicable because they enjoyed a degree of popular sympathy or support.

The Palestinians found the hijacking of civil aircraft particularly effective. As a form of blackmail it was comparatively easy (airport security being at that time rudimentary) and achieved maximum publicity, which was especially attractive to people whose hatred of Israel extended to all – in general 'the West' – who could be classed as Israel's friends.

In September 1970 members of George Habash's Popular Front for the Liberation of Palestine hijacked three New York-bound airliners, British, Swiss and U.S. (they failed with a fourth, Israeli and better guarded) and forced them to land at Dawson's Field, an airfield in Jordan. Most of the hostages were released, but 56 were held until Arab terrorists in captivity in western Europe (including Leila Khaled, in British custody after failing to hijack an Israeli airliner in England) were released. The three captive airliners were meanwhile blown up.

Other groups, with no popular cause and little support in the community, achieved even less, although they tended to be the most ferocious. In general, they gained more publicity than their activities justified. An example was the so-called Baader-Meinhof gang, a small group of less than 20 active members devoted to the destruction of 'bourgeois' society. They were responsible for the deaths of about 30 innocent people but hardly represented a threat to West German society. Their middle-class leaders, Andreas Baader and Ulrike Meinhof (motto: 'Don't argue, destroy'), were arrested in 1972. They later committed suicide in prison, though their organization, the 'Red Army Fraction', lived on into the 1980s.

The name expressed their sympathy with the most ferocious of all terrorist groups, the Japanese 'Red Army', 14 of whom were brutally tortured to death by their own comrades for expressing dissent over a policy decision. Three others, who had trained with the Palestinians in Lebanon, carried out the lunatic massacre at Lod airport in Israel in May, killing about 30 people in a suicide attack.

The most sensational terrorist attack of the year took place in Munich during the Olympic games in September, when a Group who took the name 'Black September' (after the Palestinian defeat in Jordan) broke into the Israeli athletes' quarters. Owing at least partly to a rescue attempt that went wrong, 11 Israelis were killed as well as four terrorists and a German policeman. Three terrorists were captured but later released by the Germans in exchange for hostages from a hijacked airliner.

1973

JANUARY–DECEMBER

TRUCE
IN VIETNAM

MILITARY COUP
IN CHILE

EGYPT ATTACKS
ISRAEL

Ceasefire in Vietnam

On January 27 representatives of the United States, South Vietnam, North Vietnam and the Vietcong, meeting in Paris, agreed on a ceasefire. A Council of National Conciliation was set up to prepare for elections.

Although heavy U.S. bombing of North Vietnam was renewed late in 1972, the withdrawal of troops continued. The ceasefire agreement, described by President Nixon as bringing 'peace with honour' (an unfortunate phrase: it had been used by Neville Chamberlain at Munich in 1938), merely endorsed the U.S. pull-out. It did not end the fighting between North and South Vietnam and, in fact encouraged civil war in Laos and Cambodia, where U.S. bombing was stopped only after Congress withdrew funds.

The North Vietnam delegate signs the peace agreement.

Siege of Wounded Knee

The settlement of Wounded Knee in the Oglala Sioux reservation, South Dakota, was occupied on February 27 by about 200 American Indians and sympathizers. Their leaders were members of a civil rights group, and they were protesting against the U.S. government's policy towards their people, including a long list of historical grievances.

Wounded Knee Creek, the site of the last major battle between whites and 'Indians' in 1890, was held for over two months. Two people were killed and much of the settlement was destroyed before an agreement was reached between the occupiers and federal officials.

At Wounded Knee an armed Indian stands guard over a group of government officials who were held prisoner for over an hour before being released.

Allende dies in Chile coup

In Chile, which had a better political record than most of its neighbours, democratic government came to an end on September 11. In a military coup which, unlike many such events in South America, resulted in hundreds of deaths, President Salvador Allende's government was overthrown. Allende himself was one of the victims, allegedly by suicide. With the aid of the CIA, an extreme right-wing government took over, headed by General Augusto Pinochet.

Allende had been the surprise winner of the presidential election of 1970. Sometimes described as the first Marxist to win a free national election, he led a 'popular front' type of government, which included both Communists and assorted Socialists. Attempts, covertly encouraged by the United States, were made by the right to prevent him taking office (the army commander was assassinated for adhering to the constitution), but they failed, and Allende's initial policies – nationalization of mines and banks, overdue land reforms – were generally popular in Chile. However, he was seduced by the siren call of revolution, or perhaps he was simply afraid of offending the extreme left. He alienated the middle classes by pushing ahead with less obviously just reforms, he provocatively flaunted good relations with Castro's Cuba, and he adopted an ostentatious lifestyle which irritated Socialists. On top of that, a disastrous fall in the price of copper, Chile's prime earner, led to runaway inflation, with disastrous effects on the economy and, ultimately, on Allende's government.

President Salvador Allende.

Yom Kippur War

On October 6, on the Jewish 'Day of Atonement' (Yom Kippur), Egyptian forces attacked across the Suez Canal. They took the Israelis by surprise. Blasting through sand fortifications with water cannon, they pierced the Israeli defences at several points. At the same time the Syrians, supported by units from Jordan, Iraq, Morocco and Saudi Arabia, attacked the Golan Heights.

The Six-Day War of 1967 had been followed not by peace but by a war of attrition, in which Israeli aircraft raided targets in Egypt while the Egyptians launched sporadic attacks against the Israeli defences east of the Suez Canal. By 1970 hostilities had reached such a pitch that, with Soviet pilots actually flying missions from Egypt, a direct clash between the two superpowers appeared possible. This was averted by the truce of August 1970. Both sides took steps to strengthen their defences.

The death of Nasser in September brought a more subtle strategist to power in Egypt, Anwar Sadat, who achieved greater union among Arab states, including both the 'revolutionary' regimes like Syria's and 'conservative' ones like Jordan. He got rid of Soviet 'advisers' after the Soviet Union failed to provide the support he wanted, and took a leaf out of the Israelis' book by effecting a surprise attack.

The Egyptian advance, however, was carried too far – beyond air cover – and as a result the Israelis were able to counter-attack, break through across the Canal and surround a large Egyptian force. U.S. pressure prevented a total Israeli victory. Meanwhile, the Syrian offensive was checked and, after two days' fighting, Syrian forces were thrown back.

A UN ceasefire, though not immediately obeyed, ended the war, which had lasted longer than anyone expected. The Egyptians and Syrians fought much more effectively than in 1967, and although defeated, had established a stronger moral position vis-à-vis Israel, from which Sadat was ultimately able to open negotiations to regain Sinai. Meanwhile, the Israelis pulled back a short distance on both fronts, one result of which was that the Egyptians were able to reopen the Suez Canal for the first time since 1967.

Another feature of the Yom Kippur War was the Arabs' use of the economic power they held as a result of their possession of a large proportion of the world's oil resources. By cutting off oil supplies to the United States (and to one or two other Western countries) while reducing production and sharply raising prices, they discovered a new and effective weapon – although, in its effect on the world economy generally, it proved to be a double-edged one. ▶ *page 353*

▶ *page 353*

A Syrian tank with mine-clearing equipment in operation near the Israeli border.

1974 End of dictatorship in Portugal

JANUARY–DECEMBER

COUP IN PORTUGAL

TURKEY INVADES CYPRUS

NIXON RESIGNS

ETHIOPIAN MUTINY

A coup instigated by junior and middle-rank officers on April 25 put an end to the authoritarian regime in Portugal, which had survived the retirement of Antonio Salazar in 1968. A military junta was installed under the presidency of General Antonio de Spinola.

The main cause of the rebellion was disillusionment with the anachronistic persistence of imperial pretensions in Africa, where the rebellious Portuguese colonies had imposed a devastating strain on Portugal's economy and young manhood. Students, forced to serve in the colonial wars, played a significant part in arousing opposition, and Spinola himself was a former colonial governor highly critical of Portuguese imperialism.

The movement for reform in the armed forces was far from being united. Spinola's presidency lasted only six months, and for two years Portugal appeared to be on the brink of civil war. However, an attempted Communist takeover in 1975 helped to unite moderates of both the left and right and a new constitution was introduced the following year, although for some time governments proved fragile.

General Antonio de Spinola (centre) with fellow members of the military junta which overthrew the Caetano government in Portugal.

Northern Ireland executive collapses

On May 28 the new Northern Ireland executive, which provided for power-sharing between Protestants and Catholics, collapsed. The Sunningdale agreement of 1973 had been rejected by the voters of Northern Ireland in the British general election of February 1974, and the executive was finally brought down by a succession of strikes and riots organized by Protestant extremists. Direct rule from Westminster was reimposed.

British policy in Northern Ireland was constantly thwarted by incompatibles. On the one hand, the need for thorough reforms and power-sharing was recognized. On the other, those reforms had to be democratically approved, which the Protestant majority would never do. The British government also insisted on an end to violence before beginning a dialogue with republicans, while the first priority of Sinn Fein was the withdrawal of British troops. The British feared that such a step would be followed by a massacre by the terrorist groups on either side.

Supporters of the Protestant Ulster Workers' Council standing behind street barricades.

Turks invade Cyprus

On July 20 Turkish forces invaded the island of Cyprus. The Turks acted five days after the president, Archbishop Makarios, had been overthrown in a coup backed by the military government of Greece.

The unsatisfactory political situation in Cyprus had until then remained stable largely because of the presence of UN peacekeeping troops, but no real success had been achieved in reconciling the Greek and Turkish communities. The root cause of the latest crisis was the ambition of the government of 'the colonels', who had taken power in Greece in 1967, to bring about the union of Cyprus with Greece. They had quarrelled with Makarios and supported the heirs of General Grivas, EOKA B. However, despite their attempts to destabilize the Makarios regime, the archbishop had been re-elected president in 1973 without opposition. Losing patience, the colonels then instigated the coup against him. Makarios escaped in a British helicopter, and the rebels installed an EOKA gangster, Nikos Sampson, as president. He lasted less than a week, while the Turks seized the opportunity to invade.

A ceasefire was arranged within two days and the military government in Greece, faced with mutiny among its rank and file when it ordered war on Turkey, collapsed. A conference was arranged between the three guarantors of Cypriot independence – Greece, Turkey and Britain. Turkey took a strong line and when negotiations broke down reopened hostilities, occupying nearly half of Cyprus and making thousands of Greek Cypriots homeless. A new constitutional agreement was patched up, and Makarios returned as president, but in reality Cyprus remained partitioned into Greek and Turkish regions, with economic disruption, a large refugee problem and the presence of Turkish troops adding to the island's apparently insuperable problems.

Turkish troops, part of the force that invaded Cyprus on July 20, keeping careful watch behind the ceasefire line.

Nixon forced to resign

The greatest political scandal in U.S. history culminated with the resignation of President Richard M. Nixon on August 9. Having been discredited and proved to have lied outrageously about his involvement in the Watergate affair, Nixon faced impeachment unless he resigned voluntarily.

A crucial factor was the judgment of the Supreme Court that the 'White House tapes' – incriminating recordings made of conversations among Nixon and his aides which revealed an extensive programme of 'dirty tricks' to discredit opponents – must be handed over to the Senate investigating committee.

Nixon was succeeded by the vice-president, Gerald Ford, who had only recently attained that office on the resignation of Spiro T. Agnew, disgraced by tax-evasion charges. The whole affair arguably demonstrated the inherent strength of the U.S. political system, since it survived this crisis virtually unscathed.

The Lion of Judah loses his throne

The long reign of the astute but elderly emperor of Ethiopia, Haile Selassie, came to an end on September 12. A mutiny by army officers spread to other ranks. The 81-year-old emperor was deposed and thrown into prison, where he later died, possibly murdered.

After a series of brief governments, Colonel Haile Mariam Mengistu emerged as the dominant figure in Addis Ababa. The country was, however, gravely divided, and the new Mengistu regime, which gained the support of the Soviet Union, never actually controlled Eritrea and Tigré in the north nor parts of the south. To famine, poverty and discord were added the horrors of persistent civil war. ▶ *page 384*

1975

**INDEPENDENCE
FOR ANGOLA**

**CIVIL WAR IN
LEBANON**

**SOUTH VIETNAM
FALLS**

Lebanese gunmen in Beirut
behind a barricade after the
failure of yet another peace
initiative.

Angola independent – but war continues

Serious fighting broke out in Luanda on March 27, following an agreement on Angolan independence signed in Portugal in January. Portugal's precipitate abandonment of its colonies (except Macao) after the revolution of 1974 had in Angola the effect of turning the war of liberation into a civil war.

The January agreement had been signed by the three groups which had conducted the guerrilla war against the Portuguese during the previous 15 years. They were the MPLA (Marxist), possessing close links with Cuba; the FNLA, backed by Zaïre; and UNITA, a breakaway group from the FNLA and, like it, tribally based. Apart from signing the agreement, the three groups showed no inclination to co-operate, and the first clashes took place the day after.

Angola became a cockpit of the cold war as well as the focus of African rivalries. The MPLA had Soviet aid, Cuban mercenaries and, largely for tribal reasons, it dominated the area of Luanda. It drove out the FNLA, which began to get U.S. arms through Zaïre, while Jonas Savimbo's UNITA also received U.S. support as well as active assistance from South Africa, whose troops at one point advanced to within 100 miles of Luanda. European mercenaries were also involved, and Angola collapsed into virtual anarchy. ▶ *page 385*

A parade celebrating Angola's independence.

The battleground of Beirut

On April 13 civil war began again in the Lebanon. It was provoked by a massacre of about 25 Palestinians by the Phalange, the Christian Maronite militia, which resulted in retaliation by the PLO against Christians.

The conflict escalated until, by the end of the year, it had become a civil war between Maronites and Muslims, with the front line running through the middle of Beirut. Christians attacked the Palestinian camps while Muslim and Druse forces, backed by the PLO, besieged Christian villages in the Beqa'a valley. The government collapsed and the army began to split into Christian and Muslim forces. By March 1976 the Maronite leaders were forced on to the defensive. ▶ *page 349*

The dominoes fall

Khmer Rouge guerrillas, using elephants as transport, on the move in western Cambodia.

The Communists were victorious in the southeast Asian peninsula in April, as the Khmer Rouge took over Cambodia (April 17) and South Vietnam fell to the forces of the North (April 30). The Pathet Lao gained control in Laos, which became in effect a client state of Vietnam.

Although the South Vietnamese army was one million strong and armed with the best weapons the United States could provide, it lacked the motivation to resist the Communist offensive. With

346

the fall of Da Nang at the end of March, resistance crumbled. Saigon itself fell a month later, the last Americans escaping as the North Vietnamese entered the city virtually unopposed. President Thieu had already fled to Thailand, berating the Americans. A number of army officers committed suicide and a huge refugee problem was created.

Phnom Penh, the capital of Cambodia, also deprived of U.S. support, had fallen to the Khmer Rouge two weeks earlier. The new regime was headed by Pol Pot, and its first act was to drive the two million inhabitants of Phnom Penh into the countryside in pursuit of Pol Pot's eccentric economic theories. This was the beginning of a reign of terror in Cambodia, now renamed Kampuchea, as the Pol Pot regime gained a reputation as one of the most savage in history, slaughtering its own people on a genocidal scale. An additional horror was that the killings were not massacres but were mostly individual murders, often preceded by appalling tortures and sometimes carried out by boy soldiers of the Khmer Rouge less than twelve years old. ▶ *page 356*

Australian prime minister dismissed

A rare constitutional crisis occurred in Australia on November 11, when the governor-general, Sir John Kerr, dismissed the prime minister, Gough Whitlam.

Controversy centred on the governor-general's right to take such action. Government had been virtually brought to a stop for several weeks because the opposition combined to block Whitlam's budget. The governor-general, who was appointed by the queen on the advice of the prime minister – Whitlam himself in this case – took the view that if the prime minister were unable to get parliamentary support for essential measures he was bound to resign. When he did not do so, Sir John dismissed him. A caretaker government took over, and in the subsequent election Whitlam's Labour party was defeated.

'Green March' in Sahara

On November 6 King Hassan of Morocco mounted an invasion of Western Sahara. It was unusual in that the 350,000 participants were not soldiers and carried no weapons. It was a 'Green March', a propaganda move to emphasize Morocco's claim to the region, and the marchers later withdrew.

The Spanish colony of Western Sahara was claimed by Morocco and by Mauritania. Following the 'Green March', an agreement was made in Madrid for the former colony to be jointly administered by the two claimants.

The agreement, however, ignored the strong local desire for independence, manifested by a nationalist movement known as the Polisario. The Polisario declared independence and resisted Moroccan and Mauritanian forces.

The conflict continued for years. Mauritania reached agreement with the Polisario, while Morocco attempted to take over the whole territory. Failing to do so the Moroccans built a fortified wall which divided the economically important north (Moroccan territory) from the area ruled by the Polisario.

Indonesians invade East Timor

Following civil war in East Timor and the flight of refugees to Indonesian West Timor, Indonesian forces invaded on December 7. Their purpose was to suppress communism, but they rapidly established control of the country.

With independence imminent in the Portuguese colony, a struggle for power broke out in August between the UDT, a movement favouring continued association with Portugal, and the Communist FREITLIN (which Portugal, since the 1974 revolution, tended to favour). A third, much smaller group favoured integration with Indonesia. In November, the Portuguese having left, FREITLIN declared the colony an independent republic. Following the Indonesian takeover (condemned by the UN), FREITLIN, which had a considerable army with Portuguese weapons, continued to resist. Thousands of people were killed during the next ten years. By that time FREITLIN had been virtually exterminated, but resistance persisted in the mountains, and the Indonesians continued to torture and massacre the East Timorese.

Baton-wielding police charge a group of pro-independence demonstrators in East Timor.

Military takeover in troubled Argentina

Soweto riots

A demonstration in Soweto, the black township near Johannesburg, On June 15 led to widespread violence throughout South Africa. A large crowd gathered, protesting at the new rule that some subjects in school should be taught in Afrikaans. They ignored an order to disperse and began throwing stones at the police. The crowd numbered about 5000, and the 50 policemen (mostly black), fearful for their lives, opened fire. Two students were killed and several wounded. Rioting swept through Soweto and spread to other parts of the country. By the time the troubles died down, over 250 people had been killed. ▶ *page 370*

On March 24 the president of Argentina, Isabel Perón, was overthrown by the military. She had proved a thoroughly incompetent head of government and few regretted her departure, which was effected without violence.

The shadow of Juan Perón is a long one in Argentina's history. After his overthrow in 1955 he had gone into exile in Spain. There he was a source of constant provocation to Argentina, whose dissatisfied citizens tended to look back to a Peronist golden age. In 1973 he returned, but failed to work the required miracle and alienated leftist elements previously inclined to support him. He died in 1974, whereupon his second wife, Isabel, as vice-president, succeeded him.

Extremists became more prominent. On the left, the so-called Monteneros adopted the tactics of terror, murdering a number of army officers and top businessmen. The students were in almost permanent revolt and sporadic outbreaks of violence occurred all over the country.

When the military finally lost patience with Isabel Perón and installed a junta of service chiefs, the situation became much worse. Revolutionary violence was quelled, but at a high cost, as death squads operating outside the law but with government connivance kidnapped political opponents, or people they disliked, and killed them. Mass graves were found later, but many of the *desaparecidos* ('disappeared') remained unaccounted for – in some cases their bodies had been dropped into the Atlantic. Over 10,000 people died in this 'dirty war'.

President Isabel Perón deliving a speech in Buenos Aires a few weeks before her deposition in a bloodless coup.

Armed police coming to grips with rioters during violent demonstrations in Soweto.

Syrians invade Lebanon

Syrian regular forces intervened in the civil war in Lebanon on June 9. They had entered the country a few weeks earlier, when President Assad's reluctance to embroil himself in the internecine strife of Lebanon was overcome by fear of leftist revolution and perhaps Israeli participation.

Paradoxically, the Syrian forces came to help not the Palestinians, in whose cause they had clashed with Jordan, nor other Muslim groups, but the Christian Maronites, who currently held little more than eastern Beirut and appeared to be in imminent danger of extermination.

Once more it was the unfortunate Palestinian refugees who bore the brunt of the violence. With Syrian protection, the Maronites under Michael Amoun captured the Palestinian camp of Tal al-Zaatar in August. Syrian forces advanced southwards, though not far enough to risk provoking Israel into action and, with the PLO in disarray, a cease-fire was arranged in November. According to Lebanese sources, about 35,000 people had been killed since the outbreak of civil war in April 1975.

President Assad of Syria.

Gang of Four arrested

Chiang Ching, Mao's widow.

On October 11, only a few weeks after the death of the 'Great Helmsman' Mao Tse-tung, a profound change in China was signalled by the arrest of the 'Gang of Four', Mao's closest associates (they included his widow), who had largely manipulated the old Communist ruler in his last years. The coup which struck them down was supported by government officials and the security services, not least the army, and was motivated by a determination to avoid another episode like the Cultural Revolution.

For many years the intransigence of Maoism had been balanced by the relative moderation of Chou En-lai (Zhou Enlai), the prime minister. In 1974 Chou survived another campaign by the Maoist radicals, whose attack on Confucius and the Confucian tradition was a thinly veiled attack on him. Chou died eight months before Mao, leaving as his political heir Deng Xiao-ping, who had narrowly survived the Cultural Revolution, had twice been purged from the leadership, but was probably the most powerful man in the country by 1975, when Chou and Mao were both fading away (Deng himself was well past normal retirement age).

With the disgrace of the Maoist radicals, Deng's power was confirmed, and he instituted far-reaching economic reforms, virtually abandoning the communist system and even allowing a stock market. Extensive though they were, Deng's reforms did not extend to the political sphere. The Communist party remained in total control.

Deng Xiao-ping, Mao's successor, initiated radical reforms.

1976

JANUARY
4 15 die in tit-for-tat sectarian murders in Northern Ireland
8 Gandhi government in India assumes extra powers

FEBRUARY
11 OAU recognizes MPLA government in Angola
13 Nigerian president General Mohammed assassinated
26 Spain cedes Western Sahara to Morocco and Mauritania
27 Polisario Front proclaims independence of Western Sahara

MARCH
14 Egypt terminates friendship treaty with the Soviet Union
24 President Isabel Perón overthrown in Argentina

MAY
28 U.S.–Soviet treaty limiting underground nuclear tests
31 Syrian forces enter Lebanon

JUNE
9 Syrians attack Palestinians in Lebanon
12 Coup in Uruguay
15 Over 100 die in Soweto riots
16 U.S. ambassador in Beirut kidnapped and murdered
25 Idi Amin declared president for life in Uganda
27 Palestinian terrorists hijack airliner to Entebbe, Uganda

JULY
2 Socialist republic declared in united Vietnam
2 Sudan breaks relations with Libya after attempted coup
4 Israeli commando raid at Entebbe
21 British ambassador to Ireland killed by IRA mine

AUGUST
12 Palestinian camp of Tal al Zataar in Beirut captured by Christians
31 Hundreds killed in Rhodesian raids on guerrilla camps in Mozambique

OCTOBER
6 Violent military coup in Thailand following civil unrest
6 Anti-Castro Cubans blow up Cuban airliner, killing 73
11 Gang of Four arrested in China
28 Conference on Rhodesia opens in Geneva
31 Rhodesian raids on Mozambique continue

DECEMBER
14 Geneva conference on Rhodesia ends without agreement
19 Mozambique-based guerrillas kill 27 on Rhodesian tea plantation

ENTEBBE RESCUE

THE HIJACKING of airliners proved an effective form of terrorist blackmail, hard to prevent – at least until international airlines and airports learned a few lessons in security – and even harder to defeat, once the initial action had been successful. Not surprisingly, since it was the country that faced the greatest threat of terrorist attack, Israel proved the most determined and – in spite of several botched efforts – the most adept at circumventing and defeating the airline hijackers.

On June 27 an Airbus of Air France, on a scheduled flight from Tel Aviv to Paris, was hijacked at Athens (a notoriously insecure airport) by the PFLP (Popular Front for the Liberation of Palestine). The operation was probably planned in Paris by the Venezuelan-born terrorist 'Carlos' (Ilich Ramirez Sanchez, son of a millionaire Communist), who had shot three French policemen a year earlier and led the operation to kidnap OPEC ministers in Vienna in December 1975. Two of the hijackers were Palestinians and two were Germans, members of the 'Red Army Fraction' or Baader–Meinhof gang. The pilot was forced to fly to Entebbe in Uganda, where the murderous buffoon Idi Amin, who had once declared himself a friend of Israel but had since taken up the cause of the Palestinians, received the hijackers co-operatively. They were allowed to remove themselves and their 268 hostages to a hangar. Ugandan troops stood guard, and several additional terrorists were allowed to join the hijackers.

The hijackers released most of the hostages but retained about 90 who were Israeli citizens, as well as an elderly British Jewish woman, Dora Bloch. They threatened to kill them all if 50 Palestinian terrorists held in the jails of Israel and other countries were not released.

While negotiations continued at Entebbe, the Israelis, with the co-operation of several other governments, including Kenya, were planning a rescue operation. They arrived on the night of July 4, with three large Hercules transport aircraft, having flown 2500 miles non-stop. In a brief but spectacular attack, all 13 terrorists, including the four hijackers, were killed, as well as 35 Ugandan soldiers and one hostage. Eleven Ugandan MiG fighters were also destroyed. The rescued hostages boarded the transports which flew back to Israel, refuelling in Kenya on the way.

One other hostage was missing. Dora Bloch had been taken ill and conveyed to an Entebbe hospital. Amin sent troops to find her and they murdered her at the hospital. Amin himself, having congratulated his troops for 'repelling the invaders', continued his reign of devastation and mass murder (among his victims in the next few months was the Anglican archbishop of Uganda, murdered on his orders).

Opposite. Above left. Rescued hostages being greeted by their relatives on their return to Israel.

Opposite. Above right. Seen here with her granddaughter, Dora Bloch, who was murdered by Ugandan soldiers.

Opposite. Below. Simon Peres (left), the Israeli defence minister, with members of the Entebbe rescue team.

Above left. Idi Amin, a recent convert to the Palestinian cause, speaking to journalists.

Far left. Major General Dan Shomron, the Israeli soldier in overall command of the Entebbe operation.

Left. 'Carlos', the international terrorist who was reputedly responsible for the planning of the Entebbe hijacking.

Zaïre invaded by Angolans

Moroccan troops at Kolwezi airport in Zaïre. They had been brought in to help suppress a revolt in Shaba province.

On March 8 a small force from Angola invaded the province of Shaba (formerly Katanga) in Zaïre. It coincided with a rising inside Shaba itself. The mineral wealth of the province made the revolt more significant than it would otherwise have seemed to the outside world.

The Lunda peoples of Angola and Zaïre were closely related and had combined in the FNLA, which had contested with the MPLA for control of Angola. Some of their guerrillas had been trained by Cubans in Angola and Cuba was suspected, probably wrongly, of encouraging the invasion. Since the Zaïrean army was a largely ineffective force, some 1500 Moroccan troops, transported by the French and financed by Saudi Arabia, were flown in to repel the invaders.

A similar revolt took place the following year, when Belgian and French paratroopers were sent in to evacuate Europeans.

Military takeover in Pakistan

Zulfikar Ali Bhutto, the beleaguered prime minister of Pakistan, was overthrown on July 5. The army installed General Zia ul-Haq as president of a repressive military regime. Bhutto was jailed and, two years later, hanged.

Widespread civil unrest had followed the general election in March, won by Bhutto's PPP (Pakistan People's Party). Fraud was alleged, but the rioting took place mainly in areas where the PPP was weak and, while Bhutto admitted to some irregularities, neutral observers considered that the announced results of the election were genuine.

President Zia ul-Haq, who headed the new military regime in Pakistan.

Egypt attacks Libya

Egyptian soldiers captured in the fighting with Libya.

After a series of provocative acts by Libya, which led to armed clashes on the border, Egypt retaliated in July with a limited military operation. Egyptian troops in some force crossed the border, and the Egyptian air force attacked the Libyan base at El Adem. A ceasefire was arranged a few days later, with PLO chairman Yasser Arafat and other Arab leaders acting as mediators.

Ogaden war breaks out

Guerrillas of the Western Somali Liberation Front on their way to fight the Ethiopians.

One of Africa's many simmering territorial disputes turned into full-scale war on August 8. The Somalis made a new attempt (they had twice been repulsed in the 1960s) to conquer the Ogaden region from Ethiopia, supporting the Western Somali Liberation Front with army 'volunteers' who, however, eventually comprised an invasion force numbering 50,000 men.

Having cut Ethiopia's main transport link – the railway which joined Djibouti and Addis Ababa – and overrun most of the Ogaden, the Somalis almost succeeded in capturing the vital strategic centre of Harar in November. However, the Soviet Union, having recently replaced the United States as Ethiopia's chief source of military aid, suddenly withdrew the support it had

hitherto given to Somalia. The 4000 Soviet advisers in Somalia were transferred to Ethiopia and all military supplies stopped. Cuban troops were airlifted to Addis Ababa along with weapons. In the following March the Somalis were forced to withdraw from the Ogaden, after being defeated by an Ethiopian counterattack made possible by Soviet air power.

Racial strife in Sri Lanka

The hostility between Sinhalese and Tamils broke into open violence on August 14. Over 100 people died in Jaffna, the chief town of the Tamil region. Extremism had been growing for some time, encouraged by the policies of Mrs Bandaranaike's government, which included discrimination against Tamils. Communal riots had occurred before. However, the 1977 outbreak was not only more serious, but was the prelude to greater strife. ▶ *page 366*

Sadat addresses the Knesset

The most sensational diplomatic event of the year took place on November 21 when Anwar Sadat, president of Egypt, visited Israel. Although welcomed by Israeli prime minister Menachem Begin, he had virtually invited himself, with an unexpected plea for peace a few days earlier. He laid a wreath at an Israeli war memorial and told the Knesset (the Israeli parliament) that 'we (he meant the Arabs, but most would not have agreed) welcome you among us with all security and safety'. He also pointed out that the Palesti-

nian question would have to be settled justly and that the Israeli-occupied territories would have to be given back.

Sadat's gesture led eventually to the Camp David agreements mediated by President Jimmy Carter a year later. Meanwhile, it aroused ferocious hostility in most Arab countries and, in effect, forfeited Egypt's leadership of the Arab world. The denunciations of Algeria, Libya, Syria and South Yemen were such that Egypt broke off relations with them. ▶ *page 355*

1978 Revolution in Afghanistan

JANUARY–DECEMBER

COUP IN AFGHANISTAN

SHAH OF IRAN DEPOSED

Pause in Chad's civil wars

The Chad president General Malloum declared a ceasefire on February 6. Civil war had been in progress almost continually since the mid-1960s.

The original conflict had been between the government and a liberation movement in the north, FROLINAT. By 1978 the rebels controlled three-quarters of the country, but the movement was split into two antagonistic factions – the FAN, led by Hissene Habré, and the FAP, led by Goukouni Oueddei, which had Libyan support. Their hostility was accentuated by Libya's seizure of a small strip of territory, the Aozou, which was accepted by Goukouni but was opposed by Habré. Goukouni was at first dominant and would have seized control of the government but for the intervention of French troops at the request of Malloum (who had earlier insisted on their leaving the country). Habré, commanding considerable forces himself, then joined the government at Malloum's invitation. The government collapsed in 1979, and this was followed by fierce fighting, sectarian massacres and anarchy as all three armies contended.
▶ *page 366*

Soldiers of the French Foreign Legion in Chad guarding youths rounded up after a skirmish.

In a violent coup on April 27, Mohammed Daud Khan, president of Afghanistan, was overthrown. The coup was organized by the group known as the Khalq ('the masses'), the dominant wing of the People's Democratic party (broadly Communist), which was mainly Pathan in composition. Its leaders, Nur Mohammed Taraki and Halizullah Amin, consequently came to power.

Daud had been president of Afghanistan since the monarchy was overthrown in 1973 (he was in fact a cousin of the deposed king). He had been supported at that time by the PDP, but subsequently they had fallen out. Though largely reliant on the Soviet Union for aid, Daud also attempted to exploit the East-West divide with the aim of obtaining concessions from the West. The leaders of the Khalq had been jailed in 1977 and their supporters subjected to persecution. However, they had gained support in the army, as the success of the coup against Daud showed.

The new regime introduced radical social reforms which aroused powerful opposition, especially among the landowners and the Muslim clergy. It also antagonized the Russians.

Mohammed Daud Khan, ousted president of Afghanistan.

354

Messages of peace from Camp David

The president of Egypt, Anwar Sadat, and the prime minister of Israel, Menachem Begin, agreed on September 17 to make peace. The announcement followed a week of discussions at Camp David, a rural retreat of the U.S. president (Jimmy Carter), who was given credit by both sides for negotiating the agreement.

The Camp David agreement followed from the dramatic peace initiative begun by Sadat the preceding year and Carter's eagerness to defuse the ongoing Arab–Israel conflict. The agreement itself left much undecided and was chiefly remarkable for its spirit rather than any· concrete

Sadat (left), Carter and Begin sign peace agreements.

proposals. In fact the 'spirit of Camp David' evaporated somewhat, and the signing of the treaty that was supposed to follow from the agreement at the end of the year was postponed, though it was completed five months later.
▶ page 361

Rhodesian forces invade Mozambique

On September 20 Rhodesian forces launched a series of attacks on guerrilla camps of the Patriotic Front in Mozambique. Estimates of casualties ran into four figures, and it was alleged that some targets were not guerrilla bases at all.

The guerrilla war in Rhodesia was intensifying, and the Smith government was increasingly isolated by economic sanctions, by the hostility of neighbouring regimes in Zambia and Mozambique, and by the withdrawal of South African support, as well as by the activities of the guerrillas. Smith therefore reached an agreement with moderate black African opponents such as Bishop Abel Muzorewa on a form of majority rule – to become effective at the end of the year though postponed for 'technical difficul-

ties' – which nevertheless provided safeguards for continued white dominance. The new constitution was rejected by the Patriotic Front, which consisted of a fragile alliance of two parties, ZANU, mainly Shona and led by Dr Robert Mugabe, and ZAPU, predominantly Ndebele and led by Joshua Nkomo. The guerrilla war, marked by atrocities, continued. ▶ page 359

The shah of Iran admits defeat

On December 30 an opposition leader, Shahpur Bakhtiar, became prime minister of Iran after all efforts to subdue popular opposition to the shah's government had failed. He took office on one condition: that the shah leave the country.

In the 1970s the shah's relentless drive towards greater wealth and power for Iran had resulted in inflation and other economic difficulties. His regime had also been marked by ferocious oppression, carried out by a particularly brutal security force, SAVAK. It aroused fierce resentment (seriously underrated by the shah, who was out of touch with his own people), especially among the conservative clergy, as well as among political radicals, liberals, and in fact practically all sectors of the population bar members of the police and army and the small minority of the rich and corrupt. Serious anti-government riots took place at the beginning of the year. As the disturbances gath-

Shahpur Bakhtiar, the shah's last prime minister.

ered momentum, the shah alternately promised reform and instituted suppression. Massive demonstrations in Tehran in on 'Black Friday' (September 8), in which hundreds of people were

shot, prompted a declaration of martial law. Revolution was kept on the boil by messages from the outlawed clerical leader, the Ayatollah Khomeini, in Paris.
▶ page 356

1979 Khomeini back in Iran

JANUARY–MARCH

KHOMEINI RETURNS TO IRAN

SINO-VIETNAMESE WAR

IDI AMIN FLEES UGANDA

Just two weeks after the shah had fled the country, the Ayatollah Khomeini returned, landing at Tehran on February 1. He received a huge and hysterical welcome, and announced his intention of overthrowing the government and appointing a new one himself.

An elderly, frail-looking clergyman, Khomeini was possessed of inveterate hatred of the shah and all Western influence. Since going into exile to escape arrest in 1964, he had become the focus of Islamic revolutionary activity (and not only in Iran). His return to the country was a remarkable triumph. An Islamic republic was proclaimed, and Khomeini's word became law. Though a civil government was appointed, it had little power and was subject to every unpredictable word Khomeini cared to utter from his refuge in the holy city of Qum. Fundamentalist Islamic groups rounded up anyone they suspected of less than total commitment to the cause and executed them, usually after blatantly unjust trials. The Islamic regime was as intolerant and as savage as that of the shah, though perhaps less corrupt. ▶ *page 358*

The Ayatollah Khomeini at a press conference.

Vietnamese forces take Phnom Penh

On January 7 Vietnamese forces took possession of the Kampuchean (Cambodian) capital Phnom Penh, while Pol Pot and his henchmen fled to the north. The Vietnamese attack began shortly before the New Year after months of growing conflict in border areas.

Cambodia and Vietnam were old enemies, with longstanding territorial disputes. The Vietnamese invasion was provoked by Khmer Rouge incursions and was rapidly victorious. A puppet government was then installed in Phnom Penh. It was composed largely of Khmer Rouge dissidents, and although some social reforms were attempted, the new government was crude and oppressive. However, almost any government was preferable to that of Pol Pot, who was now reduced to waging guerrilla war from the mountains.

Anti-Khmer Rouge Cambodian soldiers on patrol in difficult terrain.

China launches invasion of Vietnam

Chinese artillery in action in Vietnam.

On February 17 Chinese forces crossed the border of Vietnam. During a short but savage war, they captured the provincial capital of Lang Son, thereafter announcing that their purpose was accomplished and that they were withdrawing their forces.

China was traditionally hostile to Vietnam, although it had provided temporary support during the Vietnamese war. It was also afraid of growing Soviet influence in its own 'backyard' – one reason for its rapprochement with the United States, which was bitterly resented in Vietnam. There were other reasons for hostility too, such as rivalry in the South China Sea and the persecution of Chinese in Vietnam (many fled to China, whether voluntarily or not). For Peking the Vietnamese invasion of Cambodia was the last straw.

The Chinese attack did not prevent the Vietnamese taking control of Cambodia, but to have persevered further with the invasion would have been costly and would have risked Soviet intervention.

Idi Amin driven out of Uganda

The barbarous tyranny of Idi Amin in Uganda came to an end on March 29. An invasion by Tanzanian troops and Ugandan rebels of the National Liberation Army took the capital, Kampala, without much difficulty, and Amin fled.

Amin was one of three African rulers, heading regimes so grotesquely evil that they appeared to be mentally deranged, who were driven from power in 1979 (the others were in the Central African Empire and Equatorial Guinea). During Amin's eight-year tyranny, about 500,000 people had died violent deaths.

Unfortunately, his removal did little to restore Uganda to peace and prosperity. His immediate successor, a well-meaning academic, lasted only two months and his replacement, a lawyer, not much longer. At the end of 1980 Obote at last regained the presidency. His rule, however, was little less violent than Amin's and equally disastrous for Uganda's economic and social stability. ▶ *page 372*

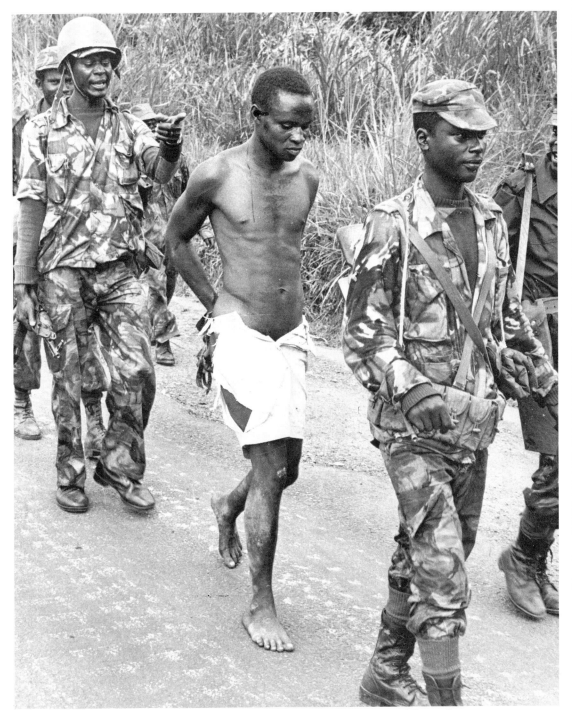

A Ugandan soldier being marched away by Tanzanians after the capture of Kampala.

1979

JANUARY
1 Formal Sino–U.S. diplomatic relations restored
7 Vietnamese take Phnom Penh
16 The shah flees Iran
30 White Rhodesians approve Smith's majority-rule constitution

FEBRUARY
1 Ayatollah Khomeini returns to Iran
6 Coup in the Congo (Brazzaville)
10 General Zia imposes Islamic law in Pakistan
12 60 die as Rhodesian airliner is shot down
14 U.S. ambassador to Afghanistan kidnapped and killed
17 Chinese invade North Vietnam
22 Renewed clashes between Kurds and Shi'ites in Iran

MARCH
3 Chinese take Lang Son in Vietnam
4 Tanzanian forces advance into Uganda
8 Women demonstrate against Islamic laws in Tehran
11 Libyan troops arrive in Uganda to aid Amin
16 Chinese withdraw from Vietnam
13 Grenada government overthrown by New Jewel movement
22 British ambassador to the Netherlands assassinated by IRA
26 Egypt and Israel sign peace treaty
29 Idi Amin flees Kampala
30 IRA bomb kills British MP Airey Neave
31 Iranian referendum approves Islamic republic

APRIL
2 Vietnamese publish evidence of Khmer Rouge massacres in Cambodia
4 Former prime minister Zulfikar Ali Bhutto executed in Pakistan
7 Prominent Iranians executed include a former prime minister
11 Idi Amin formally deposed as Tanzanians and Ugandan rebels take Kampala

MAY
8 24 demonstrators shot dead in San Salvador
9 Italian army mobilized in drive against Red Brigades terrorists
25 Israelis begin withdrawal from Sinai

JUNE
2 Huge crowds welcome Polish-born Pope John Paul II in Poland
4 Flt Lt Jerry Rawlings leads Ghana coup to restore democracy
6 State of siege declared in Nicaragua

357

1979

SANDINISTAS VICTORIOUS

SOVIET ARMY INVADES AFGHANISTAN

Somoza ejected

The Somoza dynasty which had held power in Nicaragua since 1936 came to an end on July 17. After resisting intense opposition for many months, President Anastasio Somoza fled the country. His fate had been sealed when the United States finally withdrew all support in February.

The revolutionary FSLN (Sandinista Front for National Liberation) had been waging guerrilla war for some years, but what eventually doomed the Somoza regime was the growing antagonism of the middle classes, which approached open rebellion after the assassination of newspaper publisher Pedro Joaquín Chamorro in 1978.

Soon after Somoza's flight, the Sandinistas seized power. They put in motion a genuine social revolution, but their Communist affiliations and strong links with Castro's Cuba antagonized the U.S. government. Their own speeches hardly helped: appeals for U.S. aid were accompanied by denunciations of U.S. policy past and present. When the Sandinistas themselves supplied aid to Communist rebels in El Salvador, U.S. aid to Nicaragua was cut off. The Sandinistas also alienated others, such as the native American and Afro-American people of the Miskito coast, whose traditional antagonism to Managua was heightened by Sandinista interference. Within a year the various opponents of the Sandinistas had formed a new 'liberation army', later known as the 'Contras', in Honduras; many of its leaders had been members of Somoza's notorious 'death squads'. ▶ *page 382*

Guerrilla war in El Salvador

On October 16 the military dictator of El Salvador, General Carlos Romero, was overthrown. The coup was organized by junior army officers with reformist ideals, who installed a junta that included civilian members. It promised social reform, democracy and an end to the political murders by unofficial 'death squads'.

None of those aims was achieved, and El Salvador was plunged into an interminable civil war, the horrors of which outstripped those of the military dictatorship, in which rebellious Marxist groups combined as the FMLN (Farabundo Marti National Liberation Front), named after the Communist leader killed during the *matanza* (massacre) of 1932.

Below. Menacing-looking and heavily armed National Guards on patrol in a village street in El Salvador.

U.S. embassy besieged

Militant students imbued with religious fervour demonstrating outside the U.S. embassy in Tehran.

A band of young Islamic revolutionaries besieged the U.S. embassy in Tehran on November 4 and took the 53 inmates as hostages. The act was universally condemned, except by other Islamic fundamentalists, and typified the ferocious opposition to the United States which the triumph of Khomeini in Iran had encouraged throughout Islam.

The seizure of the embassy and its staff was provoked by the presence of the shah in the United States. He had gone to receive treatment for a fatal disease, but his opponents suspected the U.S. authorities of planning to restore him to his throne.

The seizure of the hostages was naturally resented in the United States, and their release became the paramount aim of the U.S. government. Failure to secure it reduced President Carter's popularity and played a part in his failure to gain re-election in 1980. ▶ *page 360*

The end of Rhodesia

At a conference in Lancaster House, London, in December, the rebellion in Rhodesia came to an end. Agreement was reached, rather unexpectedly, on the temporary restoration of British rule (from December 12) pending fully democratic elections. All parties, some more eagerly than others, embraced the agreement.

Guerrilla warfare organized by the Patriotic Front, international opposition and economic boycott, withdrawal of South African support, massive emigration by whites – these and other factors had threatened defeat for Ian Smith's Rhodesian regime,
and in 1977 he had reached a power-sharing agreement with the moderate African leaders. On the basis of that agreement, approved by a referendum of whites, elections were held in April 1978, and Bishop Abel Muzorewa became prime minister of the renamed Rhodesia–Zimbabwe. The new constitution was not accepted by ZANU and ZAPU, the partners in the Patriotic Front broadly representing the Shona and Ndebele peoples respectively, nor internationally. Britain, in strict legal terms the responsible party, prepared a new constitution which provided for
genuine majority rule, without built-in white privileges. This was accepted at the Lancaster House conference, and Lord Soames was subsequently installed in Salisbury as British governor pending elections.

The elections held four months later, the fairness of which was disputed, gave a majority to Dr Robert Mugabe, the leader of ZANU, who had been the most uncompromising of the African opposition leaders during the years of the Smith regime. A deepening split between ZANU and ZAPU soon ended hopes for a united and peaceful state.

Soviet invasion of Afghanistan

On December 25 Soviet forces invaded Afghanistan. At least four motorized divisions crossed the border, while airborne troops seized the airport at Kabul and a special forces unit took over the government buildings, killing the president, Hafizullah Amin.

The victory of the Khalq, one wing of the Peoples' Democratic Party, in 1978 had failed to pacify the country and proved disappointing to the Soviet Union, fearful that Islamic opposition in Afghanistan would spread to Soviet Muslim republics across the border. A massacre of Soviet advisers underlined the regime's less than subservient attitude to Moscow.

Having disposed of Amin, the Russians installed as president Babrak Karmal, leader of the other wing of the PDP, the Parcham.

The Soviet invasion, prompted by fears for Soviet security, was seen in the United States as an example of Communist aggression, and the angry U.S. response was echoed in the Muslim world – paradoxically, in current circumstances. The U.S. reaction – stopping the export of grain, refusing to let U.S athletes appear in the Moscow Olympic Games, etc. – was ineffectual but the Soviet Union, opposed by Mojahedin guerrillas secure in mountain bases, soon found itself embroiled in a 'no-win' situation, analogous to that of the United States in Vietnam. ▶ *page 376*

Afghan guerrillas who formed the backbone to the ferocious resistance to the Soviet invasion.

1980
JANUARY–DECEMBER

IRAQ AND IRAN
AT WAR

ABORTIVE
U.S. RESCUE

U.S. raid on Tehran ends in failure

An attempt on April 25 to rescue the U.S. hostages seized in Tehran in November 1979 ended in failure. Although President Carter had previously ruled out the use of force to solve the crisis, he backed the attempt. Failures among the helicopters resulted in the mission being aborted while refuelling was being carried out in the Iranian desert. A helicopter then collided with a tanker aircraft and eight U.S. servicemen were killed.

The outbreak of war with Iraq made Iran eager to recover assets frozen in the United States and negotiations began for an exchange. The hostages were finally released in January 1981, on the day of President Ronald Reagan's inauguration.

A U.S. helicopter prepares to take part in the ill-fated rescue mission to Tehran.

Knightsbridge siege

Smoke and flames pour from the Iranian embassy in London.

In the latest example of an attack on foreign diplomats, terrorists seized the Iranian embassy in London's fashionable Knightsbridge district on April 30. The five terrorists took 19 hostages and demanded the release of Iranian Arabs held in prison in Iran.

After five days of tense negotiations, the terrorists shot one of their hostages, the Iranian press attaché, and threatened to shoot another every 30 minutes. An SAS (Special Air Service) unit then stormed the building, some of them abseiling from the roof through the rear windows. One other Iranian hostage was killed, together with four of the five terrorists.

Iraqi forces invade Iran

Iraqi forces launched an invasion of Iranian territory at several points on September 22. The attack, concentrated in the south, followed a series of clashes on the border.

The Iraqi dictator, Saddam Hussein, had several reasons for attacking Iran, including hostility to the Khomeini regime and fear of its effect on Iraqi Shi'ites who formed a majority, though a downtrodden one, of the population. Older sources of trouble were Iranian encouragement of the Iraqi Kurds against the Baghdad government and the Shatt al-Arab waterway, which lay between the two countries and had been a subject of dispute since the 16th century.

The opportunity for the invasion was presented by current Iraqi military strength, built up by Saddam Hussein over several years, and current Iranian weakness in the wake of the Islamic revolution and the loss of U.S. support. Saddam was banking on a swift victory, and initial advances suggested that he had obtained it. However, the Iranians rallied, held the Iraqis, and eventually took the offensive. Under their intransigent rulers, the two countries became involved in a long and bloody war.

▶ *page 368*

Saddam Hussein addressing Iraqi soldiers before the invasion.

1981

MURDER OF
SADAT

MARTIAL LAW IN
POLAND

Victory for Spanish democracy

In a remarkable episode, seen on television, members of the Spanish Guardia Civil invaded the Cortes (parliament) on February 23. They were led by a Colonel Tejero de Molina brandishing a pistol. His men carried more menacing weapons and held the 350 members hostage.

The man behind the coup was the Francoist General Milans del Bosch, who deployed troops in Valencia and declared a state of emergency. The coup was defeated when King Juan Carlos, in a broadcast message, roundly condemned it. The plot collapsed in 24 hours, and its failure marked the end of the schemes of reactionary army officers to put the clock back.

Tejero de Molina addressing the Cortes.

Sadat assassinated

The president of Egypt paid for his statesmanlike approach to Middle Eastern problems on October 6 when he was shot dead by soldiers of the Egyptian army at a military parade in Cairo. Several other people were killed, including one of the assassins, during the ensuing shootout. A state of emergency was declared and Hosni Mubarak, vice-president and heir apparent, took over as president.

Anwar Sadat, more popular in the West than in the Arab world, had plenty of enemies in his own country since he had espoused the cause of peace with Israel. He was also under attack from Islamic fundamentalists, who were inspired by the Khomeini regime in Iran and hated every aspect of Sadat's rule.

The scene after the assassination of Anwar Sadat.

Martial law in Poland

The ongoing conflict in Poland reached another crisis on December 15 when General Jaruzelski declared martial law. Solidarity was banned and its most prominent leaders, including Lech Walesa, were imprisoned. Civil rights were suspended and government was placed in the hands of a military council. Protest strikes were swiftly crushed.

The agreement that was reached between the government and Solidarity at the end of August 1980 was subject to varying interpretations. It attempted to separate political from economic functions, something difficult to achieve in a Communist state, and the demands of the workers, including free elections, became increasingly political in nature.

Conflict over the nature of the agreement kept Poland in turmoil for most of 1981, with frequent strikes on the one hand and changes in government personnel on the other. General Jaruzelski, who was in charge from February, had a reputation as a moderate, but his response to Solidarity's demands grew ever more repressive. The final crisis, which occurred not long after Jaruzelski had visited Moscow (where he was presumably encouraged to take a hard line or risk having it taken for him), was provoked by Solidarity's insistence on being given a role in running the crisis-ridden economy. Poland entered a period of stagnation, from which it was eventually to be released by *glasnost*.

Police making an arrest in Brixton, London.

Sheltering behind a wall of shields in Toxteth, Liverpool.

A burnt-out pub in Southall, London.

Petrol bomber in Belfast.

BRITISH CITIES TORN BY RIOTS

THE CIVIL CONFLICT in Northern Ireland grew in intensity in 1981, when more British troops were sent to the province and ten IRA men starved themselves to death in prison. In spite of sporadic acts of murder and sabotage in England and the Republic of Ireland, the violence had remained largely confined to the province of Northern Ireland itself. But in the summer of 1981, communal violence of another sort broke out on a large scale in England.

The first major explosion of Britain's long, hot summer, occurred in Brixton, a largely black, impoverished district of south London, in April. The spark that set off the blaze was a police operation against street crime, which was reaching epidemic proportions. When one black youth was arrested, a crowd gathered and tried to rescue him. Buildings and vehicles were burned and shops looted and smashed, as police battled with gangs of youths, both black and white. The riots raged for three days.

Black community leaders blamed the police for provoking the violence by their heavy-handed operations and prejudice against blacks. The police denied prejudice and maintained that a significant part in the riots had been played by 'agitators' from outside the area.

The worst riots of the summer occurred in July, in the run-down inner-city areas of Liverpool, Birmingham, Bristol and several other provincial cities as well as in several parts of London, including Southall, an area with a high proportion of ethnic Asians, and again Brixton. In Toxteth (Liverpool), CS gas was employed by the police (for the first time in mainland Britain) against gangs throwing petrol bombs. The Toxteth rioters succeeded in forcing the police to withdraw altogether for some time, a cause of fierce criticism from law-abiding shopkeepers whose businesses were looted and wrecked without interference from the police.

A root cause of the civil unrest, the worst in mainland Britain since the previous century, was the economic policy of the Thatcher government. Its efforts to combat inflation had resulted in high unemployment, especially among young blacks, producing resentment, frustration and sheer boredom, which found their outlet in violence. A report by a distinguished judge on the Brixton riots, published in November, blamed police harassment but also the attitude of community leaders, and drew attention to the growing distrust of authority among young people.

Opposite. Devastated buildings in Upper Parliament Street, Toxteth, bear witness to the scale of the rioting.

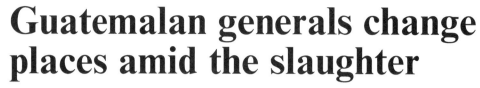

1982

JANUARY–DECEMBER

FALKLANDS
WAR

ISRAEL INVADES
LEBANON

Guatemalan generals change places amid the slaughter

In a coup organized by junior army officers on March 23, General Lucas García was removed from power in Guatemala. His position had already been undermined when President Carter ended U.S. aid to his brutal dictatorship. His replacement was Rios Montt, a dissident general who had been elected president in 1974 but prevented by the military from taking office.

Though he was an improvement on his predecessor, and checked the operations of 'death squads' in the towns, Rios Montt continued the genocidal war against the insurgent peasantry. This guerrilla war, which had gone on for many years, resulted in tens of thousands of deaths. Thousands of people had fled to Mexico. Rios Montt adopted a policy of forming peasant militias under army commanders, whose purpose was to hunt down opponents. Fearful atrocities were committed and large parts of the countryside was laid waste.

Rios Montt was himself deposed the following year and, with Washington now exerting pressure for social reforms in Central America, some reforms were introduced. Improvement was relative, however, and although the guerrillas were greatly reduced in numbers, the actions of the Guatemala government remained a particularly vicious example of contempt for human rights.

President Galtieri of Argentina.

Argentina invades the Falkland Islands

Argentine forces took over the Falkland Islands (Islas Malvinas), a British dependency, on April 2. The only defensive forces consisted of a company of Royal Marines in the capital, Stanley, who after a brief exchange of shots were ordered by the governor to surrender.

Although the Falklands had been a British colony for 150 years (the Argentine invasion was timed to coincide with this anniversary), Argentina had a long-standing claim to them, inherited from its former colonial master, Spain. The British were taken by surprise by the Argentine action, although Argentine diplomatic pressure had recently increased sharply and, a few days before the invasion of the Falklands themselves, a small party of Argentine scrap-metal dealers had landed on the associated island of South Georgia to dismantle a disused British whaling station – and raise the Argentine flag. The British government had prepared a compromise scheme on future sovereignty to submit to the Argentinian government, but had not considered so blatantly illegal an act as forcible seizure of the islands to be likely.

The main reason for Argentina's invasion stemmed from conditions inside the country. The military regime currently headed by General Leopoldo Galtieri, which had been in control since the removal of Isabel Perón in 1976, had failed to solve Argentina's problems. Inflation was approaching 300 per cent a year, foreign debts had rocketed and industry was disintegrating. New loans were unobtainable. At the same time thousands of Argentinians had been abducted and murdered. Galtieri hoped that the conquest of the Falklands, which was received with great enthusiasm in Buenos Aires, would reduce the unpopularity of his regime.

Just as the British government had failed to anticipate the Argentine attack, so the Argentinians failed to anticipate both the hostile international reaction (the UN Security Council, after intense British lobbying, voted 10 to 1 for an immediate withdrawal) and particularly the belated decision on the part of the United States to support Britain. Equally, they underestimated the British determination to retake the islands by force if necessary.

General Menéndez (left), commander of the Argentine forces in the Falklands.

Israelis invade the Lebanon

Israeli forces invaded southern Lebanon in force on June 6, allegedly in retaliation for the attempted assassination of the Israeli ambassador in London three days earlier. The operation was supposed to establish a 15-mile buffer zone north of the Israeli frontier, but in fact the Israeli forces advanced to Beirut.

There was heavy fighting, with the Syrian air force suffering heavy casualties and thousands of civilians being killed. A ceasefire with Syria was arranged after five days, but the Israeli troops continued to advance on Beirut, where they encountered greater resistance from the PLO. Muslim West Beirut endured heavy air assault, and eventually an agreement was mediated whereby the PLO agreed to evacuate Beirut, under protection of an international force. Most went to Syria; the rest to other sympathetic Arab countries. ▶ *page 366*

Argentine surrender

The military adventure essayed by the Argentine military government in the Falkland Islands (Malvinas) ended ignominiously on June 14. As British forces surrounded Stanley, a ceasefire was agreed and, after negotiations, the Argentine commanding officer, General Menéndez, accepted surrender terms.

The Falklands war was short but savage. The Argentine soldiers, mainly young conscripts, were unprepared for all-out war against a highly trained, and technically more advanced, professional force, although they were superior in numbers. The British, sending a powerful, 40-vessel task force through the Atlantic, ventured to land, at San Carlos, without secure air cover, and their ships proved vulnerable to bombs and Exocet missiles launched from Argentine ships and aircraft. The British also sacrificed some of their support internationally by an apparent reluctance to seek a negotiated agreement and by sinking the chief Argentine warship, the elderly cruiser *General Belgrano*, at a moment when she posed no real threat to British operations.

On the *Belgrano* 368 lives were lost. The total casualties in the campaign were: British 255, Argentinian 750. Besides securing the Falklands, the campaign had the widely welcomed result of dislodging General Galtieri's military regime. A civilian government now took over in Argentina and, although it was somewhat in thrall to the military, the political murders stopped.

The *General Belgrano* sinking after being torpedoed by a British submarine.

Massacre in the camps

On September 16 Christian Lebanese troops entered the Palestinian refugee camps of Sabra and Chatila in West Beirut, ostensibly to search for PLO gunmen. They then killed hundreds of helpless people.

Although Israelis were not involved, their presence in the vicinity and their tacit alliance with Lebanese Christians, whose entry to the camps was encouraged by the Israeli commander, suggested that they could have prevented the massacre if they had wanted. There were angry protests, even in Israel, and later, after an inquiry, several Israeli leaders were censured.

The slaughter was provoked, partly at least, by the assassination of the president-elect, Bashir Gemayel, a few days earlier, although it was unlikely that the PLO was associated with that killing. After the massacre, the multi-national force (U.S., French, British and Italian) was reinforced. The Israelis also remained, hoping for a peace agreement and harassed by attacks from Shi'ite militias and PLO men who found their way back into the Lebanon and eventually re-established themselves in the Palestinian camps.

Hundreds die in Sri Lanka riots

Riots in Colombo broke out on July 23 following the killing of 13 soldiers by the Tamil Tiger guerrillas. The riots were partly encouraged, by the Sinhalese terrorist group JVP, which had been quiescent in recent years.

The riots, in which hundreds of people (mostly Tamils) were killed, marked a serious deterioration in communal relations, already poor. The Tamil Tigers, who were committed to an independent Tamil state, gained many recruits, and violence increased until the country was on the verge of civil war. The JVP, too, became a threat to the government once more. ▶ *page 375*

A Sri Lankan soldier standing by a dead Tamil.

Chad gets U.S. warplanes

The presidents of Zaïre and Chad (standing left and right).

The Habré government received military aid from the United States as well as from France on August 6 when two AWAC surveillance aircraft and eight F-15 fighters landed at the capital, Ndjamena.

The interminable civil wars in Chad were renewed in 1983; and Libya, which, having acquired the Aozou strip in the far north, now coveted the whole of Chad, intervened on behalf of Goukouni and the northern rebels. The

Habre government sought, and received, help from France and the United States. The country was temporarily divided on the 16th parallel, with the Habre government controlling the south and Goukouni plus the Libyans (whose presence was denied by Colonel Gaddafi) the north.

Foreign troops were withdrawn the following year, after an agreement, and another lull set in while both sides prepared for a renewal of war.

Mass killings in Beirut

At dawn on October 23 a truck approached the residential quarters of the U.S. peacekeeping forces in Beirut. It crashed through several barriers and into the lobby of the building, where it exploded, killing 241 marines. Simultaneously, a similar suicide attack was made against the French barracks, where 58 men died.

The multinational force in Beirut had at first been welcomed but Shi'ites and Palestinians soon turned against it as it supported the Lebanese army, a predominantly Christian force. An Israeli withdrawal was agreed with the Lebanese government in May, though the terms of the agreement were unacceptable to other parties, and the Lebanese army took over from the Israelis in West Beirut. The army was soon forced to retreat by Shi'ite and Palestinian resistance and, following the Israeli withdrawal, was also defeated in southern Lebanon. U.S. forces attempted to give assistance by bombarding Druse villages from the battleship *New Jersey* off the coast. French and U.S. air attacks were also made against terrorist bases and Syrian missile sites. The multinational force, the original reason for whose presence no longer existed, was increasingly exposed. The bulk of them were withdrawn early in 1984.

The belief of many Shi'ites that martyrdom would be rewarded with a blessed afterlife in paradise explained the willingness of volunteers to give their lives in suicide attacks – the most difficult type of attack to prevent – against their enemies. The same spirit largely accounted for Iranian success in the war against Iraq, where limited territorial gains were made at tremendous sacrifice in lives. ▶ *page 370*

Aquino shot

Benigno Aquino, the chief opponent to the Marcos regime in the Philippines, was assassinated on August 21 as he left the aircraft that had brought him back (against the advice of his friends) to Manila from exile in the United States. Conveniently, his alleged assassin was also shot dead in the fracas. A set-up, organized by Marcos's chief of staff, was widely suspected.

The assassination proved counter-productive. It galvanized domestic opposition, it shocked the United States, and it provoked a demand for Marcos's resignation from the Roman Catholic primate, Cardinal Sin.

The aftermath of a bomb attack on the U.S. Marine Battalion HQ in Beirut.

U.S. marines invade Grenada

U.S. forces landed in the Caribbean island of Grenada on October 25, a week after a revolt had overthrown the government (and two days after the massacre of the marines in Beirut, perhaps a contributory reason for the Grenada action).

U.S. intervention had been requested by a group of neighbouring Caribbean governments, but the operation initially encountered widespread international criticism. Even Britain, the former colonial ruler, currently enjoying particularly close rela-

tions with the United States, attempted to dissuade the U.S. government from the operation.

In the event, the rebels were crushed with only minimal U.S. casualties and, though the prime minister, Maurice Bishop, had been killed, democratic government was restored with the apparent approval of the vast majority of Grenadans. The U.S. government's accusations of Cuban involvement and of intent to construct a Soviet airbase, however, were exaggerated and gave credence to the belief that Reagan

protested a trifle too much in his search for moral justification for the invasion. (The 700 Cubans present were mainly construction workers, though they had had paramilitary training, and the airport under construction was found to be quite unsuitable as a military base.)

At the same time, the successful U.S. operation acted as a warning to both Cuba and the Sandinistas in Nicaragua that, in the event of U.S. intervention in those countries, little help could be expected from the Soviet Union.

A U.S. soldier keeping watch over Grenadans captured during the invasion.

MARCH

23 U.S. President Reagan proposes Strategic Defence Initiative ('Star Wars')

APRIL

18 Suicide bomb attack on U.S. embassy in Beirut

MAY

4 Iran outlaws Tudeh (Communist) party
20 17 killed by ANC car bomb at South African air force HQ

JUNE

24 Syria expels PLO leader Arafat and attacks PLO bases in Lebanon

JULY

10 Polisario forces attack Moroccans in Western Sahara
15 Armenian terrorists kill seven in explosion at Paris airport
23 Communal riots in Sri Lanka

AUGUST

21 Benigno Aquino assassinated at Manila airport
22 Violent anti-government protests in Philippines

SEPTEMBER

1 269 killed as South Korean airliner is shot down
8 Contra air attacks on Managua
26 General ceasefire agreed in Lebanon

OCTOBER

5 Nobel Peace Prize awarded to Lech Walesa
6 Emergency rule imposed in the Punjab
9 North Korean bomb kills four South Korean ministers
22 Anti-nuclear-missile protests throughout Western Europe
23 241 U.S. and 58 French troops killed in Beirut suicide attacks
25 U.S. invasion of Grenada
27 Grenada revolt crushed

NOVEMBER

4 South African white referendum approves limited power-sharing
4 40 Israeli soldiers killed in suicide attack in Tyre, Lebanon
15 Independent Turkish–Cypriot republic declared in Cyprus
27 Widespread anti-Marcos demonstrations in the Philippines

DECEMBER

10 Civilian regime under Dr Raúl Alfonsín inaugurated in Argentina
17 IRA car bomb kills five at Harrods store in London
21 15 French soldiers killed by bomb in Beirut
31 Economic failure and corruption provoke new Nigerian coup

1984

**VIOLENCE IN
AMRITSAR**

**IRA BOMB IN
BRIGHTON**

Iran-Iraq war continues to escalate

Air attacks by Iraq on Iranian cities in February were a new development in the war between Iran and Iraq. On the ground, the initiative still lay with Iran, which captured Majnoon island in the south in the same month, though overall there was virtual stalemate.

Iraq had recently received help from other Arab states which, however, hostile to Saddam Hussein, were more worried by the fundamentalism of Khomeini. Iraq was thus able to fight the war largely on foreign subsidies. Iran had no such rich friends and relied mainly on its oil revenue. This explained another new tactic by Iraq which, having been frustrated on land, began attacking Iranian oil tankers and the oil terminal on Kharg Island. Unlike most Iranian cities, the Kharg terminal could be reached by Iraqi military aircraft.

This attempt to widen the war and provoke a world oil shortage was to have little immediate effect – the Iranians promptly upgraded another, safer terminal and the world price of oil did not rise significantly – but it carried the threat of international involvement. ▶ *page 374*

Libyan diplomat murders London policewoman

During a demonstration by opponents of Gaddafi outside the Libyan embassy in London on April 17, a shot was fired from inside the embassy. It killed a policewoman on duty there. The British government broke off relations with Libya and expelled all its diplomats, including the unidentifiable murderer.

Flowers laid at the memorial to Yvonne Fletcher.

Indian troops storm the Golden Temple of Amritsar

Jant Jarnail Singh Bhindranwale (centre).

Prime minister Indira Gandhi.

In a massive display of force, including tanks and artillery, the Indian army captured the chief shrine of the Sikhs, the Golden Temple of Amritsar, on June 6. About 1000 Sikhs, not all of them separatist guerrillas, were killed, including their leader, Sant Jarnail Singh Bhindranwale.

Of the many dissident groups in India, the Sikhs presented the greatest threat. Agitation for a Sikh state of Khalistan based on the Punjab had reached a violent pitch at the beginning of the 1980s, with attacks on prominent Hindus and Indian government officials as well as on Sikh moderates. The Golden Temple was turned into a terrorist fortress, and a state of emergency was declared in Punjab state. Riots, violence, terrorist murders and massacres continued. Over 100 people were murdered in the three months beginning in March, government authority in Punjab virtually collapsed, and when the Sikhs announced they would prevent grain leaving the state (which would have meant famine in the rest of India), the government of Indira Gandhi decided to act to subdue the rebels holding out in the Golden Temple.

The attack shocked all Sikhs, produced further disturbances in the Punjab and led to mutinies by Sikh troops in the Indian army. In October, Mrs Gandhi was shot dead by two Sikh members of her bodyguard, which led to ferocious reprisals against innocent Sikhs in many parts of India. Rajiv Gandhi, the late prime minister's son, took over the government and succeeded in stopping the massacres. His obviously honourable intentions combined with popular sympathy led to his election with a huge majority in December, but he, too, would ultimately fail to solve the problem of the Sikhs.

The IRA fails to kill the British cabinet

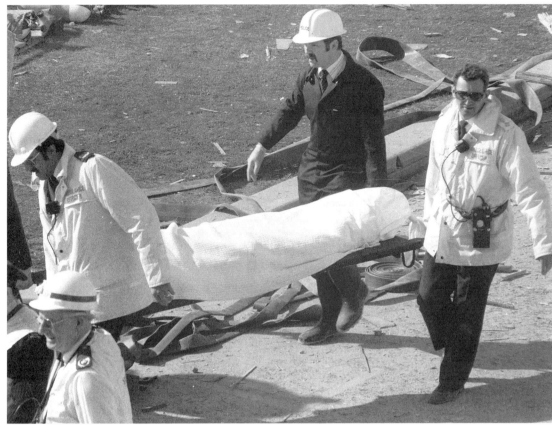

A victim is removed by ambulance men from the Brighton hotel.

On October 12 a bomb planted by an Irish terrorist exploded in the Brighton hotel where British ministers and other members of the Conservative party were staying during the annual party conference. Five people were killed, including an MP, and two cabinet ministers were among the injured. However, the bomber's main target, Prime Minister Margaret Thatcher, was not hurt.

Britain agrees to hand over Hong Kong

Following an agreement reached earlier in the year, a treaty was signed between China and Britain on December 19 providing for the return of Hong Kong to China in 1997. The New Territories, comprising 90 per cent of the area, were occupied under a lease due to expire in that year. The people of the colony of Hong Kong itself had no voice in the agreement, which granted Hong Kong special dispensation under Chinese sovereignty for 50 years. Meanwhile, Britain began to introduce greater democracy in the colony. The details of the December treaty remained somewhat vague, and there was no provision for enforcing the terms relating to the continuance of civil liberties after the colony had been handed over.

The British ambassador to Beijing, Sir Richard Evans, in close consultation with the deputy Chinese foreign minister, Zhou Nan.

369

The generals back off in Brazil

Twenty-three years of military rule in Brazil came to an end on January 15 with the election of Tancredo Nevés as president. However, his death shortly afterwards led to the succession of his little-known deputy, José Sarney.

The withdrawal of the military from government was largely motivated by recognition of its inability to deal with Brazil's huge and increasing social and economic problems. Sarney, although taking a strong and independent line – for example, by abandoning the strict monetary policy insisted on by the World Bank as the condition for loans – had too small a political power base, and, with inflation spiralling out of control, he lost the 1989 elections, giving way to the youthful Collor de Mello, who instigated a drastic monetary programme, defeating inflation at the cost of massive recession and unemployment.

Hezbollah HQ bombed

Up to 80 people were killed on March 8 when a large car bomb exploded outside the Shi'ite, pro-Iranian Hezbollah headquarters in West Beirut. The instigators were believed to be a Maronite terrorist group financed by Saudi Arabia and backed by the CIA. Though many were killed, the main target, Sheikh Mohammed Hussein Fadlallah, alleged to be the mastermind behind the kidnapping of Western hostages, escaped.

This was but one incident in the continuing havoc wrought by warring parties in the Lebanon. Israel was in the process of gradually withdrawing from all of Lebanon except for a southern border strip, where they had organized a small 'South Lebanon Army' to guard the buffer zone. As the Israeli forces fell back, war broke out between dissident Christian forces and the various Muslim groups in the area of Sidon, as a result of which the Christian population was driven out. In May the Shi'ite Amal group led by Nabih Berri launched a new attack against the beleaguered Palestinian refugees in the Shaba and Chatila camps, the beginning of a long siege.

One hopeful sign appeared in December when an agreement on a new constitution was signed by Elie Hobeiqa, the leader of the Lebanese (Maronite) forces, and the leaders of Amal and the Druse, and with the consent of the Syrians. This agreement lasted for just two weeks, until Hobeiqa was ousted.

Nimeiry toppled in Sudan

The military ruler of the Sudan, General Nimeiry, was removed from power on April 5. He was abroad at the time, and the action of the army officers who organized the coup was motivated by fear of a more radical revolution.

The main conflict in Sudan, one which long preceded its independence (1956), was between the Muslim north, linked to the Arab world, and the poorer, largely non-Muslim south, more attuned to neighbouring African countries. The Khartoum government generally followed oppressive policies in the south, and the constantly simmering conflict was punctuated by outbreaks of open civil war. Nimeiry had come to power in a military coup in 1969, and at first pursued a pro-Egyptian policy, successfully overcoming attempts to dislodge him in which Libya and Ethiopia were involved. As troubles in the south increased, the economy headed downwards; various opposition groups demonstrated against him, Saudi and U.S. economic support was cut, and the situation was aggravated by a large influx of refugees from Ethiopia and Chad. Nimeiry's fall seemed imminent. He resorted to fundamentalist Islamic policies, augmented by the activities of a ferocious secret police force, but the situation only deteriorated still further, famine being added to other miseries

Nevertheless he survived until 1985, when even the professional classes turned against him and the army decided on a pre-emptive coup. His successors, however, proved no more adept at extricating the country from the state of near ruin into which much of it had fallen.

Emergency in South Africa

After years of increasing disorders in the African townships, violence became more general with the new constitution granting representation to 'Coloureds' and 'Asians', and on July 20 President P.W. Botha imposed a state of emergency in certain areas. By that time over 500 people had been killed in the previous twelve months.

The Botha government had carried out a number of reforms in the previous few years, the effect of which had been merely to remove many of the pettier restrictions of *apartheid*. At the same time he had upheld the basic doctrine, and none of his reforms, including the constitutional change which gave representation to non-whites (but not black Africans), had impaired the white power structure. Nevertheless, strong opposition to any change had come from conservative and neo-Fascist Afrikaners.

The state of emergency – which also added to the more than 120 legal enactments that effectively gagged objective enquiry into or reporting of government or police actions against those opposing apartheid – was lifted at the end of the year but reimposed six months later and subsequently extended. By the end of 1986 deaths had reached about 2300, about half the victims being Blacks 'executed' by other blacks for collaboration. A favoured method of execution was 'necklacing' – placing a motor tyre around the victim's neck and setting fire to it. At the same time Botha's slow and cautious reform policy was maintained, with the abolition of the hated pass laws and desegregation of theatres, hotels and restaurants, and other public places. ▶ *page 382*

Black youths rioting in a South African township.

DESTRUCTION OF THE RAINBOW WARRIOR

The Greenpeace flagship *Rainbow Warrior* resting on the bottom of Auckland harbour.

ON JULY 10 the harbour of Auckland in New Zealand was shaken by an explosion. Just as people began gingerly to raise their heads again a second blast sent them diving for cover. When calm descended, a small ship in the harbour was seen to be listing badly at her moorings. The insignia of a dove in flight carrying an olive branch and the name Rainbow Warrior on her bow identified her as the property of Greenpeace, the international environmental group.

Founded in 1971, Greenpeace had a proud record of militant but non-violent opposition to states and organizations engaged in destruction or despoliation of the natural environment in pursuit of their own commercial, military or other selfish interests. Greenpeace members, young and idealistic, and the Rainbow Warrior herself, had taken part in many worthy campaigns on behalf of whales, dolphins, grey seals and other animals threatened with extinction. Particularly active on the oceans and in the polar regions, Greenpeace volunteers had risked disapproval, danger and even death as they tried to stop their targeted activities by simply getting in the way. Currently, they were aiming to get in the way of the French defence chiefs.

Their campaign was aimed at disrupting the French nuclear tests on Mururoa atoll in the Tuamotu Archipelago in the South Pacific. The Rainbow Warrior was to lead a fleet of seven vessels into the area to prevent a test being carried out. The protest was timed to coincide with Bastille Day (July 14), and no one was making any secret about it. Rather the reverse.

The explosions killed one man, a Portuguese photographer who was unlucky enough to be on board, and virtually destroyed the ship. At first the explosions were assumed to be accidental, but closer inspection revealed that they had been caused by limpet mines attached to the ship's hull under water, presumably by divers. A few days later New Zealand police arrested two people, Alain Mafart and Dominique Prieur. They turned out to be French agents, who had been acting on the orders of their government. Other agents had been involved, but they had evaded capture.

The New Zealand government not unnaturally protested very loudly indeed at this unparalleled example of state terrorism carried out within the jurisdiction of a friendly power. In France, after initial efforts to deny responsibility had collapsed ignominiously under the weight of the evidence, the defence minister had to resign, but otherwise the French treated the incident with remarkable complacency.

The two agents pleaded guilty and were sentenced to ten years' in prison. Later, however, the New Zealand government, finding that the French were able to make all manner of difficulties about New Zealand's vital trade with the European Community, allowed them to complete a shorter sentence on a remote French island in the South Pacific. Very soon they were returned to France – for health reasons, the French government brazenly asserted.

The affair played a part in increasing antagonism to nuclear weapons in New Zealand, which resulted in its withdrawal from the ANZUS pact, and in efforts to turn the South Pacific into a nuclear-free zone.

1986

**MARCOS
VOTED OUT**

**U.S. AIR RAID
ON LIBYA**

Abdel Fattah Ismail, former president of South Yemen, who died in a massacre of cabinet ministers masterminded by his successor, Nasser el-Hassani.

Slaughter in South Yemen

President Nasser el-Hassani summoned a meeting of the South Yemeni cabinet, or politburo, on January 13 which he did not attend himself. Instead, he sent his personal guards, who opened fire on the seated members with machine-guns. Several ministers were killed outright, including the vice-president, and Hassani's chief rival, Abdel Fatah Ismail (who had been president himself until Hassani toppled him in 1980). Others died later.

About 20 people died, but some ministers escaped – thanks to the intervention of their own guards – and a savage civil war broke out in Aden, largely along tribal lines. The suddenness of these events took foreigners by surprise. The Soviets, who had replaced the British as the chief foreign power (although their position was a fragile one), had a freighter in port which took off Soviet citizens. Other Europeans escaped in the British royal yacht, *Britannia*, which happened to be in the area.

The fighting lasted nearly two weeks, with an estimated 13,000 casualties and a much larger number of refugees who fled to North Yemen. Hassani was supported by the navy but his opponents had the tanks. He was defeated and fled to Ethiopia, having first ordered his men to burn down the Soviet embassy. As it happened, the Yemeni prime minister was abroad when the violence broke out, and he returned to take over.

No respite for Uganda

The government of Uganda, such as it was, led by the elderly general Titus Okello collapsed on January 26. Yoweni Musaveini, commander of the National Resistance army which had operated against Obote until he was overthrown by Okello in 1985, declared himself president.

Musaveini already exercised a reasonable degree of control over the south, but the north and west remained the territory of rebels and bandits. There were also troubles with the so-called Holy Spirit movement among the Acholi in the north, led by Alice Lakwena. The movement was virtually broken by the end of 1987 (its members having suffered grievously from their belief that they were invulnerable to bullets), but a new conflict then arose on the Kenya border, in which several people were killed.

Altogether, deaths through violence in Uganda since the deposition of Idi Amin had, by the end of 1987, reached a five-figure total. A government inquiry into atrocities in 1988 revealed appalling horrors. In most of the country, moreover, anarchy continued unchecked.

Marcos out

The corrupt and dictatorial regime of President Ferdinand Marcos of the Philippines came to an end on February 24. Elections held that month were clearly fraudulent. When Marcos announced he had won them, the opposition rose up in wrath. The opposition leader Corazan Aquino was sworn in as president, and the ailing dictator made a hasty exit from his palace in a U.S. helicopter.

Marcos had been president since 1965. From 1972, when he had declared martial law, he had been a dictator, and his regime had become autocratic, brutal and corrupt. It was increasingly unpopular but was sustained by the United States, though latterly with growing distaste.

The regime made a decisive blunder in 1983 with the murder of Benigno Aquino, the opposition leader who had been sentenced to death but reprieved during the 1972 coup. Under pressure from the Carter administration (much more sensitive than its predecessors to human-rights violations among its allies), Aquino had been allowed to go into exile in 1980 but decided to return to renew the challenge to Marcos in 1983. His murder, soon revealed as a government-organized political assassination, caused international and, more importantly U.S. opinion, to turn against Marcos while galvanizing the domestic opposition. There were constant demonstrations and protests, until Marcos made a second mistake in calling the elections of February 1986, which he claimed to have won but had patently lost. The opposition (with the exception of the Communist NPA – 'New People's Army') united behind Aquino's widow, Corazon.

The Aquino administration ended the excesses of the Marcos era but, in spite of introducing overdue reforms, had very little success in overcoming the many social and economic problems of the Philippines and failed to win over the NPA. After surviving several rightist plots, it adopted more authoritarian tactics against opponents. It survived on the immense popularity of Corazon Aquino herself.

Corazon Aquino conducting her election campaign.

U.S. launches air attack on Libya

In April President Reagan ordered a direct attack on Libya. The targets included bases in the region of Tripoli and Benghazi as well as Gaddafi's headquarters, where one of his children was killed. The attacks were launched on April 15 by aircraft from the U.S. 6th Fleet stationed in the Mediterranean and by F-111s flying from bases in England – signifying the approval of the Thatcher government for the U.S. action.

Relations between Libya and the United States, where Gaddafi was seen as the chief patron of international terrorism, had reached a nadir. The previous month he had ordered the unfortunate crews of several small naval vessels to attack the 6th Fleet exercising in the Gulf of Sirte and had launched a few SAM missiles in the same direction. The ships were sunk and the missile base was bombed, with a number of Libyan casualties.

Three weeks later terrorists bombed a discotheque in West Berlin which was a haunt of U.S. servicemen. One man was killed, together with a Turkish woman, and the United States accused Libya of complicity. As it happened, Gaddafi was probably not responsible for this attack, but U.S. conviction that he was provided the motive for the bomber strike.

BENINA AIRFIELD
15 APR 86

MIG-23/FLOGGER PIECES

DESTROYED MIG-23/FLOGGER

A Libyan airbase showing the destruction wrought by U.S. Navy planes.

New scandal rocks the White House

Shortly after the release of the U.S. hostage Dan Jacobsen on November 2 a Beirut newspaper revealed that his release had been secured by a secret deal whereby the United States supplied arms to Iran. Other evidence soon confirmed the truth of the report. Such operations were in flat contradiction to stated U.S. policy that no deals would be done with terrorists and to Congressional edicts banning arms sales to Iran.

President Reagan admitted that secret negotiations with Iran had been going on for 18 months and professed that he saw nothing wrong with that policy. The scandal became more serious when it was revealed that profits from the secret arms deals with Iran had been diverted to the Contras – the anti-Sandinista Nicaraguan rebels – whose funds had been stopped by Congress.

The people responsible for these clandestine operations were mainly members of the National Security Council, an advisory body to the president, in particular a hitherto unheard-of Lt Colonel Oliver North, who curiously enough became something of a national hero to the chauvinistic U.S. public in the course of Senate hearings on the Iran–Contras affair. A Congressional report published a year later condemned 'secrecy, deception and disdain for the law' on the part of those involved and concluded that 'if the president did not know what his national security advisers were doing, he should have.'

Although Reagan's reputation was slightly but permanently tarnished, it had little effect on U.S. power and policies.

Military coup makes Fiji a republic

Colonel Rabuka, who declared Fiji a republic.

On May 14 a small party of masked soldiers led by Colonel Sitiveni Rabuka invaded Fiji's government building and arrested the cabinet, most of whom were Indians. At the time much of the army was away in UN service, and the commander-in-chief was abroad. Rabuka demanded a new government of Fijians.

The main social division in Fiji was between the native Fijians and the descendants of Indian immigrants who had settled there when Fiji was a British colony. By the 1980s they outnumbered the Fijians, and in the elections in April they won a majority. Though the prime minister, Timoci Bavadra, was a Fijian, most of his ministers were Indians.

In the weeks following, the Rabuka coup seemed to be collapsing, as the governor-general refused to appoint Rabuka prime minister and the arrested ministers were released. A temporary compromise was arranged, in which the government was headed by a former prime minister, Sir Kamisese Mara, and contained Rabuka as well as – in a subordinate post – Bavadra. But when the governor-general announced a revised constitution which would give the two communities equal representation, Rabuka again rebelled, installing a new government in which the army was dominant. Rabuka, declaring Fiji a republic, instituted authoritarian controls, including arrest without trial. Many Indians began to leave the country.

'The tanker war'

What appeared to be a dangerous step towards internationalizing the Iran–Iraq war occurred on July 22. In response to a request from Kuwait the U.S. Navy began escorting Kuwaiti tankers in the Persian Gulf. In a move of doubtful legality Kuwaiti tankers were re-registered under the U.S. flag.

The 'tanker war' had begun in 1984 when Iraq, having failed to achieve its objectives on land, began to attack Iranian oil installations and tankers. Iran responded by attacking the tankers of Kuwait and other states on the grounds that they were helping Iraq. The intervention of the United States was seen in Iran as a hostile act.

Paradoxically, the main U.S. casualty in the Gulf was the frigate *Stark* which was hit in May by Iraqi missiles, killing over 30 sailors. Apparently the Iraqi pilot had mistaken the vessel for an Iranian ship. A similar but worse error was made the following year when the U.S.S. *Vincennes* shot down an Iranian airliner on a scheduled flight with nearly 300 casualties. Meanwhile, the Iranians had laid mines in the gulf, drawing in the ships of European nations as escorts and minesweepers. ► *page 376*

A U.S. marine stands guard over Iranian seamen captured when their landing craft was intercepted.

India intervenes in Sri Lanka

Indian troops in central Jaffna which they occupied after fierce fighting.

The Tamil guerrillas in Sri Lanka agreed to hand in their weapons to an Indian peacekeeping force in August. The Indian troops, reluctantly 'invited' by the Sri Lankan government, intervened to stop the growing violence, in particular the massacre of Tamils.

Indian policy was motivated largely by public opinion in the Indian state of Tamil Nadu (with its largely Tamil population), outraged at events in Sri Lanka, but the Indian-sponsored settlement did not stop the violence. The original peacekeeping force of 15,000, sent to protect the Tamils, was expanded to 60,000, sent to fight them. The Tamils repudiated the settlement after the mass suicide of 17 Tamil Tigers who had been captured trying to smuggle arms into the country, and the Indians occupied Jaffna after a siege in which they suffered about 500 casualties without seriously weakening the Tamil guerrillas. Sri Lanka's sorry state was further aggravated by the rising power of the JVP, the Sinhalese nationalist terrorist group, responsible for the deaths of numerous officials and policemen.

Having failed to restore peace in Sri Lanka, or to assuage the wrath of the Tamils in India, Rajiv Gandhi withdrew his troops towards the end of 1989.

Intifada

Riots took place among the Palestinians of the occupied West Bank and Gaza strip against the Israeli security forces on December 9. Gangs of youths threw stones, and Israeli soldiers opened fire, killing several. A general strike was called in the occupied territories and an underground committee formed to direct the campaign.

The riots turned out to mark the beginning of long-term violent resistance, known as the *intifada* after an Arabic word meaning 'shaking loose'. Palestinian officials resigned, reluctantly or not, and a few were murdered for alleged 'collaboration'. The Israeli government responded with draconian measures, beating up prisoners and burning villages. These tactics badly damaged its international image but failed to stop the outbreaks, which spread occasionally into Israel itself. Over 350 Palestinians were killed, as well as 11 Israelis, and thousands wounded in the first year of the *intifada*. Over 5000 young Palestinians were arrested and a few expelled.

Israeli soldiers interrogate a Palestinian family.

JANUARY
16 Reformist Chinese party chief Hu Yobang resigns
20 Hostage negotiator Terry Waite kidnapped in Beirut

FEBRUARY
13 Shi'ite militia prevent UN relief reaching Palestinian camps in Beirut
26 U.S. 'Irangate' commission report criticizes senior White House aides
27 Libyan troops withdraw from northern Chad

APRIL
8 Syrians end siege of Shatila camp by Shi'ites
13 Portugal agrees to return Macao to China in 1999
21 100 killed by bomb in Colombo bus station
25 Northern Ireland judge killed by car bomb

MAY
11 Indian government imposes direct rule in the Punjab
14 Coup in Fiji
17 Iraqi missiles hit U.S. frigate

JUNE
1 Helicopter bomb kills Lebanese prime minister Rashid Karami
19 ETA bomb kills 19 in Barcelona

JULY
14 Karachi bomb blast kills 72
22 U.S. warships begin escorting Kuwaiti tankers in the Gulf
29 Indian peacekeeping force sent to Sri Lanka
31 400 die in Iranian riots in Mecca

AUGUST
28 50 die in abortive revolt against Aquino government in Philippines
21 U.S. air attack on Iranian minelaying vessel

OCTOBER
1 Sporadic anti-Chinese riots in Tibet
6 Fiji declared a republic
6 200 Sinhalese massacred in revenge for suicides of captured Tamils
12 Heavy fighting between Indians and Tamils in Jaffna
30 French intercept ship carrying Libyan arms for the IRA

NOVEMBER
8 IRA bomb at Remembrance Day parade kills 11
25 16 missionaries slaughtered by Zimbabwe rebels

DECEMBER
8 Reagan and Gorbachev sign treaty removing intermediate-range missiles from Europe
17 Czechoslovak Communist leader Gustav Husak resigns

Soviet withdrawal from Afghanistan

On April 14, on a visit to Tashkent, where he met President Najibullah, President Gorbachev announced that Soviet troops would be withdrawn from Afghanistan. They began leaving a month later.

The war in Afghanistan had become, for the Soviet Union, a trap similar to that in which the United States had been caught in Vietnam. The Mojahedin could not be defeated, and the war was highly unpopular in the Soviet Union, where *glasnost* permitted freer reporting and TV coverage.

It was almost universally assumed that the Najibullah government would be swiftly defeated by the rebels, but this did not happen. The Mojahedin, never closely united, broke up into increasingly hostile groups and the Kabul government continued to hold its own.

Casualties in the war by 1990 were close to 500,000, and there were about seven million refugees, mostly in Pakistan. They were unable to return while the civil war continued, but since about 60 per cent of the farmland of Afghanistan had been destroyed, they had nowhere to go.

Soviet tank crews during the withdrawal from Afghanistan.

Iran accepts peace

A youthful Iranian soldier guards Iraqi prisoners.

A ceasefire in the Iran–Iraq war, on the basis of a UN resolution, was accepted by Iran on July 18. A year earlier it had refused (Iraq had accepted), but defeats suffered during an Iraqi spring offensive and the exhaustion of the economy had made even the Ayatollah Khomeini recognize that peace was essential, though he phrased his acceptance of this unpalatable fact in uncomprom- isingly hostile language. Total casualties in the war amounted to about 450,000.

Khomeini died less than a year later and was succeeded by Hoja- tolislam Rafsanjani. Although he showed no greater liking for the West, and was restricted by the fundamentalist clergy, he was a pragmatist who recognized the necessity of foreign aid if Iran were to recover.

South Africa finally agrees to independence for Namibia

An agreement signed in Geneva on August 1 provided for a solu- tion to the outstanding conflicts in southwest Africa. An imme- diate ceasefire was agreed between – on one side – the Ango- lan government, the Cuban forces supporting it and SWAPO (South-West African People's Organization, which had been fighting a guerrilla war in Nami- bia since 1966), and – on the other – South Africa. The diplomacy was mediated by the United States, which put considerable pressure on South Africa through economic sanctions, voted by Congress over President Rea- gan's veto in 1987. Namibia's independence was to follow the withdrawal of Cuban troops from Angola. Amid mutual sus- picions elections were held in Namibia in 1989 and a new constitution adopted in 1990, with the SWAPO leader, Sam Nujamo, becoming Namibia's first president.

New Caledonia remains French

On August 20 an agreement on New Caledonia was reached by the French government, the French settlers and the indige- nous people, the Kanaks. France resumed direct rule on a tempor- ary basis, and a referendum on the island's future was to be held in 1998. Those Kanaks in jail for acts of violence during the inde- pendence protests of the previous few years were, unless convicted of murder, released.

The settlement was fragile. A referendum in France approving the settlement, in which only 38 per cent voted, was rejected by the opposition, and the following May Jean-Marie Tjibaou, the Kanak leader who had negotiat- ed the agreement, was assassinat- ed by disillusioned extremists.

Military coup in Burma

On September 18 General Saw Maung led a coup in Burma and moved to break up the ongoing demonstrations in Rangoon. Within six weeks up to 1000 demonstrators were killed and student rebels left the city to join various resistance groups among the ethnic minorities.

In 1987 the regime had carried out a draconian currency reform, the effect of which was to rob most people of their savings. The first large-scale demonstrations broke out the following March, and were broken up with marked violence. Ne Win, still the effective power in Burma although he had officially resigned the presidency in 1981, admitted that reforms were necessary.

Demonstrations broke out again in June, and opposition now became more general, with General Aung Gyi, who was a former associate of Ne Win, taking the lead. Ne Win then resigned the party chairmanship, and Sein Lwin, who had com-manded the security forces against the demonstrators, took over. Aung Gyi and other leaders were arrested and martial law was proclaimed, but open opposition continued, and Sein Lwin resigned in August. He was replaced by Maung Maung, another member of the Ne Win power clique, though a civilian. As the country approached total anarchy, he promised political reform, but within a month the army stepped in.

The opposition united, and Aung San Suu Kyi, the daughter of independent Burma's first prime minister, returned from exile to become a focus for democratic hopes. Elections were

Aung San Suu Kyi, put under house arrest.

promised, and took place in 1990. Though these were disorderly, the opposition National League for Democracy appeared to have won a landslide victory. However, the results were ignored by the military regime and Aung San Kuu Kyi was placed under house arrest.

Ethnic conflict in Azerbaijan

On September 21 a state of emergency was declared in Nagorno-Karabakh, an autonomous region of the Soviet republic of Azerbaijan where the great majority of the population were Armenians. The quarrel between the Armenians and the Azerbaija-nis, itself an example of the many actual or potential ethnic conflicts within the Soviet Union, was concentrated in this region.

Large-scale demonstrations in Armenia, permitted expression by *glasnost*, took place earlier in the year, demanding the restoration of Nagorno-Karabakh in accordance with a vote taken in the region's assembly. Hostility between the two peoples degenerated into violence and massacre, particularly of Armenians in Azerbaijan. Soviet troops restored order and saw to the evacuation of some Armenians from dangerous areas, but Moscow refused to countenance revision of boundaries. Opposition and disorder continued, the party bosses of the two republics were sacked and further Soviet troops briefly restored a precarious peace. Violence on a larger scale

Armed personnel carriers in Stepanakert, Azerbaijan.

began in November, with what amounted to genocidal pogroms taking place in both republics and creating thousands of refugees. Another pause was effected in December by a disastrous earthquake in Armenia but, as the Soviet Union broke up in 1991, Armenians and Azerbaijanis continued to wage guerrilla war.

South American dictator overthrown

Alfredo Stroessner (left) with General Franco in Madrid.

On February 3, the dictator-president of Paraguay, Alfredo Stroessner, was overthrown after 34 years in power. He was given political asylum in Brazil. There was widespread popular approval for the leader of the coup, General Andres Rodríguez, who was moved to act because he was about to be politically 'neutralized' himself.

The collapse of the Stroessner regime was ultimately the result of differing views among the ruling class of what was likely to happen in future – Stroessner was 76 years old and failing. Rodríguez promised democracy and free elections (rather than the succession of Stroessner's son). The elections were held in May as promised, and Rodríguez was elected president.

Massacre in Tiananmen Square

On June 3–4 the students occupying the vast expanse of Tiananmen Square in Beijing (Peking) were dispersed by troops with great savagery. While the sheer mass of people, plus makeshift barricades, prevented some troops (who had been stationed in the vicinity for a considerable time) from penetrating to the centre of the city, the massacre that took place in the square was perpetrated by the 27th Army, a formation renowned for its brutality. Beijing was temporarily reduced to anarchy, and groups of soldiers waged gang warfare on civilians, sometimes shooting people in the back as they fled.

The demonstrations, predominantly by students from Beijing's several universities, had begun following the death of the former Communist party secretary Hu Yaobang. The students demanded his rehabilitation and protested against corruption and nepotism in the regime. Their numbers grew so rapidly that what should have been a momentous visit to Beijing by the Soviet leader Gorbachev in mid-May, was overshadowed by the domestic crisis.

The government was divided by the protests, but the hard-liners apparently had the support of Deng Xiao-ping who, although he no longer held high office, was still a dominant influence.

The protestors grew in numbers, exceeding one million by May 15. A large group of students went on hunger strike in the square, demanding a dialogue with the government about democratic reform. A growing public sympathy was manifested as professional and working people joined the protests, while similar demonstrations occurred in other cities. Some student representatives did have a meeting with the prime minister, Li Peng, but it was unfruitful. On the other hand the party secretary, Zhao Ziyang, pursued a much more agreeable line, admitting the justice of many of the students' complaints, visiting the square in person and persuading the hun-

Students grab leaflets warning them to leave Tiananmen Square.

ger strikers to call off their fast. His disappearance from the scene shortly afterwards signalled that the hard-liners had gained the upper hand.

Estimates of those killed in the massacre ranged between 2000 and 5000, though the authorities published a much lower figure. One general even insisted that the

troops had killed no one, and a transparently bogus TV film was made showing how the soldiers were innocent victims of aggressive counter-revolutionaries.

After the movement had been crushed some leaders managed to escape to Hong Kong and elsewhere. Many people were arrested and some later executed.

Fall of Ceauşescu

In a violent revolution on December 22, the Romanian dictator Nicolae Ceauşescu was overthrown. Always relatively independent of Moscow, his old-style Communist regime had survived while others were crumbling – but not for long. Taken by surprise by the intense opposition, he and his wife attempted to flee the country but were caught and, after a hasty trial, executed on Christmas Day.

The Romanian revolution was set off by an incident in Timisoara, when crowds gathered to protect a Protestant minister who had objected to the treatment of Hungarians in Romania and was threatened with deportation. Violence broke out, troops and police opened fire and several hundred people were killed.

Demonstrations spread. In Timisoara itself the troops were forced to withdraw as a massive crowd burned down the Communist party headquarters. Ceauşescu was abroad. He returned, blaming foreigners, imperialists, etc. for the troubles but, while delivering a public speech in Bucharest, he was strongly heckled, and scuffles broke out. The whole country became convulsed. Troops refused orders to fire on their countrymen (not so the large and brutal secret police force, Securitate). Martial law was declared on December 22 as a vast demonstration took place in Bucharest. The defence minister, refusing to order troops to fire, was killed, the building was besieged and Ceauşescu escaped by helicopter from the roof.

The revolutionaries now took over. They were ill-organized, but formed a National Salvation front which set up a provisional government. Securitate men and some police launched a counter-attack, and there was heavy fighting in the streets between Securitate men and ordinary soldiers. The havoc wrought by the megalomaniac Ceauşescu upon Romanian society and economy left his successors facing grim prospects.

A worried Nicolae Ceauşescu speaking to party members.

U.S. invasion of Panama

On December 20 the Panama Canal was closed for the first time since it was built. The reason was an invasion of Panama by U.S. forces (most of them in fact already present). The purpose was to remove the self-appointed dictator General Noriega and install Guillermo Endara Gallimany as president.

Several attempts had been made, with covert U.S. assistance, to topple Noriega, a gangster who was wanted in the United States on drug-smuggling charges. The decision to use force was made after he assumed dictatorial powers, announced that the country was at war with the United States and provoked a few anti-American incidents, in one of which a U.S. serviceman was killed. The U.S. attack was widely condemned worldwide, though

A watchful U.S. soldier on duty in Panama.

supported by Britain.

Noriega took refuge in the residence of the papal nuncio, where he was besieged not only by troops and guns but by highly amplified rock music – a hitherto little-exploited weapon of war. He gave himself up on January 3 and was flown to the United States for trial.

COLLAPSE OF COMMUNISM IN EASTERN EUROPE

Vaclav Havel, who had only recently been freed from prison, became president of democratic Czechoslovakia.

Tadeusz Mazowiecki was elected prime minister of Poland after the sweeping electoral victory of Solidarity.

Erich Honecker, East Germany's disgraced Communist party chief, who sought refuge in Moscow.

Egon Krenz, Honecker's successor, who gave permission for East Germans to travel abroad.

IN THE SECOND half of 1989 the Soviet empire in eastern Europe, and the ideology that supported it, disintegrated. Once Gorbachev's reformist policies had made it clear that hard-line Communist bosses could no longer rely on Soviet support and that reformers need not fear it, the whole system collapsed under popular pressure with astonishing speed and – in most countries – with very little violence.

Hungary, which was the most liberal and 'westernized' of the Communist satellites, was an exception in that reform came largely from within the Communist party itself. It even renamed itself the Hungarian Socialist party, signifying its renunciation of Communism and embracing of nationalism, the resurgence of which was one of the more ominous results of the breakdown of the Soviet system.

After Hungary, Poland led the way, with the events of 1989 concluding the unfinished business of 1980. In June elections, at which opposition parties were allowed to contest a certain number of seats, Solidarity swept the board, losing only one seat for which it was eligible. Nearly all the top government candidates were defeated: the voters simply crossed out their names. The old regime failed to form a government acceptable to Solidarity and a coalition took power with a Solidarity prime minister, Tadeusz Mazowiecki. General Jaruzelski remained president, but Solidarity and its allies were the dominant force, and within a year Lech Walesa himself was president.

In East Germany the decisive incident was the announcement by Egon Krenz (who had succeeded the elderly Erich Honecker) in November that citizens were free to travel abroad. In the previous months thousands had escaped to the West, especially through Hungary, which had opened its borders. The country appeared in danger of being depopulated, and the decision to open the borders was logical, though still unexpected. It was also a highly symbolic act in ending the division of Europe that had persisted since World War II, and opened the way for German reunification. Joyful citizens from East and West helped to chop down the Berlin Wall.

In Czechoslovakia anti-Communist demonstrations had gone on for some while and gained in strength from events in East Germany. On November 17 a police attack on demonstrators in Prague precipitated a vast protest. Half the population was in the streets, and the popular manifestations spread to Bratislava and other cities. Opposition leaders formed a party, Civic Forum, which demanded the government's resignation. Dubček returned to Prague, Civic Forum called a token general strike that demonstrated its massive support and within days the government collapsed. Vaclav Havel, the dissident intellectual only recently released from prison, became president of a free, democratic, independent state.

Bulgaria had in Todor Zhivkov Europe's longest-serving Communist party boss. As the dominoes fell round about, he was forced to resign by an adverse vote in the party central committee. The coup was led by the foreign minister, Petur Mladenov, appalled by the campaign against Bulgaria's Turkish citizens and by Zhivkov's apparent desire to pass power on to his son. It was followed by sweeping changes in personnel, although the continuation of some members of the old regime in government, combined with economic problems and racist reaction to the ending of the persecution of Turks, led to further protests.

Delighted East Berliners cross the border between East and West Berlin at Checkpoint Charlie.

MANDELA SET FREE

IRAQI ARMY ATTACKS KUWAIT

Nelson Mandela freed

In his address at the opening of the South African parliament in February, President De Klerk announced that Nelson Mandela was to be released. The veteran ANC leader had been in prison since 1962. His release (on February 2) was not unexpected: he had been moved to progressively more comfortable accommodation in recent years and had been offered release before on conditions that he would not accept. Somewhat less expected was De Klerk's other main announcement that, after 30 years, the ban on the ANC was to be lifted.

De Klerk's decision was evidence of his recognition of the need to negotiate with responsible leaders within the black community and bring to an end the violence that was threatening to engulf the state. He had already acknowledged the need to accept power-sharing, although he had rejected the ANC objective of majority rule. By recognizing the ANC, he began a long, sometimes hesitant reform process in which the structure of apartheid was steadily dismantled and the first steps were taken towards the establishment of democracy. He also secured the lifting of some international sanctions, notably by the European Community, though this move was very strongly resisted by the ANC who

Sandinistas lose election

Elections were held in Nicaragua on February 25. Although the Sandinistas emerged as again the largest party, they lost to a coalition led by Mrs Violeta Chamorro, widow of the Managua newspaper editor whose murder in 1978 had galvanized opposition to the Somoza regime.

To the surprise of those who had been seduced by U.S. propaganda, the Sandinistas carried out their promise to abide by the outcome of the democratic process, and Daniel Ortega handed over the presidency with good grace.

Thus democracy had accomplished what the United States had spent so much money and effort trying to achieve by non-democratic means – the downfall of the Sandinista regime. However, the main reason for its declining popularity was the deterioration of the economy, which had been brought about partly by Sandinista inefficiency and corruption but partly by the expensive campaign against U.S.-backed rebels and by the effects of U.S. economic sanctions.

Violeta Chamorro celebrates her election victory.

Nelson Mandela and his wife Winnie greeting well-wishers after his release.

regarded it as premature.

Two particular threats to the reform process soon emerged. The first was the danger that the Afrikaner extreme right, opposed to virtually all liberal reform, would widen its appeal among the

white community sufficiently to threaten the viability of the government – perhaps even the loyalty of the army and police. The second was the outbreak of violence between supporters of the ANC and those of the Inkatha

movement led by Chief Buthelezi, more conservative and predominantly Zulu. There was widespread suspicion that some of these outbreaks were initiated by whites, perhaps by the security forces themselves.

Iraq invades Kuwait

Soon after midnight on August 2 Iraqi forces crossed the border into Kuwait. In spite of the extreme tension of the previous two weeks, the Kuwaiti forces were taken by surprise and put up little resistance, though a few aircraft escaped to Saudi Arabia. Within hours the Iraqis had overrun the country and occupied Kuwait City.

Relations had been critical since mid-July, when the Iraqi leader, Saddam Hussein, had made a speech fiercely attacking Kuwait. With Iraq's economy in dire straights after the Iran–Iraq war he was anxious to boost the price of oil, and blamed over-production by Kuwait (and Saudi Arabia) for keeping it down. He also accused Kuwait of infringing on Iraqi territory during the recent war and of stealing Iraqi oil. Beneath all that lay Iraq's longstanding claim to Kuwait, sporadically aired since Kuwait's achievement of independence nearly 30 years earlier.

The Kuwaiti forces were put on a state of alert, and several Arab leaders tried to mediate, but talks soon collapsed in the face of Iraqi intransigence. Meanwhile, Saddam Hussein moved 100,000 men up to the Kuwaiti border.

International condemnation of the invasion was immediate and widespread. The UN Security Council passed a resolution demanding Iraq's withdrawal and the United States rushed forces into Saudi Arabia, which also seemed to be threatened – while Kuwait was declared an Iraqi province.

A majority of the members of the Arab League supported a subsequent UN resolution calling for sanctions. However, to some Arabs (and other Muslims) Saddam Hussein appeared as a hero, and in countries like Algeria, Tunisia and Jordan there was strong popular pressure on governments to support Iraq. The emotions of the Palestinians compelled Yasser Arafat to adopt an openly pro-Iraqi stance, while South Yemen (currently a member of the Security Council) withstood heavy U.S. pressure to cast a dissenting vote in the series of resolutions passed against Iraq in the ensuing three months.

Nevertheless, no international conflict since World War II had occasioned such general agreement. The ending of the cold war was not advantageous to Saddam. The day after the invasion, the foreign ministers of the United States and the Soviet Union (traditionally Iraq's chief supplier of arms), who were meeting in Moscow, published a joint condemnation of Iraqi aggression and called for a ban on arms supplies. ▶ *page 384*

Iraqi tanks take up position in Kuwait City. Saddam Hussein's overwhelming superiority in armour and manpower led to a rapid victory.

Flight of the Kurdish refugees

A serious refugee problem arose in April as large numbers of Kurds in northern Iraq fled to Turkey and Iran. The Kurds, continually persecuted by Saddam Hussein, had rebelled in the wake of the Gulf War. In spite of some initial success, the Kurdish guerrillas were defeated by Iraqi forces and thousands of Kurds were forced to take refuge in the mountains. A U.S.-led international rescue operation was mounted, at first to bring emergency supplies, then to establish 'safe havens' in northern Iraq where the Kurds were protected. By the end of the month Kurds were beginning to return to their homes.

Kurdish refugees moving through mountainous terrain.

Coalition forces attack Iraq

On January 16 coalition forces, concentrated mainly in Saudi Arabia, launched an offensive against Iraq with the intention of forcing it to evacuate its army from Kuwait. The attack followed the expiry of the deadline, after which the use of force against Iraq's occupation was countenanced by a UN resolution. Last-minute diplomatic efforts to prevent hostilities had failed owing to Iraq's refusal to agree to withdraw.

The UN-supported coalition forces were dominated by the United States, but there was a sizeable contingent from Britain (especially strike aircraft) and smaller forces from almost 30 other countries. The total coalition forces numbered about 700,000 (500,000 U.S.), against about 550,000 Iraqis who included 120,000 elite Republican Guards but otherwise consisted largely of conscripts.

The war began with an air offensive, the main targets being airfields, missile sites, power stations, etc. After two weeks, the attack was largely diverted against troop formations and supply lines. The attacks were mostly very accurate – precision bombing seemed at last to have earned its name – but the Iraqi air force mounted only minimal defence, being mainly intent on saving aircraft (a number were flown to Iran, where they were impounded for the duration of the campaign).

In an effort to broaden the war by turning it into an Arab cru-sade, Iraqi fired a few missiles at Israel, a non-participant. Under heavy U.S. pressure, Israel made no response, thus regaining some of the international respect it had lost as a result of the *Intifada*. The Iraqis also pumped oil into the Gulf, causing serious pollution and threatening Saudi Arabian water supplies, and set fire to Kuwait's oil wells.

The air assault was sustained longer than expected in the hope that Saddam Hussein would give in, and the land attack did not begin until February 24. Against all expectations, it encountered only slight resistance. Kuwait was swiftly liberated and part of southern Iraq occupied. President Bush called a halt four days later, when Iraq agreed to carry out the requirements of 12 UN resolutions, which included unconditional withdrawal.

The destruction of Saddam Hussein's government was not among the aims countenanced by the UN, though U.S. (and other) leaders hoped that this would be accomplished from within.

General Norman Schwarzkopf, the overall commander of the coalition forces during the Gulf War, is an acknowledged expert in the art of desert warfare.

Rebellion broke out among the Shi'ites in the south and the Kurds in the north, but both uprisings were crushed and Saddam Hussein remained in power.

Casualties in the Gulf War were about 150 in the coalition forces, and about a thousand times as many, among the Iraqis. In addition, an estimated 7000 Kuwaitis had been killed since Iraq's invasion.

Ethiopian revolution

The beleaguered Mengistu government of Ethiopia fell at last on May 21. It had been fighting against separatists and other rebels for many years and had displayed remarkable incompetence and corruption. Though the famine of the 1980s could not be blamed on the government, its efforts to alleviate the suffering lacked conviction.

The forces of the Ethiopian People's Revolutionary Democratic Front entered Addis Ababa towards the end of the month, soon after Mengistu fled the country. The EPRDF set up a transition government in co-operation with other groups, notably the Eritrean separatists, with whom they had waged war against Mengistu's regime.

Peace comes to Angola

On May 31, following agreement reached a few weeks earlier, a settlement was signed which promised peace for Angola. Civil war had continued since independence in 1975, complicated by the presence of South African and Cuban troops, and SWAPO guerrillas, and the conflicting interests of the superpowers. The international settlement, which had brought independence to Namibia and removed South African and Cuban forces from the arena, had ignored the rebel movement in southern Angola, UNITA, led by Jonas Savimbi, which, with U.S. support, had been able to hold its own against the MPLA and its Cuban mercenaries. The May agreement between UNITA and the government effected a ceasefire and promised multi-party democracy in Angola.

UNITA leader Jonas Savimbi.

Soviet coup

An announcement was made in Moscow on August 19 to the effect that presidential power in the Soviet Union had been transferred to the vice-president because the president, Mikhail Gorbachev, was 'unable to perform his duties for health reasons'. In fact, Gorbachev was held prisoner in a holiday villa in the Crimea, the victim of a plot by old-style Communists determined to put an end to *perestroika* and *glasnost*.

Several prominent reformists in the Soviet Union had warned of such an eventuality, and Gorbachev had attempted to undermine opposition among conservatives by giving many of them high office – thus bringing protests from reformers. In the event, the coup proved a damp squib, collapsing within three days. Its leaders were evidently unsure of the extent of their support in the armed forces, hesitating to order the troops to act against opponents for fear of their refusal to obey. Moreover, although many prominent citizens managed neither to support nor condemn the coup, resistance was vigorous, especially on the part of Boris Yeltsin, president of the Russian republic.

The results of the coup were contrary to the intentions of its instigators. It vastly strengthened Yeltsin vis-à-vis his rival, Gorbachev, and it encouraged the Soviet republics to declare their sovereign independence – the

majority did so before the end of the month. It also demonstrated the need for a fundamental reform of the political system,

which in turn meant the rapid and total collapse of the Communist party. Gorbachev, forced to concede the dissolution of the party, fought a determined rearguard action to keep the Soviet Union together, but at the end of the year it was replaced by a loose and fragile-looking federation called the Commonwealth of Independent States. Gorbachev, out of a job, then resigned.

A defiant Boris Yeltsin with his supporters in Moscow.

GULF WAR

U NTIL *1991 the term 'Gulf War' referred to the Iran-Iraq conflict. The engagement between Iran and the U.S.-led forces had some similarities with the earlier war, although it was far shorter-lived. Both resulted from a naked act of aggression by Iraq, aggression which was partly caused by Iraq's desire to control the Shatt-al-Arab waterway connecting the Rivers Tigris and Euphrates (both in Iraq) with the Gulf.*

Iraq is an artificial creation, resulting from the carve-up of the former Turkish Empire after 1918. The main components are the Kurds in the north, accounting for nearly 20 per cent of the population, the Sunni Arabs from whom the ruling elite is drawn, and the Shi'ite majority, who are mainly poor and sympathetic to the fundamentalist Shi'ite regime in Iran.

After the coup of 1968 power fell into the hands of the al-Takriti clans, from the town of that name north of Baghdad. The strong man of the regime was Saddam Hussein, though he did not establish his personal dictatorship until 1979.

Meanwhile Iraq was growing very rich, thanks to oil. By 1979 it was the world's second largest oil exporter with plenty of money for arms expenditure. The Soviet Union was the chief supplier, though Iraq also bought arms elsewhere.

Saddam Hussein's first effort to expand in the south resulted in the savage war with Iran, which ended in 1988. His attempt to gain control of the Shatt had failed and he therefore turned against Kuwait.

For 200 years Kuwait had been ruled by the al-Sabah family, under the Turkish sultan and, after 1918, under British protection. As early as the 1930s Kuwait was claimed by the new state of Iraq. When the British protectorate ended in 1961, this claim was revived, and British troops returned briefly at the Sheikh's request to discourage any Iraqi moves to enforce it.

Kuwait offered rich pickings for a country in economic straits after the Iran-Iraq war. Saddam Hussein may have expected a welcome from at least some of the people in Kuwait, such as the Palestinians who provided most of the labour without enjoying citizens' rights. He certainly did not anticipate such international opposition. The United States had tacitly supported Iraq against Iran (even the use of chemical warfare against the Kurds had not provoked any serious complaints). In the Iran-Iraq war U.S. interests were not involved. In Kuwait, a major oil supplier, they certainly were. Another factor overlooked by Saddam Hussein was the ending of the Cold War, which denied him Soviet support. President Bush, by untiring telephone diplomacy, constructed an impressive coalition against which Iraq could not hope to prevail. At the same time he was careful not to exceed the authority granted by a series of UN resolutions, culminating in the invocation of Article 42 of the UN charter on November 29, which sanctioned the use of force.

Once all attempts to prise the Iraqis out of Kuwait through diplomacy had failed, one of the shortest and most one-sided wars of the century began on January 15 and ended six weeks later. The Iraqis were expelled from Kuwait, thereby fulfilling the stated objective of 'Operation Desert Storm' and the only goal on which the members of the U.S.-led coalition agreed. The real objective, to rid the world of Saddam Hussein's brutal and dangerous regime, was not realised, because it could not have been achieved without breaking up the fragile coalition. President Bush expressed the hope that Saddam Hussein would be deposed by his own people. The Kurds took him at his word, with devastating effects for themselves since Saddam Hussein's army, though defeated, had not been destroyed.

Iraqi vehicles scattered in confusion after a U.S. air attack.

A British soldier guarding Iraqi prisoners.

The aftermath of a Scud missile attack on Israel.

Kuwaiti oil wells set alight by retreating Iraqis.

Saddam Hussein.

1992

CONFLICT IN ARMENIA

CIVIL WAR IN YUGOSLAVIA

COLLAPSE OF AFGHAN REGIME

Armed opponents of Gamsakhurdia embrace after his flight.

Georgia's president deposed

The popularly elected president of Georgia, Zviad Gamsakhurdia, fled the country on January 6 as political conflict spiralled into civil war. Opposed by former associates, he was forced to make a hasty and surreptitious flight to Armenia when deserted by his own security guards. A new provisional government was set up in Tbilisi.

A few days later Gamsakhurdia returned to his home town, Zugdidi, in western Georgia, but he showed little will to lead a counter-revolt and resistance soon crumbled. In March a truce was patched up by the Tiblisi government, now led by the respected former Soviet foreign minister, Eduard Shevardnadze.

Croatia and Slovenia gain recognition

On January 15 the members of the EC, along with other countries, officially recognized the independence of Croatia and Slovenia. The driving force behind the decision to acknowledge the break-up of Yugoslavia was Germany – a sign of reunited Germany's increased diplomatic weight in Europe.

Macedonia's independence was not recognized because of Greek objections: part of historical Macedonia lies in Greece. Nor was that of Bosnia, where the Serbian minority declared an autonomous Serbian republic. The Bosnian government called for a referendum on independence at the end of February.

Ethnic separatism and opposition to the dominance of the Communist party had increased in Yugoslavia since the death of Tito in 1980. Conflict was aggravated by economic failure – poor industrial management, declining agriculture and crippling foreign debts. In 1989 the federal government initiated drastic reforms in the direction of a free-market economy. Runaway inflation was conquered, but at severe social cost. The Serbian demagogue, Slovodan Milosevic, transformed from Communist boss to Serbian nationalist, helped to exacerbate ethnic tension by his ambition to restructure the country under Serbian dominance, taking over the autonomous provinces of Kosovo and Vojvodina. Croatia and Slovenia opted for independence in preference to inclusion in what looked increasingly like a Greater Serbia, provoking a bitter conflict, especially in those areas of Croatia where Serbs formed a large part of the population.

Croatian guardsmen at the funeral ceremony of a comrade.

Massacre at Khodzhaly

The bitter conflict between Armenia and Azerbaijan, focussing on the enclave of Ngorno-Karabakh, reached a new pitch on February 25 with the massacre of the Azeri villagers of Khodzhaly.

At the beginning of the year the Azerbaijani president, Ayaz Mutalibov, had imposed direct rule on Ngorno-Karabakh, though with little practical effect. Azerbaijani forces bombarded Stepanakert, while Armenians attacked the Azeri city of Shusha. The Khodzhaly massacre was a factor in the resignation in March of Mutalibov, generally regarded as a moderating influence.

Riots in Algeria

A state of emergency was declared in Algeria on February 9 following violent protests by the Islamic Salvation Front (FIS) against the assumption of presidential powers by the so-called High Committee of State.

Muslim fundamentalists were angry at being deprived of a probable victory in democratic elections, which had been postponed to prevent their gaining power.

An Algerian killed in a clash is taken for burial.

Moldavian separatists hold out

Renewed fighting broke out in Moldavia (Moldova) on March 3 between the nationalists and Slav separatists, mainly Russian and Ukrainian, and supported by Cossack bands, who had established a mini republic on the River Dnestr. The old hard-line Communist leaders retained control there because of the fear that Moldavia would seek union with Romania. The adoption of Romanian as the state language exacerbated the conflict. There were other ethnic problems too, for instance with the Gagauz, ethnically Turkish but Russian-speaking, who proceeded to set up their own mini republic in southern Moldavia.

Yugoslav civil wars spread to Bosnia

Violence broke out in Bosnian cities on March 2 after the vote in a referendum supported independence. This was rejected by the Serbs, who formed a minority of less than one-third. However, unlike the Croats and Muslims who were in the majority, they were better organized militarily, and had at least the tacit support of units of the Yugoslav national army. The independence of Bosnia-Herzegovina was recognized by the EC and other countries and Serbian aggression was widely condemned.

Artillery damage in Bosnia.

Crisis in Afghanistan

The regime of Dr Mohammed Najibullah in Afghanistan finally collapsed on April 16. Though universally believed to be on the point of defeat when Soviet forces withdrew in 1989, the 18-stone former athlete and qualified physician had survived over three years.

His position had deteriorated in recent months as a result of acute economic problems, continuing ethnic rivalry and declining morale in the army. A few days before, as mojahedin elements captured Charikar and the nearby airbase of Bagram, less than 30 miles from Kabul, he had agreed to surrender power to a UN-sponsored Afghan Council, the latest effort to bring the 14-year civil war to an end. Given the divisions among the mojahedin and the conflicting ambitions of Pakistan and Iran for influence in Afghanistan, Najib's disappearance made peace no more likely.

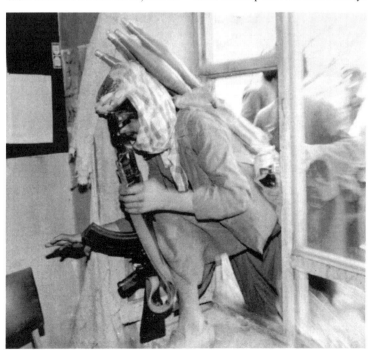

A heavily armed Mojahedin fighter makes a forceful entry.

INDEX

Numbers in **bold** type indicate text and illustration references. Numbers in ordinary type refer to entries in the chronology.

390

391

393

400